BACKPACKING

BACKPACKING

Sixth Edition   **Revised and Updated**

R. C. Rethmel

Follett Publishing Company/Chicago

Book design by Karen A. Yops
Front cover photo by Keith Gunnar/TOM STACK & ASSOCIATES

Library of Congress Cataloging in Publication Data

Rethmel, R. C.
  Backpacking.

  Bibliography: p.
  Includes index.
  1. Backpacking.   2. Backpacking – Equipment and
supplies. I. Title.
GV199.6.R47 1979   796.5   78–10895
ISBN 0–695–81144–4

123456789/8382818079

Contents

TABLES

APPENDIXES

INDEX

Preface

Backpacking has been an intriguing subject to, and a favorite outdoor activity of, the writer for many years. Most of us have a certain "explorer instinct." We would like to know and see what is beyond the next bend in the river, or over the next mountain, or in the canyon far below. A backpacker can find out firsthand—and enjoy the healthful exercise, the fun of camping out, and many other benefits in doing so.

An experienced backpacker can go into a remote area for a week with a thirty-five- to forty-pound pack on his or her back and live very adequately, shut off from all outside communication. In fact, in many cases the backpacker will live more comfortably and eat equally as well as others who take to the highway with a full trailerload of equipment, in spite of the fact that the highway travelers will probably make daily stops to replenish certain supplies.

A primary purpose of this book is to set forth information on clothing, equipment, and food needed for a successful backpack trip, and to describe techniques for the trail, the camp, and the pretrip preparations. The distinction between luxury gear, good satisfactory gear, and make-do is emphasized. A particular effort has been made to be very specific, rather than to discuss the various subjects in general terms.

My background includes a considerable period as a boy scout and as a scout leader. For many years I have made frequent trips into the Gila Wilderness in southwestern New Mexico and into some of the other wilderness areas. On many of these trips I have been organizer and informal leader of small groups of adult backpackers. Checklists and pretrip plans, as well as notes made during and after pack trips, led to the original publication of *Backpacking*. I never make a backpack trip that I don't learn something. Hence there has been a frequent updating of the material in this book.

A few years ago I spent the summer backpacking in the Canadian Rockies. Much of the time I made a particular effort to travel those trails on which I knew there would be a fair population of other backpackers. I did this so that I could meet and talk with some of the most experienced backpackers and also see their equipment in action on backwoods trails and in backwoods camp areas. I wanted to get other viewpoints and compare them with my own experience and background. I also spent considerable time in visiting and talking with Canadian wardens who were backpackers and with other government personnel who were knowledgeable on the subject of backpacking.

Please keep in mind as you read through this book that the material herein applies specifically to backpacking. Otherwise you may squirm a bit in your chair when you read such recommendations as to take no duplicate clothing on a week-long backpack trip except for socks, to use a sheet of plastic for rain protection (under some conditions), or to use certain freeze-dried foods that may cost a dollar or more for one ounce.

For those readers who are old hands at backpacking, it is hoped that you will be broad-minded about the amount of detail included in this book. After reading the book, you may feel that you would like to express your opinion on some recommended procedure, technique, or item of equipment, based on your backpacking experience. If you have comments of any kind, either general or specific, I would appreciate receiving them in a letter or note addressed to me at P.O. Box 1526, Alamogordo, New Mexico 88310.

Well, we were going to talk about backpacking—so pull up a log, and we'll get started.

R. C. (Bob) Rethmel

Alamogordo,
New Mexico

Acknowledgments

Important photographic contributions to *Backpacking* have been made by Lou Clemmons, of Gig Harbor, Washington. Lance Olsen, of Wolf Creek, Montana, made worthwhile suggestions and provided some illustrations. For the back cover photo, and certain other photographs and comments, I am indebted to Bill Lee, of Edmonton, Alberta, Canada, with whom I did some backpacking in the Canadian Rockies. J. R. Guinn, of Alamogordo, also contributed photographs and suggestions.

Opinions on eating patterns, general nutrition, proper backpacking foods, renewal of glycogen stores, and so on, vary considerably, even among qualified and experienced backpackers. For the comments that I have included in this edition in these subject areas I sought the advice and opinions of a number of qualified physicians and nutritionists and also used my own experience and background in this area. Many of these persons were backpackers themselves. Those to whom I would like to give particular mention are William W. Forgey, M.D., Gary, Indiana (and Churchill River country, Canada); Albert P. Rosen, M.D., Fair Lawn, New Jersey; Mrs. Dorothy Wehnau, Washingtonville, New York; and Mrs. Joy Peterson, Greenacres, Washington.

Chapter 14, Backpacking with Children, is based largely on my experience of backpacking with my own children, plus some backwoods observations I have made. However, photographic contributions and some suggestions in this subject area were made by Fred Mulholland, of Tampa, Florida, and Owen Thero, of Lompoc, California. Both Owen and Fred are accomplished backpackers. They can be very proud of having carefully and thoroughly initiated their children to wilderness backpacking.

Certain photographs were furnished by various manufacturers. To these firms I am very appreciative.

Credit for photographic and other illustrative material that was furnished by other persons or firms is acknowledged where it appears in the text. The acknowledgment is in the form of the name of the person or firm enclosed in parentheses at the end of the caption.

Again, to all of those who assisted in any way in the preparation of this edition, my sincere thanks.

R. C. R.

28 June 1978

1
Introduction

WHY GO BACKPACKING?

People go backpacking for a variety of reasons. Backpacking can take you into beautiful unspoiled scenery that may lie just a few miles beyond the roadhead. It can provide an inexpensive vacation that is a complete escape from the boredom of the asphalt and concrete "jungle." It is certainly healthful exercise, if one is in reasonably good physical condition to start with. There is an endless variety of trails and terrain available, and the backpacker can select a route and a trip plan that are commensurate with his or her ability and physical stamina. Entire families—some with young babies, toddlers, or children five or six years of age—have backpacked into some of our forest and wilderness areas.

In addition to being able to pursue such objectives as photography, nature study, fishing, relaxation, or whatever, there is a tremendous satisfaction just in being able to carry your "house" on your back for a week and to live comfortably in the woods, shut off from all outside communication. It takes some skillful planning, and this too is part of the fun in backpacking. Selecting an area that suits your particular objectives can be a pleasant spare-time activity, and it will be time well spent.

People interested in technical mountain climbing find that backpacking is useful and necessary for carrying their climbing gear and supplies to a base camp from which they will do their climbing. Sportsmen use backpacking equipment and techniques in getting to good hunting and fishing grounds, which are frequently more than a day's travel from the roadhead. Thus, to some people, backpacking is simply a necessary means of moving equipment and supplies into an area in order to accomplish another, more primary, objective. Many others find backpacking itself to be an enjoyable and exhilarating sport, especially when done in an area that is isolated and attractive from a scenic standpoint. To them, exploring the area and simply enjoying what it has to offer, step by step, is reward enough. For some people, walking or hiking is an addiction like jogging, baseball, or some other sport. Their basic explanation is that they feel at their best when they are trudging along a mountain trail with a pack on their back.

In our modern-day civilization it is possible for a person to go from the cradle to the grave and hardly draw a deep breath. He may never have a problem in seeking shelter from the elements or a need to cook his own food in a wilderness setting. One can go through life and never experience the fatigue and pleasure resulting from prolonged and pleasurable physical exertion. As the progress of civilization continues to make our lives easier and more comfortable, it becomes more evident that we need some primitive physical activity and experiences to break the monotony and to achieve a "balance" in our activities. A drink from a cool mountain stream on a hot day, the smell of a pine forest, and the taste of a freshly caught mountain trout are pleasures that are available to practically everyone in reasonably good health, if we will but make the effort and take the necessary initiative. Psychologically it is good for us to have new problems and new experiences to provide a contrast to the pattern of our everyday living. We all need some adventure in our lives—if only for a few days each year. Backpacking is a wholesome, invigorating activity that provides a physical and mental atmosphere that is a pleasant change from our daily routine.

PHYSICAL CONDITION

Some people picture a typical backpacker as a sun-bronzed youth with bulging muscles waiting to be unleashed against the "ferocity" of the wilderness. There *are* those types. There are also many people well past middle age who are backpacking the trails of our parks and forests. Grandfathers and grandmothers have hiked the full length of the Appalachian Trail, from Mount Katahdin in Maine to Springer Mountain in Georgia—about 2,000 miles in all. Many of these people had led fairly sedentary lives for most of their working years. The legendary Grandma Gatewood hiked the full length of the Appalachian Trail for the first time at age sixty-eight. She then went on to do it twice more in her lifetime. It is interesting to note that she did not carry a packframe. She carried her equipment in a homemade duffel bag slung over one shoulder. And she wore tennis shoes for much of her hiking!

Admittedly, a person who plans to backpack should be in reasonably good physical condition. It is obviously important to select a pace, terrain, and pack load commensurate with age, hiking ability, and backpacking experience. Some preconditioning hiking and other exercise is recommended for *all* who backpack. For older people, such preconditioning can be of major importance and should never be taken lightly. At the same time it should be recognized that there are many adults of middle age and past who are in essentially as good physical condition as they were fifteen or twenty years earlier. These are usually people who have learned over the years the benefits of a regular exercise program and a nutritious diet—matters that are often taken lightly in the

early years. Even more important perhaps, they have learned to pace themselves in their physical activities. The do-or-die attitude common in youth has been replaced by a more realistic outlook.

BE PREPARED

On a backpack trip into a remote area it is necessary to be not only a hiker but also a camper, cook, doctor, pathfinder, and many other things. Careful planning and preparation is called for. Those who like to "throw a few things together and take off" when they go camping had best prepare for a drastically different approach if they plan to do any serious backpacking. It is easy to take too much equipment, clothing, and food—that is, until you have carried it up a few miles of switchbacks with the hot sun bearing down. Forgetting essential items of equipment or running out of certain supplies can be equally serious. On an automobile camping trip (or on any other trip that keeps in touch with civilization) forgotten items of equipment can be bought at the nearest store. If certain equipment needs repair, someone requires medical attention, the group needs a change from their own cooking, or some other service is required, the service can usually be had for a little cash. Money won't help on a backpack trip in a wilderness area. You are on your own. To a considerable degree a backpacker's technique and know-how are deciding factors on how long he can stay out on the trail and how comfortable he will be, that is, whether he will enjoy the trip or will decide to give up backpacking.

GOALS

Most people go backpacking because they enjoy the activity. They will plan routes that will take them through interesting country, perhaps reaching one or more "special" objectives. The goals that they have in mind are usually flexible and can be modified if weather, terrain, or other conditions so dictate. With a few backpackers, however, goals are more rigid. Consciously or otherwise they plan activities that they think will impress friends and others at home. Examples are setting time records for certain stretches of the trail, setting distance records, catching as many fish as possible, and scaling mountain peaks in record time. Unfortunately (for those backpackers), the folks back home could probably care less about such accomplishments.

To most hikers, backpacking, like life itself, is

a *journey* rather than a *destination*. The backpacker who wants to get the most satisfaction from his backwoods trek should resolve to go slowly and to keep a flexible and relaxed itinerary. He should take time to observe the birds, animals, plant life, rock formations, and the overall scenery. He should give some thought to ecology—the study of life systems and their interrelationships with the environment. To go a bit further, he can consider what effect his passage, and that of many other backpackers, is having on the ecology and what can be done to minimize that effect.

Unfortunately, a few backpackers set out with the goal of somehow "conquering" the wilderness. This is definitely the wrong approach. A major objective should be to live in *harmony* with the wilderness. An important consideration of every backpacker should be *to leave no trace* of his passing. He should take pride in packing out not only all his own trash but also a part of someone else's. The ax was touted for many years as one of the most important items of equipment that a "genuine" woodsman could carry. With it he could cut balsam boughs for a bed, cut saplings for a lean-to shelter, and split logs for a roaring campfire at night. That day is long past. The modern backpacker carries neither an ax nor a hatchet.

EQUIPMENT

A beginning backpacker can easily spend several hundred dollars on special equipment for use in backpacking. On many items, however, he can improvise or make do, with equipment that is already around the home or with inexpensive substitute items that are locally available. A plastic tarp can be used for a shelter, for example. It is recommended that he do this, particularly in regard to such major items as sleeping bag, tent, and expensive clothing. He can talk with knowledgeable backpackers, make short backpack trips in mild weather to gain experience, or perhaps join a club that backpacks regularly. In some areas many items of backpack equipment can be rented. In this way he can get a good feel for the relative merits of various brands and discover his preferences before he spends any great sum of money.

A packframe and packbag will probably be the first items that a budget-conscious beginning backpacker will want to buy. Carried on a poor packframe, even a modest load will be uncomfortable. The possibility of purchasing used equipment should not be overlooked. Like those in any other sport or hobby, backpackers go "in and out of business." Some invest in expensive equipment (perhaps hastily) and then give up the sport. Others may "outgrow" good, serviceable equipment and purchase more sophisticated gear as they advance and become more knowledgeable. Still another way to save dollars in backpack equipment is to buy the do-it-yourself kits that are now available for a wide variety of items. Some of the sources for such kits are listed in Appendix A.

A list of some of the firms that sell special equipment for use in backpacking and publish good catalogs is given in Appendix A. These catalogs are recommended for beginners, as well as others, as being worthwhile material to order and browse through. This "window shopping" won't cost anything, and it will add to any backpacker's knowledge just to read through them.

Backpacking should not be considered an elitist activity. As I review my own early experiences in backpacking, and those of acquaintances, I am amazed that we had so very little special-purpose gear. In my first hike of the Grand Canyon an army surplus canteen and an army blanket were the only items carried that could even remotely be considered special-purpose. Yet, at the time, the equipment, clothing, and food that we carried seemed appropriate. Certainly in no sense did we feel that we were handicapped by the caliber of our gear. Another thought comes to mind. Fifty pounds of the most sophisticated and expensive ultramodern backpacking equipment that money can buy is just as heavy as fifty pounds of less expensive equipment. This is emphasized because some hikers, in their efforts to "get away from it all," attempt to take it all *with them*. They take far too much equipment, clothing, and food for the occasion. Most *expeditions* will want the best gear that money can buy. They frequently encounter situations where the quality of their gear may decide a matter of life and death. However, very few backpack trips even come close to the conditions encountered by most expeditions.

These thoughts are mentioned, in particular, for the beginning backpacker, hopefully to deter him from investing hastily in a lot of expensive backpacking equipment. If he keeps on with backpacking, he will probably want to replace some of the items with better equipment. It is recommended that this be done *gradually*, however, as experience and knowledge are gained, so that his dollars can be spent most wisely.

In various parts of this book there are references to specific brand names of equipment and food. These are brands that I have personally tried on backpack trips and found to be satisfactory. For the most part, rather than naming brands, I have detailed important *features* to look for in selecting clothing and equipment. In the area of foods, however, this is not possible; that is, you cannot tell by looking at the package in the store how the food is going to taste. Therefore, for foods, in particular, I have spelled out the kind of food and brand that I have found to be satisfactory. Where brands are named, this is *not* meant to imply that there is not another product that may be equally good. Hikers may wish to try other brands or their own substitute items, and it is certainly their choice to do so. However, before you take off on an extended backpack trip, it is recommended that all new equipment and food items be tried out at home or on a very short backpack trip. Then, in case anything does not work out as planned, necessary changes can be made. This cannot be emphasized too strongly. For a hiker to be thoroughly familiar with his or her equipment and clothing, to know just what it can do and what the limitations are, is one of the most important aspects of backpacking. To carry a supply of good food that has been tried before—to be assured of tasty snacks and meals when it comes time to eat—is almost equally important.

PACK WEIGHT

As for every other kind of outdoor activity, there are equipment, clothing, and techniques that are especially pertinent to backpacking. Some of the gear is very sophisticated and also quite expensive. It would not require nearly so much skill and planning for a backpack trip if the matter of weight did not need to be continually considered. The pack weight, in turn, is interrelated with equipment, clothing, food, and technique. Equipment and clothing can be perfect for a backpack trip, but if the wrong foods are planned for and taken, the pack weight will grow out of bounds. Assuming that the group possesses proper equipment and the necessary know-how to plan and conduct an interesting and safe backpack trip, then the most significant factor affecting the hiker's enjoyment of the trip is doubtless the *weight of the pack*. It should receive careful consideration.

Normally a person should not plan to carry a loaded pack totaling more than 40 pounds. This applies to the average adult male backpacker with average experience, for a trip lasting up to a week or ten days. A 50-pound pack may feel quite comfortable when one is walking around in the living room or back yard at home for a few minutes, but five or six hours on a mountain trail can be quite different. If a person has a special purpose for going into the wilderness, say for commercial-type photography, and chooses to carry 10 to 15 pounds of photographic equipment, then it is going to be very difficult to keep the total pack weight from growing over 40 pounds. However, the average backpacker should not be carrying that much special-purpose gear. For persons of small body build, or those not accustomed to backpacking, it is recommended that they eliminate all nonessential equipment and clothing so as to keep the total pack weight between 25 and 30 pounds. The irony of it is that experienced backpackers will have the least difficulty in keeping their packs light, while the beginners (who are most apt to really suffer from a heavy pack) will find it more of a problem. However, for those who are willing to spend sufficient time in planning and preparation, it can be done. The chapters that follow tell how.

2
The Pack

Your pack is your home on your back. In your pack you will need to carry shelter, food, extra clothing, cooking and eating utensils, and all the other gear required to travel and live comfortably in the back country. If your trip is to be pleasurable, your pack load must be comfortable. Your pack is your most important item of equipment (except for boots, which are really an item of clothing).

Over the years many styles of packs have been devised for carrying loads on the trail. The human back, in relation to the rest of the skeletal structure, was not properly designed for carrying heavy loads. Yet, by trial and error, the back has been proven to be the optimum place to position large loads that are being carried for relatively long distances.

When I was of high school age, I made a four-day backpack trip from the south rim of the Grand Canyon to the north rim and back again. My "pack" for that trip consisted of an army blanket with essentially all equipment rolled inside. The blanket was then tied into a horseshoe shape and was worn over one shoulder. A canteen was carried on a strap over the opposite shoulder, and a cooking pan dangled from the blanket roll. By frequently changing the pack from one shoulder to the other, I endured the trip. However, I would have welcomed almost any of the packframes that are commercially available today in place of that blanket roll.

In the early history of packframes and packboards two of the most frequently used designs were the army packboard and the Trapper Nelson. The army packboard used a piece of plywood formed into a shallow U shape for mounting a canvas backpanel that rested against the back. The load was lashed to the packboard with lashing cord that passed around metal hooks mounted along each of the two vertical edges. There was no hip belt. The load was borne entirely by the shoulders. In years past I have used such a packboard, and they are still available in some army surplus stores today.

The Trapper Nelson packboard has been carried and used by many thousands of backpackers

Author backpacking in the Grand Canyon at 16 years of age. Note the horseshoe-shaped blanket roll, which served as a pack.

Typical tubular aluminum packframes, of good design, with matching packbags. (Stuff bag mounted to packframe is also shown.)

The packframe-packbag combinations shown above are typical of many that are available from mountaineering and backpacking equipment shops, sporting goods firms, and large mail-order firms. This general type of packframe-packbag is the most widely used by backpackers today.

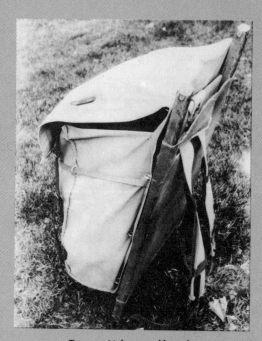

Trapper Nelson packboard.

Army packboard.

For serious backpacking, these packs have been largely replaced by the contoured, tubular aluminum packframes, which have better weight distribution, waist belts or hip belts, and other desirable features. The army packboard will carry large and odd-shaped loads. In hunting, it is sometimes useful in packing out a quarter of game. For normal backpacking use, it leaves much to be desired.

over the years, and I have also owned and used one of these. This packboard has straight, wood side rails connected by several horizontal members formed of curved wood. Two canvas backpanels—sometimes a single large one—are mounted to this frame so as to hold the load away from the wearer's back. This packboard has a single large canvas packbag, much too deep to keep the load close to the hiker's back, but has no side pockets and no hip belt. The Trapper Nelson is still available in some stores today, but its design is obsolete.

Since the days of the army packboard and the Trapper Nelson there have been some very significant changes in packframes and packbags, both in materials and in design.

THE MODERN PACK

In order to have a comfortable pack load, it is important to start with a good packframe. The packbag, although it is also important, is secondary to the packframe. If your packframe does not fit properly or feel comfortable, the best packbag in the world will not make it right. You will be miserable while carrying it. This is pointed out so that in the event that you cannot afford both a good packframe and a good fitted packbag, it would be most wise to invest in a good packframe first. If necessary, you can get by with a "cheapie" packbag, or make one yourself. With many packframes you can even lash a "bundle" of gear to the frame. If at all possible, however, buy a good fitted packbag with your packframe, and you will be off to a good start. A good preliminary step to buying a pack would be to *rent* a packframe-packbag combination of the style and size you have in mind and try it out on a field trip before you buy.

The general requirements for a good packframe and packsack are fairly well agreed upon among backpackers. There is, however, some disagreement about details, as is reflected in the numerous variations in individual design, particularly with respect to the packframe. However, to the average backpacker the variations in design among the many *good* backpack frames currently available are not earthshaking in importance.

Important considerations in choosing a pack are the kind of use and type of trip that the pack is intended for. A person who uses a pack for day hiking and short weekend trips does not need nearly as much pack as one who takes to the trail for three to five days, or perhaps a week or two. In fact, for short trips a rucksack may do the job better, at less cost, and with greater comfort to the hiker.

This discussion on packs will be mainly concerned with those used by the typical backpacker. The length of the average trip will probably be somewhere between several days and two weeks. Most of the hiking will be done over reasonably good mountain trails. The total pack load will probably be in the range of 30 to 45 pounds. The most widely accepted pack for such usage is the contoured aluminum packframe with a fitted packbag to match.

Construction. The packframe should be constructed so as to hold the load close to the hiker's back and to place the heavy part of the load as nearly as possible over the center of gravity of the body. Because of this objective a good packframe will have the general shape of an elongated S when viewed from the side.

The usual packframe, when viewed from the rear, will have the appearance of a very short ladder. There will be three or more horizontal crossbars. A minimum of four crossbars is recommended for the average frame and five for larger frames. The lowest crossbar should be curved outward so that the packframe does not rub against the backbone in this area. The crossbars will usually be constructed from aluminum tubing of 5/8- to 7/8-inch diameter. The vertical rails will usually be 3/4- to 1-inch-diameter aluminum tubing. The top horizontal member will in some designs have the shape of an inverted U and will be directly connected at each end to the top of the vertical members so as to be a continuation of those members. In many designs, however, the vertical side rails are not connected at the top. The open ends of the rails on such designs should be plugged (usually with a simple plastic plug) to prevent entry of dirt and water. The bottom ends of the rails should be similarly plugged. The main crossbars are curved outward to provide for holding the load away from the wearer's back. Two or more small-diameter vertical tubes connecting the horizontal crossbars are often used to provide greater strength and rigidity.

Aluminum alloy tubing is the material most often used in packframe construction. Commonly used alloys are 6061, 6063, and 7001; there are others. Magnesium tubing is a bit lighter and has been used to a very limited extent in packframe construction. However, it is more difficult to work with than aluminum, and the higher prices dictated by manufacturing techniques have essentially ruled it out as a basic packframe material.

A few frames have been constructed of PVC (polyvinyl) tubing. Aluminum alloy tubing remains the accepted material.

The tubular aluminum members in many of the best packframes have heliarc-welded joints where the horizontal cross members join the vertical rails. Helium gas is used in the welding of such joints. They have a somewhat rough, irregular, and homemade appearance, but they are strong. The manufacturer's description will generally state whether or not the frame is heliarc welded. Good workmanship in the welding process is of the utmost importance. Soldered or brazed joints may also be used in the construction of rigid packframes. Such frames *may* be satisfactory, depending primarily upon the particular design and the quality of workmanship. Before buying a packframe of rigid construction (welded, brazed, soldered), you should carefully inspect each individual joint and reject the frame if any joint has even the slightest crack.

Some very good packframes are being produced that do *not* have rigid joints. A few (such as Jan Sport and Alpine Designs) use couplings or fittings to join frame members. Such couplings permit some flexing, and the joints thus absorb more stress than those of a rigid frame. In many of the packframes that have coupled construction the coupling can be replaced if it fails. This is not true of frames that have welded or similar rigid construction. Some assembled frames are adjustable. The crossbar on which the shoulder straps are mounted can be moved up or down, thus allowing for some variation in fit.

The joints are a very vulnerable part of any packframe. Their failure in the backwoods can mean a real hardship. Regardless of the type of joint, the quality of the *joints* is frequently a good index to the *overall* quality of the packframe. The reputation of the manufacturer and the warranty provided on the packframe are very important considerations. Some backpackers are probably too concerned about the strength of their packframe. Most frames that are produced by reputable manufacturers are very unlikely to fail under the use to which they are subjected by the average backpacker.

In buying a packframe, you can make a simple test of rigidity and strength by setting the frame upright on the floor, bracing the bottom ends of the rails with your feet, and then attempting to twist the tops of the rails, using a reasonable amount of force. In frames that have welded or other rigid construction there should be very little give, and the joints should remain intact. In an assembled or bolted construction there may be some give, but the frame should regain its original configuration, with no detrimental effects, when the force is released. An even more severe test is to place the bottom end of one of the vertical rails on the floor and exert pressure on the frame. This is a severe test and should be done judiciously. It is a fairly realistic test, however, in that it duplicates a condition that frequently occurs in the field. As a backpacker swings the pack off his or her back and drops it to the ground, one leg may strike the ground with the full force of the loaded pack and the momentum of the fall bearing on it. Some reasonable caution in removing the pack in the field can save the frame from a lot of unnecessary stress.

A few manufacturers of backpacks use a wraparound design for the lower part of the frame. In these designs the lower end of the frame is extended forward on either side of the wearer to a point near the hip sockets of the body. The packframe is then suspended from the waist belt that is attached to the frame at approximately these same points. The theory of such designs is to place the pack weight in line with the person's normal center of gravity, directly over the legs.

All packframes should be fitted or adjusted to the individual wearer. However, it is generally agreed that for the wraparound frames a *careful individual fit is of major importance*—more so than with conventional packframes. The projections that support the waist belt come very close to the body. An improper fit could make for an uncomfortable load.

Some users of these frames claim that there is a distinct backward pull at the shoulders and that it is necessary to lean significantly forward to compensate for this. Other users state that there is no such backward pull. I personally know some backpackers who are using wraparound packframes and are very well satisfied with them. I know of other users who are not so satisfied. I believe two factors are particularly important in evaluating such a frame for your own use. First, there are some design differences among the various wraparound frames so that all do not perform equally well. The wraparound frame of one manufacturer may suit you fine, but the frame of another manufacturer may not. Secondly, I believe a person's body build is an important factor. If the backpacker is very slim waisted or bulges in the wrong places, possibly no wraparound design would be satisfactory. Thus, the matter of an individual fit and trial before buying cannot be overemphasized. Quite a few places rent packframes,

Wraparound packframe. Note the horizontal frame extension at hip level. *(J. R. Guinn)*

and this would be a good way to start if you are considering such a frame.

The waist-level projections make these packframes somewhat more prone to damage than the more conventional designs. This particularly applies to damage incurred in car trunks or baggage compartments of commercial carriers while the frame is being transported to the trailhead. Some designs provide for the extension bar assembly to fold when not in use, which would minimize the possibility of damage.

Backbands and Backpanels. The load of the pack presses against the hiker's back through backbands or a backpanel. These keep the frame and packbag away from the body and prevent odd-shaped objects in the packbag from poking into your back. They also distribute the weight of the pack evenly and provide space for circulation of air between the load and your back.

A common arrangement has two nylon backbands positioned on the vertical side rails of the frame so that one or both may be adjusted up or down to fit the wearer's back. If they cannot be adjusted up or down on the frame, or if only one of the backbands is adjustable, much more care will be needed in selecting a frame that will fit your particular body build. Tall or long-waisted people will require a different packframe than those who are short.

Rather than two separate backbands, some designers use a backpanel, often constructed of nylon mesh, for better ventilation. Some people feel that full-length backpanels compress too much of the clothing against the body and hamper ventilation. Others prefer the full-length mesh panels to the two-band design.

Some backbands are padded for greater comfort. Whether you choose the arrangement of two nylon backbands (padded or unpadded) or a larger mesh panel is largely a matter of personal choice. Any of these can be quite comfortable when properly designed and fitted.

To accomplish their function, backbands (or backpanels) must be kept very taut. Quite a few packs have a turnbuckle arrangement for this purpose. This is a very convenient and quick method of tightening the backbands. Other designs use nylon cord tightly laced through a series of grommets.

On packframes with two backbands the upper band should contact the back in the area of the shoulder blades. The lower band should fall on the upper part of the buttocks.

Shoulder straps. The top ends of the shoulder straps should be attached relatively high on the frame, except on those frame designs that have extensions at the top. The attachment point may be the top crossbar or the one just below it, depending upon the frame design and the number of crossbars. The standard means of attachment is by clevis pins and keeper rings through grommets in the shoulder straps. The straps should be wide where they bear on the shoulders and narrow where they pass under the arms. Normally the crossbar should have a number of holes to which the top end of the shoulder straps can be attached, to provide for varied placement of the straps to fit the wearer. The straps should ride close to, but not touching, the neck, and never far out on the shoulders. They should always be firmly attached to the frame, rather than have a floating arrangement that allows the pack to move either up or down or from side to side.

Padded shoulder straps will be found on most good packframes. The padding is usually Ensolite or other dense foam encased in coated nylon duck cloth. You should give the foam parts of the harness a good squeeze. Soft foam will not hold its shape after a period of use and should be avoided. For those few packframe designs that do not have padded shoulder straps, shoulder pads may be purchased separately and installed on the straps.

The points of attachment of the shoulder straps to the pack are subjected to heavy stress. Some backpackers lift the entire pack by the shoulder straps, at the upper end, prior to swinging the pack onto the back. (This is not correct. It should be grasped at a crossbar.) Even while the pack is being worn, the stress at the point of attachment of the shoulder straps may be considerable. Therefore, the grommets at the top of the shoulder strap, as well as the fittings at the bottom, need to be strong and securely fastened to the shoulder strap. The grommets at the top need to be heavy-duty. Where they are inserted into the strap material, the strap should be well reinforced with extra stitching. Grommets should be checked to see that they are tight. A loose grommet can be a real problem. If it pulls out on the trail, it can be a disaster. In checking the grommet, you will need to remove the clevis pin. Hold on to the grommet between your thumb and forefinger and try to turn it. If it moves at all, it should be rejected. Grommets used in the hip-belt assembly and at the points of attachment of pack-bag to frame should be similarly checked.

Buckles near the bottom ends of the shoulder straps provide for length adjustment to suit the individual wearer. This adjustment is also important for shortening or lengthening the straps as protective layers of upper clothing are removed or added during the day. It is also a good idea to loosen shoulder straps in such situations as crossing hazardous streams. Since the shoulder straps may be adjusted quite a few times during the day, the buckles should be capable of being quick-

Hip belt on packframe. This type of hip belt is available as a separate accessory and will attach to many packframes.

ly adjusted and, once adjusted, should hold positively, with no slippage. To facilitate quick adjustment of the shoulder straps, I mark each strap with a black felt-tip marker. I make a horizontal line across the strap at the "normal" position of the buckle. As the straps are tightened or loosened during the day, this reference mark is a big help in getting the buckles properly repositioned and the straps of equal length.

Packframe belts.   In recent years there have been many changes in the design, construction, and method of attachment of belts that are fastened to the lower end of the packframe. Some are waist belts and some are hip belts. They are not the same thing, although some suppliers' catalogs and other literature use the terms somewhat interchangeably.

Waist belts appeared on packframes long before the modern hip belt came into existence. The first waist belts were fairly narrow unpadded webbing. They were intended primarily to hold the lower end of the pack load in position and close to the body. Depending on the fit or adjustment of the packframe to the particular wearer, the waist belt might simply encircle the hiker's body about where the trouser belt would normally fall. Or, again depending on how the frame fit the individual, the waist belt might ride above or below the trouser-belt line. It might, indeed, transfer some of the pack load to the hips. Many packframes were equipped with waist belts when purchased, whereas a wide, fully padded, true hip belt was not often a standard feature of the packframe. It had to be purchased separately and installed by the owner; this is still the case with some packframes today.

In contrast to most waist belts, a true hip belt is a wide (4 inches or more), fully padded belt. It is intended to be worn with the frame and shoulder straps adjusted in such a way that a major part of the pack load is borne on the protruding bone shelf of the hips. When the packframe is properly adjusted to the wearer and the hip belt falls into proper position, it is possible for the hip belt to support as much as 75 percent or more of the pack load with comfort. Thus, the shoulders and back, which structurally are not suitable for carrying heavy loads for long distances, can be relieved of much of the pack weight. Wide, fully padded hip belts have been available as a separate packframe accessory for some years. In more recent years a fully padded, true hip belt has become standard equipment on many quality packframes.

Belts are usually attached near the lower end of the packframe rails in one of several ways. With some designs the clevis pin that holds the lower end of the shoulder strap is used to accommodate a grommet on the belt and thus fasten it to the frame. Half-belts are often fastened in this manner. Another configuration uses a short length of strap attached to the belt, with several grommets in the strap permitting some variation in positioning of the belt. Wraparound packframes have other methods of attachment.

Some manufacturers furnish belts with their packframes that are not true belts. Rather they are two half-belts, each attaching near the bottom end of one of the vertical rails, and each half meeting in front of the wearer in a buckle arrangement. The two-half-belt approach is considered by many backpackers to be less desirable, less effective, and less comfortable than a full belt. However, there are some satisfied owners of packframes which have the two-piece belts.

A true hip belt—at least 4 inches wide, fully padded, and completely encircling the body—is generally considered to be the best belt arrangement. If your packframe does not have such a belt, one can be purchased (for about $10) and easily installed. Hip belts will fit most packframes. All belts should have a quick-release buckle so that the pack can be quickly jettisoned in an emergency.

A hip belt should encircle the hips below the waist, resting on the flare of the hips and on the upper buttocks. It needs to be very tight when in use. It is important to keep your trouser belt free of canteens, sheath knives, and similar equipment that will interfere with the hip belt. In fact, your trouser belt itself will probably interfere a little bit. Heavy-duty suspenders or trousers with an elastic waistband are somewhat preferable to a conventional belt.

Accessories. There are a number of accessories that can be purchased for use with your packframe. Some will increase the load-carrying capacity of your pack. Others (such as hip belts) make for greater ease in carrying the pack. Certain replacement parts are available for repair.

HIP BELTS. As previously mentioned, wide, padded hip belts are available as a separate accessory. If your pack does not come with a padded hip belt, you will probably find such a belt to be a very worthwhile investment. The cost is about $10.

POCKETS. A pocket that mounts high on the pack strap is convenient for carrying a small

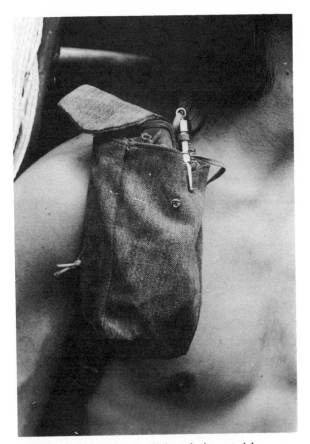

Pocket for pack strap, handmade from denim material. Pockets can be used to carry items such as sunglasses, compass, notepad, and pencil. *(Lou Clemmons)*

Extension bar. A useful addition to the packframe is this extension bar that fits into the top vertical rails. *(Lou Clemmons)*

A useful addition to the packframe is four of these D rings attached to the two top and two bottom clevis pins. Rope, drinking cup, and so forth, can be suspended from the rings. *(Lou Clemmons)*

Some useful spare packframe parts. Clockwise, from upper left: aluminum U ring for attaching lower end of shoulder strap to frame, end plug for frame, split rings, clevis pin. *(Lou Clemmons)*

notebook, pencil, sunglasses or eyeglasses, and so on. The cost is about $2. You can easily make such a pocket yourself.

TUMPLINE. An accessory sometimes used with packframes is a tumpline. This is a strap that generally fastens near the bottom of the frame and that has a padded area that bears on the top of the head. However, unless your head and neck are thoroughly accustomed to use of a tumpline, you probably will not find it very comfortable to use for more than a few minutes at a time. It is not recommended for the average backpacker.

SPARE PARTS. Clevis pins, lock rings, plastic plugs and caps, eye bolts, and so on, can be purchased for replacements or as spares for a possible emergency on the trail.

OTHER ACCESSORIES. Clamps that mount along the vertical members of tubular packframes are available for lashing various items of equipment. Some backpackers find a removable shelf that mounts to the lower part of the packframe to be a convenience. Extension bars can be purchased that can be mounted on the top of some packframes (H frames) by removing the plastic plug or cap and inserting the smaller-diameter tubing of the extension bar. This is useful for carrying light, bulky loads (such as an additional sleeping bag for a family group, a foam pad, or similar item).

THE PACKBAG

A good packbag is an important complement to a good packframe. It should be large and commensurate with the size of the packframe. This is not so that you can carry an extra heavy load, but rather because it is easier to pack equipment in a roomy bag in a systematic manner — so that it can be found more quickly when you want it. In general, packbags come in full length (covering essentially the full length of the packframe) and in three-quarter length. The three-quarter-length bag is the least expensive and remains the most popular. With a full-length packbag the sleeping bag is usually placed in the bottom compartment. However, it is somewhat more difficult to stuff a sleeping bag into a compartment of a packbag than it is to get it into a stuff bag. Most backpackers prefer to use a stuff bag for their sleeping bag and strap it to the lower part of the packframe.

There is also the matter of cost. A three-quarter-length bag plus a stuff bag for your sleeping bag will cost considerably less than a full-length packbag. Some three-quarter-length bags have the added feature that they can be moved up or down on the packframe to change the center of gravity of the load. This is an advantage if you will be hiking over varied terrain and under a wide range of hiking conditions.

As to proportions, the packbag should be fairly high, have a good width, and not be too deep (front to back). As was previously mentioned, a major objective in packframe design is to place the load as nearly as possible over the center of gravity of the body. If a packbag that is too deep (front to back) is then mounted to the frame, it defeats the objective of holding the load close to the body. The hiker will need to lean forward to compensate for the excess depth of the packbag, which, when loaded, will exert a backward pull on the body. A depth of 7 or 8 inches for the packbag is about right.

Attachment. If possible, purchase a bag that is intended for the frame you buy. This will provide a better fit and ensure that the points of attachment and method of attachment of bag to frame are compatible with one another. The method of attachment of bag to frame is usually by clevis pins, using either a long locking wire going through all pins along one rail of the packframe, or individual split rings in the clevis pins. The grommets through which the clevis pins fit to attach the bag to the frame are worthy of careful inspection to see that they are properly inserted and not likely to tear loose. There should be at least three points of attachment (on each side) where the packbag is fastened to the frame.

Some packbags are not mounted to the frame with clevis pins. Instead, the top of the bag has, at each corner, a 4- or 5-inch sleeve that fits over the top of the vertical rail. These are points of stress and abrasion. Tie tapes on the bottom corners of the packbag, and in some cases at intermediate points, hold the packbag to the frame. This method of attachment is much less desirable than the use of clevis pins.

Materials. Many quality packbags are made of waterproof urethane-coated nylon. Some bags are only water repellent, but waterproof is preferable. If it is raining, you will want to keep every drop of water that you possibly can out of the bag. The question of "breathability" of the fabric is not applicable here, as it is for tents or clothing. If you have a damp article of clothing in your packbag, it should be inside a plastic bag or other waterproof cover where it cannot dampen the other contents of the pack. If the sun is shining, damp articles are best hung on the outside of the pack, where they can dry as you hike along the trail.

The side of the waterproof nylon that has the waterproof (urethane) treatment should be on the *inside* of the packbag. The outside surfaces of your packbag are subject to scuffing and abrasion, which has a tendency to rub away the waterproof coating. Although the inside surfaces of the bag are subject to a certain amount of rubbing and abrasion, it is not nearly so severe as that on the outside surfaces, if the bag is properly packed.

In recent years Cordura, a rough-textured nylon duck weighing about 10 or 12 ounces per yard, has been used in some packbag designs. Where the bag may be subjected to unusually rough wear, Cordura is a good material. For all normal usage, 6- to 8-ounce waterproof nylon duck is sufficiently tough and quite adequate. In some designs Cordura is used only on the bottom of the packbag, which may be particularly subject to scuffing and abrasion. If the packbag is three-

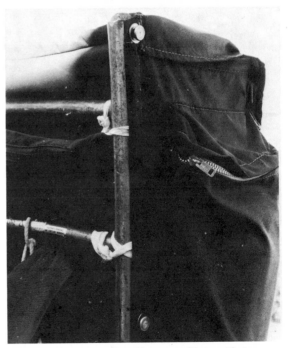

One method of attaching packbag to frame. Clevis pins are a somewhat better method.

Clevis pin attachment of packbag to packframe. Tie tapes hold in place a small homemade zippered bag containing trail snacks.

quarter length and is mounted on the frame above a stuff bag, there is little more wear on the outside bottom of the bag than in other areas.

Packbags should be sewn with synthetic thread, since cotton thread is subject to rot. The sewing of the seams on the bag should be carefully scrutinized. Stitching should be even and the stitches close together. Rows of stitches should be straight. Double rows of stitching should be used in areas of high stress. Reinforcing material and extra stitching should be used at the top corners and in places such as where the packbag fastens to the frame. The sewing of all zippers, compartments, pockets, and the pack bottom should be carefully checked. The sewing and workmanship in the areas of grommets and D rings is important, since these are subjected to high stress.

Compartments.   The basic packbag may be one large compartment, or it may be divided. A common arrangement is to have one large upper compartment and a comparatively roomy lower compartment extending the full width of the bag, with a generously long zipper for separate access to contents. This makes for easy access to certain items, especially items that may be used frequently during the day, without opening the large main compartment. Some bags incorporate a light metal frame in the upper compartment for the purpose of holding the compartment open for easier loading or unloading.

Some packbags have other compartments in addition to a large upper compartment and a small lower compartment with outside access. Some have a vertical divider in the upper compartment. Other designs have multilayered horizontal compartments stacked on top of one another, extending the width of the bag. Too many compartments or dividers can be a nuisance. I believe it is far easier to pack a bag that has few compartments in the main bag. A good arrangement is one large upper compartment and a smaller lower compartment. If various items of equipment and clothing are placed in plastic bags before packing, they are easily packed into the larger compartment and readily found when needed. In a normal hiking day I find that there are very few times while on the trail that I need access to the main compartment of my packbag, and there is never a need to rummage through its contents. I may remove or replace a protective garment that I usually carry at the top of the compartment contents. The lower zippered compartment and the packbag pockets hold most of the items that I need during the day on the trail.

A common arrangement of outside pockets on a packbag is to have two on either side — usually one deep pocket and another roughly half the depth of the first. The large pockets should be of sufficient size to hold a water bottle or canteen. Generous-sized pockets with good zippers are important features of a good packbag. Some manufacturers use synthetic zippers; others use metal zippers. The important thing is that the zippers be of good quality and that they operate freely. All zippers on a bag should be checked before buying to assure that they operate properly. A very important feature of all zippered closures is a generous-sized protective flap that completely covers the zipper when the pack is loaded (and the zippers are under tension). All zippers are potential sources of water leakage in a rainstorm. The flaps should keep out water and dirt. When you shop for a new packbag, check over the inside of the packbag pockets for possible loose ravelings of thread or excess cloth along the zipper opening. When these get stuck in the zipper, either in camp or along the trail, it can be very annoying. In general, the manufacturing processes used in the better packbags eliminate this problem.

The main compartment of most packbags opens at the top. The top opening on a pack is another feature that may quickly cause a packbag to leak if it is improperly designed, even though the bag may be made of waterproof material. The top flap on the packbag should be of generous size, so as to cover the main (top) opening completely and also to provide protection to a jacket or other article of clothing, which may be rolled and placed under the flap in the final step of packing the bag. A map pocket located in the flap is an important feature and it, also, should be of generous size. A Velcro tape closure for this pocket may be helpful. The flap is usually fastened by nylon cords tied to the flap at the corners through grommet holes and fastened to D rings located about two thirds of the way down the back side of the bag. (The back side of the packbag is the side that opens — the side farthest to the rear when the bag is on the hiker's back.) A strap and buckle closure may also be used.

Some packbags, in addition to side pockets and a map pocket on top, have a pocket at the rear. Added to the depth of 7 or 8 inches for the main bag, this places the contents of such a pocket still further away from the packframe and the center of gravity of the body. Therefore, if there is such a compartment, it should never be loaded with heavy items.

In a few packbag designs the large compartment has a zippered opening which arcs across the *back* of the bag. This allows quick access to the contents at all levels of the compartment without digging from the top. Such designs usually provide two horizontal straps across the rear of the bag for stabilizing the load and to relieve the zippers of excess stress.

Some packbags feature leather patches or loops for fastening such gear as ice axes, hammers, crampons, and so on. Most backpackers do not require these.

Packbag accessories. There are some accessories available for your packbag that will add to its usefulness. One of these is a good stuff bag to contain your sleeping bag. With a three-quarter-length packbag the stuff bag is usually strapped to the lower part of the frame. Straps, rather than shock cord or rope, are recommended for fastening the stuff bag to the frame. Shock cord will frequently catch on branches or other projections along the trail, and you may lose your sleeping bag. Cord will have a tendency to cut into the stuff bag contents, and it is more difficult to fasten the load tightly to the frame. Straps provide a fairly wide bearing surface, can be made very tight, and can be quickly tightened and loosened.

STUFF BAG. In the purchase of some packframe-packbag combinations a stuff bag is included. More often, however, it must be bought separately. A stuff bag is also frequently included in a sleeping bag purchase. However, sleeping bag manufacturers often furnish a stuff bag that is too small. The sleeping bag will fit into the stuff bag under ideal conditions, and with sufficient time. However, field conditions are seldom ideal. If your stuff bag appears a bit small, it is recommended that you try to convince the sup-

plier to furnish a larger one. If this fails, it may be desirable to purchase another stuff bag.

The size of the stuff bag will be dictated primarily by the size of the sleeping bag and the amount and compressibility of its filler material. Stuff bags are generally about 8 to 12 inches in diameter and 18 to 22 inches long. It is recommended that the length be such that you take advantage of the full width of your packframe. A fairly long stuff bag of modest diameter is easier to handle and pack than a short, stubby one of large diameter.

It cannot be stressed too strongly that the stuff bag should be of strong, abrasion-resistant, waterproof nylon. It should have a drawstring opening and a generous-sized flap to protect the opening. Your sleeping bag is not a rugged piece of equipment. If it gets torn or wet, it is not going to do the job that you want it to. As a further aid to ensuring that your sleeping bag will stay dry, it is recommended that it be contained in a large polyethylene bag in addition to its regular stuff bag. The polyethylene bag can be somewhat larger than the regular stuff bag, but never smaller. The best approach to getting the sleeping bag inside both bags is to first partially stuff the sleeping bag into the polyethylene bag. Next, insert the polyethylene bag into the regular stuff bag and continue stuffing the sleeping bag simultaneously into both bags.

As you travel along the trail, there will be rest stops and other stops during the day when you will be removing your pack. In setting your pack on the ground, use reasonable care to select a spot that is free from stones, sticks, or any sharp objects that might penetrate the stuff bag and perhaps damage the sleeping bag inside.

POCKETS. Perhaps there is room on your packbag for extra outside pockets, and you would like more. Pockets that you can sew onto the packbag are available from some suppliers. Side pockets are usually sold in pairs; rear pockets are sold as single units.

PACK COVER. Although your packbag may be made of waterproof material, it is worth some extra effort and some additional weight to ensure that its contents will stay dry. Zippers, seams, and top openings are points of potential leakage. Backpackers who do much hiking in rainy weather will probably want a pack cover. A pack cover made of coated nylon weighs about 4 ounces and costs $8 to $10. It is one of those items that is relatively easy to make yourself, if you are so inclined.

Stuff bag, containing sleeping bag, strapped to lower part of packframe.

SHOPPING FOR A BACKPACK

You will probably have your packframe and packbag for a long time. Some careful shopping is called for if you are to have a combination that you will be satisfied with. A poor pack load can mean many hours of misery on the trail, whereas a substantial load contained in a good packbag that is mounted on a good frame can be carried in relative comfort.

Talk to other backpackers about their packs. Visit mountaineering stores and other shops and try on some of their packframe-packbag combinations. If possible, rent or borrow a pack for a short trail trip. If your budget is limited, it is recommended that you concentrate on first obtaining a good, well-fitting packframe. The best packbag will never make a comfortable load if mounted on a poor packframe. On the other hand, an inexpensive packbag that will do the job can be purchased or even made at home. Or you can place your equipment in a tarp and lash it to the packframe. It may not be as convenient as a good packbag (with pockets, and so on), but if the load is properly fastened to a good packframe, it will be comfortable.

Quite a few cheap imitations of good packframes, many foreign made, have appeared on the market in recent years. It is particularly recommended that your packframe-packbag combination be purchased from a reputable backpacking equipment supplier. Be sure to check it over thoroughly and determine that it meets the basic requirements as outlined herein. You cannot get much of a feel for the comfort of a packframe-packbag combination by simply putting it on with no load in the packbag. Some stores will have a simulated load you can use. Or you can carry your own, say a package of books wrapped in a blanket and tied into a bundle.

In fitting a packframe to your particular body build, the important criterion is the measurement from the top of your shoulders to your waistline. Your height is not necessarily important, because the trunk of your body could still be either long or short. Most packframes come in a small, medium, and large size, and one of these sizes will usually fit the average person. Some manufacturers also provide an extra large size. A very few backpacks come in one size only. If that one size doesn't fit, you have to look to another brand, unless it can be adjusted to your size. Some adjustability for the individual is provided by moving the backbands up or down on the frame. On some frames the height of the shoulder straps is adjustable to fit the individual torso. A few frames are telescopic and can readily be shortened or lengthened. Such a frame may well be worth considering for a child or teenager who is still in the growing stage. For those people who are inclined toward a wrap-around frame design, the fit becomes more critical. A competent and knowledgeable salesperson is always a definite help when it comes to selecting a packframe size to fit your particular build.

You can expect to pay from $30 to $75 or more for a good packframe-packbag combination. Some expedition-type backpacks and some with wrap-around frame designs will cost considerably more. (The average backpacker has no need for an expedition-type backpack.) A good basic packframe and packbag in a youth size may cost as little as $25. Packframes and packbags can be bought separately. Prices for a packframe range from about $18 to $35 or more. Packbags range in price from about $20 to $45 and up. Most packframe-packbag combinations will generally weigh from 3½ to 4¼ pounds, with 4 pounds being a good average weight for an empty pack in an adult size.

LOADING A BACKPACK

The pack load should ride both close to the back and high on the back, but it should not be top-heavy. Where the terrain is very rugged or steep climbing is to be done, the center of gravity of the load needs to be kept low so as not to throw the wearer off balance. In most backpacking, over reasonably good trails, the heaviest items in the load need to be near shoulder level. This is accomplished by mounting the packsack high on the packframe and by packing light objects in the bottom of the packsack and heavier objects near the top. The sleeping bag is usually fastened to the lower part of the packframe.

When a good packframe is properly loaded, the center of gravity of the load will be very nearly over the hiker's hips. The hiker will feel comfortable when walking in essentially an upright position, bending forward only very slightly to balance the load. In order to keep the center of gravity of a substantial load close to the back, the frame and the load on it need to be high, wide, and not very deep (front to back).

RUCKSACKS

A rucksack is a small pack that is usually supported entirely by the shoulders. It rides quite low on the back, compared to a packframe. Rucksacks are used primarily for day hikes and overnight trips, where light loads are to be carried. They are of particular use to climbers and skiers because the center of gravity of the load is much lower than with a packframe. They do not have the tendency to throw the wearer off balance, as does a packframe load with a high center of gravity. However, with most rucksacks a load of more than 20 to 25 pounds is uncomfortable. (With some designs the limit of comfort is reached with a much lesser load.) Even with a nominal load you need to lean forward to keep your balance. Some incorporate a belt, mainly to hold the load in position. There are frameless rucksacks and also rucksacks with light metal frames to give shape to the load and make it more comfortable. Many backpackers never use a rucksack. For the average hiker their primary use is for day hikes.

Frameless rucksacks.   For carrying a jacket, rain gear, lunch, first aid equipment, and so on, on a day hike, a frameless rucksack is often used. For loads of 10 to 20 pounds a frameless rucksack is usually preferable to carrying a large packframe and packbag. With the frameless type the load will bear directly against the back. If it is a large load, it can generate quite a bit of heat and sweat and be uncomfortable on a hot day. It is best to buy a fairly large rucksack and plan to fill it only loosely. If a loaded rucksack is packed tightly, it will tend to bounce against the back with each step and make for a very uncomfortable load. It is also important in packing the rucksack to have clothing or other soft material in the area that will be riding next to the back.

Rucksacks are often made roughly triangular in shape, with the peak of the triangle riding near the nape of the neck. They are frequently made of canvas, which is relatively rugged and tends to retain the original shape of the sack. Nylon is also used, sometimes in combination with canvas. A small, all-nylon rucksack has the capability of being folded and compacted into a very small bundle for stowing. Some backpackers carry such a rucksack inside their packbag for day trips that they plan to make from a base camp. The average frameless rucksack weighs about 1 to 2 pounds. The cost ranges from about $10 to $35.

Framed rucksacks.   For greater loads, roughly 15 to 30 pounds, framed rucksacks are available. The frame tends to give shape to the load and to keep various objects in the rucksack from poking into the hiker's back. With a few exceptions (a few sophisticated designs have weight-bearing belts) the load is still borne entirely on the shoulders. When it reaches the 25- to 35-pound category, it is often best to go to a packframe-packbag combination.

Framed rucksacks are usually somewhat larger and a pound or more heavier than the frameless type. The cost ranges from about $20 to $60.

Most backpackers would do well to avoid the sophisticated, expensive rucksacks and go directly to the packframe-packbag combination that has been described in previous paragraphs.

BELT POUCH

Rather than stuffing your pockets with a few items of equipment needed for a very short hike, it is a good idea to use a belt bag or pouch. This usually takes the form of a small zippered compartment that simply slips onto your belt. The cost usually ranges from about $5 to $8. However, it is not difficult to make a simple belt pouch if you choose to do so.

Small rucksack for day hikes. (Lou Clemmons)

FANNY PACK OR WAIST PACK

The fanny pack, or waist pack, is usually a fairly large zippered compartment measuring roughly 4 by 4 by 12 inches. It is contoured to fit around the back at waist level and is fitted with a waist strap and buckle. Its use is generally limited to day hikes in good weather, where a minimum of gear will suffice. This type of pack is also used by skiers. The cost is usually about $10 to $15.

The waist pack is useful for day hikes. When it is certain that a few small items of equipment and lunch will suffice for the planned day hike, this is a good way to carry those few items of gear.

Waist pack being worn by author.

3
Sleeping Gear

SLEEPING BAGS

Backpacking requires the expenditure of a lot of physical energy. If you are to recover this energy and be prepared to start each day with renewed strength and enthusiasm, then you must sleep soundly and comfortably at night. Few things are more important on a backpack trip than your bed. It is one of those factors, like a good pack and good boots, that can mean the difference between an enjoyable trip and one where you wish you had stayed home. In adverse weather the characteristics of your sleeping bag may be a deciding factor in whether you survive or not. Don't try to drive any hard bargains in purchasing a sleeping bag for backpacking. A good sleeping bag, purchased from a reputable manufacturer or supplier, is a wise investment, a pleasure to pack, and a joy to use. With reasonable care it will probably last for many years.

The first backpackers carried blankets. Later ones tried old-style rectangular bags that left much to be desired from the standpoint of weight, warmth, bulk, and other important factors. It was not unusual for a backpacker in the old days to carry 10 to 12 pounds of blankets or a rectangular-shaped bag weighing 8 or 10 pounds. This is no longer necessary. Modern methods of construction and modern filler materials have made available good sleeping bags weighing from 3 to 6 pounds that will provide the necessary warmth

and comfort required by the most discerning backpacker.

For backpacking use, the rectangular sleeping bags have given way to the "mummy" style. A mummy bag, in contrast to the rectangular-shaped bag, essentially conforms to the shape of your body, being wide at the shoulders and tapering toward the feet. The rectangular bag has much more room in it than is necessary to confine your body, and it thus weighs more than a mummy bag that will provide equivalent warmth. The air inside the sleeping bag must be heated by your body before you will become warm. It takes considerably longer to heat the excess volume of air in a rectangular bag than that in a mummy one.

Filler material. In the past few years there have been some very significant changes in regard to sleeping bag construction. The most important of these changes has been the result of the development of new insulating materials, particularly Hollofil II* and PolarGuard. Sleeping bags and protective garments made from these materials have become popular with many backpackers. They will therefore be discussed in some detail in

*In 1977 Du Pont, the manufacturer of Fiberfill II, changed the name to Hollofil II. Therefore, you will find that recent literature refers to Hollofil II, although there is no change in the product itself.

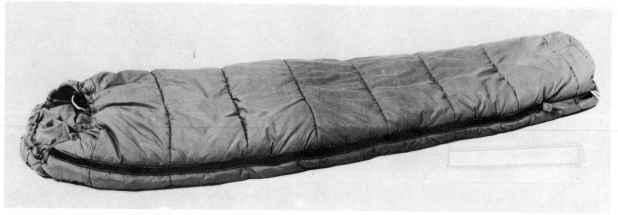

Sleeping bag insulated with Du Pont Fiberfill II. *(Mountain Products Corp.)*

this section. Still another synthetic insulating material that has gained favor with some backpackers is open-cell polyurethane foam.

Down insulation (both goose down and duck down) has been used for many years in the manufacture of quality sleeping bags and garments. Many backpackers still prefer down as an insulating material. The primary differences—and very important ones—between down and the synthetics are the latter's ability to insulate when wet and the comparatively shorter time that they take to dry.

Cheap sleeping bags are available that contain inexpensive filler materials such as kapok, Orlon, Celacloud, and a long list of others that can be quite confusing to the inexperienced. Many of these fillers have a tendency to mat and pack into lumps, thus losing their insulating value (which was probably very poor to start with). Some of the fillers are attractive to vermin. Sleeping bags made from these materials are not worth consideration by most backpackers and will not be discussed.

The *warmth* of a sleeping bag is a primary consideration. Warmth in turn is determined by the *loft,* or thickness, of the insulating material. The greater the thickness, the greater the dead-air space that is created around your body, and thus the warmer the bag will be.

Other important considerations are *compressibility* and *weight.* For backpacking, it is desirable to compress the bag into a reasonably small space for ease in carrying. Weight is also a primary consideration for any item that must be backpacked.

DOWN. The down of the northern domesticated goose has long been used as a filler for high quality sleeping bags for backpacking. Some down comes from Canada, some from northern Europe, and much from other sources. There is

also considerable variation in the quality of goose down. A particularly attractive characteristic of goose down is that it can be compressed repeatedly and still regain its original volume when the pressure is released. An ounce of high quality goose down will fill a space of more than 500 cubic inches.

Top quality goose down has become quite scarce and expensive in recent years. As a result, some manufacturers are substituting duck down, or a blend of goose down and duck down, in their sleeping bags.

Good duck down comes quite close to being the equal of goose down insofar as the factors of compressibility and loft are concerned and it is used in many good quality bags. Incidentally, in goose down the color of the down makes no difference in the quality. Gray goose down is as satisfactory as white down. Also, a few small feathers are present even in the best quality down.

As a rough check on the quality of down, you can feel through the covering of the bag for lumps that indicate the presence of pinfeathers. You can also check the bag label, which is required by law to state the nature of the filling, but there can be a great deal of variation in fillings covered by the various descriptive tags on sleeping bags, even

Sleeping bag insulated with open-cell urethane foam. *(Trail Tech)*

though the tags would all appear to indicate high-quality filler. *Avoid* any sleeping bag whose label indicates that it contains *reprocessed down*. Bags can be compared somewhat by laying them out on a flat area, fluffing them up, and noting the loft. The bag with the most loft will be the thickest and warmest. Since you cannot see the filler material, this is another important reason for buying your sleeping bag from a reputable manufacturer.

One of the major advantages of down as a filler for sleeping bags is also a disadvantage. For packing and carrying, it compresses easily into a small, compact bundle. It will therefore compress under your body during the night and provide less insulation in that area. Another disadvantage is that a down bag completely loses its insulating value when it becomes wet. Further, it cannot be dried quickly. Under field conditions it may take four or five days, or even longer, to dry.

A good down sleeping bag, purchased from a reputable supplier, will range in price from about $75 to over $200. The price depends primarily on the quality of the down, the amount of down, and the workmanship used in construction. Sleeping bags in the $200 price range are intended for use in very cold weather and will not be required by most backpackers.

HOLLOFIL II (FIBERFILL II). For many years Du Pont Dacron "88" (polyester fiberfill) was the best of the synthetic filler materials used in making sleeping bags. However, it was heavy and virtually noncompressible. Many of the large rectangular sleeping bags used in car camping are made from this material. In recent years Du Pont has marketed a greatly improved Dacron material known as Hollofil II (Fiberfill II), which is now one of the leading synthetic materials used in lightweight sleeping bags for backpacking. It re-

covers quickly from compression and can be re-fluffed. In fact, its compressibility is roughly 90 percent of the compressibility of goose down. It takes about 1½ pounds of Hollofil II to equal the insulating value of 1 pound of goose down.

An important characteristic to the backpacker is that Hollofil II is virtually waterproof. Hollofil II fibers absorb less than 1 percent water. A sleeping bag that uses this material as an insulator can get thoroughly wet and still retain essentially its original loft. Also, a wet Hollofil II sleeping bag is much easier and quicker to dry than a wet down bag. In the field, water can be squeezed from a wet Hollofil II bag and the bag dried for a short period, and it is ready for use. In fact, after being squeezed out by hand, the still damp bag can be used immediately with relative comfort.

Hollofil II is made of hollow polyester fibers. The fibers are relatively short and are sometimes referred to as chopped fibers. The Hollofil II material is furnished to the sleeping bag manufacturer in the form of batts. The material is nonallergenic, odorless, and mildew resistant.

Hollofil II is a relatively inexpensive material. The cost of a sleeping bag that uses this material is dependent primarily on the method of internal construction and quality of workmanship, rather than on the amount of Hollofil II that is used as insulation. A good Hollofil II sleeping bag will cost from $50 up to about $90.

POLARGUARD. PolarGuard is a synthetic material having characteristics very similar to those of Hollofil II. Basic differences are that PolarGuard filaments are solid and are essentially continuous, in contrast to the short, hollow, chopped filaments of Hollofil II, and that a light resin coating is used to hold the PolarGuard filaments together. Thus, it does not feel quite so soft as Hollofil II, but it is very satisfactory in that

Parka and footsack. This sleeper is using Hollofil II parka (made by the author) in combination with a PolarGuard bivouac bag, or footsack. The footsack weighs about 32 ounces and the parka about 40 ounces. For such use, the parka should have a zipper that functions from the inside as well as the outside. Parka sleeves would normally be pulled inside the parka for nighttime use.

respect. PolarGuard will not compress quite so much under the weight of a sleeping person's body as Hollofil II will. Thus, it requires less added insulation between the sleeper and the ground. Both PolarGuard and Hollofil II are far superior to down in this respect.

PolarGuard absorbs less than 1 percent moisture. Thus, it dries in a comparatively short time. Even when wet, it retains over 80 percent of its loft; therefore, its effectiveness as an insulator is good when wet. Like Hollofil II, PolarGuard is nonallergenic, odorless, and resistant to mildew.

Some very reliable manufacturers of quality products are making both sleeping bags and protective clothing using Hollofil II as insulation. Other manufacturers, equally competent and reliable, are making such products using Polar-Guard as an insulator. If a clear superiority of one filler over the other does exist, it has not been conclusively demonstrated. Both are excellent materials. A good sleeping bag that uses Polar-Guard as an insulator will range in price from about $50 to $90. As with Hollofil II, the method of construction and quality of workmanship have a greater bearing on the cost of the sleeping bag than the amount of filler used.

OPEN-CELL FOAM.   Some sleeping bags used for backpacking utilize open-cell polyurethane foam as an insulator. Open-cell urethane foam is another of the few materials that will still insulate when damp. A thoroughly soaked sleeping bag that uses this material as an insulator can be squeezed out in the field and used immediately with relative comfort. A disadvantage when it comes to packing these sleeping bags is their relative bulk and stiffness. They compress very little and require about twice the storage volume that an equivalent down bag would. However, an advantage in this regard is that a sleeping pad or mattress is frequently not required when using such a bag. The urethane foam used as an insulator is often a sufficient pad in itself between the sleeper and the ground. These bags do not conform to or drape about the body as do most sleeping bags made from more conventional materials. However, some backpackers have found these bags to be quite acceptable. From a weight standpoint such sleeping bags are competitive with conventional bags, especially if the backpacker eliminates a separate pad or mattress. These sleeping bags range in price from about $50 to $70.

Construction.   In buying a sleeping bag, the head and shoulder area should be carefully in-

spected. Some mummy sleeping bags are designed so that a single drawstring at the head end can be adjusted to completely enclose the shoulders and head. Others have a drawstring at the shoulders and an extended hood. In this design the hood can be left flat (in warm weather), or it may be drawn tight around the head and face with another drawstring. A few bags are made with hoods that can be completely detached from the sleeping bag.

A popular design is one wherein the head end of the bag is closed by a single drawstring that provides for drawing the bag tightly about the head and face. Since the opening at the head and shoulder area is important to proper ventilation on a warm night and is equally important in shutting out cold air on a cold night, good adjustment in this area is called for.

When you are snug in your sleeping bag, you reach up from the inside with your hands and tie a nice bowknot in the tie tape. However, this frequently presents a problem later on. When you wake up, either during the night or in the early morning, and sleepily reach up to quickly undo the bowknot in the tie tape, you may find that it has relapsed during the night into a good solid knot. Not being able to see the knot that you are trying to untie makes the job no simple matter, and being somewhat captive inside the sleeping bag may give you claustrophobia quickly. Most quality sleeping bags come equipped with a spring-loaded fastener or a slide fastener so that it is not necessary to tie a knot in the drawstring. If your sleeping bag does not come equipped with

Spring-loaded drawstring clamp, installed on sleeping bag drawstring.

such a fastener, one can be purchased separately and readily installed.

The outer and inner fabric used in the shell construction of down sleeping bags must be down proof so that the down will not work its way through the bag covering and be lost. Many manufacturers of quality down sleeping bags use 1.5- or 1.9-ounce ripstop nylon. This material is essentially down proof, breathable, and strong (highly tear resistant). It is also wind resistant. Taffeta is a nylon material with characteristics similar to those of ripstop nylon. It is also used for shell construction in some of the quality sleeping bags.

A basic aspect of sleeping bag design is the cut of the inner and outer shells. In a differential cut, the inner shell (next to the sleeper's body) is cut smaller than the outer shell. This type of cut supposedly has the advantage of allowing the filler to loft more freely about the sleeper's body. Also, knees and arms apparently do not poke into the filler and thereby create a thin spot in the insulation. However, some quality bags are made with the inner shell having the same circumference as the outer shell. Manufacturers who use this design claim that the inner shell drapes more closely around the sleeper's body, thus leaving fewer air pockets to be heated. Both designs are being used in quality sleeping bags. How the shells are cut is probably of less importance than good workmanship—which means that the bag should be purchased from a reputable manufacturer or supplier.

A well-made sleeping bag will have additional room at the foot end in the form of a special elliptical or box-shaped construction, rather than a flat envelope. This prevents the feet from thrusting into the filler material and thereby creating a thin spot or cold area.

One of the indications of quality in a sleeping bag is the stitching. It should be uniform. Nylon thread is generally used. Check the stitching in difficult-to-sew places, such as the hood of the bag and along the zipper. There should be a double row of stitching at points of stress. Eight to ten stitches per inch is about right. Cheaply made bags may have much longer stitches. Backstitching or tacking should be used at the end of a row of stitching, for reinforcement.

In shopping for a sleeping bag, be sure to get one that is long enough. If you are six feet tall or taller, this requires special consideration. If you should purchase a sleeping bag that is a bit too short, you will regret every night that you spend in it. You should get inside the bag. With the hood closed, there should be ample room at the shoul-

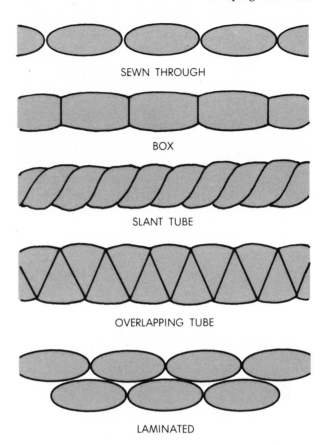

SEWN THROUGH

BOX

SLANT TUBE

OVERLAPPING TUBE

LAMINATED

Down sleeping bag construction.

ders and at the foot end. With your body stretched out your feet should *not* press against the ends of the bag. Make sure you can draw the hood tightly and securely about your head.

CONSTRUCTION OF DOWN BAGS. The internal construction of the sleeping bag is of primary importance. A well-constructed sleeping bag having 2 pounds of high grade goose down filler material may easily keep the sleeper warm at temperatures down to 5° or 10° F. A poorly constructed sleeping bag using exactly the same filler material may be cold at temperatures well above freezing. Good construction means extra labor and good workmanship—and a higher cost—but it is a very important factor.

To provide uniform warmth in a sleeping bag, it is important that the filler material be kept evenly distributed around the sleeper's body. In down bags the filler material is contained in tubes or panels. In a very few inexpensive sleeping bags these tubes run longitudinally, from the head to the foot. However, the filler tends to shift within the tubes, and in the longitudinal tubes shifts toward the foot of the bag. The better sleeping bags have circumferential filler compartments or a variation of this called the chevron pattern.

Panels are usually constructed of nylon netting, which is light and compressible and does a satisfactory job of preventing the shifting of down between compartments. Some manufacturers use nylon cloth, rather than netting, for panel construction.

There are essentially five basic types of internal construction, or compartment design, used to contain the down.

A *quilted*, or *sewn-through*, construction is used in some of the inexpensive sleeping bags. It is the least satisfactory of the various types of construction because it permits cold spots at the stitched-through points. The best quality sleeping bags have panels, or baffles, sewn to the inner and outer shells.

In a *box* type of construction, baffles that form individual compartments at right angles to the inner and outer fabric are used. In this type of construction there is some tendency for the down to fall away from the baffles. This may result in cold spots.

The *slant tube*, or *slant wall*, type of construction is used by many manufacturers of high quality sleeping bags. The slant tube minimizes the shift of the down. At the same time, when the pressure is released from the bag, the down regains its maximum loft.

The *overlapping tube* type of construction is efficient in restricting down shift. However, it somewhat restricts the down from reaching its maximum loft when the pressure is removed. There is also some penalty in added weight and cost, because of the additional paneling required.

The *laminated* type of construction is essentially two quilted sleeping bags sewn together so as to eliminate the cold spots. Such construction makes the bags heavy, because of the extra layers of fabric. Very few sleeping bags use this design.

CONSTRUCTION OF SYNTHETIC-FILLED BAGS. Both Hollofil II and PolarGuard are purchased by the sleeping bag or garment manufacturer in the form of batts. Both materials are machine processed to form a batting of desired thickness. Since these batts are a far different raw material to work with than goose or duck down, the various methods of internal construction used to contain the material in down sleeping bags do not apply to Hollofil II or PolarGuard bags.

The methods of containment of the batts within the sleeping bag to prevent thin or cold spots and to prevent shifting vary among the manufacturers. In one of the high quality designs of a Hollofil II bag the batts are sewn in an overlapping slanted configuration, with each batt extending completely around the circumference of the bag. At any point on the bag there are two full thicknesses of batting. The most inexpensive bags use only a single layer of batting. Stabilization of the batts is accomplished by sewn-through seams. Such bags will have cold spots at the seams, where the two sides of the nylon shell are pinched together.

As was pointed out previously, PolarGuard is essentially a continuous filament. It therefore lends itself to a minimum of sewing to keep the batts from pulling apart and shifting. One construction method, often used with this material in medium-priced bags, is simply stitching around the edges of the shell to hold it to the batting. This is referred to as edge stabilization. Since Hollofil II batts consist of many very short filaments, this method is not applicable to that material. The filaments would shift, leaving cold spots. Some manufacturers who use PolarGuard as an insulator feel that the batts will eventually shift if only edge stabilization is used to hold them in place. Therefore, some employ a quilted construction. Still others use a laminated construction in which the PolarGuard batt is laminated to a supporting material. It can be seen that the technology of construction is still developing and that further changes in manufacturing processes will undoubtedly be made. Regardless of the insulating material used in your prospective sleeping bag, the reputation of the manufacturer remains an important consideration.

It is not necessary to have a ripstop fabric in a polyester bag (as it is in a down bag). The matter of a very tightly woven fabric is not so important here. Down and small feathers will find their way through the sleeping bag shell if it is not made of tightly woven cloth. This does not apply to polyester batting, however. You may get a small rip in your bag, but the Hollofil II or PolarGuard will not come pouring out the gap (as will goose down), since it is in the form of batts. An uncoated nylon taffeta is frequently used as shell material for polyester bags. As with down bags, the material must *not* be waterproof. It must be able to breathe, or it will become wet from the perspiration given off by your body. Some manufacturers use ripstop nylon for all sleeping bag shells—those of both down-filled and synthetic-insulated bags.

Whatever the internal construction of the synthetic-filled bag may be, construction is an important aspect. When you shop for such a bag, if the construction is not apparent and if the salesperson does not have convincing information on this aspect, I would recommend that you take time to write to the manufacturer for such information before going ahead with a purchase. To repeat an earlier statement, your sleeping bag is one of your most important items of equipment. Take your time and shop carefully.

Zippers. Some sleeping bags are made without zippers. You simply put them on like a sock. If the weather is warm, you push the bag down from the head and shoulders for more ventilation. Such bags are not as difficult to get into and out of as one might think. Lightweight sleeping bags, in particular, may perform very well without a zipper.

Most sleeping bags have zippers. A zipper adds a bit to the weight and is a possible source of heat loss. However, the possibility of heat loss at the zipper can be countered by a well-designed insulated flap. The insulated flap or tube should be constructed so that it cannot be easily moved out of position when the sleeper rolls over. It should

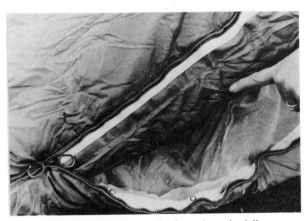

A down-filled baffle on the sleeping bag, along the full length of the zipper, prevents cold air from entering the bag.

Down-filled sleeping bag with side-mounted zipper. *(Lou Clemmons)*

be generous in size and thick, and it should cover the zipper fully. Draft tubes in some sleeping bag designs have a tendency to get caught in the zipper. You should test the operation of the zipper for its full length to check this feature and also the smoothness of operation of the zipper. The foot end of the zipper should be checked to make sure that the draft tube extends the complete length of the zipper and that there is no cold spot at the very end.

Metal zippers are cold. They also jam and break more easily than nylon zippers do. They have a tendency to rip the shell fabric when snagged. The best zippers are heavy-duty nylon or Delrin. They do not feel cold to the sleeper and are less subject to snagging than metal zippers are. A #10 YKK zipper is a good heavy-duty zipper. A #5 YKK is the smallest that should be used on a sleeping bag. A good quality zipper is very important. Most of the heavy-duty toothed zippers are very dependable. Coil zippers are somewhat more snag proof and easy to free, but they seem to vary in quality more than the toothed zippers do.

Whether to buy a sleeping bag with a full-length or half-length zipper depends primarily upon intended use. If you are going to be using your sleeping bag for a significant amount of warm-weather backpacking, you will probably want a full-length zipper for a wider range of temperature control. The zipper should have two-way operation, opening from both the head and foot ends. In a bag used mostly for cool-weather backpacking, a half-length zipper may suffice. Since the zipper is a potential area for significant loss of heat, the lesser length of zipper should tend to make the sleeping bag warmer. Also, if a full-length zipper becomes jammed in cold weather, it takes a lot of safety pins or other improvisation to keep the cold air out.

Some zippers are mounted on the top center of the sleeping bag; others, at the side. Top-mounted zippers can be operated while the sleeper is lying on his back. However, a top-mounted zipper will have some tendency to reduce loft. Ventilation control is probably somewhat easier with side-mounted zippers. In the long run it probably does not make a lot of difference whether zippers are top mounted or side mounted. However, most quality sleeping bags have side-mounted zippers. Full-length zippers should be 70 inches or more in length. If sleeping bags are purchased with the thought of zippering two bags together, it is important to check the operation of the zippers to see that they are compatible.

Liners and covers.   A liner can be used in your sleeping bag to aid in keeping it clean. Depending upon material and construction, a liner may also add some warmth. Also, some people prefer a material other than nylon next to their skin. Commercially made liners are available from some manufacturers of sleeping bags. It is not difficult to make a sleeping bag liner yourself from muslin or other suitable material. If you plan to use a liner, it will be necessary to purchase a sleeping bag that has an internal system of snaps and tie tapes, in order to keep the liner in place during use. Otherwise it will get hopelessly and uncomfortably twisted around your body during the night. I have used a liner in my sleeping bag in the past but found it to be generally unsatisfactory. When it wasn't caught in the zipper, it was frequently twisted uncomfortably about my body (sometimes both at the same time).

There is no doubt that it is desirable to keep your sleeping bag clean. However, this can be accomplished by other and simpler means than using a sleeping bag liner. First, you can bathe fully before going to bed. This is not always practical. However, it is no great chore to wash at least your head and face and hopefully your feet. In addition, you can sleep in a pair of pajamas. These can be very lightweight, as an aid only to keeping your bag clean, or they can be of such material (flannel, Dacron, and so on) as to provide additional warmth. If you feel you may overlook washing your feet before crawling into your sleeping bag at night, sew a "foot" or "bootie" to each leg of the pajamas. The pajamas will then keep the foot area of your bag clean, as well as the main portion. The area of your sleeping bag that will often become soiled rather soon is the head end. This is usually the result of oil and dirt in the hair. A small homemade nightcap or hood to cover your hair will prevent this soiling. In cold weather a wool knit cap is often worn by backpackers at night for warmth. If kept clean, this will suffice to protect the bag from hair oil and dirt. You will find that wearing the items described will keep your sleeping bag just as clean as using a liner, and it will be much more comfortable to sleep in.

A cover for your sleeping bag, to keep it clean, is generally *not* recommended. Most people find that it has about the same nuisance aspects as a liner. If you use a tent, or an adequate ground cloth, with a pad or mattress of at least hip length, the outer shell of your sleeping bag will stay reasonably clean for a long time. The ground cloth, plus sleeping pad or mattress, will also give protection from abrasion on the ground side.

The bivouac sack is a somewhat different type of sleeping bag cover that may be of interest to some backpackers. For moderate-weather backpacking, those who wish to dispense with a tent or tarp may want to try a bivouac sack.

If you have a synthetic-insulated sleeping bag (not down), you can afford to be a bit more adventurous as far as weather and the possibility of getting your sleeping bag damp or wet are concerned. You would not want to put a waterproof cover over your sleeping bag because that would *ensure* a wet bag from your own body moisture. Some manufacturers are producing a bivouac sack made of Gore-Tex. This slips over a sleeping bag and reportedly provides both a waterproof cover and breathability. Since stakes and poles are not required, this combination would be lighter than even the lightest tarp. I have not yet had the opportunity either to try such a combination or to observe one in use under trail conditions, so I cannot vouch for its practicability. (See discussion of Gore-Tex on pages 46 – 47.)

Stuff bag.   A good stuff bag is an important complement to your sleeping bag. A few backpackers have oversized packbags to fit their packframes, and the sleeping bag is simply stuffed into a lower compartment of the packbag. The majority, however, carry their sleeping bags in a stuff bag, which is strapped to the lower part of the packframe.

The stuff bag should be made of coated waterproof nylon, so as to protect the sleeping bag from moisture. Another function is to protect the bag from abrasion by tree branches and other sources along the trail and from repeatedly setting the pack on the ground at trail stops. The waterproof coating should be on the *inside* of the stuff bag, so that it is not abraded away in spots, thus losing its waterproofness. Typical dimensions of a stuff bag that accommodates a sleeping bag are 8 to 12 inches in diameter and 18 to 22 inches long.

A *down* sleeping bag is usually stuffed handful by handful into the stuff bag. I have found that manufacturers' instructions for getting a *synthetic*-insulated sleeping bag into its stuff bag vary. Some say that the synthetic bag should be stuffed handful by handful into its stuff bag, just as is done with a down bag. Others instruct the owner to first roll the synthetic bag into a tight roll somewhat longer than the stuff sack. This roll is then inserted into the stuff sack, and pressure is exerted on the exposed end so that the sleeping bag then fills the stuff sack.

Some manufacturers and suppliers furnish stuff sacks that are too small for their sleeping bags. These are a real nuisance and time-consuming to use. A stuff bag should be generous in size in proportion to the sleeping bag it is to accommodate. Try the stuff sack out in the store before completing your purchase. If your sleeping bag does not easily fit into its stuff sack in the store, under ideal conditions, reject it. It will require herculean effort on a cold, wet morning on the trail when the sleeping bag is *not* in the best condition for stuffing and you may be working with numb fingers, probably in a bit of a hurry to get going. Not too long ago I purchased a name brand synthetic-insulated sleeping bag that came with a ridiculously small stuff sack. I finally got another, roomier, stuff sack, but such experiences are long remembered.

A heavy plastic bag placed inside the stuff sack will provide added assurance that your sleeping bag remains dry. I have found that a plastic bag slightly larger than the stuff bag is easiest to use.

A compressor bag with an external lacing system can be used to compress a stuff bag into a still more compact bundle. For most sleeping bags this is not essential. However, for those who have sleeping bags insulated with polyurethane foam, it is virtually a necessity. Otherwise they will end up with a sleeping bag bundle that is too bulky for their packframe.

A stuff bag is usually included in the purchase of a sleeping bag. A stuff bag that is bought separately will cost from $4 to $6. It is not difficult to make your own.

Cleaning sleeping bags. Spot cleaning of a sleeping bag shell is relatively easy. Soiled spots are simply sponged with lukewarm water and mild soap and then rinsed with plain lukewarm water. The bag is then hung up to dry.

Thorough cleaning of the entire sleeping bag is something else. Synthetic-insulated sleeping bags are rather easily cleaned, in contrast to down bags. Generally accepted procedures for cleaning sleeping bags, and precautions to be taken in cleaning, are given in the following paragraphs. If they differ from the manufacturer's instructions for your particular bag, the latter instructions should, of course, be followed.

CLEANING DOWN SLEEPING BAGS. When thoroughly dirty, a down sleeping bag is not easy to clean. It is also very easy to permanently damage a down bag in the cleaning process if it is improperly carried out. Most backpackers take more than casual care of a down bag and see that it does not quickly become dirty in the first place. Because of the hazards in cleaning, the average owner also probably tolerates a soiled bag somewhat longer than he otherwise would. However, dirt and oils from the sleeper's body eventually get worked into the down. These inhibit proper lofting of the down and decrease the bag's efficiency. A thoroughly dirty bag is also a smelly one, and it is unpleasant to sleep in. A down sleeping bag can be cleaned by either hand washing or dry cleaning. Correct procedure in either case is *very important.*

Whether a wet down sleeping bag is being handled in camp after being soaked by a rain or being washed at home, it should *never* be lifted by its shell. The weight of the wet down may tear out the internal baffling of the bag.

The best place for washing a sleeping bag is in your bathtub. Lukewarm water and mild soap should be used. Detergents are apt to remove the natural oils from the down. Place the dry bag in the tub of water and work it with your hands, being very careful not to scrub, twist, or yank the bag. You can gently press, squeeze, and massage the bag while it is lying in the bottom of the tub. Again it must *not* be lifted, even partially, by its shell.

Two or three changes of soap and water may be required to get the bag clean. When you are satisfied that the soap and water have done the job, drain the tub, leaving the bag lying in the bottom. Then slowly refill the tub again with clear lukewarm water. Continue to massage and manipulate the bag until all evidence of soap has been removed. This will require the tub to be drained and refilled a number of times. In the last rinsing, gently *squeeze* (not wring) as much water from the bag as possible. You can then remove the bag from the tub very carefully by placing both arms under the folded bag so that the entire bag is supported. It can then be put in a *front-loading* clothes dryer that is set for *low heat.* Placing a pair of clean tennis shoes in the dryer will help in breaking up clumps of wet down and will also assist in the building up of static electricity, which is necessary for the bag to regain full loft. Repeated cycling on low heat will be necessary. When the sleeping bag is dried to the point where it is only slightly damp, it may be removed and hung outdoors for final drying. If the entire drying process is done outside, rather than by machine, the down clumps must be continually broken up by hand. Otherwise they will matt permanently. Machine drying is recommended.

An alternative to hand washing your sleeping bag is to find a reputable dry cleaner who is *experienced* in the dry cleaning of down sleeping bags. This may prove to be difficult. Inquiry should be made of the dry cleaner as to what cleaning agent he uses. If he uses anything other than a mild petroleum-base solvent, pass him up. Stoddard's solvent is a satisfactory, commonly used cleaner. It is best to select a dry cleaner who has a known reputation for the satisfactory cleaning of down sleeping bags, and this narrows the choice considerably. Your bag may need to be mailed to an out-of-town cleaning establishment. If you are in doubt as to where to send your sleeping bag for dry cleaning, consult with a backpacking and mountaineering equipment supply firm for their recommendation.

The sleeping bag should be carefully air dried after the dry cleaning, for two reasons. First, any cleaning solvent remaining in the bag may deteriorate the down. Second, dry-cleaning fluids are toxic and have been known to kill sleepers who used recently dry-cleaned bags before they were thoroughly aired. Eight to ten days of air drying is not too much.

CLEANING SYNTHETIC-INSULATED SLEEPING BAGS. Normally neither Fiberfill II-nor Polar-Guard-filled sleeping bags should be dry cleaned, inasmuch as the cleaning agent may degrade the material. There is really no point in dry cleaning them anyway, since they can be machine washed if you do not wish to hand wash them. The manufacturer's instructions for cleaning should always be followed.

When machine washing these sleeping bags, a *large front-loading* machine should be used. They should be washed on slow cycle, using a mild non-detergent soap and lukewarm water. Fabric softeners should not be used. Zippers on bags should be closed prior to either machine washing or hand washing.

In hand washing, as for a down bag, a bathtub is ideal to use. The bag should be kneaded gently in a tub of lukewarm water to which a mild soap has been added. Clear lukewarm water should be used for rinsing to get out all the soap and dirt. Two or more washings may be necessary if the bag is very dirty.

Before you lift the bag from the tub, it should be *squeezed* (not wrung) to remove most of the

water. The bag should then be lifted by placing both hands under the bulk of the bag, rather than lifting by one corner.

Bags can be dried by hanging over a line, or they can be machine dried. For machine drying, a large front-loading dryer should be used, with *low heat*. Several cycles may be required for complete drying.

Sleeping bags that are insulated with polyurethane foam can be washed in a bathtub in the same manner as described for Fiberfill II-and PolarGuard-insulated bags. They should be dried over a rope line, rather than in a machine dryer.

OTHER SLEEPING GEAR

Roughing it.   A bed made on the bare ground will not provide the comfort that most people need for a good night's sleep. Most of us require something a bit softer. There was a time when a person could take an ax or hatchet and cut limbs from live trees in order to make a bough bed. That time is past. Don't do it! Leaves, grass, and other similar materials can also be used to provide a foundation for your sleeping bag. However, the time required to gather such materials and the likelihood that you won't find them when and where you want them add up to the fact that you should plan to carry a pad or mattress of some sort on which to lay your sleeping bag. It should also be pointed out that most bough beds, as well as beds made from other natural materials, would look pretty sad in comparison with a good air mattress or foam pad. Especially after such beds have been slept in for four or five hours, they leave much to be desired. Try to imagine, too, some nice, large, sticky, stained areas on your good sleeping bag, caused by the pitch in the pine or balsam boughs.

Most important is the fact that the gathering of any natural materials for making a bed (including grass, leaves, and so on) can no longer be condoned from an ecology standpoint. Wherever you make such a bed, the signs will be there for a long time, an eyesore to others who use that campsite.

Air mattress.   The average person will sleep comfortably if his head, shoulders, and hips are properly supported. Your legs can extend past the edge of the mattress onto the ground and it will make little difference. A hip-length air mattress weighing under 2 pounds is suitable for backpacking. For very short backpack trips the added weight of a full-length mattress may not be im-

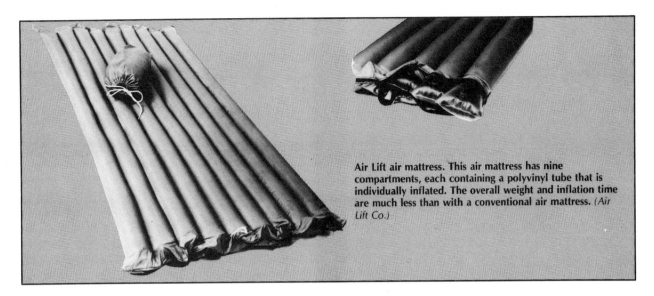

Air Lift air mattress. This air mattress has nine compartments, each containing a polyvinyl tube that is individually inflated. The overall weight and inflation time are much less than with a conventional air mattress. *(Air Lift Co.)*

portant, but on longer trips it will be. An air mattress made of vinyl will be lightest in weight for a given size. Such a mattress will also be the most subject to tears and pinholes from twigs, pine needles, sharp stones, and other material lying on the ground where you choose to make your bed. You should go over the ground very carefully (on your hands and knees) and remove all such objects before you put down an air mattress. If you use a plastic air mattress, be sure it is in new condition. After they have been lying around for a few months (even though they are not used much), plastic air mattresses will start to develop pinholes that will about drive a person crazy trying to keep them patched. Your ground cloth (discussed later) will give some protection from puncture, but plan to spend some valuable camp time (and sleeping time) in locating and patching air leaks if you use a plastic air mattress. A few years ago a discarded plastic air mattress was one of the more common items of trash that one sometimes found at abandoned campsites in the backwoods. Today very few backpackers use them.

A good air mattress for backpacking is made of coated nylon fabric. A typical air mattress of this type, in hip-length size, with no pillow, measures about 22 by 48 inches and weighs about 28 ounces. Cost is about $11. Such mattresses will take a lot of fairly rough treatment. Air mattresses made from other materials are available, but most of them are too heavy for backpacking use. A patch kit should always be carried with an air mattress so that any necessary repairs can be made on the spot.

Blowing up an air mattress, if you should decide to use one, might be considered one of the "oc-cupational hazards" of backpacking. It takes a lot of huffing and puffing. After a hard day on the trail you may get light-headed and pass out. In a group a lightweight air-mattress pump might be a justifiable item of equipment. However, it would be unusual to find a group with many people using air mattresses. A good way to blow up an air mattress by mouth is to lie down alongside it and simply "breathe" into it, not blowing hard and taking plenty of time.

There are several brands of lightweight air mattresses available that are compact and rather durable. The shell is made of ripstop nylon. The mattresses have longitudinal compartments into which individual vinyl tubes are inserted. Each tube is blown up separately, and the total inflation time is less than for a conventional air mattress of comparable size. If a puncture develops, it is likely that it will only affect one tube, which can be patched or replaced. The mattress usually comes with one spare tube, and extra tubes can be bought separately. These mattresses are available in a number of sizes. A typical size (short version) measures about 20 by 42 inches and weighs about 20 ounces. Cost is about $20. The literature on some of these mattresses states that they are *not* recommended for temperatures below freezing.

A distinct disadvantage of an air mattress is that it provides only very poor insulation between your sleeping bag and the ground. This is an area where you particularly need good insulation. This is because the filler material on the ground side of your sleeping bag (especially down bags) is compressed when you are lying on it.

When you inflate an air mattress for the night,

don't blow it up too full. It should be fairly limp. When you lie on it and can just barely feel your hip touch the ground at one point, it is about right. Lay it out so that the valve end is near your head. Then you can easily reach over and let a bit of air out if it is too hard. Or if it is too soft, roll off to one side and blow it up a little. When you first wake up in the morning, reach over and open the air valve while you are still lying on your mattress. This will save a little time later on in getting the air out. Lying on the hard ground will also provide additional incentive for getting up. In packing your air mattress, try not to fold it in the same pattern each time, since this will cause the mattress to weaken along the seams where it is repeatedly folded.

Urethane foam pads (open-cell). The urethane foam pads, ranging in thickness from 1 to 2 inches or more, are quite popular with backpackers. Many people find that the cushioning effect and the relatively firm support provided by a foam pad are superior in comfort to an air mattress. A foam pad also provides fair insulation between the sleeper and the cold ground, but an air mattress provides essentially no insulation at all.

A short urethane foam pad 24 by 48 inches and $1\frac{1}{2}$ inches thick weighs about 20 ounces. A disadvantage of these foam pads is their bulk, and this is a major factor. A pad of the above dimensions rolls into a bulky package having a diameter of about 9 inches. When rolled tightly for carrying on your packframe, the roll must be secured by wide straps. If rope is used, the pressure exerted by the tightly rolled cylinder will cut into the foam.

Another disadvantage of the urethane foam pads is that they are of open-cell construction and will readily absorb water. They should therefore be enclosed in a cloth cover to keep out moisture. A cover that uses waterproof nylon on the bottom side of the foam pad and cotton on the top side is good. Your sleeping bag would have a tendency to slide around if the top side (next to the bag) were nylon.

Closed-cell foam pads. The Ensolite pads are closed-cell foam. No cover is needed for these pads. They will not absorb water, and they provide excellent insulation. An Ensolite pad will provide about three times as much insulation as an open-cell foam pad of the same thickness.

A popular size Ensolite pad is 21 by 56 inches with a thickness of $\frac{3}{8}$ inch and weight of 20 ounces. Although a $\frac{3}{8}$-inch-thick Ensolite pad is not as comfortable as the thicker urethane foam pads, many backpackers find Ensolite pads to be a very acceptable compromise, considering weight, bulk, insulation, and general comfort. I have used a $\frac{3}{8}$-inch-thick Ensolite pad on many backpack trips and find it to be very satisfactory. When rolled for attaching to the packframe, a 56-inch pad is about 5 inches in diameter.

Another popular type of closed-cell foam pads is Volarafoam. Blu-Foam is similar. These foam pads weigh less than an equivalent size of Ensolite pad, and they also cost less. They are somewhat less durable than Ensolite but are very satisfactory.

I have observed that on the trail many backpackers are seen carrying Ensolite and other closed-cell foam pads. This applies to summer backpacking as well as to cold-weather backpacking. Evidently many hikers consider the lighter weight, less bulk, and waterproofness of the closed-cell pads to be a good trade-off for somewhat less comfort.

Ground cloth. It is important that your sleeping bag be kept dry. It should also be kept clean, insofar as possible. If you are sleeping inside a floored tent, a ground cloth should not be necessary. If you are sleeping in the open, a ground cloth is recommended.

If you lay your sleeping bag directly on the ground, the bag will probably get dirty, and possibly wet. Even though you may be sleeping on a full-length mattress or foam pad, you cannot count on these to keep your sleeping bag from touching the ground. Also, most backpackers carry hip-length mattresses or pads, not full-length ones. You will be rolling around a bit during the

Closed-cell foam pads. Left, Ensolite; right, Blu-Foam. *(Lou Clemmons)*

night, and some parts of your bag will contact the ground. For one person a ground cloth about 3 feet wide by 7 feet long is recommended.

The least expensive groundsheet will be a piece of plastic (polyethylene) of 3- or 4-mil thickness. A ground cloth made of coated nylon will be much more durable. Some of the backpacking equipment supply firms sell such cloth by the yard. It is certainly not difficult to make your own groundsheet out of coated nylon, and it is recommended that you try it.

Stones, sticks, pine cones, and so on, should be removed from your bed site before spreading out your groundsheet. It is suggested that you mark the top side of the groundsheet with the word UP, using a felt-tip marker, and that you always place the reverse side next to the ground. In this way you will avoid getting your sleeping bag and mattress dirty by putting them down on the side of the groundsheet that was next to the ground the last time it was used.

Pillow. Most backpackers improvise a pillow in preference to carrying one as an additional item of equipment. A jacket or other item of clothing placed inside the stuff bag used for your sleeping bag makes a satisfactory pillow. For maximum comfort the stuff bag should be filled only loosely, not full.

Some backpackers may purchase an air mattress with an attached pillow. If you do this, make certain that the pillow and the main mattress each have separate valves for filling. If there is only one valve, air will enter the pillow part when you lie on the mattress, making the pillow much too hard for comfort.

If you want to carry a separate pillow, there are air pillows available that weigh 4 to 6 ounces. As with an air mattress, the pillow should never be blown up hard. It should be quite limp for maximum sleeping comfort.

SLEEPING GEAR SUMMARY

There is considerable difference among people as to how warm they sleep under the same conditions. Thus, the temperature ratings that a manufacturer may list for various sleeping bags is only a rough guide at best. For estimating weight of sleeping gear, it is assumed that a 4½-pound sleeping bag will suffice for the average person in moderate weather. Your sleeping bag may be a little heavier or a little lighter. A foam pad is also assumed, with a weight of 14 ounces.

TABLE 1. RECOMMENDED SLEEPING GEAR*

Item	Approximate Weight (in ounces)
Sleeping bag	72
Sleeping pad, ⅜" closed-cell foam, 21" X 56"	14

*Use of tent assumed; no ground cloth necessary.

TABLE 2. OPTIONAL SLEEPING GEAR

Item	Approximate Weight (in ounces)
Air mattress, 20" X 56"	20
Air pillow, inflatable nylon	5
Ground cloth, coated nylon, 3' X 7'	10
Sleeping pad, 1½" open-cell foam, 20" X 50"	28

4
Shelter

It is recommended that some type of shelter be taken on every backpack trip. If it is the time of year when rain is very unlikely, then the shelter can be regarded as an emergency measure and the simplest type of protection may suffice. If you are going into an area where rain may be expected, you will want to provide yourself with more substantial protection. Travel in the high mountains at a time of year when rain or snow, and possibly high winds, may be encountered requires good protection, usually in the form of a well-made commercially designed and fabricated tent.

The background and experience of the hikers is also important. When you are taking young children on a backpack trip under any conditions, some type of *tent* is desirable. It gives them an added sense of security, which is important when they are being introduced to backwoods travel. The psychological aspect should not be important to experienced backpackers, and they may be willing and ready to take some gamble with respect to the weather. However, even the latter types will generally take some emergency shelter. Getting thoroughly soaked, and possibly chilled, and having a camp full of wet gear is no fun, regardless of your experience and background.

In recent years the increased use of Hollofil II and PolarGuard in quality sleeping bags and certain protective clothing has had its effect on the

shelter situation. With these items you can afford to be considerably more adventurous with respect to inclement weather than when using down-insulated articles. With down-insulated gear you will not want to take *any* chances of getting your sleeping bag wet. This essentially dictates the use of a well-made tent. With a Hollofil II- or Polar-Guard-insulated sleeping bag minimal shelter may suffice if only infrequent rains are to be expected. Thus, if the rain blows in the end of a tarp shelter and partially dampens, or even wets, your synthetic-insulated sleeping bag, you are in no great trouble. The water can be squeezed out (if the bag gets that wet), and you will sleep warm. The bag can be aired and dried relatively quickly the next day.

In some areas a tent or enclosed shelter of some kind may be required simply for reasons of privacy. In a crowded backwoods campground a sheet of transparent plastic doesn't offer much privacy. Getting dressed and undressed inside a sleeping bag, or trying to, is usually not very practical. However, it should not be overlooked that plastic sheeting is available in black and other nontransparent colors if privacy is the main concern. A coated nylon tarp is also nontransparent and, with some improvising, will offer privacy that would be acceptable to most backpackers.

Depending on the particular locale, in some seasons protection from insects is just as important as protection from adverse weather. Insects may be in the form of hordes of mosquitoes or black flies, or crawling ants, bugs, and no-see-ums on the ground. These can make for a poor night's sleep.

On a cool and windy night the wind sweeping unchecked over your sleeping bag can greatly reduce the bag's ability to keep you warm. In a stiff wind a tent can increase the effectiveness of a sleeping bag by as much as 10 to 20 degrees.

Just as for sleeping bags, a basic aspect to be considered in tent design is the familiar problem of waterproofness versus breathability. Good ventilation is required both for comfort and for safety. In general, most quality tents are constructed of breathable fabric, usually uncoated nylon. Positive protection from rain is achieved by use of a waterproof fly erected over the main tent. (However, see the discussion of Gore-Tex on pages 46–47.)

A tent can be one of your most expensive items of backpack gear. It is not unusual to pay $90 for an average good tent for use in moderate weather. Tents for high mountain use and very severe weather may cost $200 or more. As in choosing many other items of equipment, it is recommended that you go slowly in your evaluation of your shelter needs. Otherwise you may end up with "too much tent" and will have wasted some money. I own a good two-person tent purchased from a reputable supplier. Yet I have spent about a hundred and fifty safe and comfortable nights in the backwoods in a simple one-person tent (described in Appendix C) that I designed and fabricated myself for less than $15. One of the pleasures of backpacking is sleeping in the open, or as nearly so as is safe and comfortable, rather than being cooped up inside a tent.

PONCHOS

A poncho can be used as an emergency rain shelter. An adult-size poncho will be roughly 54 by 90 inches in size. Ponchos made of polyethylene material are available, but a coated nylon poncho is much more durable, is generally more comfortable to wear, and is recommended. Many such ponchos are provided with grommets (you can easily add more) and can be used as emergency tarp shelters for rain protection at night. Ponchos are also available that cover not only the hiker but also his pack. Such ponchos will measure about 54 by 105 inches, and those made of coated nylon will weigh about 16 ounces. The cost of a nylon poncho of this size is about $18.

A poncho such as described above, when used for rain protection at night, should not be laid directly over your sleeping bag. It should always be pitched over a ridgeline (see page 54) and maximum ventilation provided, even though the size of the poncho may limit the peak height, when pitched, to 1½ to 2 feet. There must be free circulation of air under any such waterproof covering, or excessive condensation will result.

TARPS

Polyethylene tarps are available in many thicknesses. Some are sold at hardware stores as painters' drop cloths. The very thin variety may weigh as little as 6 ounces for a 9-by-12-foot size. However, these are very fragile and must be very carefully handled and kept away from bushes or tree limbs while being erected. Otherwise they will billow with the slightest breeze and be torn before they are erected the first time. They are usually pitched over a ridgeline, in pup-tent fashion, and weighted along the ground edge with smooth, round rocks. Unless you have had experience with such tarps and are willing to take the time and patience to erect them properly (and keep them patched), don't bother with them, even for emergency protection against unlikely rain.

Heavier polyethylene tarps are available in 2- to 4-mil thicknesses. A 9-by-12-foot size will weigh about 2 to 4 pounds. Some will have grommets for tying in place. If not, you can install

Visklamp. These clamps are useful for anchoring tarps that do not have grommets.

some grommets yourself if you have the equipment. In installing grommets, glue an extra square of polyethylene or cloth over the area where each grommet is to be inserted and they will not be so likely to tear out in a stiff breeze. Tarps without grommets can be guyed in position by placing small, smooth stones on the inside surface and tying the guy rope around the stone where its outline protrudes through the other side of the plastic. An even better method of fastening such sheets where no grommets are present is to use Visklamps. These are small rubber-ball-and-clamp arrangements that work like garters. They are inexpensive and are available from mountaineering supply shops.

Polyethylene tarps that are reinforced with nylon thread are available from some mountaineering shops. These are much more durable than the same weight of nonthreaded poly tarp.

If you are "tarp-minded," the best tarp will be a sheet of coated nylon varying in weight from about 2 to 4 ounces per square yard. Coated rip-stop nylon weighing about 2½ ounces per square yard is good. It is strong, tear resistant, and waterproof. Tarps purchased from mountaineering shops will have grommets installed, and the area around each grommet will be reinforced with an added square patch of cloth. It is not difficult to make a nylon tarp. It will be less expensive than buying the same size made commercially. The coated nylon cloth can be purchased by the yard from a number of mountaineering and backpack equipment supply shops. If you don't have a grommet-setting kit and don't want to purchase one, a shoe repair shop can install the grommets. All seams should be coated with urethane seam sealant. For sewing nylon cloth, cotton-covered polyester thread is recommended.

Tarps can be pitched in many configurations. The configuration used will often depend upon the particular terrain where you find yourself when it comes time to make camp. Sometimes a large log, 3 or 4 feet or more in diameter, can be used as the "front" of your tarp shelter, and the tarp can be erected in a position slanting from the top of the log to the ground. Probably the most used configuration is with the tarp pitched over a ridgeline in an A-frame or pup-tent fashion. In this configuration, with a steep sidewall, it will usually shed water readily. In other configurations it is quite likely that there will be some places in the roof that will sag and collect water. If it rains, this will mean that you will have to dump water from these sagging places at regular intervals by pushing up from the inside with your hand. If you

are asleep at night while the water is collecting in puddles on certain portions of your roof, it may start to leak long before you are aware that there is a puddle there.

TUBE TENTS

Some backpackers use the plastic tube tents, primarily as emergency shelters. They are waterproof (when new), but there are drawbacks. Even though the ends of the tent are open, there will be some condensation inside. Rain falling on the outer edge of the ground side will usually run toward the center, wetting your sleeping bag and other articles that are on the ground surface of the tent. If you attempt to partially close the ends of the tent, be particularly careful. It is extremely important that the tent *not* be closed tightly. The sleeper in a tightly closed tent may use up the available oxygen and wake up panic-stricken. If you decide to try a tube tent, you should mark a particular section (with a felt-tip marker) that is to go next to the ground. Thereafter, always pitch the tent with that section on the ground side, rather than as a wall. The ground side will develop pinholes and leaks, and if the tent is pitched so that that side is on a wall, your tube tent will leak.

Another drawback of these tents is that you should carry poles for the front and back ends. Trying to find a level spot with good drainage between two trees that are positioned so as to accommodate a ridgeline is quite a task.

The polyethylene tube tents leave much to be desired. This is evident from the number of such tents that one sees discarded at campsites in the backwoods. (The owners "forgot" to carry them out with other litter when they found that the tents didn't do the job intended.) Some mountaineering shops have discontinued selling tube tents because the tents have become such a common item of backwoods litter.

If you are on a limited budget and are seriously considering a tube tent, I would recommend that you first consider making a tent yourself from reinforced plastic sheeting. This refers to polyethylene sheets that have been reinforced with nylon thread, making them much stronger and tear resistant. Buy a sheet about 8 or 9 feet long and of sufficient width to accommodate the desired number of persons when pitched over a ridgeline or between poles. The "floor" will be a separate ground cloth, spread over pine needles or whatever the terrain offers. Reinforce the edges of the front and rear ends of the tent with cloth ad-

One-person backpack tent. Note the "bathtub" floor construction. A waterproof fly is used over the tent to give protection from the elements. Instructions for making this tent are given in Appendix C.

hesive tape. To these reinforced edges sew a triangular piece of mosquito netting, fore and aft, of sufficient size to accommodate the end opening when pitched. The mosquito netting at the front end should be provided with two zippers (similar to the one-person tent shown in Appendix C) to provide for access. Additional cloth adhesive tape can be used at intervals along the longitudinal ground edge to provide for insertion of grommets at those points. You now have a tent that will not sweat and is essentially mosquito proof, and rain blowing in a bit from the open ends will not run the length of the floor (as in a tube tent) and wet the contents. Some overhang at the peak, fore and aft, will be helpful in preventing excess rain from blowing in at the open ends.

ONE-PERSON BACKPACK TENT

Sleeping in the open, with only the sky for a roof, can be a delightful experience. You can watch the tall pines sway in the breeze and view the starlit sky, unhampered by a roof over your head. Depending on the season, however, mosquitoes and other "peskies" may make your night in the open pretty uncomfortable. With a little ingenuity it is not difficult to make a one-person tent, suitable for moderate-weather backpacking, that will provide protection from insects, rodents, and reptiles. If you require protection from rain, a nylon fly sheet is pitched over the main tent. I planned and fabricated a one-person tent that meets these requirements, and I use it frequently. This tent is essentially a cover for your sleeping bag, with some additional room at the head end for a few items of clothing or equipment. The tent is about 8 feet long, 28 inches high at the head end, and 17 inches high at the foot end. The main

tent is made of nylon mosquito netting. A plastic fly sheet can be used for rain protection, although I generally use a coated nylon fly. Including the coated fly sheet and stakes, the tent weighs about 2¾ pounds. With such a tent you dress or undress outside. There is not room inside unless you are a real contortionist. You slip into your sleeping bag at the same time you slide into the tent. However, this tent answers the requirement for a lightweight, inexpensive shelter. Instructions for making this tent are given in Appendix C.

It is a pleasant experience to lie in this tent at night, with the head end of the fly sheet drawn back, and watch the starlit sky overhead. If you want protection from rain or wind, you simply fasten the head end of the nylon fly sheet back into place, and you are in business. A tree or bush at the head end, for fastening the ridgeline, is all that is required for supporting the tent. A stick 18 or 20 inches long, under the ridgeline at the foot end, keeps that end off your sleeping bag.

Backpacking literature frequently shows a ridgeline strung between two trees, supporting a tube or other type tent. However, even in a forest of trees, you will seldom find two trees the right distance apart with level ground between them suitable for pitching your tent. It is possible, but not very likely, that you will find such a spot when you need it. Finding one tree or large bush with fairly level ground nearby, as required for the one-person backpack tent just described, is not so much of a job.

FOREST TENTS

There is a wide range of tents available for general backpacking use that are generally referred to as forest tents. Such tents are intended for use below timberline, where the primary requirements are protection from rain (or snow) and insects and, to some extent, the storage of gear out of reach of birds and rodents. The effectiveness of a sleeping bag is also increased when used with a tent. Very high winds, deep snow, and severe cold are not normally encountered in the use of such tents, as contrasted with tents designed for mountaineering use at high altitudes.

The conditions expected to be encountered in your backpacking are important factors to consider in the selection of such a tent. The number of persons who will be using the tent (possibly a family with children) is also a factor. The most popular-size tent in this category usually accommodates two or three adults. If you are buying your first tent, it is suggested that it be a two-person size, unless there is a special reason for buying a larger one.

A waterproof floor is important. If much camping in wet weather is expected, it is best to choose a floor construction in which the floor material extends up the sides of the tent (also the front and back ends) about 6 to 8 inches. This is generally referred to as bathtub, or simply tub, construction. Even though the site selected for the tent has imperfect drainage, a tub floor will usually keep water out of the tent.

A prime consideration is breathability of the tent material. If the tent does not breathe so as to allow body moisture given off by the occupants to escape, it will be damp inside, regardless of the weather outside. This requires that the main tent be made of water-repellent, rather than waterproof, material. Maximum ventilation should be provided in the tent design, even though the material is breathable, to keep condensation to a minimum.

A common style of forest tent is the A-frame. It will normally have a screened front and a screened rear "window" of generous size. A modified A-frame may have low side walls, and possibly additional netting along the top edge of the side wall, for maximum ventilation. Such a tent will usually serve the purpose in mild rain showers, shedding the rain satisfactorily and still not soaking the occupants with their own sweat. Selecting a tent site in a protected area or in the woods, rather than in open terrain, will increase the tent's effectiveness.

In hard rain, or in a prolonged rain, a water-repellent tent will sooner or later start to leak. Therefore, with many such tents a waterproof fly is used. This is pitched over the main tent, and the combination will usually provide protection in the most severe and prolonged rain.

You may have possibly located a water-repellent A-frame tent that is generally satisfactory for your intended use but that does not have a separate rain fly. In that case, especially if you are on a limited budget, you should seriously consider buying the waterproof material and making a rain fly yourself. For an A-frame tent a fly sheet is not difficult to make. It should extend well out over the fore and aft ends of the tent. If you anticipate the need for a sheltered area for cooking with a backpack stove, it is particularly important that a generous overhang be provided at the front end, since that is probably where you will be using your stove in foul weather.

A-frame tents may have a true A-frame pole arrangement at the front and back ends. Some

Typical A-frame tent. This type tent is good for all-around use at normal altitudes. *(Lou Clemmons)*

have A-frame poles at the front, for easy access to the tent, and a single pole at the back end. Others have single poles at both ends. An A-frame pole arrangement withstands high winds much better than single poles do, but this would not normally be a problem in camping below timberline. Some A-frame tent designs have a lesser height at the rear; these are often referred to as low-enders. This design saves a bit on weight with no significant decrease in utility.

There are many other shapes of tents in the general category of forest tents. Some are of pyramid shape, with stand-up room. Others are igloo shaped, without ground stakes. In general, a tent with waterproof floor and separate rain fly should weigh about 3 to 3½ pounds per person, including poles and stakes. That is, a two-person tent should weigh about 6 or 7 pounds. The cost of forest tents varies from about $40, for a simple two-person A-frame tent without a separate rain fly, to over $100 for the more sophisticated tents.

ALPINE, OR MOUNTAINEERING, TENTS

For use in high mountains and above timberline an alpine, or mountaineering, tent made by a reputable manufacturer of mountaineering equipment is recommended. Such tents must not only withstand snow and rain but also winds of 50 to 100 miles per hour. Two-person tents of this type are often of the A-frame design, but they must have much better materials and workmanship, and other features, than an ordinary A-frame tent intended for relatively low altitude use. Good design and adequate performance of such a tent are not merely matters of convenience and comfort. They can mean the difference between life and death in severe adverse weather.

A very important feature of a mountaineering tent is its stability. The A-frame design provides good stability in high winds. Double poles are used both front and rear in a good A-frame tent. These double poles take the form of an inverted V. It is important that they be securely joined at the top. The poles generally fit through "sleeves" sewn to the upright edges at the front and rear of the tent. The bottom of these poles should rest in a cloth "pocket" sewn to the edge of the tent, or they may be held in place by grommets set in webbing tabs sewn into the tent. Without such provision for anchoring the ends of the poles, they would sink in sand, snow, or mud, and the tent could not be erected.

Flapping of tent walls in the wind makes for a poor night's sleep. Even more important, it is hard on the tent fabric and seams. A quality A-frame tent will have one or more pullouts on the sides. These are flaps of cloth sewn to the tent, with a grommet inserted to accommodate a guy line. They help to eliminate flapping and sagging of tent walls. They also provide a somewhat more spacious interior.

Mountaineering tents, as well as other quality tents, will be constructed with a catenary cut. A line stretched between two points will never be straight. It will always sag, even from its own weight. This curve is called a catenary. All tent ridges that are sewn straight across between suspension points will sag, and this causes wrinkles in the fabric. Pulling on the ridge of the tent to correct this will *not* do the job and will put a lot of strain on the tent. A catenary cut helps to make for smooth, tight walls in the pitched tent. It distributes the wind strain on the tent evenly along the seams and also reduces the wind flap. With a good catenary cut there will be sag in the ridge-line but no wrinkles or sag in the sides of the tent.

Ventilation tunnel, viewed from inside and outside tent. *(Lou Clemmons)*

Cooking inside the tent is sometimes necessary in prolonged severe weather. Therefore, a vestibule at the tent entrance or a cook hole in the floor (and frequently both) is desirable. The cook hole is a section of floor, often semicircular, that is zippered in place so that a bit of ground can be exposed for placing the cook stove. Thus, the stove and some cooking equipment can be set on the ground and some spillage can occur without soiling the tent or other equipment. A vestibule at the front of the tent is very worthwhile. Oftentimes, cooking can be done in the vestibule (which is much safer than cooking inside the tent) in weather that would preclude cooking outside the tent.

A good mountaineering tent will have the customary separate fly for rigging over the main tent. It may also have double entrances, with one entrance being of tunnel design. With a tunnel entrance two tents can be joined together. Also,

Typical mountaineering tent for high-altitude use. This tent has a semicircular zippered cook hole in the floor and loops at front and rear peaks (inside) for clothesline. A rain fly (not shown) extends below the sidewalls to keep the tent dry in all weather. The design provides good stability in high winds. *(REI, Inc.)*

zippered entrances may freeze up under certain weather conditions, and a tunnel entrance is desirable from this standpoint. Where zippers are used, nylon zippers are much preferred to metal zippers.

Snow flaps, or sod flaps, are frequently attached around the base of mountaineering tents. These are 10- or 12-inch strips of coated fabric that extend out from the floor line. In use these strips are covered with snow or dirt that is tamped in place; this provides considerable additional support. They prevent wind from getting beneath the tent, which makes for a more stable and warmer tent. In the event that snow and soil are lacking above timberline, smooth rocks can be placed on the snow flaps and will usually work satisfactorily. Jagged rocks should obviously be avoided.

The size of a mountaineering tent will be somewhat more important than the size of a forest tent. In most backpacking that is done with forest tents, protection from the elements for periods other than for sleeping is usually a comparatively negligible matter. In contrast, you and your companions might be confined for many hours, or even days, during foul weather at high altitudes. Therefore, somewhat greater attention needs to be paid to the living space provided by the mountaineering tent.

Some mountaineering tents come equipped with frost liners. These liners are for extended winter camping in cold temperatures. During a very cold night the moisture in your breath will form frost on the roof of the inner tent. A frost liner, usually made of cotton, will allow the moisture to pass through. The frost on the tent roof is thus separated from the occupants and does not "shower" them during the night.

A good alpine, or mountaineering, tent will cost upwards of $175. A tent of this type will not be required by the average backpacker backpacking in moderate weather and camping at timberline or below.

CONSTRUCTION DETAILS

A good tent is a substantial investment, not only in dollars, but in comfort, protection from the elements, and satisfaction. Under some adverse conditions it can save your life. The circumstances under which you expect to use your tent, and conditions that may develop during its use, should be continually considered while you are shopping for a suitable tent. If at all possible, visit a few backpack equipment shops where they have

a tent erected and on display. Talk with the salespeople about the tent. They may not have all the answers, but you should learn something. Notice whether the pitched tent appears ship-shape or whether there are wrinkles and sags in the material. If it doesn't pitch well on the salesroom floor, which is smooth and even, it is going to be more difficult to pitch properly on uneven ground.

Materials.   Commonly used materials in tent construction are ripstop nylon and nylon taffeta. Quality tents are made from both materials. Cotton poplin is sometimes used, but only to a very limited extent. It is too heavy for a typical backpack tent, and the material must be dried carefully if it gets wet. Otherwise it is subject to mildew and rot. Nylon does not have these disadvantages. It is also very light and has high tear strength.

Nylon is not waterproof. It must be coated with polyurethane, vinyl, or some other coating to provide waterproofness. Tent floors are made of waterproof nylon, and the coated fabric generally extends up the walls of the tent to provide a tub effect. The main tent is made of water-repellent material so that it can breathe. The fly sheet, like the floor, is made of coated nylon.

Tent floors need to be somewhat rugged. They are frequently made from 2.5- to 3-ounce coated nylon, although a few tentmakers use nylon of up to 4.5 ounces. Coated 1.9-ounce ripstop nylon is commonly used for other parts of the tent. In contrast to a section of the tent proper, a tent fly sheet can be fairly easily repaired or replaced. Fly sheets are therefore quite light, often being made of 1.2-ounce nylon.

Workmanship.   The sewing and general construction of the tent should always be closely scrutinized. The points where guy lines are attached to the tent are points of stress. Such points should be reinforced by patches of fabric sewn to the inside of the tent. *Any* place on the tent that grommets are attached should also be so reinforced. The reinforcement patch should be large enough to distribute the stress over a considerable area. The stitching should be uniform and even. There should normally be six to ten stitches per inch. There should be two or more rows of stitches wherever the fabric is subject to stress. Most quality tents are sewn with flat-felled seams (see sketch). A flat-felled seam is folded in such a way as to protect the edges of the material. Four layers of material are provided where the seam is sewn. This reduces seam leakage and provides a strong seam. Such a seam sheds water

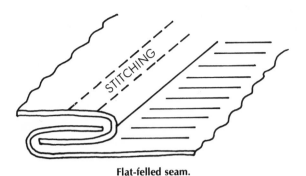

Flat-felled seam.

in much the same way that a house shingle does. Stitch holes are potential sources of leakage and should be sealed with a seam sealant, preferably on both sides of the seam.

The waterproof coating of the floor fabric should be on the *inside* of the tent, rather than next to the ground. If it is on the ground side, the coating will suffer abrasion from rocks, sticks, and so on, and the floor will lose its waterproofness. The floor needs to be cut, folded, and stitched at the corners, where the box construction is formed. These seams will need to be periodically sealed during the life of the tent. In some newly purchased tents the seams are *not* sealed. If the tent is sealed at the factory and then folded for packing before the sealant is thoroughly dry, the wet sealant may work its way onto other parts of the tent and damage them. The instructions that come with the tent should be checked to determine whether the purchaser is required to seal the seams in the tent. If so, a tube of sealant will usually be furnished with the tent.

Ventilation. Even though a tent is made of breathable fabric, specific provisions should be made for good ventilation in any tent design. A vent at each end of the tent, covered with nylon netting, is preferable, so as to provide cross ventilation. Warm, moist air will rise, so at least one of the vents should be located high on the tent wall. It is important that the vents be protected from blowing rain or snow by suitable closures. The tent fly will usually be generous in the area of vents, so as to offer some protection. If a tent is essentially waterproof and has no fly, the vents should be particularly generous, since there is going to be more than a little condensation inside the tent.

You should pay more than casual attention to the ventilation provisions of your prospective tent. It can mean a matter of life or death. Good ventilation is just as important in cold weather as it is in warm weather, possibly more so. When the tent occupants breathe, they take oxygen from the air and give off carbon dioxide. If the tent is not vented, the concentration of carbon dioxide will build up and will cause the occupants to become ill. Usually nausea, headache, and so forth, signal the occupants that more fresh air is needed. A person will normally be awakened, even from deep sleep, by the symptoms caused by a heavy concentration of carbon dioxide. Cooking in a tent can be very dangerous, but it is sometimes necessary under severe weather conditions. A cook stove in use will give off carbon monoxide. Unlike carbon dioxide, this gas does not give warning signals to the occupants. It is odorless and colorless. More than a few persons have died in tightly sealed tents, during adverse weather conditions, because a burning cook stove produced a high concentration of carbon monoxide. Deep snow around a tightly battened down mountaineering tent provides an ideal setup for carbon monoxide poisoning.

Poles. Normally it is best to carry tent poles for erecting a tent. Finding suitable trees with a level space in between for erecting a tent without poles cannot be depended upon, even in a forest. Tent stakes should also be carried.

Tent poles are most commonly made of aluminum tubing. Some A-frame forest tents use a single vertical pole (I pole) at each end of the tent. Some use two poles at the front, A-frame style, to facilitate entry, and a single I pole at the rear. Single poles do not provide nearly the stability that two poles joined in A-frame fashion do, but they are generally satisfactory in moderate winds and for very light snow loads. For mountaineering tents, two A-frame poles joined at the top are required front and rear, because of the stress imposed by severe snow and wind loads.

Poles are usually broken down into sections for easy storage and carrying. In some pole designs the several sections fit into the largest section in telescoping fashion. They require more time to assemble than sections connected by shock cord do. In good weather, where time is not critical, such designs may be entirely satisfactory. Reasonable care must be exercised not to lose a pole section. Also, such poles must be kept clean, to prevent jamming.

For tents having A-frame design poles, each pole is usually broken down into sections 14 to 18 inches long, and the sections are joined together by shock cord running through the center of the hollow poles. The shock cord not only serves to keep the pole sections together (to prevent loss of

Collapsible tent pole. Sections are fastened together with shock cord.

some sections) but it also greatly facilitates quick assembly of the poles and rapid erection of the tent.

In A-frame tents the A-frame poles frequently fit into sleeves or pockets sewn to the front and rear edges of the tent. This serves to hold them in place and to keep the tent taut. It also assists in eliminating flapping of the tent in the wind—as do pullouts, which are flaps of cloth fastened to the sides of the tent, with grommets and ropes which, when fastened to additional stakes, will keep the tent ship-shape, provide additional room inside, and add to its overall stability. A good set of A poles (two sets required per tent) will cost about $20 to $25.

Some tent designs utilize fiberglass wands to provide additional stability and somewhat more interior space. The wands also help minimize flapping of side walls. They fit into sleeves that run up one side of the tent and down the other. They create an arch effect, bowing the sides of the tent outward.

Stakes and Guys. Tent stakes come in a variety of sizes, shapes, and materials. Aluminum wire skewer stakes are very light and will generally hold well in the soil of a forest floor or in moderately rocky ground. Steel skewers are heavier and stronger and can usually be used in soil that is quite rocky. In sand and light soil a broad aluminum (half-tube) stake 8 to 10 inches long will usually do the job. Still other stakes are made of high-impact plastic. They drive easily and have good holding power. Since there is considerable variation in the weight of tent stakes, for a particular trip you should chose the lightest stake that is compatible with the soil where you expect to camp. Tent flies should generally be anchored by their own stakes, rather than to the tent stakes.

A guy line tightener usually takes the form of a small piece of bent aluminum with guy line holes in each end and near the center. It is used to quickly adjust the tension in guy lines for the tent and fly without relocating the tent stakes or pegs. Shock cord is frequently added to guy lines to allow the line to stretch in a gust of wind and then return to normal length. Shock cords should generally *not* be used in the inner tent, since they permit additional flapping, which is a strain on the tent fabric. They are helpful when used on the guy lines for the fly sheet. Since the fly sheet is coated, the coating could deteriorate if the fabric were repeatedly strained, rather than having the gust load transferred to the shock-corded guy line.

The peg loops used for securing the tent to the ground should be carefully inspected. They place considerable strain on the tent when it is erected, and it is desired to distribute this strain, insofar as possible. In a good quality tent the loops are frequently made of heavy nylon webbing. It is recommended that each loop be inspected. Where it is sewn to the tent floor, there should be a patch of reinforcement cloth to distribute the stress. On some tents the peg loops are simply small loops of nylon cord threaded through grommets inserted in a patch of reinforced cloth. Grasp a grommet between the thumb and forefinger. If you can turn it, or if it appears weak, the workmanship is poor.

Zippers. Large zippers are strong, do not snag as easily as smaller ones, and are thus recommended. A #5, #6, or #7 zipper is a good size. They should preferably be nonjamming. Nylon or plastic toothed zippers are frequently used. YKK nylon self-repairing coil zippers are found in many quality tents.

Tent stakes. Left to right: of high-impact plastic, of aluminum (half-tube), skewer type. Stake bag (homemade) is shown at left.

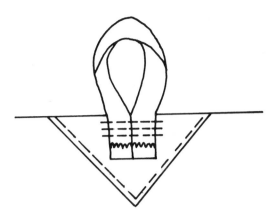

Typical peg loop, showing sewing pattern important to a strong loop.

TENT STYLES AND COLORS

There are many styles of tents, as well as variations in the basic styles. The most common is the A-frame, which has been referred to in the previous discussion. This style is found in many tents, both in the forest tents and in the alpine, or mountaineering, tents. A variation of the A-frame is the low-ender, wherein the rear end of the tent is somewhat lower than the front end. Some weight is saved in this design, and if the tent is used primarily for sleeping, there is no great sacrifice in comfort.

Other tent designs include the dome, half dome, igloo-shaped, pyramid, and other variations. If you should decide on one of these styles, rather than on an A-frame, the general construction features previously mentioned are generally applicable. An important consideration, especially if your tent is to be used under severe weather conditions, is the reputation of the manufacturer. When the only thing between you and a raging storm outside is the thin nylon cloth of your tent wall, you will want to be sure it will hold together and do the job it was intended to do.

Backpack tents come in a variety of colors, from very bright hues to those that blend with the surroundings. Green and blue are rather inconspicuous. Orange, red, and yellow give forth a brightness and a cheery feeling on a cloudy day. A bright color would be more easily seen by a search party, if that aspect seems worthy of consideration. All in all, color is mostly a matter of psychological appeal.

TENT STUFF SACK

The tent stuff sack should be of generous size. If you buy your tent in a local shop, try the stuff sack for size in the store. Remember, it is one thing to stuff a tent into its carrying sack under ideal conditions, when everything is warm and dry (including yourself), but quite something else to be breaking camp in a hurry, perhaps in adverse weather, and with cold, numb hands trying to stuff a wet tent, maybe with a little snow and dirt on it, into a tightly fitting stuff sack. The waterproof coating should be on the *inside* of the sack, rather than on the outside.

INSTRUCTIONS

It is a good idea to check, before purchasing a tent, to see that a set of instructions is furnished for setting it up. Seemingly ignoring part of their responsibility, some tentmakers fail to provide such instructions even though every tent design has certain peculiarities. Although the average experienced backpacker could eventually get an A-frame tent, or one of another design, erected without directions, this should not be necessary. The manufacturer is best qualified to furnish directions for setup. Hopefully, you will purchase your tent in a shop where you can inspect it beforehand and the salesperson will be willing to furnish a trial setup in addition to the printed directions. In some cases setting up a tent improperly, without instructions, could unduly stress the fabric or otherwise damage it.

USE OF TENT

Selection of a tent site when backpacking should not be done too hurriedly. A grove of small or medium-sized scattered trees is frequently a good choice. A single large tree is a poor choice. It may attract lightning, and there are usually some dead limbs on such a tree that may come down on your tent if there is wind during the night. Drainage is always a foremost consideration. The tent site should not be in a depression where water will run if it should rain. It may not *look* like it is going to rain, but moving an improperly placed tent to another location during a rainstorm is not very practical. Also, sitting up all night with a mess of wet gear and a wet sleeping bag is no fun. The nature of the ground surface is also important. A grassed area or a forest floor covered with pine needles will soak up much more water than the bare ground. Your tent will also stay cleaner on such a surface, in contrast to bare ground. Small rocks, sticks, and so on, are easily moved from the tent site, if there are not too many. However, it is important to determine that a small projection of rock above the ground is not a part of a large rock beneath the surface that cannot be moved. Similarly, a large tree root that barely projects above the ground can be a problem. Rocks, sticks, and so forth, that you may remove from your tent site should normally be replaced when you leave the area, so as to return the site to its natural appearance.

The floor of even the best tent is not very rugged. Nylon has good tear strength, but it can be punctured rather easily. It is recommended that you go over the ground on your hands and knees and remove pine cones, rocks, twigs, and anything else that may cause abrasion and possibly make a hole in the tent floor. Some backpackers carry a poly sheet, of 2- to 4-mil thickness, to be placed under the tent floor. This keeps the ground side of the tent floor clean and also provides additional protection from abrasion from an irregular ground surface. In trimming such a subfloor sheet to size, it should be cut slightly smaller than the tent floor. If the edges of the groundsheet extend beyond the tent floor, rain will fall on the exposed part of the plastic sheet and will then probably run under the tent—just where you don't want it.

Wilderness ethics do not permit ditching of tents. This makes selection of a proper site with respect to drainage even more important. Ditching leads to erosion and mars the ground surface. Contouring the ground to form "hip holes," in preparing a bed site, is in the same category.

Setup. In setting up a tent, it should normally be pitched so that the *back* of the tent faces into the wind. Another satisfactory arrangement may be to have a back corner facing into the wind, with the back and one side each at a 45° angle to the wind. The front, or entrance, will be downwind. Few sites will be absolutely level. You will normally want to sleep with your head at the higher end. If there is a fire site and you plan to use it, the tent should be kept far enough away from the fire so that it is out of range of sparks.

Prior to staking out a tent, it is important that nearby tree limbs be observed; the tent should be kept far enough away from them that even in a strong wind the tree branches cannot blow against the tent and possibly damage it. It is also important not to tie guy lines, or any other lines connected to the tent, to tree limbs. The tree limbs may whip in a wind, strain the tent fabric, and damage the tent. Tying guy lines, or other support lines, to sturdy tree trunks or to small solid bushes that cannot whip in the wind is normally a safe practice.

Before erecting the tent, you should zip shut any zippered openings, such as the front entranceway and any large nylon mesh paneled areas. Stakes, poles, a pounding tool, and other accessories should be within easy reach, especially if you are erecting your tent in a wind and must get it up quickly. Skewered stakes can often be pushed into the ground with the hands. For other stakes a smooth, round rock that you can hold in one hand will usually suffice as a pounding tool.

It is recommended that the peg that will guy the rear pole and center guy line be driven in place first. The floor of the tent is then unfolded, positioned in place, and staked so that it is taut and free of wrinkles. A peg for the front-end guy can then be placed. Once the floor is staked out and the pegs for the two end guys are in place, the tent can be quickly raised and the poles placed in position. You will probably need to make a few adjustments in position of stakes after the tent is up, to get it wrinkle free and ship-shape.

If your tent is not of the A-frame type, the procedures may vary somewhat from those outlined above. Also, the manufacturer's directions should be followed if they vary from the foregoing remarks. In general, you will probably find the above recommendations to be applicable as a basic guide.

Packing. Before rolling the tent for packing, it is recommended that you use a small whisk broom, or your hand, to brush off twigs, pine needles, leaves, bird droppings, and so forth. (A tent whisk broom weighs as little as 1 ounce.) While the tent is being rolled to fit its stuff sack, such debris should continue to be brushed off. Tent poles and pegs, especially the latter, can abrade and puncture tent cloth. It is therefore recommended that poles and pegs be carried in a small cloth sack, which you can easily make yourself, rather than be rolled with the tent. I carry pegs and skewer stakes in a small cloth bag that has the bottom half sewn with heavier cloth than the top half, to prevent puncturing by the stakes while on the trail.

Sometimes it is necessary to strike camp and hit the trail while the tent is wet. A damp tent can be rolled loosely and tied to the D rings on your pack. It will then continue to dry as you hike. Dampness will not harm nylon as it will cotton, but tents, as well as clothing and other gear, should be aired and dried whenever it is convenient—on the trail, in camp, or during layover days. All nylon items should also be thoroughly aired and dried at home, before storage.

SHELTER SUMMARY

The shelter that you choose for your backpacking trip will depend upon a number of factors. Of primary importance will be the anticipated and possible weather conditions. If you are to be camping in a forest, your choice will be different than if you will be camping above timberline. The number of people in the group makes a difference.

If the group is composed of three people and a three-person tent is available, it might be the best choice (assuming that the three are compatible as sleeping companions). Perhaps a tarp will suffice. These are matters to be discussed in the planning stages. Tables 3 and 4 are intended to be used as guidelines only, to assist in your choice of a suitable shelter.

TABLE 3. RECOMMENDED SHELTER

Item	Approximate Weight (in ounces)
Tent, one-person: tent, fly, pole, and stakes	44
OR	
Tent, two-person: tent, fly, poles, stakes, small whisk broom, and sponge	52†

†Half of total weight. One person carries tent and other carries compensating load of remaining common equipment.

TABLE 4. OPTIONAL SHELTER

Item	Approximate Weight (in ounces)
Tarp, coated nylon, 8′ X 10′ (for one person)	26
Parachute cord for tarp, ⅛″-diam. nylon, 30 ft.	2
Stakes and poles for tarp	22
OR	
Tarp, coated nylon, 10′ X 12′ (for two people)	20†
Parachute cord for tarp, ⅛″-diam. nylon, 45 ft.	1½†
Stakes and poles for tarp	12†

†Half of total weight.

5
Clothing

Few areas of preparation are more important than selecting the proper clothing and combinations of clothing for a backpack trip. Your choice will depend to a large extent on your previous experience in backpacking in the chosen area at the same season or on information obtained from knowledgeable people, with the added help of a forecast on the probable weather. Regardless of what the anticipated weather may be, however, it is essential to be prepared for unexpected changes in weather. The matter of preparing for unexpected foul weather can make the clothing aspect of preparation considerably more complicated than it would be otherwise. In certain seasons, or under adverse conditions at almost any season, it can mean the difference between an enjoyable trip and a thoroughly miserable one. In a few situations the difference can mean life or death. Many people take to the mountains when they backpack, and mountain weather is particularly subject to sudden and extreme changes.

Experience is an important factor in selecting clothing. If you know that certain clothing or combinations of clothing previously kept you warm, dry, and comfortable under adverse conditions, you are better prepared to choose your clothing for the next trip where similar conditions may be met. The length of trip is important. If you are going to be a good distance into the backwoods, the situation can be much more critical than if you are relatively close to the roadhead.

It is recommended that the factors of season, previous experience, weather forecast, and so on, be carefully and deliberately evaluated at home during your planning of the trip. Last-minute decisions to alter your clothing plan that may be made in the warm sunshine of a bright day at the trailhead may be disastrous. The more backpacking a person does under varying conditions, the more automatic his choice of clothing becomes, but overconfidence and taking the matter too lightly can result in trouble.

There is always a temptation to plan clothing around existing or apparent weather, rather than around possible adverse weather. A windshell jacket may weigh 4 ounces, an insulated vest 16 ounces, and a knit cap 2 ounces. Any of these items may mean the difference between being comfortable and uncomfortable.

Two very important functions of clothing are to keep you dry and to keep you warm. Keeping dry and keeping warm are directly related. You can get chilled in a hurry if you are wet, the weather is a bit cool, and there is a wind. Protective clothing is usually worn in layers. For example, over an undershirt might be worn a light cotton shirt, then a light or medium-weight wool shirt, perhaps an insulated vest or sweater over the wool shirt, and an outer garment consisting of a light windshell parka. It is recommended that various clothing combinations be tried out near home. You can go walking or hiking in the rain, in a cold wind, in snow, and so on, and determine what clothing and clothing combinations do the best job for you. If you carry a small pocket thermometer on such hikes, it will be helpful to record the temperature for future reference. The estimated wind speed and precipitation should also be recorded during such tests. If you make and keep some notes on these home tests, they will be helpful in planning your clothing for an actual backpack trip. Similar notes made during and after actual backpack trips will also be helpful. The experience and confidence gained in this manner will be well worth the effort. Most people are probably inclined to do their practice hiking in good weather, but purposely doing some hiking in inclement weather will be very beneficial. A rucksack or small pack should be carried so that you can add or shed layers and protective garments as you would on an actual backpack trip.

Obviously, clothing has other important functions to perform in addition to keeping the hiker warm and dry. Clothing should normally provide maximum protection from the sun. There will be less risk with heat exhaustion, sunstroke (heatstroke), and sunburn if this is kept in mind. Heatstroke is very serious—frequently fatal. Sunburn is painful, and sunburned shoulders, in particular, can be a catastrophe on a backpack trip. Therefore, long-sleeved shirts, long trousers, and a broad-brimmed hat are recommended. At the same time you will get more protection from nicks and scratches caused by rock projections and bushes, as well as protection from poison ivy. At certain seasons protection from mosquitoes, black flies, or other insects will be a major concern. Maximum coverage of all bare skin will be needed, including a head net for the head, face, and neck, and perhaps light gloves for the hands. Compared to bare skin, long-sleeved shirts and long trousers also offer significant additional protection against snakebite in areas where rattlesnakes (or other poisonous snakes) may be encountered. All clothing should be a little loose, rather than a little too tight.

Maybe you prefer hiking shorts for your backpacking. Perhaps you like to hike with no shirt at all. If that's your cup of tea, go to it. After all, you are taking your backpacking trip for fun, so "do your thing." It is recommended, however, that long-sleeved shirts and trousers be handy in your pack, just in case you need the additional protection from the elements or from insects.

MATERIALS

In choosing fabrics for making clothing, the familiar problem of breathability becomes a very important factor. There are excellent strong and lightweight synthetic materials available today that are waterproof. However, since the body gives off about a quart or more of water each day, the use of truly waterproof materials must be limited and various design techniques that will permit this water to escape to the outside air must be used in clothing construction. Otherwise our skin and clothing would soon be sopping wet, which would at the least be very uncomfortable and, in many circumstances, a threat to our health and even our life. Thus, in general, clothing must breathe. This is demonstrated when you wear a pair of rubber hip boots or a rubber slicker on a warm day. Your perspiration cannot escape to the outside and evaporate. Depending upon the amount of exertion, humidity, and other factors, your clothes soon become damp and clammy.

One of the challenges of backpacking, related to the clothing aspect, is to avoid sweating, or to keep perspiration to an absolute minimum, particularly in cool or cold weather. This is accomplished partly through controlling the level of exertion. Equally important, however, is the amount of clothing worn under varying conditions and, in particular, the *kinds* and *combinations* of clothing.

Wool. One of the most widely used materials in the making of outdoor clothing is wool. In years past it was *the* material. In more recent years some of the synthetic materials have replaced wool in certain applications, but wool still retains a prominent place in the manufacture of some items; for example, wool shirts, wool trousers, and wool socks. The use of wool socks is fairly standard as an outer sock for use in boots. Wool shirts and trousers remain in high favor, particularly for cool and wet weather use.

An important advantage of wool is that a wool garment will retain much of its insulating ability and warmth even when wet. It traps air in tiny pockets between the curly fibers. Due to its waviness and crimp, it is resilient and durable. Wool garments are not as easily torn on brush as some of the synthetics. Wool has many small dead air pockets, which are good insulators. If an article of wool clothing is wet, a person can sleep with it on, next to the skin, and in the morning it will be dry. A disadvantage of wool is its weight, and heavy wool garments are not recommended. Also, some people are allergic to wool and others find it uncomfortable and irritating when worn next to the skin.

Virgin (all-new) wool provides the greatest warmth and is most comfortable when worn next to the skin. Reprocessed wool has shorter fibers and is not so soft and comfortable. However, garments made from reprocessed wool will be considerably cheaper.

Cotton. To most people, cotton feels comfortable when worn next to the skin. Cotton underwear and socks, as well as cotton shirts and trousers, are relatively inexpensive and commonly used. Cotton quickly looses its insulating qualities when wet. Therefore, it is primarily suitable for clothing to be used in warm, dry weather.

Some people like to wear a lightweight cotton shirt under a wool shirt if they find the wool shirt irritating to the skin.

Synthetics. One of the common synthetic materials used in clothing construction is nylon. It is lightweight and very strong. It is breathable but can readily be coated, usually with polyurethane, to make it waterproof. It is resistant to mildew. It is used primarily in the construction of protective garments, such as rainwear, wind jackets, and pants, and as the outer material for cold-weather clothing containing various insulating materials. When used next to the skin, it feels slippery and somewhat cold. Thus, it has limited use in this application. The nylon most commonly used in clothing is either ripstop or taffeta.

Fabric blends. Two commonly used fabric blends are referred to as 60/40 cloth and 65/35 cloth. The purpose of blending the cloth is to obtain certain of the better qualities of cotton and of nylon (or Dacron) through the blending process. A blend of 60 percent cotton and 40 percent nylon is referred to as 60/40 cloth. This cloth has the inherent toughness and lightweight of nylon and the softness of cotton. Also, the cotton swells upon contact with water. Garments made of 60/40 cloth offer good wind protection and water repellency. They are not waterproof.

A blend of 65 percent cotton and 35 percent Dacron is referred to as 65/35 cloth. This cloth has somewhat greater strength than 60/40. It is also somewhat superior in its ability to provide more uniform water repellency. In 60/40 cloth the nylon threads run in one direction and the cotton threads in the other (fill) direction. In 65/35 cloth the Dacron and cotton are blended together before

they are used to make the cloth, so the blended yarn runs in both directions in the cloth.

There are still other fabric blends which are blended to provide various properties in the finished cloth. The 60/40 and 65/35 are two of the most commonly used.

Waterproof breathable cloth. Elsewhere in this book it has been stated that in order for a fabric to have breathability, its waterproofness must be compromised. After many years of intense experimentation by many qualified manufacturers, that seemed to be a solid and indisputable fact. Yet, about the time that the sixth edition of this book was being prepared, a new material that appears to have the qualifications to disprove that "fact" was being introduced to the market. This material is called Gore-Tex.

Gore-Tex is a membrane that is made from the same resin as Teflon. Technically speaking, it is a microporous polymeric film of polytetrafluoroethylene (PTFE). It is very thin and flexible and not rugged in itself. Therefore, other fabrics are laminated to it in various combinations. The Gore-Tex is frequently sandwiched between layers of nylon or other material. Tents, sleeping bags, and clothing are being made from Gore-Tex laminated material. The material is rather expensive, costing a minimum of about $10 per square yard.

The company responsible for the development of Gore-Tex is W. L. Gore and Associates, North Elkton, Maryland. Gore-Tex has about 9 billion pores per square inch. Each pore is smaller than the smallest bacteria that exist. A film of Gore-Tex is about 1 mil thick. Water vapor, since it is gaseous water, will pass through Gore-Tex. Liquid water will *not* pass through Gore-Tex. When Gore-Tex is laminated to a breathable material or uncoated fabric, it prevents the penetration of water in liquid form but allows moisture vapor to pass through. When a Gore-Tex jacket or other garment is being worn, heat from the body makes the temperature on the inside of the garment higher than the outside temperature. This creates a vapor pressure greater than that on the outside, and the vapor diffuses through the Gore-Tex to the outside air. The same process would apply to a sleeping bag or similar article made from Gore-Tex laminates.

Gore-Tex laminates were made commercially available as outerwear materials in January 1976. It will be some time before the various products made from Gore-Tex have been in use by enough backpackers for a sufficient period to thoroughly evaluate the material and to verify its unique properties and practicability under various field conditions. Some limited preliminary experience indicates that it is important to keep a Gore-Tex garment clean in order for its unique properties to be effective. Also, its practicability as a material for tents had not been fully demonstrated at the time of publication of this edition.

Insulating materials. There are several insulating materials, or "fillers," used in jackets, vests, parkas, and other garments to provide warmth. The most common are goose down, Hollofil II, and PolarGuard. Open-cell foam (polyurethane) is used to a lesser extent. The characteristics of these materials were discussed in Chapter 3 on sleeping gear. Hollofil II, Polar-Guard, and open-cell foam are particularly useful under conditions where the garment may become wet, since dampness does not seriously affect their insulating value. Just as it is for sleeping bags, goose down or duck down is restricted to use where it is fairly certain that they can be kept dry. When they become wet, for all practical purposes they completely lose their insulating value, which is a very serious consideration. Equally serious is the lengthy time (usually days) required for drying out a wet down garment.

SHOPPING FOR CLOTHING

There is a vast array of special, sophisticated, and (very frequently) expensive, clothing available to the backpacker. Much of this special clothing has "blossomed" during the past few years, with the tremendous increase in popularity of the sport of backpacking. It might be well to emphasize that people were backpacking many, many years before the current deluge of sophisticated clothing (and equipment) was available, or even thought of.

The point is, you don't need a lot of special clothing to go backpacking. In fact, you may need very little of it. This is particularly emphasized to those who are fairly new to backpacking. Unless you have a lot of money to spend, it is strongly recommended that you first gain some significant experience in backpacking before making any substantial purchases of expensive special clothing.

These remarks are in no way intended to belittle the manufacturers of special clothing (and equipment). This includes those firms who have spent good sums of money to research and develop materials, fabrics, and construction techniques that would serve vital purposes on backwoods trails, and do it better and with less total weight than previously available equipment. There are many manufacturers and researchers who have contributed immeasurably to the overall enjoyment and safety of the sport. My purpose is rather to *caution* those who are a bit short on experience against hastily buying items before they gain the insight and knowledge that they will need to make such purchases *wisely*. Even old hands at backpacking, with a vast background of information and experiences to draw from, often let their enthusiasm outweigh their good judgment and frequently come up with some real "bummers." If you are fashion-conscious and want to look your best even in the backwoods, then these remarks will have little effect. So be it.

Backpacking and wilderness living are not elitist activities. Ordinary folks make up the vast majority of persons found on backwoods trails and in backwoods camps. However, shopping for clothing for your backpacking, and studying the price tags on some articles, may raise doubts in your mind about these statements. For most moderate-weather backpacking, you will need very little, if any, special clothing. Usually some of the clothing that you already have will do the job. This does not mean that "any old thing" will do the job for clothes on a backpack trip. It won't. You need to be a bit selective in choosing your clothing, particularly if you are faced with the possibility of cool, wet weather.

Almost any old trousers, if they are full cut and not binding in the seat or legs, will do the job. Most work trousers are roomy and satisfactory. Any comfortable shirt—preferably a *nonsynthetic* one—will suffice. For cool, wet weather, it is highly desirable that shirt and trousers be wool. An old, loose-fitting wool sweater will provide warmth. Two of medium weight are preferable to a single bulky one. A lightweight windshell jacket and an inexpensive vinyl poncho will essentially complete the wardrobe, to start. If you don't have suitable old clothing around the house, a visit to an army-navy store or some rummage sales will probably provide the desired items at a very modest cost. All clothing should be in reasonably good condition. It is a poor beginning to take a worn-out article of clothing (or equipment) on a backpack trip with the hope that it will hold together until you can get back home and throw it away. As I have stressed many times (it's my theme song), try out your chosen articles of clothing on local hikes and very short trips. Dashing off into the backwoods on a full-scale backpack trip with a collection of untried clothing is poor business. Knowing when and how to use the clothing is almost as important as the clothing itself. Avoid sweating, when at all possible, and use the layering system. Dress so as to be a bit cool (not cold), rather than overheated, when hiking.

HATS

A few people backpack without a hat; however, a hat is definitely recommended. The head and neck are very sensitive to changes in temperature. If your head is uncovered, a lot of heat loss will occur from the head in cold weather. In the summer sun a hat can mean the difference between being comfortable and being too hot, or possibly becoming sick and dizzy from the sun. It can also prevent sunburn, which is important. Most people who spend much time in the out-of-doors consider their hat to be a very vital item of clothing. Quite a few backpackers carry two hats—a broad-brimmed hat for protection against the sun, and a stocking cap for cold temperatures.

Summer hat. For mild-weather backpacking, any comfortable hat, reasonably soft and flexible, with a broad brim, should be satisfactory. An old felt hat is good. A few holes cut in the crown will make it cooler. The crusher hat, sold in many backpack equipment shops, is a good hat for backpacking. It weighs about 3 ounces. The white tennis, or glacier, hats, with wide brim, are also good. In the hot sun your hat should be worn with the brim turned down so as to shade the eyes and provide protection for the upper face and ears. Hats made from preshrunk, water-repellent poplin material are also good. Summer hats should be light in color to reflect the sun's rays. In hot weather it is best to wear your hat with the crown pushed up, rather than creased, so as to provide maximum air space around the head. Your hat may not look very stylish with the crown pushed up, but doing this serves a very definite purpose.

To avoid losing your hat in a brisk wind, a chin strap is important. You can easily attach a chin strap. Punch a hole in the brim, just above each ear, close to the crown, and thread a leather thong or nylon cord around the back half of the brim circumference on the top side and down through the holes. Tie the thongs or cord under the chin, or use a slide fastener (more convenient). If you decide to go for brief periods without wearing your hat, it can be tied to the outside of your packframe. The

Crusher hat. Note that the top of the pack is well above the hat. The hat is soft and flexible. The annoying bumping of the rear part against the pack, which occurs with many broad-brimmed hats, is avoided.

Glacier hat. This type provides good protection from the sun.

crusher and glacier-style hats can be rolled up and stuffed inside the packbag.

It will usually be necessary to roll the brim of the hat up in back (or to turn it down) to keep the top of your pack from bumping against the hat as you hike. This bumping can be very annoying.

Cold-weather hat. You may be accustomed to going without a hat, and in cold weather your head and neck may not be *noticeably* cold. However, in cool weather, blood vessels near the surface cause large amounts of heat to be lost in this area. When this happens, more blood flows to the torso, which contains the vital internal organs, and also to the brain. The hands and feet receive less circulation and thus become cold. The saying "If your feet are cold, put your hat on" is scientifically valid. A wool knit cap makes a good cold-weather hat. It is also very helpful when worn in your sleeping bag if you are sleeping a bit cool. For very cold weather, a balaclava makes a good head cover. It protects not only the head but also the neck and lower face.

Rain hat. A separate rain hat will not normally be necessary. For rain protection a poncho or rain jacket will usually be carried, and this will have a hood that protects the head and neck area. If for some reason you plan to hike in predominantly rainy weather, you may prefer a separate rain hat. The sou'wester type of rain hat, with a wide brim that pulls down to protect the face and neck, is popular.

SHIRTS

For summer, a light cotton shirt, worn next to the undershirt, is recommended. Synthetic shirts do not absorb sweat satisfactorily. A wool shirt worn over this will provide significant additional protection. Many people find that wool, when worn next to the body, causes their skin to itch and become uncomfortable. The cotton shirt underneath the wool shirt will usually take care of this problem.

The heavy cotton flannel shirts (also called chamois shirts) are quite popular among some backpackers. They are very soft on the skin and absorb sweat readily. People highly allergic to wool usually like these shirts.

In cool, wet weather, wool has an advantage in that it will keep you warm even though it is wet. Two popular brands of wool shirts are Pendleton and Woolrich. A light or medium-weight wool

Knit cap. This is good headgear for cold-weather daytime use and for wearing in the sleeping bag on cold nights.
(Lou Clemmons)

shirt is recommended over the heavy jacket type. A heavy wool shirt not only adds excess weight but does not provide much versatility. It may quickly become too warm, and it does not lend itself to the accepted practice of removing or adding *layers* of garments as the day warms or cools. Also, the space *between* the multiple layers of garments is important added insulation.

If the shirttail is worn outside the trousers in hot weather, you will be cooler because of the added ventilation provided. For wearing outside the trousers, a square-cut shirttail is a little more convenient than a long, tapered one. However, a long shirttail provides needed additional warmth in cool weather. Shirts should normally have long sleeves. These will give protection against sunburn, insects, and cuts and scratches from brush, and provide added warmth in cool weather. A plaid design will not show dirt as readily as a solid color will. Light colors will be cooler in hot weather. Two generous-sized pockets will prove useful. They should have a button top, preferably a flap top with button. Small items are easily lost from shirt pockets that do not have button tops. Before you start out, *all* buttons should be checked and any that are loose resewn.

TROUSERS

Long trousers, without cuffs, are recommended. In cool weather they are needed for warmth. They also protect the legs from scratches and insects. In the hot sun they perform the important function of preventing sunburn.

Trousers should always be loose, even a bit baggy, rather than formfitting. You will be doing a lot of stooping, bending, squatting, and stretching. Trousers that fit too tightly in the seat or crotch, or that are too narrow in the legs or thighs, will bind and chafe. They will also be hot in warm weather. Large, roomy pockets, with at least one of the hip pockets having a button-down flap, are desirable.

Some hikers prefer blue jeans for backpacking in mild weather. Some blue jeans may be satisfactory, but many are formfitting and too narrow and tight. They do not allow sufficient freedom of leg movement. You can make a simple test for the fit of trousers to be worn in backpacking. Put them on and place one foot on a chair or step stool, about 18 to 20 inches off the floor. Any binding in the crotch, the thighs, or around the knees should be cause for rejection. Work trousers are usually generously cut and satisfactory for mild-weather backpacking. They are usually made of cotton, which is a poor material for wet weather.

In cool, wet weather, wool trousers should be worn. An old pair of dress trousers may be satisfactory. A tightly woven material is superior to a loose weave, which may catch on brush. Some materials that are mixtures of wool and nylon are quite satisfactory.

An elastic waistband, rather than a belt, to hold your trousers in place, will be most comfortable. When the waist strap on your pack is drawn tight, a conventional belt and buckle is going to interfere a bit. One solution to the problem is to wear heavy-duty suspenders to hold up your trousers. Even if you don't normally wear suspenders, you will probably find them useful and comfortable in backpacking.

I sometimes wear a web belt and buckle arrangement that is very much like the straps used to strap sleeping bags to the packframe. My preference, however, is to wear wide, heavy-duty, "police style" suspenders. As you hike along, your trousers are going to tend to sag if you wear a belt, and you will need to keep hitching them up to keep them in place. I have found that suspenders do not interfere at all with the hip belt on your pack; they keep your trousers at the proper height, there is no tightness at the waist (as with a trouser belt), and they simply feel good. A word of caution. Heavy-duty suspenders are frequently available with either clips or button slots at the ends, for fastening to the trousers. Always get the type with slots for attachment to buttons on your trousers. Then sew four heavy-duty buttons to

your backpacking trousers at the proper points—and sew them on well. When you stoop or bend, there is stress at these points of attachment. I have used the clip-attachment type and have found that the clips won't take the stress. They lose their grip on your trousers at odd times during the day and are a nuisance.

Trousers should be a little short, rather than too long, and should fall 2 or 3 inches above the heel of your boot. Large, roomy pockets are desirable, but pockets should not be loaded down with small items of equipment or other material. If you have a packsack with outside pockets, most of the items that you would normally want to carry in your trouser pockets will be almost as accessible in the packsack pockets. Otherwise you can put such items in a small bag near the top of the main packsack compartment.

Some hikers prefer shorts, rather than long trousers, for added freedom of movement and ventilation. If you do wear shorts, it is also recommended that you carry long trousers in your pack for cool weather and for part-time protection from the sun, insects, and so on. If you want to be stylish, there are some good-looking hiking shorts available at about $10 to $15 per pair. If style isn't important to you, suitable hiking shorts can be readily improvised from an old pair of long trousers. Simply cut them off at the desired height above the knee. They will do the job.

Knickers are frequently worn by climbers; a few hikers also use them. They are not recommended for backpacking, however. The full-length socks worn with knickers are easily torn on brush and projecting rocks. The lower leg has much less protection against brush, damp grass, and so on, than it does in full-length trousers.

UNDERCLOTHES

On a backpack trip you can wear the same underclothes that you normally wear. However, after a period of strenuous hiking in warm weather, the undershirt (in particular) will usually become sweat soaked. It will cling to your skin and wick the moisture into your clothing. A fishnet style of undershirt (and drawers also) that will prevent this is available. These fishnet underclothes are cooler and drier in summer and warmer in winter. The material used in fishnet underwear is commonly cotton, or 50 percent cotton and 50 percent polyester. Wool-cotton material is also used and is good for wet-weather use. When wearing fishnet underwear in warm weather, you loosen up your shirt at the neck and

Net undershirt. The fishnet construction holds an outer shirt away from the skin. Such an undershirt will provide good warmth and comfort in winter. In summer it will provide for more air circulation, ventilation, and comfort than will a conventional undershirt. Fishnet shorts and "longjohns" are also available.

sleeves, and maybe open the front, and also allow the shirttail to hang outside the trousers (if it is really warm). This allows free circulation of air. The skin will "breathe," and your perspiration will evaporate. In cool weather you button up the neck of your shirt and the sleeves. The small pockets of dead-air space in the fishnet underwear are thereby heated, and you will then be warmer.

When not backpacking, most women usually wear undergarments of nylon or other synthetics. However, these do not absorb moisture, and they are quite uncomfortable next to the skin when wet, in contrast to cotton or a cotton-polyester blend. When they go backpacking, it is advisable for women to wear cotton underclothing. The fishnet style commonly worn by men is also worn by many women.

Thermal underwear is available for cold-weather use. This is usually two-piece, with long sleeves and long legs. Such underwear usually consists of two layers. The inner layer, next to the skin, is cotton. The outer layer is frequently a mixture of cotton and wool. Duofold is one such brand of underwear. However, most backpackers depend upon extra layers of outer clothing, rather than on this type of underwear, or other "longjohns," to keep warm.

SWEATERS

A medium-weight sweater can be a good addition to your protective clothing. A wool sweater is a fairly common item of everyday clothing, and it is quite possible that you already possess one that will be quite suitable. Heavy, bulky sweaters are to be avoided. Two light sweaters would be better. A light or medium-weight wool shirt and a light sweater make a good combination. Heavy, bulky ski sweaters are generally unsatisfactory. When used with a windshell jacket, these layers of clothing can keep out a lot of weather. A loose-weave sweater is best. It will assist the escape of body moisture. It will also permit more stretch and will thus not restrict body movements as will a tightly knit sweater. Extra length in a sweater is desirable. It should preferably extend to the hips. Otherwise, during trail activity, the sweater tends to work its way up above the waistline and protection is minimized. One way of achieving extra length in a sweater is to buy an old one at a thrift shop, cut it roughly in half, and sew the bottom section onto your "good" sweater. Another approach is to have some capable individual knit an additional bottom section for your sweater. It can be sewn to the "upper" sweater, using an additional piece of cloth. A turtleneck sweater will be warmer than a V-neck, but some kind of opening at the neck is preferable.

There is sometimes a bit of confusion in nomenclature between sweaters and jackets. Some manufacturers' literature includes in the sweater category jackets that are insulated with down or synthetics, and may even refer to vests as sweaters. I believe most people think of sweaters as woven or knitted garments consisting of a single layer of material, usually unlined. Some are pullover style, with no buttons, and you get into them by slipping them on over the head. This style is a bit harder to get into and out of than the type that simply buttons down the front. Also, the latter type can readily be partially or fully opened to allow for variation in temperature, whereas the pullover type does not permit such adjustment to be made.

JACKETS

You can find jackets in many styles and types of construction, and for wide temperature ranges. The mornings and evenings in the mountains can be very cool, even in summer. Thinking back on such periods when it was very cool (or downright cold), you may be tempted to pack a heavy jacket.

Down jacket. A lighweight garment providing good insulation and warmth when dry. The collar of such a jacket will become dirty quickly. A piece of lightweight cloth was fastened over the collar of this jacket with a basting stitch to prevent soiling of the jacket collar.

This may weigh 2½ to 4 pounds, and many times it would only be used for an hour or two in the evening and again in the morning.

It is very important to keep in mind that the *layer system* should be considered in selecting clothing for protection against cold. You should not rely on a single heavy garment. The layer system not only provides greater versatility for comfort in a wide range of temperatures, but for a given weight it will provide the most protection. That is because the air space between the layers of clothing provides added insulation. As the temperature changes during the day, or as your level of exertion changes, you can shed or add clothing as necessary to stay comfortable.

As discussed under sleeping bags, there are now two excellent synthetic insulating materials available—Hollofil II and PolarGuard. These are also being widely used in the manufacture of jackets and other protective clothing. As with sleeping bags, a goose-down garment will be the lightest in weight for the protection afforded. However, also as with sleeping bags, once the down garment gets wet, you are essentially out of business for a few days or longer.

Thus, in your search for a suitable jacket or other protective clothing, it is recommended that you give serious consideration to those that use one of the synthetic materials Hollofil II or PolarGuard for insulation. If you are certain you can stay dry on your trips, then down has advantages—primarily its very light weight and bulk (when packed) for a given insulating value. In the back country, depending upon the season and altitude, it is very difficult to assure that at some time during a trip you will not get wet. At such time you will be thankful for a protective garment that has synthetic filling. The water can be squeezed out, the garment will have much of its original loft, even though wet, and it will provide warmth immediately. Not so with goose down. It is not difficult to visualize adverse field conditions in which the choice of insulating material in your protective clothing could mean the difference between life and death.

On the trail or working about camp, you may snag and tear your jacket on a tree limb. In a down garment the down will immediately start falling out through the torn spot. This will require a fairly good repair job. This is not true of the synthetics. Since the material is sewn into the garment in the form of batts, it is not readily lost if a rip occurs, and a fairly simple repair job in the field will suffice.

A quilted construction is usually used to hold the insulation in place, and it may be either single quilted or double-layer quilted. For extreme cold, there should be no sewn-through seams. However, the average backpacker will not usually require a jacket in this category.

Ventilation control is important. A full-length zipper in front provides for good ventilation adjustment and for easily putting the garment on or taking it off. On quality garments the zipper flap may have snaps, for complete closure and additional ventilation flexibility. A draw cord at the waist should be provided to control loss of warm air in that area, when desired. Elastic cuffs will often be provided to prevent loss of warm air at the wrist openings. Some quality garments will have cuff closures fitted with snaps or Velcro tape, for better ventilation control.

Pockets should be well insulated and roomy. Collars are occasionally skimpy on insulation, but they should not be.

A down jacket designed for moderately cold weather will weigh about 1½ pounds. An equivalent (temperature-wise) synthetic-filled jacket will weigh about 2 pounds. A good down jacket will cost from $50 to $75. Synthetic-filled jackets usually range from $30 to $60. Garments intended for use in very cold weather will cost considerably more.

Since a lot of heat is lost from the head and neck area in cold weather, the next logical step in improving an insulated jacket is to add an insulated hood. The jacket then becomes a parka. In some designs the hood is a separate item that is attached at the neck, with snaps or something similar. Prices for such garments usually start at about $40, depending on the quality of design and insulating material used, and go to well over the $100.

VESTS

An insulated vest is a popular garment with many backpackers. When worn over a wool shirt or sweater, with a windshell jacket or parka, the combination can provide a surprising amount of warmth.

A down vest will weigh about 12 to 14 ounces. Many are made with an extra long back panel that protects the lower back and buttocks and provides additional warmth in that area. This is a good feature.

Down-insulated vests have been popular for many years. Vests are now available that use Hollofil II and PolarGuard as insulating materials. An insulated vest is a relatively easy garment to make at home. It is recommended that you try it if you are so inclined. Prices of store-bought insulated vests range from about $15 to $25.

PARKAS

There are many variations in the construction of parkas as well as variations in the function that the parka is intended to perform. The jacket-style parka opens completely in front and is easy to put on and take off. The pullover type must be donned by pulling it over the head and wriggling the arms and shoulders until the garment is in place. The primary feature that parkas have in common is that the garment extends above the shoulders to cover the head and neck area.

As was mentioned earlier, some types of jackets have an attached hood. On insulated jackets the hood should also be insulated, so as to give complete and adequate protection to the head and neck. A well-insulated parka of this type is generally suitable for very cold weather and is usually too much garment for the average backpacker. A detachable hood will add to its

versatility. A well-designed, well-insulated parka of this type, with attached hood, will range in price from $40 to over $100. Weight will usually be about 2 to 3 pounds.

Still other parkas are primarily designed for storm protection—to keep out wind and to provide moderate rain protection. They are usually generously cut, so as to fit over insulated clothing worn for warmth. Drawstrings at waist and hood and cuffs that can be tightly closed are important features. Some parkas of this type are referred to as mountain parkas or wilderness parkas, or simply as storm parkas. They are frequently made of 60/40 cloth, which is a blend of approximately 60 percent cotton and 40 percent nylon. This material is strong, has good water repellency, and is breathable. Such garments usually weigh about 1½ to 2 pounds and cost $35 to $60.

Parka shells, or windshells, are versatile and useful outer garments. The material used is often uncoated nylon (frequently ripstop nylon). Lightly coated nylon is also used. These shells are intended mainly for wind protection, thus increasing the warmth of the insulated clothing over which they are worn. Since the insulated garments over which it is worn are generally bulky, the windshell should be generously cut. Length is important; a good windshell should fall well below the hips. Windshell parkas may weigh only 6 to 8 ounces. Cost is usually about $10 to $20.

Hollofil II parka. This parka, made from a pattern by the author's wife, uses Hollofil II as an insulating material. By itself it will provide comfort in temperatures down to 25° F. In combination with other protective garments the comfort range can be extended considerably lower.

RAIN GEAR

A discussion of rain gear involves the familiar problem of *waterproofness* versus *breathability*. Just as in tent design, you cannot make a rain suit that will "breathe" and yet give absolute protection from rain. (However, see the discussion of Gore-Tex on pages 46–47.)

Ponchos. Ponchos were briefly discussed in Chapter 4 on shelter. A full-sized poncho, about 54 by 90 inches, can be used for rain protection on the trail and will serve as an emergency shelter. Ponchos are not formfitting. They are loose and floppy. In a strong wind you will probably have difficulty keeping your poncho from blowing about, and you will usually end up with wet legs (unless you wear rain chaps). If the trail goes through terrain that is thick and brushy, the poncho will frequently catch on bushes. The disadvantage of a poncho (being loose and floppy) is also its advantage. Air circulates much more freely under it, and you will not become so wet from your own body moisture as you will in a formfitting rain suit. The poncho is one of the most widely used of all the various garments designed for emergency rain protection. The larger sizes are designed to cover the pack as well as the hiker. Inexpensive vinyl ponchos are available for $1 or $2. However, they snag and tear easily. A good nylon poncho is much more durable and will cost from $15 to $18. Weight is about 12 ounces.

Raincoats. A plastic raincoat can be carried for possible protection against infrequent rain. However, these raincoats are not very popular with most backpackers. Ordinary rubber slickers are much too heavy for backpacking.

If the weather is warm and it starts to rain, one way to keep your clothes dry (from perspiration) is to take off all clothes except shoes, socks, and underclothes. You can then put your outer clothes in your pack where they will stay dry until the rain is over. Put your poncho or other rain gear on over your underclothes and continue hiking. Admittedly, the company you are in will have a bearing on whether this procedure is practical.

Rain parkas. A rain parka, in contrast to a wind parka, is made of coated waterproof nylon. Most are of hip length. Some have a zipper in front, which makes them easier to put on and take off and also provides for ventilation when the weather does not require complete closure. However, the zipper does make for a vulnerable area

Coated-nylon poncho, covering both pack and hiker. *(Lou Clemmons)*

Rain gear.

Poncho being used as "tent" shelter. *(Lou Clemmons)*

through which rain may penetrate in a storm. A good rain parka will avoid seams at the shoulders, a potential source of leakage. The *anorak* is a variation of the rain parka. The main distinguishing feature is that it is a pullover, with no zipper in front, except for perhaps a very short one to adjust the opening at the neck. When made of uncoated fabric, it is primarily intended for wind protection. Like any other pullover, an anorak should always be of generous size. In shopping for one, if you should choose to do so, you must constantly keep in mind any bulky garments that you may want to wear under it. Getting into and out of a pullover that is a bit too tight can be an unpleasant and irritating exercise. Parkas with a full front opening with zipper or snaps are generally more popular than anoraks. In general, the anoraks are most popular with climbers, rather than backpackers.

Cagoules. You may have seen cagoules advertised in some of the backpacking equipment catalogs. Cagoules are very similar to anoraks. However, they are cut much fuller and are longer, usually coming down to the knees or slightly lower. To hike or backpack in a cagoule would normally be like walking in a portable sauna. Cagoules were originally designed for bivouac use by rock climbers. If you sit down with your knees drawn up in front, the drawstring at the bottom of the garment can be tightened around the lower legs or boot tops, and you have a relatively storm-proof temporary shelter. Cagoules are not practical for most hiking. However, under certain combinations of temperature and humidity, and with a low level of exertion, they could be used.

Rain pants. Rain pants are sometimes carried and worn as a complement to a rain parka. These are full-length pants, extending from the waist to the ankles. Many have no pockets or fly opening; others do. Since the nature of rain gear dictates that you may want to put it on and also take it off quickly and easily, an important consideration is that the legs be large enough to permit donning the rain pants without removing your hiking boots. This requires that the legs be extra large. Provision is usually made in the lower legs for a short length of vertical zipper, a drawstring at the cuffs, or a similar closure to permit snugging the pants about the lower leg. A primary disadvantage of rain pants is that they are usually very hot, making perspiration great. After a rainstorm you can remove your rain parka, poncho, or whatever, and probably also your

Rain parka. This rain parka was made from a kit. It was purposely made large and is being worn here over a Hollofil II parka. This combination is ideal for cold, wet, windy weather, and when using rain pants or rain chaps to protect the trouser legs.

shirt and even your undershirt, thus drying out (from your own sweat) and cooling off a bit. You can also remove your rain pants, but that's about as far as you can go. It probably isn't very practical to take off the trousers you hike in, even though they are wet with sweat. Because rain pants are hot and sweaty, many backpackers prefer rain chaps.

Rain chaps. Rain chaps are two separate waterproof "legs" that fit over the trouser legs and have loops for hooking to the belt. If suspenders are being worn, you can use safety pins to fasten the loops to your trousers. They are much cooler in warm weather than rain pants are, and they are often worn in combination with a rain parka or poncho. As was true for rain pants, an important consideration is that the rain chaps be wide enough that they can be pulled on over your boots. There should be some provision for snugging the legs at the ankles—zipper, drawstring, or Velcro tape—after you get the chaps on. If tall grass borders the trail, rain chaps are helpful even after the rain stops. They will protect your trousers from getting wet as you brush against the wet grass. Rain chaps are relatively simple to fabricate; you can probably make a pair yourself, as I have. Precut kits are also available if you prefer to take that approach. Both rain pants and rain chaps also offer protection in cold wind.

GLOVES AND MITTENS

For normal summer backpacking, few hikers bother with gloves. However, at certain seasons a pair of lightweight gloves may be desirable to protect the hands and wrists from insects. In a work party, where clearing of brush, digging, and similar jobs are to be done, gloves will offer some protection against blisters. Some backpackers keep a pair of lightweight cotton gloves with their cooking utensils and use them while cooking.

Heat is lost from the body mainly through the extremities, and this includes the hands. When your hands get cold, you can put them in your pockets. However, if much cool weather is expected, a pair of gloves may be desirable for warmth. Gloves offer greater versatility than mittens when you are working. You can do many jobs while wearing gloves, but mittens must usually be removed even for very simple tasks. However, mittens offer much more warmth in cold weather. (Your fingers need the "companionship" of one another in cold weather, if your hands are to stay warm.) In really cold weather some backpackers wear mittens over a very thin pair of wool or silk gloves. Simple tasks can usually be performed by removing only the mittens, and the thin gloves offer some protection during such periods.

HANDKERCHIEF

A handkerchief is not generally essential. This is usually used for blowing your nose, and no hiker should start a backpack trip with a cold. A handkerchief will soon get dirty, and carrying dirty laundry in your pack is not recommended. A small package of tissues or some toilet tissue will do the same job. If you usually use your handkerchief or bandana for wiping your hands and face, as many hikers do, a 10-inch square of old, thin toweling carried in your hip pocket will do a better job.

If you do use disposable tissues, they should be pocketed after use and burned later, if a fire is available, or carried in a litterbag. Littering the trail with them is absolutely inexcusable. Those who cannot resist the temptation to toss paper tissues down along the trail after each use are implored to please stay with the handkerchief.

A bandana or very large handkerchief is frequently useful when worn as an item of clothing. When placed around the neck it will help keep out dust. The neck, particularly the back and sides, is very susceptible to sunburn. A bandana worn as a neckerchief will protect this sensitive area. It will also feel comfortable in a cold wind. To a degree, it provides protection from insects in the neck area.

PAJAMAS

Many backpackers do not bother with pajamas. Some sleep in the raw; others, in their underclothes. Various items of clothing are sometimes worn in the sleeping bag. Wool clothing or underwear, even though damp, will provide additional warmth if worn in the sleeping bag and will probably be dry in the morning. A pair of formfitting pajamas, or possibly "longjohn" underwear, can be worn in the sleeping bag at night and can also be used for daytime wear in unexpected cold weather.

Under the discussion of sleeping bags it was pointed out that some people use a liner in their bag to help keep it clean. There is no question that it is desirable to keep a sleeping bag clean. However, pajamas can do essentially the same job as a liner in keeping the sleeping bag clean, and they will generally be more comfortable than sleeping with a liner. During the night a liner will often get completely twisted about the body. A pair of socks, when worn with pajamas, can prevent the feet and legs from soiling the foot end of the bag. By wearing a small cap (similar to a stocking cap) in the sleeping bag, you can prevent the head end from being soiled. In cold weather a hat can also provide considerable additional warmth.

SOCKS

The socks that you wear with your hiking boots are very important. They should either be new or in new condition, without darns or patches. Well-worn socks or the thin socks that you usually wear with street shoes simply won't work. Blisters and sore feet will be the result. Socks made especially for hiking boots are available from many suppliers of backpacking equipment.

Socks provide insulation, and they cushion the feet as you walk. They absorb perspiration from the feet. A particularly important function is to reduce friction between boots and feet. Some people wear only one pair of socks—a single, thick, heavy pair. However, most hikers agree that wearing two pairs of socks (simultaneously) gives better results than wearing a single pair. These can be two pairs of medium-weight wool socks, but the usual preference is for a thin inner sock (next to your foot) of wool, cotton, or synthetic material, and a thick outer sock of wool. Many people cannot tolerate wool next to the skin. Those people, in particular, will want to use an inner sock of cotton, cotton and nylon, or perhaps an all-synthetic material. Heavy "wool" socks are frequently about 70 to 80 percent wool, with nylon added for greater durability. Toes and heels, in particular, may contain a high percentage of nylon because of the greater wear at those points.

It is important to keep feet dry when on the trail. This will help prevent blisters, tender feet, and other problems. The moisture in wool socks will more readily evaporate than that in cotton socks. Wool socks will also provide warmth even when wet. Wool socks have the added advantage that when they get wet, they do not *feel* wet in the way that cotton socks do.

Try different combinations of socks for your local hiking and for short backpack trips, to see which provides the most comfort. It is recommended that one or more duplicate sets of socks, in whatever combination you prefer, be carried on all backpack trips, and even on extended local hikes. As socks become worn, I mark them with a felt-tip marker and use them for local hikes. I reserve new socks for backpack trips. If you have hiking socks in more than one size, it is also a good idea to mark the size on each sock. The store marking soon becomes faint.

At the end of each day it is a good practice to rinse out the socks you have worn that day. Some hikers carry Woolite for washing socks and other woolen items. Woolite works well in cold water.

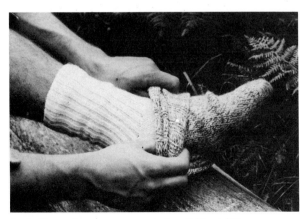

Socks. Two pairs are recommended – a lightweight inner sock of cotton or wool, and a thick, outer sock of wool. *(Lou Clemmons)*

Soap (not detergent) can also be used, or the socks can simply be rinsed. Perspiration contains salt, which is an irritant to the skin. It will accumulate in sweat-soaked socks. Rinsing socks washes out the salt. Damp socks may dry overnight in good weather, or they can be hung on the outside of your pack to dry as you hike. For hanging socks on your pack, safety pins provide a more positive fastening than clothespins do. If your route goes through brush, you may need to put the damp socks inside your pack. When this is necessary, a plastic bag will keep them from dampening other articles. Drying wet socks and other articles near a fire is *not* recommended. It is a hazardous procedure. In camp they can be spread out on a rock, to dry in the sun. They should be weighted down with other rocks, or they may blow away when they become dry (and light).

If your feet perspire a lot, the use of a good foot powder will generally be helpful. Some people, in addition to using foot powder on the feet, sprinkle some powder on their outer sock, next to the shoe. A few hikers with particularly tender feet massage their feet with rubbing alcohol once or twice daily, just before and during their backpack trips.

Before putting on your socks, run your hand carefully over the outside to detect and remove any tiny stones, twigs, burrs, balls of thread, and so forth. Then turn the sock inside out and repeat the process. Also check the inside of your boots for such tiny particles, which can easily cause a blister or tender spot on your foot.

GAITERS

Many backpackers do not use gaiters. However, under some conditions they are very useful. In deep snow they are practically a necessity.

In traveling through wet grass or snow, the exposed part of your sock will usually get wet very quickly. This will be followed by moisture wicking down to the lower foot, and you will soon be walking in wet (and perhaps cold) boots. On a trail covered with deep dust the dust can usually be counted on to find its way into your boots. Small stones and various other debris will do likewise.

A short gaiter fits over the ankle and lower leg. These are usually 7 to 9 inches high. They are frequently made of uncoated nylon, occasionally of waterproof material. The waterproof material will prevent circulation of air around the foot. It is frequently used, however, particularly in long gaiters (about 18 inches high) that are primarily used for wading deep snow. Gaiters are usually held in place at the top and bottom by elastic cord, with one or more cords under the instep. One must be careful that the elastic is not too tight; this will hamper circulation and cause cold and frostbitten feet (in cold-weather conditions). Zippers or snaps (sometimes both) are usually used for closing the gaiter at the back. Some gaiters, particularly long gaiters, open at the front and use cord and eyelets for lacing.

For those backpackers who opt to wear gaiters for normal backpacking, a short gaiter, water repellent and weighing about 4 ounces, is recommended. In the absence of gaiters an elastic band (not too tight) near the top of your hiking sock will retard (but not prevent) dust and small stones from entering your boot.

SWIMSUIT

On some backpack trips a swimsuit may be desired. For those people backpacking in the high mountains, swimming can usually be ruled out. If swimming is not actually forbidden, the cold temperature of the water in many high mountain lakes makes it a dangerous practice. However, there may be some backpack routes at relatively low elevations where swimming would be allowed and would be enjoyable. On a very few routes it may be advisable to carry a swimsuit for use in the crossing of deep rivers. The latter would probably also call for the use of an air mattress to float the pack across the river.

DUPLICATE CLOTHING

The term *duplicate clothing* is used to refer to clothing that is carried primarily so that you will be able to have change from a soiled or dirty garment to a similar or duplicate clean one. It does not refer to clothing taken as extra protection against the elements.

On trips lasting up to a week or two, the only duplicate clothing recommended is extra sets of socks (duplicates of whatever combination of socks you hike in). Some hikers may want more duplicate clothing, but the added weight and the nuisance of carrying around dirty laundry in your pack are seldom justified. As stated previously, socks can be washed or rinsed in the evening. They can be dried on a rope line, on a sun-bathed rock, in your sleeping bag, or on your pack as you hike. You can also wash out underclothes or any other item of clothing. Hopefully, you will choose a layover day, or a day when you make camp

early, for such washing. There should be a good sun for drying; a damp, rainy day makes a poor washday in the backwoods.

Your shirt and trousers are going to get soiled with dirt, soot from the campfire, and many other things. However, it is not "dirty" dirt, and it is surprising how you hardly notice it after a few days. It is recommended that you have a complete change of clothes, including comfortable shoes, along with soap, towel, and washbasin, to leave in your vehicle at the roadhead. If you wash up and change clothes before starting the trip home, you will be much more comfortable. You may also avoid a "cool reception" when you stop somewhere at a restaurant.

Incidentally, if you should try to dry articles of clothing near an open fire, don't get them too close to the fire and watch them almost continuously. Many hikers have "lost their (damp) shirts" by attempting to dry them near the fire while going about other camp jobs. A slight, momentary shift in wind, and you may be without that article of clothing for the rest of the trip.

A large group may find it desirable to carry (as common equipment) a washbasin or bucket of the folding plastic type while on the trail. This will facilitate personal bathing and washing of clothes, as desired. If much washing of clothes is anticipated, you may want to carry a special soap for the purpose. Local stores carry a number of cold-water soaps that will do a fairly good job of getting your clothes clean. If a wood fire is available, it will be worthwhile to heat water for washing of clothes.

TRYING OUT CLOTHING

The clothing that you wear on a backpack trip is not normally the clothing that you would wear for everyday use. For example, on a backpack trip your preference for clothing may be fishnet underwear, a lightweight wool shirt worn over a thin cotton shirt, and wool trousers. If the weather turns windy, you may take a nylon shell jacket from your pack and put it on. In the mornings and evenings when it is quite cool you may add an insulated vest or jacket under the wind-shell jacket. There are a great many types of clothing and variations in combinations of clothing that can be used under different weather conditions. To have confidence that your clothing is going to do the job you want it to do, you should try out your clothing and combinations of clothing on short weekend trips near home, or even on day hikes. Carry a thermometer with you, and you will gain additional confidence as to just how effective your chosen clothing combinations are for various temperature and weather conditions. This will give you assurance when planning a week-long backpack trip that the clothing you select is going to do the job. Get out your pack and rain gear occasionally and go hiking in the rain near your home. You may want to take along your chosen shelter (tarp or tent) and practice putting it up in the rain. There is nothing like practice to give you confidence when you are deep in the backwoods and faced with adverse weather and other unfavorable conditions.

CLOTHING SUMMARY

By *extra clothing* is meant clothing that is normally carried in your pack for additional warmth (on cool mornings and evenings) and for protection against adverse weather. A sweater, windshell jacket, extra wool shirt, and a vest or jacket would be extra clothing. As was previously stated, *duplicate clothing* is that which duplicates an item of clothing that is normally worn and is taken so as to have a change from a dirty garment to a clean one while on the trail. The following tables set forth recommended and optional duplicate and extra clothing. You will probably want to make some changes in these lists to suit your particular situation. The length of trip will have its effect on the clothing to be taken, as will the anticipated and possible weather conditions. Weights given may need to be adjusted for your particular items.

TABLE 5. RECOMMENDED DUPLICATE CLOTHING

Item	Approximate Weight (in ounces)
Socks: duplicate of the combination of socks worn while hiking	5

TABLE 6. OPTIONAL DUPLICATE CLOTHING

Item	Approximate Weight (in ounces)
Bandana	1½
Socks: additional combinations (one heavy pair, one light)	5 (per set)
Underclothes: duplicate of underclothes worn while hiking	6 to 18

TABLE 7. RECOMMENDED EXTRA CLOTHING

Item	Approximate Weight (in ounces)
Poncho, nylon	15
Shirt, medium-weight wool	16
Vest, insulated	16
Windshell jacket, nylon	4
	51

TABLE 8. OPTIONAL EXTRA CLOTHING

Item	Approximate Weight (in ounces)
Anorak	8
Balaclava	4
Cagoule	15
Cap, knit	2
Gaiters (short)	4
Gloves	4
Mittens	8
Moccasins	15
Pajamas	11
Rain chaps	5
Rain hat	5
Rain jacket	14
Rain pants	7
Shorts, hiking	10
Sweater	18
Swimsuit	3
Tennis shoes, canvas	22

6
Boots

The boots and socks that you wear on a backpack trip are your most important items of clothing. Choose them carefully. Tender and sore feet can make you thoroughly miserable. Blisters or a bruised Achilles tendon (the tendon at the rear of the heel of your foot) can put you completely out of business. Problems with your feet and shoes that never occur in the walking required by your usual daily routine will often show up on a backpack trip. If you take the matter of footwear too lightly, you can easily ruin the trip for everyone.

TYPES

There are several categories of boots. *Trail shoes* are intended for use where the trails are good or for city walking. They are not intended for carrying heavy loads over rough trails. *Kletterschues* are lightweight shoes, mostly foreign made, that are intended primarily for technical rock climbing. They are not intended for trail use and are generally unsatisfactory for hiking. Certain brands may be suitable for light trail walking. *Mountaineering boots* are heavy-duty, heavyweight boots weighing 5 to 6 pounds or more per pair. They are intended for use on very rugged terrain, in ice, snow, and rock. A *hiking boot* for typical backpacking use generally falls between a trail shoe and a mountaineering boot as far as general characteristics are concerned and may have some of the features of

both. In general, this represents the best all-purpose boot for backpacking. Such boots are heavier and tougher than trail shoes but lighter and less stiff than a mountaineering boot. Most boots for general backpacking use fall in the weight range of 3½ to 4¾ pounds per pair for men and 3¼ to 4¼ pounds for women. There are many boots, varying in style and construction, that fall into this category. It is important to choose a boot that will be tough enough to stand up to the most rigorous terrain you expect to encounter in your backpacking. Rubber or canvas footwear is not recommended for hiking or backpacking. A good boot for normal backpacking use will range in price from about $35 to $55.

The weight of the boot should receive very careful consideration. Carrying one extra pound on the foot is equivalent to carrying four or five extra pounds on your back. Providing they have good construction and sufficient cushion and protection for the feet, your boots for backpacking should not be one ounce heavier than necessary. If you have an average stride, you lift each boot and set it down again about 1,100 times in traveling one mile. If your boots are a few ounces heavier than necessary, this represents a lot of energy going to waste. For example, if each boot is four ounces heavier than necessary, this amounts (energy-wise) to walking one quarter of the distance traveled with a one-pound weight strapped to each ankle.

THE UPPER BOOT

Top grain leather is high quality leather and is used in quality boots. A tanned cowhide in its original form is too thick to use. It is therefore split into sheets. The outside, or top, layer is called top grain. It is most used for construction of boot uppers in quality boots.

A good boot may be made either with the smooth side of the leather on the outside of the boot or with the smooth side inside the boot. The latter type is usually referred to as a rough-out boot and has a suedelike appearance. Rough-outs are not necessarily made of suede leather, which is split leather with the cut surface on the outside. On the contrary, the rough-out construction may simply mean that the leather grain is reversed (smooth side in, rough side out). High quality boots are available in both "smooth side out" and "rough-out" constructions. A true suede leather is generally satisfactory for only light boots. It is not normally satisfactory for rough usage and wet trails.

Minor imperfections in the leather are most readily apparent in boots having smooth-finish leather on the outside. Such imperfections are frequently found in good quality boots and are not necessarily a detriment. Smooth leather is also somewhat more susceptible to scratches and abrasions during trail usage than rough-out leather is. If these scratches and abrasions penetrate the relatively thin, tough outer layer, the boots become less water repellent. Some people feel that if the leather grain is reversed in boot construction, the rough-out side offers somewhat more resistance to scratches and abrasions. Incidentally, rough-out boots can be treated with waterproofing compound as easily and effectively as smooth-finish leather can.

In quality boots there will be a minimum of seams in the upper boot. That is, ideally they should be made from one whole piece of leather. This is possible, but from an economy standpoint it may be impractical. Seams are potential sources of leakage and separation of leather, but good workmanship will usually obviate this problem. A moccasin-style construction in the toe area is seldom found in quality hiking boots. This style is particularly susceptible to wear and leakage. In general, there should be as few seams as possible in the boot construction. An extra piece of leather on the outside at the heel should cover the heel seam. There should be no rough surfaces or edges inside the boot. Carefully examining the inside of the boot and feeling the inside surfaces with your

Typical boots used for backpacking. The boot at top is a fairly heavy-duty boot with padded tongue, padding at ankle, and scree collar. The boots weigh about 4½ pounds per pair for size 9½. The boot at bottom is a lightweight boot lacking some of the features of the heavier boot and weighing about 3¼ pounds per pair for size 9½. Both boots have the Vibram Montagna lug sole.

hand are important in your initial examination of a new boot.

A boot may be lined with a thin sheet of leather, or unlined. Many quality boots are lined to provide a smooth surface for the foot and ankle. Boots should not be insulated. If insulated, they cannot "breathe," and they become too hot for normal hiking use. The insulation would soon become sweat soaked, and you would be hiking with wet socks and feet.

A scree top, or "collar," will be found on many quality boots. This is an extra piece of leather sewn around the top edge. Its intended purpose is to keep small stones (scree), dirt, snow, and so on, from entering the boot. It should be well padded. Otherwise it will probably cause chafing of the leg in that area and possibly a bruised Achilles tendon, which can be very painful. Even though a boot may not have a scree collar, the back of the boot may slope forward in such a manner that it will irritate this area of the leg and be a problem. Some backpackers feel that the scree collar does not perform its intended purpose of keeping debris out of the boot. They would rather depend on gaiters for this purpose. Most do not actually object to the scree collar, however. I have two pairs of backpacking boots that have scree collars. I have never found them objectionable, even though I may need to take off a boot occasionally to remove a small stone.

Boots may be padded (most often with foam or felt) in the ankle area or in other areas of the boot. Padding in the ankle area and under the inside tongue is very common. However, if too many areas of the boot are padded, it can be a disadvantage. The boot will probably be too warm, and moisture that gets into the padding can take a long while to dry out.

A good quality boot should have a heel counter. This must cup the heel snugly in such a manner that it anchors the foot to the sole at that point. The counter is frequently made of leather or plastic and is positioned inside the boot at the heel. There must be minimum lift (not more than 1/8 inch) of the foot at the heel when the boot is being worn. Otherwise you will have blisters and other problems. Some boots have a "hinge" above the heel counter, allowing the upper part of the boot to flex forward and back. The leather forming the upper part of the boot is usually joined at the heel. The outside seam at this point is covered with a cap, generally referred to as a back stay.

A hard toe will be found on most hiking and backpacking boots. This is frequently formed of extra pieces of leather. The front of the boot tends to hit against rocks, roots, and other projections, even in walking over trails and moderately even terrain. The hard toe tends to take the sting out of these bumps and protects the boot as well as the foot.

An arch support should be neither excessive nor absent, because in either case pain and damage to the foot (and maybe to the lower back) could develop. High quality boots will provide shanks in the sole to support the arch and protect the instep. These shanks may be made of steel, plastic, or laminated wood.

Some of the quality boots will have a double tongue sewn on each side of the boot, essentially all the way to the top. This tongue keeps water (to some extent), small sticks, stones, and dirt out of the boot. The extra leather folds inward when the boots are laced. Under the outer tongue will be found a separate padded inner tongue. This padded tongue keeps the bootlaces from cutting into your sock and foot when your boot is snugly laced, and prevents chafing of the foot in that area. There are also boots with split outer tongues to facilitate getting in and out of the boot.

On a frosty cold morning you can just about dislocate an arm or your back in trying to pull a stiff boot on. A split tongue is an advantage in such a situation, but it is somewhat of a disadvantage in the overall picture because it is a potential source of leakage. Also, the problem of stiff boots in the morning can be solved in several ways, or by a combination of these. First, you can put your boots in a bag (so as to keep your sleeping bag clean) and put it in the foot of your sleeping bag at night so that the boots don't get stiff. A stuff bag, turned wrong side out, is good for this purpose. Secondly, when you first get up in the morning, you can put on just your thin inner sock. Even a stiff boot will slide over this fairly easily. Lace the boots loosely and walk around camp for a while, while you do some morning chores. Soon the boots will have warmed up, as well as your fingers (and you will have the added advantage of being more fully awake). You can then sit down, remove the boots, and put on the heavy outer socks—after checking them for burrs, tiny stones, balls of thread, and so on. Next, put on your boots and lace them snugly, but not too tight. You are now in business, and the process was much less painful than if you had tried to accomplish the entire act when you first got up.

Hiking boots vary in height from about 6 inches to 8 or 9 inches. For normal usage 6 or 7 inches is high enough. An 8-inch boot may be satisfactory, but the higher the boot, the more tendency toward sagging of the leather at the ankles and the greater possibility of a tender or bruised Achilles tendon. Also, the higher the boot, the more tendency to restrict the calf muscles of the leg.

SOLE

Outer sole. The outer sole of most quality hiking boots is of the synthetic-rubber lug type. The Vibram lug sole is one of the most commonly used. The deep lugs provide good traction on most surfaces. There are a number of different lug styles, lug thicknesses, and rubber compositions used in Vibram lug soles. The Montagna has deep lugs and is commonly used in hiking and backpacking boots. The Roccia sole has lugs that are shallower and softer in composition. They are used primarily on lightweight trail boots and climbing boots. Labels on the soles of Vibram boots indicate the rubber hardness. A yellow label indicates that the rubber is quite hard. A brown label indicates that the rubber is relatively soft; it will not have good wear characteristics.

In addition to the Vibram, there are other lug soles, such as the St. Moritz and the Galiber. The Vibram is most commonly used, however.

Midsole. The midsole is a double or triple layer of material between the inner sole and the outer sole. A double midsole is frequently used, and often consists of an upper layer of leather and a rubber midsole below. In some constructions both the upper and lower midsoles are leather. There may be a third midsole, also of leather.

In some boots the layer nearest the outer sole is made from wood or fiberglass, with the addition of a steel shank for arch support and rigidity. A hiking boot should have some flexibility in the sole. Otherwise it will be uncomfortable, and blisters will be a problem. The steel shank does not affect the longitudinal movement as much as it does the "twisting" of the sides of the boot.

The midsoles are usually glued to the outer sole. In addition, nails and screws are sometimes used.

CONSTRUCTION

One of the most important features to consider in shopping for a boot is the method used to fasten the soles to the uppers. The construction methods most generally used are cemented, injection molded, inside stitched, and welted.

Cemented construction. In cemented boots or shoes the upper leather is folded under a light, narrow insole. The outer lug sole is then glued on. No midsole is used. There is no stitching. This is not only a weak construction structurally, but it provides very little protection for the foot. The boots cannot be resoled. The construction is simple and inexpensive, but no manufacturer of quality boots uses this method of construction. It is found in some trail shoes. It is not suitable for a boot to be used in backpacking. This construction is readily recognized by the absence of any stitching and the lack of a midsole.

Injection-molded construction. In the injection-molded method of construction no stitching or cement is used. Molten neoprene is applied under pressure, which takes the place of stitching or cement. Injection boots fall into two categories. In one method the sole is molded directly to the upper. It is inexpensive and is found only on cheap shoes or boots. Resoling of such boots is not practical. In the second method a separate midsole, usually of rubber, is used. It is inserted between the molded section and the outer sole. Such boots can be resoled. There is no stitching, and waterproofing is easier than with a stitched construction. A sacrifice in both foot comfort and breathability is inherent in this method of construction. This type of injection molding is used primarily in mountaineering boots and in those used for technical rock climbing. It is *not* used in boots that would be suitable for backpacking.

Inside-stitched construction. The construction of inside-stitched boots is also referred to as Littleway construction. In this method of construction the lower part of the upper is turned under and sandwiched between the inner sole and the midsole. These layers are fastened together by a double row of lockstitching within the boot. There is no exposed welt. The stitching is thus protected from abrasion, moisture, and drying—which is an advantage. The inner sole and midsole are stitched tightly together, and this stiffens the entire sole—but this is a disadvantage, since flexing is important to comfort in a boot used for hiking and backpacking. The boot must be removed from the last prior to sewing, and the uppers do not always conform well to the shape of the foot. If workmanship is not up to par, the inside stitching may be a source of irritation to the foot. The Littleway construction is used on some trail shoes and very lightweight hiking boots. The soles can be closely trimmed. This can be an important feature in boots to be used in technical rock climbing, but does *not* apply to a backpacking boot. In fact, it is really a disadvantage.

Welted construction. The wider sole used in welted construction provides a wide, stable platform, distributing the weight over a greater area. This is important to a backpacker carrying a loaded pack over mountain trails. A commonly used type of welt construction is the Norwegian. In this construction the upper boot is turned outward. It is sewn to a lip on the bottom of the inner sole by stitching running diagonally inward. A second line of stitching runs straight down to fasten the upper or the welt directly to the midsole. Some heavy-duty boots have a storm welt, which is an extra piece of leather sewn on top of the normal welt for the purpose of sealing stitch holes against water seepage. Both midsole and outer sole are relatively easy to replace on boots having this type of construction.

The Goodyear welt is somewhat similar to the Norwegian. The upper is stitched directly to the insole. Then the welt is stitched to the midsole.

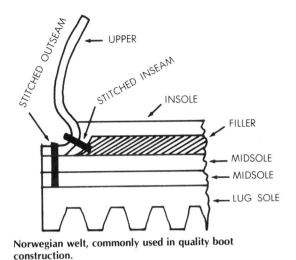

Norwegian welt, commonly used in quality boot construction.

The Goodyear welt construction is used in many boot designs; however, it is not considered as durable or as practical as the Norwegian welt. The outer sole can easily be replaced in this type of construction, but the midsole is difficult to replace.

In a welted construction the sole usually extends beyond the outside edge of the upper boot about ¼ inch or more. A welted construction generally conforms well to the shape of the foot, thus resulting in optimum foot comfort. Synthetic thread should be used in sewing of the welts, as well as for the upper boot construction. Some people feel that the thread holes in the welted construction are possible sources of water leakage. This is not generally true. The swelling of the leather will usually seal the holes. Also, the welt is usually sealed at the factory with a special compound or, in some designs, covered with a thread cap, or storm welt, as mentioned above.

LACING

A common arrangement for lacing of boots is eyelets or holes in the leather reinforced with grommets. This is the type of eyelet usually found on street shoes. The eyelets are strong and seldom pull out. There is some disadvantage in that it takes longer to lace up your boots than with some of the other lacing arrangements. Some boots have eyelets partway up the boot, and a hook system the remainder of the way. This combination of eyelets and hooks is common in many boots. Some boots use a combination of swivel eyelets (which resemble D rings) on approximately the bottom half of the boot and hooks the remaining

distance. Speed lacing uses closed tunnellike hooks. To some extent speed lacing reduces the versatility and effectiveness of the bootlaces. A more "precise" lacing, a better grip, and a greater variation in lacing patterns are possible with hooks, eyelets, swivel eyelets, or a combination of these.

Braided nylon laces are very strong and durable and are commonly used in hiking boots. They do not rot, nor do they absorb water and freeze when they become wet and cold. Porcupines and other rodents do not eat nylon laces, as they sometimes do leather laces. Leather laces will absorb water and stretch. Even when fairly new, they are subject to occasional breakage. If your bootlaces are too long, it is recommended that you cut them off and seal each end by holding it in a match flame. Tying extra long laces in big bowknots or wrapping them around the leg is not recommended. The large bows can catch on brush, rock projections, and so on, and may cause you to trip and fall.

In lacing boots for downhill travel, some hikers lace the boot snugly in the lower part, tie a square knot there, and then continue to lace the upper part, but more loosely than the lower. This is to keep the toes from jamming into the front of the boot in downhill travel. When you are traveling in other terrain, if your feet and toes feel cramped, the procedure can be reversed, with the lacing being somewhat loose in the lower part of the boot and tighter in the upper part. If the knot at the top of the boot is uncomfortable and causes chafing and discomfort at that point, try lacing the boot to the top and then back down again a couple of rows, before tying the knot. Before you start on a backpack trip, take the laces out of your boots and give them a hard yank. If they break, or appear weak, replace them.

SHOPPING FOR BOOTS

Shopping for a good boot to be used for backpacking is not an easy job. This is partly due to the vast array of boots listed in retailers' catalogs and displayed in backpack equipment stores. Only a relatively few can be considered truly suitable for backpacking. Therefore, to the shopper looking for a good backpacking boot, it is particularly important to look for certain features and construction details, rather than to depend on whether the boot is listed as a trail shoe, backpacking boot, mountaineering boot, or whatever. This situation probably contributes to the fact that many backpackers on the trails today are overbooted. They are wearing too much boot, at the expense of their pocketbook and unnecessarily expended energy on the trail, picking up and setting down the clodhoppers that some salesperson passed off as backpacking boots. Also, it seems to be the "in" thing to buy and wear the biggest and heaviest boots that you can find. This is the wrong approach. For backpacking, a medium-weight boot, if it has the basic desirable construction features, and *fits*, is a much better choice than the heavy mountaineering boots.

It is strongly recommended that, if at all possible, you *avoid buying boots through the mail*. Before you buy, you need to see the boots, try them on, walk in them (in the store), and talk to the salespeople. It is also important to have a firm understanding that you can *return* the boots if, after you wear them around the house for a few days (indoors), they do not prove up to your expectations. As with other important and expensive gear, the reputation of the manufacturer and the general quality of his products are very important factors.

When shopping for boots, you should wear the combination of socks that you plan to wear while hiking. The size of your street shoes will serve only as a rough guide, at best, as to the size hiking boot that you will need for a comfortable fit. No one has two identical feet. One foot will usually be larger than the other. Be sure there is adequate room in the boot for your larger foot. Carrying a heavy pack over mountain trails causes the feet to expand. Blood and body fluid tend to collect in the feet during the day, making the feet somewhat larger in the afternoon. It is therefore recommended that you shop for your boots in the afternoon and that you also try to be on your feet for a significant period, and do some walking, in the morning of the day you do your shopping.

When you try on new boots, they should be laced snugly. You should notice whether or not there is sufficient gap between the eyelets to allow space for further tightening as the boots are broken in and conform to your feet. In general, the length of boots should be generous enough so that you can wiggle your toes without having them touch the front end of the boot. If your boots are a bit too short, you will suffer real agony in downhill travel, and your toes may become so sore that you are essentially out of business. You should not be able to press your toes against the front of the boot when the boots are laced tightly and you are standing on a slope. (Carry a short board and improvise a slope in the salesroom.)

When the boot is unlaced and the toe is pushed against the front of the boot, you should be able to slide a forefinger down into the gap remaining at the heel.

The heel counter should cup the heel so that it anchors the foot to the sole and allows only minimum lift. Stand up and, with the boots snugly laced, have the salesperson hold one of your feet to the floor. Then try to lift your heel within the boot. There should be no significant lifting of the heel (not more than 1/8 inch). The ball of the foot should be held firmly to the sole. There should be no perceptible sideways movement.

Leather will stretch. Your boots will never be any longer, but they will become wider with use. To allow for this future stretch in girth, you may prefer to wear a single pair of heavy socks during your boot shopping, rather than the combination of two pairs that you intend to wear on the trail. At any rate, visual inspection, feel, and judgment must be used in selecting the proper width boot.

The foot of the average American is bigger, longer, and narrower than that of most Europeans. Thus, it is recommended that you purchase boots made on American lasts. It should be emphasized, however, that not all American lasts are the same. Each boot manufacturer has certain ideas of his own as to what constitutes the "average" American foot. The answer is to simply try on boots made by a few different manufacturers, to see which gives the most comfortable fit on *your* feet. A friend may have a pair of boots that he is quite enthusiastic about, but it does not necessarily follow that the same brand and design of boot will be satisfactory to you. If possible, women should purchase boots that have been made on lasts for women's boots, rather than buy men's boots.

Some boots are built on lasts that provide a "rocker" effect. That is, the soles curve slightly upward at the toe and heel. As you hike, this rocker allows the boot to rock, and this, for many persons, permits a better stride. If you can, try some boots that have a built-in rocker and some that do not. On most backpacking boots that are used for a time, you will note that the toe of the boot takes on a slight upward curve, illustrating this effect.

When you finally decide on a style and fit of boot that suits you, there is another important step to be accomplished before you leave the store. Arrange an understanding with the salesperson that you can try out your new boots inside your home for several days and return them if you are not satisfied. Then wear your boots as much as possible in your home for a few days to see if they fit as well as they should. Also find out from the store where you buy your boots how the boot leather was tanned. This will be very important in taking proper care of them (see below).

You may not have access to a shop that has quality hiking boots, and you may find it necessary to order your boots through the mail. If you do so, *always send along an outline of your foot* (the larger foot if one is larger than the other). Better yet, send outlines of both feet. These should be made with your hiking socks on and by tracing onto a piece of paper with a pencil held vertically (preferably by a helper). Make the outline in the evening, while you are in a standing position with your full weight on the foot. It is a good idea to state your street shoe size and width, but stress in your order that the foot outline, and not your street shoe size, is to govern the size of hiking boot. Again, have an understanding with the firm from which you order that the boots can be returned for replacement or refund if they are not satisfactory. When you receive them, wear them around the house for a few days to be sure you have a boot that you will be satisfied with. Once they are worn outdoors, they are yours.

CARE OF BOOTS

Most leather boots are water repellent and will stay that way with reasonable care and periodic treatment. You should be able to wade wet grass and puddles in the trail, but wading streams is something else. If you are going to be wading streams, it is recommended that you carry a pair of canvas tennis shoes for this purpose. Some hikers wade across streams by removing their socks

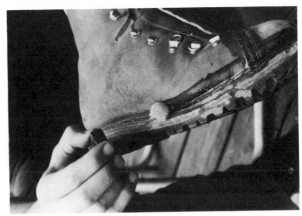

Leath-R-Seal is applied to the welt area of the boot and to the seams of the boot upper. *(Lou Clemmons)*

and crossing while wearing their hiking boots. When the crossing is accomplished, they then dump the water from their boots, put their dry socks and the wet boots back on, and continue on their way. If there is dirt or dust on the trail, some of it will cling to the wet boots. The boots can thus become caked with mud, which is neither pleasant for the hiker nor particularly good for the boots. They're your boots; suit yourself. Also, wet feet will soften the skin, and this frequently results in blisters. I prefer dry feet at all times. Wading streams is more fully discussed in Chapter 11.

Heat can do a lot of damage to leather boots, and many good boots are permanently damaged by artificial heat. Forced drying of wet boots beside an open fire is an excellent way to ruin them. Using dry socks and a change of socks, you can walk the dampness out of your boots with much better results than those from forced drying. If you like to sit in front of a campfire and toast your outstretched feet, fine. However, do this only after you have removed your boots.

At home, after a trip, dirt can be cleaned from boots by washing with a scrub brush and cool water. If mud is left to dry on boots, it will dry out the leather. It will also dry out the cement holding the boot together, and the boot may come apart. It is a good idea to stuff the boots with crumpled paper towels or newspaper, which will absorb the excess moisture. Boots should be stored at room temperature or below—and *never* near a source of artificial heat.

From time to time, boots will require treatment in order to retain their water repellency and preserve the leather. This is the point at which you will need the information on how the leather in the boot was tanned. In general, for an oil-

Trail areas like this are not uncommon at certain seasons of the year. Well-made boots and good boot care are required. *(Lou Clemmons)*

Sno-Seal is rubbed into all parts of the boot upper by hand. The process should not be hastened by heating the boot. About 24 hours should elapse between coats. *(Lou Clemmons)*

Sno-Seal and Leath-R-Seal are good products for treating boots. They maintain water repellency and preserve the leather. *(Lou Clemmons)*

tanned boot, treat lightly with oil or a grease, keeping the oil away from the sole. For chrome-tanned leather, treat lightly with wax or silicone, again keeping it away from the sole. Sno-Seal is a commonly available wax-and-silicone mixture. Use any shoe preservative in moderation and not too often. Using too much waterproofing compound, or making too frequent applications, will soften the leather too much. It is important that the leather be able to breathe; otherwise your feet will sweat, and you will be walking with water-logged boots. Leath-R-Seal is a good liquid compound for keeping soles and seams waterproof.

BREAKING BOOTS IN

A backpacker should never start a trip with new boots. They should always be well broken in; otherwise, serious foot problems will result. The boots should not be so old that there is any doubt about their lasting for the trip, however. It is a poor risk to wear any pair of boots on a backpack trip with the thought of getting just a few more miles out of them before they are thrown away.

There is more than one way of breaking a new pair of hiking boots in. However, the best way is to simply start wearing them around home for brief periods. To start with, you probably won't want to wear them for more than five or ten minutes. Increase this period by five or ten minutes each day until you can wear them comfortably for an hour or more. Then start taking short hikes. After a few short hikes, do some hiking on trails, carrying a light pack load. Gradually increase the distance and load. It will take four to six weeks to break in a pair of new boots by this method, but it is time well spent.

If you find it essential to break your new boots in quickly, one approach is to use the "water treatment." Fill each boot with lukewarm water. After a few *seconds* have elapsed, dump the water out. Then put the boots on, with hiking socks, and go walking until the boots dry on your feet. I have never tried this method, so I cannot recommend it from experience, but it reportedly works. I prefer to break my boots in the "old-fashioned" way—by simply wearing them for longer periods on consecutive local walks and hikes. *Soaking* boots in water is *not* recommended. Since most serious backpackers are more or less systematic personalities, I have never quite understood the need for quickly breaking a new pair of boots in. I prefer the approach recommended under Spare Boots, below. At any rate, sufficient advance planning should avoid the necessity of having to rapidly break new boots in.

SPARE BOOTS

For those who backpack regularly, it is recommended that they always have at least two pair of boots for backpacking. One pair should be essentially new, insofar as miles of wear on the boots is concerned, but should be well broken in, so that you can take a full-scale backpack trip in them with no fear of foot discomfort or boot problems. Let's refer to this "new" pair as your "A" boots. There should also be a second pair of boots. These will be a much older pair that has seen many miles of trail travel. They will still be suitable for the trail, but you would not want to take a full-scale backpack trip in them because you know they are nearing the end of their useful life. If you took them on a full-scale trip, there would be an element of doubt in your mind as to whether they would come apart while you were on the trail—a disaster, even from the most optimistic viewpoint. Let's refer to this second pair as your "B" boots.

Almost everyone who regularly takes backpack trips does some local hiking and takes weekend trips so as to keep himself and his equipment in shape for longer trips. The "B" boots are the ones that he should wear for these local trips. If the boots start to come apart on the trail, he will probably be only a few miles from the roadhead, and it is not a serious emergency situation. If he were many miles into the backwoods, the same situation would take on a very different aspect.

The "A" boots will be reserved for full-scale backpack trips. They will be well broken in and ready to hit the trail, but will then be shelved until time for the next backpack trip. As was stated earlier, your boots are your most important item of clothing. If you use the approach outlined above, you will have the peace of mind while on the trail that you are well shod, and will have no fears that your footwear is going to give any trouble.

SOCKS

In general, it is recommended that you also use the above approach in regard to hiking socks. After you have worn new socks or a combination of socks on a few local hikes, put them away to be used for the full-scale trip, rather than for local hiking and backpacking. I usually identify such socks with a big A made on the foot of the sock with a felt-tip marker. Socks that have become somewhat thin and worn, or that may be patched, are used only for local hikes.

I usually mark the size on my socks also. For jogging and some other activities, I use socks similar to those used for backpacking, only in a different size. After some use and repeated washings the store marking of the size becomes faint and cannot be read. This causes difficulty when a batch of socks is washed and you have to sort them afterward according to size and use. For example, without a legible marking, the difference between a size 12 and size 13 sock is not readily apparent.

7
Foods and Recipes

WATCH THE PACK WEIGHT

There are a number of books available on camp cooking. It may be interesting to learn to cook a variety of foods using different types of fires and equipment. In this book it is assumed that the backpack trip you are about to take will be for the purpose of exploring, climbing, observing wildlife, fishing, photography, or some similar objective and that you won't want to spend any more time than necessary to prepare and cook your meals and still have good nourishing food to eat. Food and cooking equipment, more than anything else you will pack, will have a tendency to get out of hand by leaps and bounds as far as weight and bulk are concerned. Yet it is certainly important that you eat well. Therefore, some skillful planning and preparation are needed in this area.

The above remarks are not intended to discourage those who like to do "gourmet" cooking on the trail. If that is your cup of tea, take along your reflector oven, or whatever else you need, and go to it. Your pack will be heavier, however, so such cooking should generally be pursued only on relatively short trips.

DRIED AND DEHYDRATED FOODS

On a backpack trip the use of dried and dehydrated foods is important. Water is heavy; a pint weighs about a pound. It should be added to the foods after you get to the campsite, rather than carried in with the food. Macaroni, spaghetti, rice, flour, oatmeal, and so on, are dry foods by the nature of the product. *Dried* prunes, peaches, apricots, raisins, and so forth, are foods that have been dried to remove much, but not all, of the water that is present in their natural form. *Dehydrated* and *freeze-dried* fruits, meats, and vegetables have been specially processed to remove substantially all of the water. The longer the trip, the more important it is that meals be planned around dehydrated or freeze-dried foods. A No. 2 can of peaches, for example, will weigh about 16 ounces and will serve four persons. If freeze-dried peaches were used, about 1½ or 2 ounces would serve four persons. In general, the freeze-dried foods are lighter and are more expensive than ordinary dehydrated foods. Some are more tasty, also, but this certainly doesn't apply to all freeze-dried foods.

TRY FOODS AT HOME

As with every product, there are good dehydrated foods and poor dehydrated foods. If you were to start experimenting with various dehydrated foods and brands of dehydrated foods, it would probably take a long while and you would run up quite a bill before you settled on a full line of foods that you liked. This book therefore suggests particular foods and brands for your guidance. I have tested these at home and on the trail

70

and have found them to be acceptable to most backpackers. There are quite a number of producers and suppliers of dehydrated foods, and if you wish to experiment a bit, order some of their foods and go ahead. Appendix B lists some sources of special foods for backpacking. Many of the firms in Appendix A, as well as some local sporting goods stores, carry the products of those suppliers. One word of caution. You should not take any food on a backpack trip that you have not cooked at home, in your own kitchen, to prove to yourself that you like it. Then you can hit the trail with confidence that you are going to enjoy good food. The experience of cooking the food at home will also provide better assurance that you will cook it properly when you are on the trail and cooking under somewhat less than ideal conditions. Further, cooking such foods at home and keeping some simple records will provide good firsthand information on cooking time and possible recipe complexities, as well as on the amount of uncooked food required for realistic, nominal servings.

There is almost no limit to the kind and variety of food you can take on a backpack trip. However, some foods are much more *practical* than others and at the same time will provide good, wholesome fare. These are the foods to which I have devoted maximum space in this section.

KEEP REQUIREMENTS SIMPLE

Cooking can be done with a Dutch oven, over a grill, with a reflector oven, and so on. These all have a place in general outdoor cooking. However, in backpacking, it is desirable to keep cooking gear and other equipment to a minimum. The food recipes listed in this chapter are therefore chosen for light weight and for simplicity of preparation. They have also been proven on the trail to appeal to most hikers' appetites. Every food recipe listed here can be suitably cooked in one of two basic utensils—either a pan or a skillet. It is possible and practical to plan an entire backpack trip around foods that require only pans (no skillet) for cooking. In general, the cooking periods listed are for altitudes of 6,000 to 8,000 feet. For a higher or lower altitude the cooking time will need to be adjusted accordingly.

MEAT

Bacon. All bacon should be cooked by starting it in a cold skillet and cooking it over a medium fire. Do not grease the skillet. The fat on the bacon provides more than enough grease for cooking.

STORE BACON. A pound of store bacon will serve from three to five persons, depending upon how much other food you have with it. The bacon you buy in the store will have considerable fat on it. Unless this fat is saved and used for other cooking, it must be looked upon as excess weight in backpacking. Take along a small can with a tight-fitting lid to store the grease in. As the bacon cooks, pour off the excess grease into the can. About ten to twelve minutes of cooking is usually sufficient, depending upon how crisp you like it.

Ordinary bacon, in addition to being heavy, is difficult to pack. It should be carefully wrapped and carried in a double thickness of heavy poly bags. Otherwise, the grease in the bacon will probably soil adjacent items in your pack.

CANNED BACON. A convenient bacon for backpacking is Swift's canned bacon. It requires no refrigeration. It is precooked and only requires heating over a low fire for five to eight minutes. The can weighs 7 ounces (gross), and it contains the equivalent of 16 ounces of regular store bacon. The bacon is packed in a roll inside the can, with the layers separated by a heavy paper. The entire contents can be put into the skillet, including the paper. When the bacon starts to warm, the paper can be easily separated. There is not much excess grease on this bacon, but you should save what there is. Although this bacon is very tasty, it will be too heavy and bulky for all but short backpack trips.

BACON BAR. Many suppliers in Appendix A stock a bacon bar that is a concentrated prefried bacon. A 3-ounce bar is equivalent to about 12 to 14 ounces of uncooked bacon. It can be eaten hot or cold. This is the favorite form of bacon to many backpackers, and these bacon bars are widely used.

OTHER BACON. There are other canned bacons available, including Canadian bacon. Some suppliers listed in Appendix A carry a type of canned Canadian bacon. Several varieties of canned bacon are also available in some of the local stores. Most of these are too heavy and bulky for any except very short backpack trips, however.

Sausage. Most local stores carry small cans of sausage links with a gross weight of about 10 ounces. The Libby's brand is good. One can is usually sufficient for three persons for one meal (medium servings), with other food. Canned sau-

TABLE 9. INFORMATION ON SOME FOODS FOR BACKPACKING

These foods and brands are those with which the writer is familiar from personal experience and that he can recommend. This list represents a lot of trial-and-error testing of many dehydrated foods over a period of years. No aspect of backpacking is more important than having good, tasty foods. Yet to find a full range of appetizing foods—meats, main dishes, salads, beverages, and so on—requires more time and expense than many backpackers can afford. With a few exceptions this list is concerned with foods for which no equivalent is available in local stores.

Item No.	Item	Brand	Approximate Weight (in ounces)	No. of Servings
1	Bacon, canned	Swift	7	3 to 4
2	Bacon bar	Wilson	3	2 to 3
3	Beef, dried	Peacock	2	2 to 3
4	Beef jerky		2	2 to 3
5	Beef stick	Hickory Farms	16	6
6	Ground beef patties, freeze-dried	Mountain House	3¼	2 to 3
7	Hamburger, freeze-dried	Rich-Moor	2	2
8	Sausage patties, freeze-dried	Mountain House	2¼	2 to 3
9	Egg, dehydrated	Durkee	1¼	1 to 2
10	Egg, dehydrated	E-Z (Marshall)	6	4 to 5
11	Beef Almondine	Tea Kettle	3½	2
12	Chicken Stew	Rich-Moor	3¾	2
13	Shrimp Creole, freeze-dried	Mountain House	4	2
14	Tuna a la Neptune	Tea Kettle	3½	2
15	Turkey Tetrazzini	Tea Kettle	3	1 to 2
16	Beans, Boston style	Seidel	12	3 to 4
17	Carrots, freeze-dried	Mountain House	1	3 to 4
18	Green beans, freeze-dried	Mountain House	½	3 to 4
19	Peas, freeze-dried	Mountain House	2	3 to 4
20	Sweet-potato flakes	Pantri-Pak*	10	6 to 7
21	Vegetable salad, dehydrated	Pantri-Pak	1½	3 to 4
22	Applesauce	Pantri-Pak	5¾	3 to 4
23	Applesauce	Rich-Moor	4½	3 to 4
24	Apple slices, freeze-dried	Mountain House	1	2
25	Banana chips, dehydrated	Rich-Moor	4	3 to 4
26	Fruit mix, dehydrated	Seidel	3½	3 to 4
27	Peaches, freeze-dried	Mountain House	1	2
28	Pineapple Waikiki	Rich-Moor	4	3 to 4
29	Pancake syrup, maple	Rich-Moor	6¼	3 to 4
30	Chocolate, tropical	Hershey's	1	1
31	Gorp (trail snack)	Rich-Moor	6	3 to 4
32	Trail candy	Traubenzucker	2	(8 pieces)
33	Fruit bar	Pem (H & M)	1	1
34	Granola bar	General Mills	1	1
35	Wafer, rye	RyKrisp	8½	6 to 7
36	Wafer, whole wheat	Wheat Thins (Nabisco)	9¾	7 to 9

37	Wafer, whole wheat	Triscuits (Nabisco)	$9^3/_4$	7 to 9
38	Cottage cheese, freeze-dried	Mountain House	2	3 to 4
39	Ice cream, freeze-dried	Rich-Moor	$2^1/_4$	3
40	Lemon powder	Pantri-Pak	4	6
41	Lemon crystals	Lemon Queen	$2^1/_2$	3 to 4
42	Lime crystals	Lime Queen	$2^1/_2$	3 to 4
43	Fruit flavor drink	Wyler's	3	3
44	Iced tea drink	Wyler's	$1^1/_2$	3
45	Pan-coating oil	Vegalene	1	—

*The Pantri-Pak brand is made by Perma-Pak. See Appendix B for address.

TABLE 10. MEASURING UNITS FOR FOODS USED IN BACKPACKING

Food	Volume	Approximate Weight (in ounces)
Beef stick	$2^5/_8''$ x $5''$ cylinder	16
Cocoa, instant	3 heaping tsp.	1
Coffee, instant	6 rounded tsp.	$1/_2$
Cornmeal	1 cup	4
Cream substitute	3 rounded tbs.	1
	1 cup	$4^1/_2$
Flour	1 cup	4
Lemon powder	3 level tbs.	1
Macaroni, small elbow	1 cup	4
Margarine	1 cup	8
Milk, dehydrated	1 cup	$2^1/_2$
Noodles, fine, short	1 cup	3
Oatmeal	1 cup	3
Pepper	4 level tsp.	$1/_2$
Popcorn	1 cup	6
Raisins, store variety	1 cup	5
Rice, Minute	1 cup	4
Salt	1 level tbs.	1
	small cardboard shaker, $3^3/_4''$ high	4
Sugar, white	2 tbs.	$1^1/_4$
	1 cup	8
Sugar, brown	$1^1/_4$ cups	8
Shortening, liquid	2 level tbs.	1
	1 cup	8
Tea, instant	6 rounded tbs.	$1/_2$
Wheatena	1 cup	5

3 level teaspoons (tsp.) = 1 level tablespoon (tbs.)
2 level tablespoons of water = 1 ounce
16 tablespoons of liquid = 1 cup

sages that are packed in natural juices have a better flavor than those packed in water. Dried sausage sticks, which do not require refrigeration, are available from some suppliers of trail foods and occasionally from local corner grocery stores. About 1 or 2 ounces per person per meal is a sufficient ration.

The Mountain House brand of freeze-dried sausage patties can be particularly recommended. In fact, this is one of the best dehydrated meats I have found. There are four patties in a package, having a total net weight of 2¾ ounces. They are reconstituted by simply soaking them in warm water for three to five minutes. I like these sausage patties well enough that I frequently use them as a meat base for a main dish such as sausage and noodles. Instead of having chicken and noodles, I substitute sausage because I have not found a brand of dehydrated chicken that I like as well as these sausage patties.

Salami.   This is available in most local stores. It will keep for several days if the weather is not too hot. Summer sausage is sometimes available from local stores and will keep better than salami.

Fish.   On many backpack trips trout will be caught. They should be eaten soon after being caught, preferably within several hours. There are special drying processes and other means of keeping fish without refrigeration, but they are not recommended for the usual backpack trip. Soon after being caught, fish should be rough-cleaned by removing the contents of the body cavity and bleeding the fish. Never soak cleaned fish in water; keep them dry until time to cook. Salt and pepper the fish lightly, inside and out, before cooking. Trout are very good without being floured before frying. However, if you must flour them, a mixture of half flour and half cornmeal is good. Put the flour and fish together in a large plastic bag, using just enough of the flouring mixture for one meal. Shake the bag vigorously, and the flouring job is done. The simplest method of cooking trout is to fry them. Bacon grease, cooking oil, peanut oil, or margarine (least satisfactory) can be used for frying. Have the grease medium hot before putting the fish in. Cook over a medium-hot fire. While they are frying, fish may be basted with a mixture of melted butter and lemon juice, but this is not essential. About fifteen minutes of frying is sufficient for medium-sized fish.

Some backpack groups will not be using a frying pan for other purposes and will not want to carry one just to fry fish that they may catch. If open fires are permitted, there are at least two other very satisfactory methods of cooking fish, which do not require the use of a frying pan. One method is to use aluminum foil. The fish are individually wrapped in the foil. They are salted, and margarine is added to the foil package. The foil-wrapped fish are placed in the coals of a fire for about fifteen minutes, depending upon the size of fish. Still another method is to bake the fish on a rock. Select some smooth, flat rocks that are not porous. It is more important that they be fairly smooth than perfectly flat. Wash the top of the rock free of dirt, using your hand and a bit of water. Then set the rocks in an open fire and heat them thoroughly. The side of the rock that you intend to cook on should be facing upward. When they are well heated, pull the rocks to the edge of the fire so that you can get close enough to them to do your cooking. Add salt to the fish, and grease the fish with bacon grease or margarine. Lay the fish on the rock and bake it until the flesh is flaky and the bones can be readily removed. The skin may stick to the rock, but that is no problem. Pull the rock away from the fire and, using it as a plate, eat directly from the rock. When the meal is completed, scraping the rock with a small stone will remove most of the fish still on the rock.

Some cooks prefer to prepare trout of 10 to 12 inches long by cutting into the body cavity from alongside the backbone, rather than splitting the belly side. When this is done, the belly acts as a hinge, and the thick back section is reduced to a better size for more uniform frying. Removing the bones before eating is a bit more difficult with this method, but the faster and more uniform frying improves the taste so much that it is well worth the effort. Trout that are 13 or 14 inches long or more, as well as many other fish of this size, should be prepared for the frying pan by filleting.

I fillet a trout by first making a fairly deep cut completely around the fish, just behind the head and gills. I then make a similar cut just ahead of the tail, completely encircling the body. Next, I push the point of the fillet knife through the skin along one side of the backbone, from head to tail, and work the knife downward along the "rib cage," close to the bones, all the way to the belly. I then repeat the process, starting the knife through the skin on the other side of the backbone. When this piece is cut along the rib cage to the belly, the fillet will come loose, leaving the remainder of the fish in one piece, to be disposed of.

It is frequently difficult to maintain a firm grip

on fish while you are cleaning them. Trout, especially, are hard to hold on to. One method that helps hold them is to put salt on your fingers before handling the fish. However, if you have any small nicks in your fingers or hands, then getting salt in these cuts will probably send you into orbit. A better method to hold your fish is to carry a 6-inch square of waterproof, automotive-finish sandpaper for this purpose. Hold the sandpaper in the palm of your hand, rough side up. Now lay the trout on the sandpaper, close your grip, and you have it. Wearing an old cotton glove on the hand that you hold the fish in will also help hold the fish while cleaning it.

If you are going to be cleaning a lot of fish at once, say for a large group, an old toothbrush is handy for cleaning away the kidney and other bloody material that lies along the inside of the backbone. Break this up with your knife or thumb to start; then it can be quickly removed with the toothbrush.

When fish are cleaned, it is frequently a problem to find something to put them in until you are ready to fry them. A spare pan is not always available, and if you use a pan, it must be washed before it can be used for another purpose. A good solution to the problem is to make a small bag about 8 inches by 14 inches in size out of ordinary muslin or percale. Mark the bag plainly on the outside with the word FISH, using a felt-tip marker before leaving home. After they are cleaned, the fish can be kept in this bag until you are ready to fry them. Rinse the bag out after each use and dry it on a rope line. The wet sandpaper and the toothbrush for fish cleaning can be carried in this bag between meals. Fold the whole business into a small compact package and carry it in a plastic bag, so that you will not have a fish smell on other items in your pack.

Chicken. Most local groceries carry small cans of boned chicken in a number of brands, such as Swanson and Richardson. These are convenient to use as a meat base in a number of dishes, such as those explained later in this chapter. Most of these small cans have a gross weight of about 7 ounces and a net weight of about 5 ounces. Some suppliers in Appendix A carry dehydrated chicken that can be used and will have considerably less weight for the same food value.

Beef. There are several forms of beef that are commonly used by backpackers. Quite often these are added to soups, stews, or a main dish prepared for supper.

CANNED HAMBURGER. Small cans of hamburger, usually containing five or six small patties, are available in some local stores. The Libby's brand is good. Gross weight is about 14 ounces and net weight 12 ounces. These can be heated and eaten separately or used as a base for a main dish like spaghetti and hamburger.

DEHYDRATED GROUND BEEF. A dehydrated ground beef will save weight; some of the brands are very good. Follow the directions for cooking, which are usually very simple. One method is to put the meat in a skillet, barely cover it with water, and simmer it about fifteen minutes, until the water is gone. Then add a small amount of butter to the skillet and fry very slowly for about five to eight minutes. Do not try to fry the beef to the point of crispness. It can also be added directly to soups or stews before cooking.

FREEZE-DRIED GROUND BEEF. The Mountain House brand of freeze-dried ground beef can be recommended. There are four patties in a package, ample for three persons — or for four persons if used to flavor a pot of spaghetti or macaroni. Net weight of the package is about 3½ ounces. The patties are prepared by soaking them in warm water for five to ten minutes and then frying them lightly for several minutes. If used as a meat base for a main dish and cooked with the other ingredients, the frying can be eliminated.

The Rich-Moor freeze-dried hamburgers are also quite good. Two 2-ounce packages provide four patties, about enough for three persons. Used as a meat base for a main dish, they will suffice for four.

BEEF STICK. A good beef product for trail use is the Beef Stick manufactured and sold by Hickory Farms, of Toledo, Ohio. It is tasty when eaten cold. It can also be heated in a skillet or cut into bite-sized pieces and added to soups or stews. This beef product will keep well without any refrigeration, even in warm weather.

Beef jerky. This is a dehydrated form of beef that will keep almost indefinitely without refrigeration. It is usually eaten cold and is good food for lunch or as a trail snack. Most of the suppliers listed in Appendix A carry beef jerky, but it is relatively easy to make yourself, and it is recommended that you try this.

Top round steak with very little or no fat is recommended for making beef jerky. With a sharp knife cut ½- to ¾-inch-thick round steak into slices about ⅛ to ¼ inch wide and 6 to 10 inches long. Using the blunt edge of a cup or similar tool, pound the strips as thin as possible, being careful not to tear them apart. Salt and pepper these strips quite heavily. Using a wire basket strainer like those used for making french fries, lower the strips into a pan of heavily salted boiling water. Leave the strips in the water about fifteen seconds, just long enough to "blanch" the meat. Then take them out and place them on paper towels to drain.

Make a tube or cylinder out of cheesecloth, about 3 to 5 feet long and 8 inches in diameter. You will also need a piece of stout clean cord about 6 feet long. Using a large needle and strong white cotton thread, pierce the cord near one end, then pierce a piece of jerky and run it up the thread to about 1 inch from the first point. Continue in this manner, "sewing" the jerky to the cord. Now slip the cheesecloth cylinder over the jerky and snap a rubber band or clothespin over each end of the cylinder to keep out flies.

Holding on to the two ends of the cord that protrude from the cheesecloth cylinder, carry the line of jerky outside and fasten it between two tree limbs or to a clothesline (safest place) where cats and other animals cannot reach it. Select a place in the sunlight where there will be free circulation of air. If it rains, cover the jerky or take it inside. Leave it in the open for about five days, and you will have finished jerky. It will get stiff and brittle and very dark, but it is good to eat and very nourishing. It will keep practically indefinitely. Store it in plastic bags, which in turn can be kept in a closed container such as a coffee can.

You may prefer to dry your jerky indoors in an oven, which is also satisfactory. In rainy weather this method is preferable, since the jerky must be kept dry. The oven temperature should be set for about 175° – 200°, and the oven door should be left open just a crack. In placing the jerky in the oven, it is best to lay the strips directly on the oven racks. Cookie sheets or foil should be placed under the jerky to catch the drippings as the jerky dries. It should be dry in about eight to twelve hours. When it is dry, the strips of jerky should crack when bent, but should not break.

Generally, 16 ounces of fresh meat will provide about 4 ounces of jerky when the process is completed. A good way to eat jerky is to spread mustard on it and eat it cold. A tangy mustard such as horseradish mustard is particularly good. It makes a good trail snack.

Meat bars. Some companies market a dehydrated meat bar that weighs about 3 ounces and makes a satisfactory trail snack. It can also be

Beef jerky drying on clothesline.

used in cooking, to flavor a pot of stew, and so on. Quite a few backpackers prefer the flavor of the bacon bar to the meat bar, however.

Canned meats. Some other meats that might be considered suitable for very short backpack trips are available in canned form from local groceries. Some of these are Swift's Prem, Hormel chopped beef, Spam, and so on. Most of these only require to be cut into thin slices, placed in a skillet with a little shortening, and thoroughly heated. Gross weight of cans is usually about 14 ounces and net weight 12 ounces.

EGGS

Fresh eggs. It is not safe to keep fresh eggs for more than a couple of hours without refrigeration, and at high temperatures (70° F and up) even this exposure may be too long. For an overnight camp with temperatures below 50° F, they may be satisfactory. They must be carefully packed, as they make a fine mess if they are broken in your pack. Aluminum egg carriers are available from several of the suppliers in Appendix A. Another way to carry eggs is to use a small can with a tight-fitting lid, about the size of a baking powder can. Push a pint plastic bag down into the can as a liner. Now break the eggs out of their shells and into the can. Close the bag and seal the top with a small rubber band. Then put the lid on the can and seal it with tape. As soon as you get to camp, put the can in a stream or other place where it will be kept at below 50° F until ready to use.

Dehydrated eggs. There is a wide difference in the taste of dehydrated eggs. Whatever brand you choose, you should by all means try it out thoroughly at home, to be sure you are going to like it. A good-tasting brand of dehydrated eggs that I have found is Durkee, available in some local stores. Another very good product is Marshall E-Z Eggs. The latter brand is available from some backpack equipment firms; it may also be ordered directly from the Marshall Produce Company, P.O. Box 1088, Marshall, MN 56258. These two brands not only taste good but are among the least expensive of all the dehydrated eggs.

Dehydrated eggs are very easy to fix. You simply mix them with water to make a paste (instructions are on the package) and put this into a greased prewarmed skillet. Cook over a low fire for two or three minutes. Be careful not to overcook. When your eggs are a nice golden brown, they are overcooked. Throw them out and start over. Stir the eggs in the skillet almost continuously while they are cooking. One very good way to cook these eggs is to first crumble part of a bacon bar into a greased skillet and cook that for several minutes over a low flame. Then add the scrambled egg mixture and continue to cook for about two minutes longer, stirring continuously. Remove the eggs from the fire and add plenty of salt and pepper. Omelets made from dehydrated eggs frequently end up tough and rubbery (and tasteless). Most cooks prefer the scrambled version. A good addition to scrambled eggs is dehydrated onions, which can be put to soak the evening before (for breakfast), if desired.

A particular advantage of scrambled eggs is that you don't need to have a skillet. They can be cooked in a pan. In preparing the mix, add a very small quantity of water to the powder to start with and blend it into a paste before adding the remainder of the water. A generous quantity of shortening should be put in the cooking pan. After it is heated to medium hot, add the scrambled egg mix. During the several minutes that the eggs are being cooked over low to medium heat, they must be stirred constantly. At the same time scrape the bottom of the pan to keep them from sticking.

Some egg mixes contain imitation ham, bacon, or sausage, or small bits of such meats in freeze-dried form. I have found many of these to be quite disappointing. The meat is often tough and tasteless. I prefer to add my own separately prepared bacon or sausage.

Some "instant" eggs require only the addition of hot water (no cooking) in their preparation. A few of the brands are quite good tasting. However, they are also rather expensive. Some backpackers may consider them worthwhile.

Once you have settled on a good brand of dehydrated eggs and taken the time and patience to learn to cook them properly, I believe you will find, as I have, that they are a good addition to any backpack food list. Don't overlook the possibility of using them for meals other than breakfast. About 1½ to 2 ounces of dehydrated egg powder provides a very ample portion for one person.

CEREALS

Oatmeal. Many people who wouldn't think of eating oatmeal for breakfast at home find it very much to their liking on a backpack trip. A number of brands of "minute" oats are available, such as Mother's oats. For each person, you will need ½ cup of oats, ¼ teaspoon of salt, and about 1 cup of water. You can start the oats in cold, warm, or boiling water. If creamy oatmeal is desired, start it in cold water. For a thicker, less creamy oatmeal, start it in boiling water. Cook for a minimum of three to five minutes, even for one-minute oats. At high altitudes ten minutes on the fire is not too much. Eat with sugar and milk or cream.

There are some instant oatmeals available, such as Quaker, that are quite popular with some backpackers. Individual serving size packages are available, if desired. About ¾ cup of boiling water is added to the individual serving; stir, and the oatmeal is ready to eat. The instant variety is the kind to use if you are cooking over a backpack stove. Fuel will be saved in preparation and there is no cooking pan to wash afterward.

Good additions to oatmeal are raisins, banana chips, brown sugar, and nuts (such as almonds). You can put any or all of these items right in the plastic bag with the oatmeal when it is packaged. Some margarine can also be added to the oatmeal during preparation. It will improve the taste, and it is a good way to get additional calories.

Other cooked cereals. You may prefer some other type of cooked cereal, such as Wheatena. There are a number of such cereals. Most of them have a relatively short cooking time.

Cold cereal. Most of the cold cereals that are commonly eaten for breakfast at home are too bulky and too low in calories to be suitable for backpacking. However, there are some exceptions. Grape-Nuts, Heartland, and Quaker granola cereals are good for backpacking use and are available in many local stores. Birchermuesli (Familia) is very good and is available from some of the suppliers listed in Appendix A.

Storage of cereals. It is best to observe a bit of caution before using cereals and other grain products such as cornmeal, white flour, wheat flour, and so on. By the nature of such grain products, and their handling, there will be some inert larvae in these foods. Storage of the foods for a long period under favorable conditions will cause these larvae to come to life. Thus, you may end up with bugs or weevils in your cereal (not a pleasant thought).

Therefore, in packaging cereals, cornmeal, and similar products in plastic bags prior to hitting the trail, it is recommended that they *not* be poured into the plastic carrying bag directly from the container in which they were stored. Instead, they should be dumped into a large bowl. Then, using a large spoon, you can ladle the food from the bowl into the bag, watching closely while doing so for the presence of the tiny worms which will signify that you need to purchase a fresh supply.

PANCAKES

A traditional camp food is pancakes with butter and syrup. A number of prepared pancake flours are available, such as Aunt Jemima brand, and they are very satisfactory. Add water or milk to the flour (not vice versa). Stir the mixture just enough to get the lumps out. A fork is a good stirring tool. Do not beat the batter. Hold back a little flour just in case you should get the batter too thin to start with. There is nothing worse than using up all your flour in one grand start and then having the batter come out too thin.

Dip out 3 or 4 tablespoons of batter onto a hot greased skillet and cook over a medium-hot fire. Turn only once, when bubbles have appeared over the top surface of the uncooked side. It is much easier to make one large pancake in an average-sized skillet than to make two or more small ones. Cut the large pancake into two or more pieces as soon as it is removed from the skillet and divide it among several persons who are eating, so that each will have a hot piece. One large pancake will get partly cold just while it is being eaten.

A satisfactory pancake syrup can be made from brown sugar and water. Good prepared syrup mixtures are also available. In making syrup from brown sugar, use about 1 cup of sugar to ½ cup of water. Bring the mixture to a boil and stir until the sugar is dissolved. Be very careful not to use too much water, or the syrup will be too thin.

There are several disadvantages to having pancakes as a food item in backpacking. First, the pancake flour and the sugar from which to make the syrup are relatively heavy, compared to other suitable breakfast items. Also, not all backpackers will be carrying a skillet, which is necessary. A wood fire is also desirable. A pancake breakfast takes considerable time in preparation, eating, and getting the dishes washed. If you are trying to get an early start down the trail, better skip the pancake breakfast. For short backpack trips and for layover days in camp, it may be entirely satisfactory. Pancakes should not be overlooked as a possibility for supper, instead of breakfast.

About 10 ounces of pancake flour and 6 ounces of sugar or prepared syrup mix provides a sufficient ration for three persons.

FRUIT

It is recommended that at least one meal each day include fruit. It is a good supplement for almost any menu. The dried and freeze-dried varieties make good trail snacks without any preparation. Contrary to many dehydrated and freeze-dried products, fruits seem to be the one item that is usually quite tasty, regardless of brand. (There are some exceptions.) Most people find fruits to be very satisfactory for use in backpacking. From a general nutrition standpoint they are a good food. They provide bulk, and many are relatively high in calories per unit of weight. There are several types of dehydrated fruits available, as described below.

Ordinary dried fruits. Most grocery stores carry dried fruits. Prunes, apricots, and peaches are common. In drying, not all the water is removed. These dried fruits are still soft and chewy. About 2 ounces of dried fruit per person per meal is the right amount. Pitted prunes are available (pits represent extra weight). The usual cooking procedure for dried fruits is to cover them with cold water and simmer them in a pan for fifteen to twenty minutes. However, if you are cooking on a backpack stove, these fruits can be eaten cold, without cooking, in order to save fuel. Just soaking them overnight will soften them, and they will have very nearly the texture of cooked fruit. Some people add up to 2 level teaspoons of sugar for each 2 ounces of fruit; others prefer the fruit unsweetened. These dried fruits also make a good trail snack just as they come from the package.

Vacuum-dried fruits. Vacuum-dried fruits are available from many of the suppliers of trail foods. They have had most of the water removed — to the point where they are hard and brittle. They are *not* suitable as a trail snack. Like ordinary dried fruits, simply soaking overnight will make them suitable for eating without cooking. Simmering them over a fire for about five minutes, after soaking, will improve their texture and flavor, however. Adding some sugar, if this is not already provided in the package, will also improve the flavor. About 1 ounce per person per meal provides an ample serving.

Freeze-dried fruits. Most of the freeze-dried fruits are quite tasty. They are also more expensive than the vacuum-dried variety. They are very light; about 1½ to 2 ounces provides ample portions for three persons. A particular advantage, in addition to good flavor, is that they are very quickly and easily prepared. They can be eaten directly from the package, or they can be soaked in cold water for a few minutes, if desired. They are a very good trail snack. You can pop a piece of freeze-dried fruit into your mouth, suck on it until it softens, and it is quite good.

Applesauce. A good side dish for some meals is provided by applesauce. There are several instant types of applesauce available. To prepare them, you simply mix the applesauce granules with cold water and let stand for ten to fifteen minutes. No cooking is required. A number of suppliers also carry apple nuggets or diced apples. Some of these can be eaten cold as a trail snack, but a more tasty dish results if they are cooked for about five minutes. The cooked apples are somewhat superior in taste to the instant applesauces. A bit of cinnamon is a good addition to applesauce and can be put in the poly bag when the applesauce is packaged at home.

BEVERAGES

What you drink on a backpack trip, and especially *how much* you drink, is important. You will be exerting and perspiring, and your body will lose a lot of fluid that needs to be replaced if you are to feel well. If you were to drink only water, you would probably not take in as much liquid as if you drank a few beverages. Therefore, some variety of beverages and a beverage with every meal is important.

Coffee. The best coffee for backpack use is the instant or freeze-dried kind. No coffee pot is required (it would mean added weight), and instant coffee is light in weight compared to the

regular kind. Normally, 2 ounces of instant coffee will make about thirty cups. It can be made in either of two ways. One way is to simply bring water to boiling in a pan, pour the hot water into cups, add a rounded teaspoon of instant coffee to each cup, and stir. Another way is to put the desired number of cups of water into a pan, bring to a boil, and add the instant coffee directly to the boiling water in the pan. Let it boil for several minutes on the fire before removing it, and pour into cups. Add cream substitute or sugar to taste.

Tea. The instant variety of tea is also recommended. Bring water to a boil in a pan and then pour it into cups. Then add about 1 teaspoon of instant tea per cup, depending on the strength desired. Sweeten to taste. Never add tea to boiling water. The water must always be removed from the fire before adding the tea. Tea is very light in weight. Thirty-five to forty cups can be made from 1½ ounces of tea. If you prefer to use tea bags, rather than instant tea, you will find that two cups of tea can usually be made from one tea bag.

It is interesting to note that many who are strongly in favor of coffee as a drink at home revert to tea as a mealtime drink in the woods. It somehow seems to fill the bill better.

Many people add a teaspoon or more of margarine (or butter) to their tea. This gives it an interesting flavor, and it also provides some calories in the form of fat — an important consideration.

Bouillon, instant soups. Bouillon is carried in most local food stores. The instant broth and instant soups carried by many of the suppliers of trail foods are much more flavorful and satisfying, however. Instant beef broth, chicken broth, pea soup, and potato soup are common. Several good brands are conveniently packaged in individual size foil envelopes, providing for some variety at the same meal. All that is required is to add the contents of the package to a cup of freshly boiled hot water and stir. These soups and broths will have a place on most backpack food lists. While hikers are settting up camp or preparing other food items and waiting for them to cook, it is convenient and most satisfying to sip a cup of hot soup or broth. Bouillon may also be used to flavor rice and noodle dishes, giving a gourmet touch to meals in the woods. As with tea, adding a bit of margarine to the bouillon or soup will add to the flavor and also provide calories.

Hot gelatin. Most persons are surprised to find that they like hot gelatin for a drink. The

Royal and Jell-O brands are good. About 1 ounce of gelatin powder is required for a 1-cup serving. Simply heat water to boiling and dissolve the gelatin in the hot water. Drink it at the same temperature that you would drink hot tea or coffee. Any flavors are satisfactory, but orange and lemon flavors are particularly recommended as a hot trail drink.

Cocoa. The instant variety of cocoa is recommended for its convenience. Place about 3 heaping teaspoons (about 1 ounce) of cocoa in a cup, add hot water, and stir. The Swiss Miss, Nestle, and Hershey's brands are available in individual (1-ounce) packages. These are convenient for backpacking, since you can make cocoa, tea, coffee, and so on, from the same pan of hot water. Dishwashing is also simplified. A 1-ounce serving of cocoa contains more than 100 calories.

Lemonade. Hikers will frequently develop a craving for something tart and sour while on a backpack trip. There will be times when you would give your kingdom for a dill pickle. It is not convenient or practical to carry dill pickles on a backpack trip. However, you will find that a lemon drink strongly on the tart side will satisfy your craving for something sour, as well as help make for a balanced diet.

Many people, myself included, prefer to use the pure lemon powder, without sugar or other additives, in making a lemon drink. The Pantri-Pak brand (made by Perma-Pak) is quite good. For each cup of lemonade, about 1 level tablespoon of lemon powder is required. First, add a small amount of water and mix it thoroughly with the powder to make a paste. Then fill the cup with water, sweeten only very slightly, and you will have a very tart drink. If you prefer the ready-to-use type of lemonade (with sugar already added), the Wyler's brand is good.

SOUPS

Most soups are ideal backpack foods. They are easily and quickly prepared and readily digested. They supplement beverages in replacing fluids lost from the body. Lipton, Knorr-Swiss, Wyler's, and Campbell are some of the brands of dehydrated soup most commonly found in local stores. The directions will be found on the package, and since they vary from brand to brand, they should be followed carefully. For example, some of the soup mixes are added to hot water and others to cold water (which is then heated). A glob of butter or margarine added to soup will improve the flavor and will provide additional calories.

VEGETABLE SALAD

After a few days on the trail I frequently have a craving for fresh raw vegetables. It seems like a dish of coleslaw with a vinegar dressing would really hit the spot. I know of other backpackers who often have the same food desire. I always take along one or more packages of dehydrated vegetables with which to make a fresh vegetable salad; these really fill the bill.

Some of the dehydrated vegetable salads require boiling in hot water for a short period. Others (such as the Pantri-Pak brand) only require soaking in cold water. This latter type is recommended, since most people prefer their salads cool and preparation is simplified. The Pantri-Pak brand has an excellent taste and is recommended. Usually, 1 ounce of salad provides ample servings for three persons. Before you break camp in the morning, you can put your salad to soak in a tightly capped jar. When you stop for lunch (or supper), your salad is ready. Most salad dressings purchased in the store require refrigeration once they are opened. A good salad dressing that does not require refrigeration is made from the following ingredients. (It can be made at home and carried in a small plastic bottle.)

¼ cup	wine vinegar
⅛ cup	salad oil
½ tsp.	salt
½ tsp.	black pepper
several	cloves of garlic

Simply put the ingredients in the plastic bottle, shake them well, and your dressing is ready for use. If the garlic cloves are left in the bottle for a trip of several days or a week, the garlic flavor will gradually get stronger, but this spicy flavor tastes good in the out-of-doors, even to most people who do not eat highly seasoned foods at home. The salad oil and the vinegar will quickly separate in the bottle, so shake well each time before using.

Another salad dressing that does not require refrigeration is made from the following:

1½ tsp.	lemon powder
6 tsp.	water
1½ tsp.	sugar
3 tsp.	Pream or other cream substitute
½ tsp.	salt
¼ tsp.	black pepper

Mix the above ingredients together, first making a paste of the lemon powder and water, being sure to get all the lumps out. Because of the nature of the ingredients, this salad dressing can easily be made up fresh at each meal where you use it.

BREAD

The bread that you normally buy in the store is not suitable for backpacking. It is bulky, it usually ends up in crumbs if carried, and it molds easily. It is therefore recommended that you use a bread substitute that does not have these undesirable qualities. If you want to sacrifice some trip time that could be spent in other pursuits, you can, of course, bake bread or biscuits in camp. To bake consistently good camp bread or biscuits requires an open fire and the use of a reflector oven or similar device. A reflector oven will weigh about 2 to 3 pounds. In addition to the weight that a reflector oven adds to the pack, there is some problem in keeping it clean enough to pack from place to place. This means extra time required during the dishwashing operation. Additional utensils are usually required. Assuming that all the cooking in the oven turns out perfectly and that none of the "results" are thrown away (that would be rare), there is still a considerable investment in weight. For a lesser total weight you can probably provide an ample bread ration for each person by using canned bread and cakes, hard crackers, wafers, or other bread substitutes. The most food value per unit weight will result if you use a fortified biscuit, fruitcake, nut bread, or similar product.

For those who feel that they must have bread, some pumpernickel, rye, and black breads are sufficiently durable that they will last for several days. They must be carefully packed, however.

VEGETABLES

Many backpackers seldom bother with a side dish of vegetables. Beans and potatoes are sometimes an exception. Beans, with the addition of a meat bar, can be a main dish. Potatoes, corn, peas, and string beans can be good additions to a stew that you concoct yourself. Dehydrated spinach, in my experience, is better left at home (or in the store).

Potatoes. Dehydrated potatoes are now a common item in most local food stores. In cooking, the potatoes are covered with salted water and boiled for about fifteen minutes or until soft.

Presoaking will reduce the cooking time to just a few minutes. About 4 ounces of dehydrated potatoes is sufficient for three persons. A tasty addition to boiled potatoes is to add ½ cup of powdered milk (or equivalent cream substitute) and about 3 ounces of cheese during the last five minutes of cooking. Cut the cheese into thin slices and stir these and the powdered milk into the potatoes after most of the water has boiled off (or has been poured off).

Instant dehydrated white potatoes are also available in local food stores. In preparation of most of the instant potatoes, a measured amount of water is first brought to a boil. It is then removed from the fire, and a measured amount of milk is added. (Dehydrated milk or cream substitute can be used to make the required milk.) The instant potato granules or flakes are then quickly added and stirred so as to obtain a uniform "mashed" potato. Instant sweet potatoes are also available. Some are available in local stores. The Perma-Pak (Pantri-Pak) brand is also quite good. It is very important to carefully measure the amount of liquid used in preparing the instant potatoes. Otherwise they will turn out to be too soupy or too gummy.

There are some very good prepared gravies, such as the French's gravies, that are an excellent addition to the instant mashed potatoes. They can also be used on the dehydrated potato buds. Most of these gravies are available in local stores.

Beans. Precooked dehydrated beans are available in some local stores and are also carried by some of the manufacturers of trail foods. However, the cooking time required is usually too long for them to be convenient for trail use. There are some freeze-dried bean dishes available, that have meat or other additions, making some of them suitable for a main dish. These are discussed later.

Corn. Some local stores carry dried corn. The John Cope brand is quite tasty. It is desirable that the corn be presoaked for eight to ten hours before cooking, however. Even with such lengthy presoaking, a minimum of twenty minutes cooking time is required. Thus, its use is generally restricted to cooking where a wood fire is available. The John Cope corn does make a good trail snack when eaten dry, with no soaking or cooking.

Freeze-dried corn is available from some suppliers of trail foods. The Mountain House brand is good and only requires hot water (no cooking) for its preparation. It can be used as a side dish for some meals or added to soups or stews. About ½ to 1 ounce per person provides an ample serving as a side dish.

Peas, string beans. The freeze-dried peas and string beans, available from some of the suppliers in Appendix A, are much more tasty than the ordinary dehydrated variety. About ½ to ¾ ounce (before cooking) of freeze-dried peas or string beans is sufficient for one person. The Mountain House brand requires only hot water (no cooking) for preparation.

MAIN DISHES

Some meals, especially supper in the evening, are frequently planned around a main dish. A main dish should not be complicated to cook, nor should it require a long cooking period. It should be tasty, and it should be filling. Unless you have fish or other meat with the meal, the main dish should preferably contain some meat or meat substitute.

Some foods suitable for main dishes can be found in local stores. I have found spaghetti, macaroni, noodles, and rice to be excellent basic ingredients for main dishes. When I started to do a lot of cooking on a backpack stove, I thought at first that I was going to have to eliminate spaghetti, macaroni, and noodles because of their relatively long cooking time. However, I did some experimenting and found that the cooking time could be greatly reduced by presoaking. Some people will scoff at the idea of presoaking these food products, but it works. After macaroni and spaghetti are soaked in cold water for about an hour, they will cook satisfactorily in about five minutes. Fine-cut noodles presoaked for ten minutes will cook in three to five minutes. It is easy to try this for yourself. Use just a few tablespoons of each item for your experiment. It works! The soaking time varies with the size and shape of the individual pieces. The times given are for the "average size" of those products.

Various packaged macaroni and spaghetti dinners can be bought in supermarkets. I have tried many of these and have found them to be less than satisfactory. If they are cheese flavored, the cheese is often too strong or has an off taste. The same applies to various other ingredients in these prepared dinners. I much prefer to make my own dishes, starting from scratch. I find that it only takes a few minutes longer in the packaging process, and they are much tastier.

In the recipe for a main dish, meat is frequent-

ly a problem. Small cans of chicken, sausage, hamburger, and so forth, can usually be found in local stores, but they are too heavy, except possibly for very short backpack trips. Lightweight freeze-dried meats are available, but they vary greatly in taste. After considerable experimentation I have found a few freeze-dried meat products that I consider palatable and suitable.

Several freeze-dried dinners that I have found to be satisfactory are also listed in this section. Many such dinners are available, and I have tried a lot of them. Most are fairly expensive, but the high cost does not assure a palatable dinner. I would strongly advise against trudging off to the backwoods with your pack loaded with freeze-dried (or any other) foods that you have not previously tried. You will surely have some disappointing meals.

You will probably consider some of the freeze-dried dinners to be too expensive. In defense of that aspect, however, I would say that if the dinner is flavorful and satisfying, you should probably not be too critical of cost. If a main dish for four costs approximately $4 or $5 and will, with the addition of beverage, dessert, and so forth, satisfy three hungry backpackers, then that price compares very favorably with what you would pay for a comparable amount of food in a restaurant. Backpackers on a modest budget may not be so broad minded with respect to cost. In that event concentrate on the use of suitable foods that you can buy in the supermarket, repeat certain dishes and menus that you particularly like, and use a minimum of the special trail foods.

Some main dishes that I use frequently and that I can recommend are described in the following paragraphs.

Spaghetti and beef. The following ingredients will provide a main dish sufficient for three persons:

7 oz.	elbow spaghetti
1 pkg.	spaghetti sauce mix (about 2 oz.)
2 tbs.	dehydrated bell peppers
2 tbs.	dehydrated onions
3½ oz.	freeze-dried beef patties (Mountain House)
	or
1 can	cooked hamburger (about 10 oz.)

(Both the bell peppers and dehydrated onions can be packaged at home in the poly bag with the spaghetti.)

Cover spaghetti with water and presoak it for about an hour. It can be soaking while you hike, if you desire. When you are ready to cook, prepare the beef patties by reconstituting them with warm water according to directions on the package. Next, cut the patties into small pieces.

Place the spaghetti, bell peppers, and onions in a pan and cover with lightly salted water. Add the cut up beef patties and spaghetti sauce. Bring the mixture to a boil and simmer for 5 minutes. Stir frequently and thoroughly while cooking and add water — a small amount at a time — if necessary. (Since it is not possible to pour off excess water after the cooking is started, considerable care must be used in adding the water.) A tablespoon of butter or margarine added to the pot during the last minute or two of cooking improves flavor and provides more calories.

If canned hamburger is used rather than the freeze-dried variety, it should be cut into bite-sized pieces and added to the spaghetti prior to cooking.

Noodles and chicken. The following will provide a main dish for three persons:

6 oz.	fine-cut noodles (short pieces, break if necessary)
1 pkg.	dehydrated chicken noodle soup (such as Wyler's or Lipton)
2 tbs.	dehydrated bell pepper
3 oz.	freeze-dried chicken
	or
1 can	boned chicken (about 7 oz.)

Presoak the noodles for about 10 minutes. When you are ready to cook, prepare the freeze-dried chicken by soaking it in hot water according to directions on the package. Separate the chicken into small bits.

Place the noodles and bell peppers in a pan and cover with lightly salted water. Add the diced chicken and the package of chicken noodle soup. Bring the mixture to a boil and simmer it for 3 to 5 minutes. Stir frequently and thoroughly while cooking and add water — a small amount at a time — if necessary. A tablespoon of butter or margarine added during the last minute or two of cooking is recommended.

If canned, rather than freeze-dried, chicken is used, cut it into small pieces and add it to the noodles prior to cooking.

Macaroni and cheese. The following quantities are recommended to make a main dish for three persons:

7 oz.	elbow macaroni
4 oz.	cheese (mild or sharp, as preferred)
2 tbs.	dehydrated bell peppers
3 tbs.	dehydrated milk or equivalent cream substitute.

(The bell peppers can be put in the poly bag with the macaroni, when packaged at home.)

Cover the macaroni and bell peppers with water and presoak them for about an hour. If you prefer, they can be soaking while you hike. Cut the cheese into small, thin slices.

Place the macaroni and bell peppers in a pan, cover with water, and add about ½ teaspoon salt. Bring the mixture to a boil and simmer it for about 5 minutes. During the last several minutes that it is on the fire, add the cheese and dehydrated milk. Stir frequently and thoroughly while it cooks and add water, a *small amount* at a time, if necessary. A tablespoon of margarine should be added just before the cooking is finished.

Rice and gravy. This is an inexpensive dish, quickly prepared and very tasty. For three persons you will need the following:

6 oz.	Minute rice (about 1½ cups)
1 pkg.	chicken flavor gravy mix (about 2 oz.)

Use equal quantities of rice and water. Bring the water to a boil. Add ½ teaspoon salt and 1 tablespoon margarine to water. Stir in the rice and remove the pan from heat. Let stand about 5 minutes. Fluff with a spoon.

Another person can make the chicken gravy, which is usually prepared with boiling water in 2 or 3 minutes. (Other flavors of gravy can be used if you prefer.)

Spread the gravy over the rice and eat immediately.

Bacon hash. The following ingredients will provide a main dish for three persons:

4 oz.	dehydrated potatoes
2 oz.	dehydrated onions
3 oz.	bacon bar

If the dehydrated potatoes are the kind consisting of small, hard cubes, they should be presoaked at least an hour, or even all day. The onions can be soaked with them. Dehydrated potatoes that are in the form of small, thin shreds should be presoaked 15 to 30 minutes.

Place a heaping tablespoon of margarine or other shortening in a skillet and heat it until it is quite hot. Then transfer the potatoes and onions from the pan to the skillet, using a pancake turner, so as to drain off the water in the process. If you fry about half the potatoes at once, they will fry faster. After the potatoes and onions are in the skillet, shred the bacon bar and add a portion to the skillet. Fry all over a medium-hot fire for about 10 minutes, stirring frequently. Salt to taste.

Hash can be fried in a pan as well as in a skillet. A smaller quantity should be fried at one time, and the contents of the pan must be stirred frequently.

Hash makes a good dish for some breakfasts. Soak the onions and potatoes (together) all night, and they will quickly fry to a finish in the morning. With other food for breakfast, the ingredients recommended for three persons will be reduced to:

2½ oz.	dehydrated potatoes
1 oz.	dehydrated onions
3 oz.	bacon bar

Chili mac with beef. The Rich-Moor brand of this freeze-dried chili dish is very good. The "dinner for four" has a dry weight of 11½ ounces and provides generous servings for three persons. Cooking requires boiling for about 10 minutes. An easily prepared and satisfying dish.

Beans and franks. The Mountain House brand of this freeze-dried main dish is particularly good. It is reconstituted with hot water; no cooking is required. Dry weight is about 13½ ounces for a four-serving package (which I recommend for three persons). A tasty dish.

Beef chop suey. This is a good freeze-dried main dish. The Mountain House brand is very good. It is rehydrated with hot water. You will need two packages, each weighing about 3½ ounces, to provide good portions for three persons.

DESSERTS

Your appetite for ordinary food will usually be so sufficient that you won't need to pamper it with elaborate desserts. A few suggestions are discussed below.

Candy. The need to sustain physical energy is sometimes used as a reason for eating a lot of candy on a backpack trip. Some increase in candy consumption over what you would normally eat at home may be justified, but constant nibbling on candy is neither necessary nor desirable. To sustain your energy at a high level, it is recommended that your *protein* and *fat* intake be in-

creased somewhat over the amount you would normally eat at home. Beef Stick, beef jerky, cheese, nuts, fruit bars, and chocolate are good energy sources, and some of these are suitable as desserts.

A *reasonable* amount of candy can be recommended. Specially prepared candies are available from some of the suppliers listed in Appendix A — for example, the Tex-Schmeltz Traubenzucker. Each 2-ounce package contains eight individually wrapped squares of lemon-flavored candy. Other special candies, such as Hershey's high-melting-point chocolate, Hi Energy bars, and so on, are available from some of the suppliers listed. The M&M's peanut chocolate candies, locally available, have a fairly high melting point. Peanut bars are also good. You can readily buy peanuts and other nuts in bulk and repackage them into single portions.

Gorp is an arbitrary name given to a mixture of about equal parts of nuts, raisins, and chocolate. There are many variations of this mixture.

For a hot day on the trail sour hard candies can be very refreshing. It is best to get individually wrapped candies, whether for hot weather use or otherwise.

Puddings. Instant puddings, such as the Jell-O instant brand, are found in most local stores. Many are fairly good and make a good dessert for supper or a good evening snack. They are very easily prepared. Many of the suppliers listed in Appendix A carry various brands of instant puddings (and cobblers). I have found also that most backpackers like fruit and that a ration of fruit, either in the pudding or separate, is readily accepted as a dessert or as a trail snack.

Popcorn. Popcorn is a real favorite as an evening snack. It is most easily prepared over a wood fire. About ⅔ cup of unpopped popcorn is sufficient for three persons.

For a cooking utensil, you can fasten a wood-stick extension handle to an aluminum pan, as described for the skillet in Chapter 9, page 118. If the pan does not have a lid, you can make one from a piece of aluminum foil slightly larger than the pan opening — about 10 inches square. (By repeated folding, you can work this foil into a 2-inch square and put it right in the bag with the popcorn when you pack the food.) A piece of stove wire around the pan, just below the rim, will help hold the foil "lid" in place.

The cooking pan can also be set on a grill positioned over the wood fire.

To cook, first add a rounded tablespoon of shortening to the pan. When this is hot, add about 1/3 cup of popcorn. Place over a medium-hot part of the fire, shake it frequently but gently, and you will have popcorn in about five minutes. Don't leave it on the fire too long, and as soon as it is removed, dump it quickly into another utensil (such as a pan or skillet) before it burns. Sprinkle it liberally with salt, and then get back so that you don't get stepped on in the rush.

If you don't have a wood fire, you can try making the popcorn on your backpack stove. In this case you will need rags, a towel, or heavy gloves for holding on to the pan. Remove the pan from the stove momentarily when you shake it.

Popcorn has psychological as well as food value. To a neophyte backpacker sharing a pan of popcorn with other backpackers, the blackness of the night in the backwoods somehow seems less forbidding.

Other desserts. There are many other possible desserts. There are cookie mixes, cobblers, cake mixes, no-bake pies, and so forth, available from the suppliers of trail foods. Some are very easy to prepare; others are quite complicated. Some involve a number of utensils that may not be readily available—and also extra dishwashing, which may be a problem. Also, you may be disappointed in the taste. Just because a food is labeled as a dessert does not necessarily make it good. Before you take these more elaborate desserts on a backpack trip, it is recommended that they be tried out at home.

OTHER FOOD ITEMS REQUIRED

A few other food items and condiments are going to be required for your cooking. The basic items that will be needed for the foregoing recipes will be briefly discussed.

Sugar. If you use sugar in fruit drinks, on fruit, for cereal, and for certain other cooking, it can add up to quite a bit. This, in combination with a greater amount of candy than you normally have in your daily diet, can result in more sugar than is necessary. It is recommended that you be a bit conservative in the use of sugar in various foods where it is called for. About 1 1/4 pounds of sugar should be sufficient for three backpackers for a week-long trip.

Shortening. Margarine can be used as shortening in most recipes. If you want a spread for bread or pancakes, margarine is usually acceptable. Butter will turn rancid much more quickly in hot weather than margarine will. Margarine can also be used for frying, although it has a lower burning point than Crisco or a similar product. If you are frying fish regularly, much more shortening will be required than if you are not. Analyze your menus to determine your requirements. Running out of shortening can be a real inconvenience. Several shortening products, such as Vegalene and Golden Clear, are packaged specifically for backpackers in convenient nonbreakable dispenser bottles. Coating the entire inside surface of a cooking pan with one of these products before cooking a food such as oatmeal, spaghetti, or stew will reduce the tendency of the food to stick.

It should be emphasized that margarine (or butter) is an excellent source of fat and high in calories (about 200 calories per ounce). It is recommended that it be used fairly liberally as a spread for crackers or bread, in oatmeal, soups, stews, and main dishes. Some backpackers even add margarine to tea. It gives a unique flavor and is a good way to get extra calories.

Milk or cream. Many brands of dehydrated milk and cream substitutes are available in local stores. The cream substitutes will weigh a bit less and are a little richer when used in recipes that call for milk. If you like milk to drink, Carnation, Pet, and Lucerne are good brands found in many local stores. There are many others. If you have cool water at hand for mixing, they can be mixed in a poly bottle and will taste almost as good as the real thing.

Condiments. Don't take too many condiments. On many backpack trips salt will be the only condiment. Catsup, mustard, fruit preserves, and various spices may be desired in some cases, but be prepared for a real mess if they are not packaged properly. Also, rummaging through a lot of small bags or other small containers in which condiments are packaged can be pretty exasperating when the cook is trying to find something that is really needed. When you are trying to find a certain food item, having all foods grouped together in a few large bags is far different than having them arranged neatly in a pantry at home.

The salt requirement is roughly 1/4 ounce per person per day. If you use table salt in water, rather than salt tablets, to avoid dehydration, you may want more than this. Some people use crystals of rock salt, rather than salt tablets.

PREPACKAGED MEALS

Complete prepackaged meals are available from some of the firms that sell dehydrated foods. You can buy a variety of breakfasts, lunches, and suppers that contain everything from beverage to dessert. These prepackaged meals are *not* particularly recommended, however, unless you are short on time for putting together your own menus.

Many of the prepackaged meals are fairly expensive, considering the food items that they contain. They will also frequently weigh more than a similar meal that you would put together yourself. There will be too much of some foods and too little of others. There will probably also be some foods that you do not like, and you may throw away some of them. In general, you cannot rely on a package labeled Dinner for Four to feed four people. For healthy appetites, the number of people that a package of dehydrated food will feed is frequently overstated. Experience with certain foods and brands of foods — and keeping records — is the solution to this problem.

FOOD SHOPPING

Many foods suitable for backpacking can be found in supermarkets and other local stores. Some of these are listed here.

    Beans, precooked
    Bouillon
    Breads: pumpernickel, rye, other hard
        breads
    Breakfast bars
    Candies, hard nonmelting
    Cereals: Grape-Nuts, Heartland, granola
    Cheeses: Gouda, cheddar
    Chicken, canned boneless
    Chocolate, Baker's semisweet
    Cocoa, instant
    Coconut
    Coffee, instant
    Condiments: salt, pepper, sugar, catsup,
        mustard
    Cookies, hard
    Dates
    Fruit, dried
    Fruit drinks: Start, Tang, Wyler's, others
    Gelatin desserts
    Granola bars
    Gravy mixes
    Jam
    Lipton dinners
    Macaroni

    Margarine
    Meat, potted
    Meats, canned
    Milk, dehydrated
    Mincemeat, condensed
    Mushroom slices, freeze-dried
    Noodles
    Nuts: peanuts, filberts, cashews
    Oatmeal, instant and regular
    Onions, dehydrated
    Oysters, canned smoked
    Peanut bars
    Peanut butter
    Peppers, dehydrated bell
    Potatoes, dehydrated: cubed, sliced, mashed
    Puddings, instant
    Raisins
    Rice, Minute
    Salad spreads
    Salami
    Sardines
    Soups, instant
    Spaghetti
    Summer sausage
    Sunflower seeds
    Tea, instant
    Tuna
    Wafers: RyKrisp and Triscuits

In addition to shopping in conventional supermarkets and food stores, try specialty food stores. These include health food stores, Japanese and Chinese food stores, and gourmet shops. You will find numerous food items that are satisfactory for backpack trips.

If there are some mountaineering and backpacking equipment shops in your area, you will want to include these in your shopping for foods for backpack trips. Although their products are generally more expensive than similar foods found in conventional food stores, such shops will usually have many specially prepared backpacking foods which cannot be found elsewhere. You may also need to purchase some of your foods from the mail order firms that carry mountaineering and backpacking equipment. If you do, allow plenty of time for ordering and receiving merchandise. It can make for some hectic last-minute preparations and a lot of extra work if mail-ordered items arrive just prior to takeoff. (Or they may *not* arrive before the trip starts — more problems!)

8
Menus and Food Lists

GENERAL PLANNING

Whether you are to be on the trail for several days, a week, or more, it is recommended that you have a written menu plan for every meal that you expect to eat. There is certainly no rigid requirement that you must eat each and every meal in the exact order and amount as planned, but there should be a plan. With the menu plan you can then make up the food list, adding some extra food for a possible emergency. The amount of extra food will depend upon the length of the trip, the distance from the roadhead, and your experience and skill in planning food lists. Some important factors to be considered in menu planning are discussed in the following paragraphs.

Whether you are going to do most of your cooking on a portable stove or over a wood fire will have a definite effect on the planning of menus. Many backpackers are accustomed to cooking on a backpack stove, and they will probably continue to do so even though there may be a sufficient wood supply for cooking. Others prefer to cook over a wood fire if there is a sufficient wood supply and wood fires are not prohibited. However, even where wood fires are normally allowed, they may be prohibited at certain times because of forest fire hazard. If there is any doubt about the availability of wood, it is important to check into this aspect before the trip. In many popular backpacking areas, adequate wood for cooking is simply not available.

To avoid long cooking times—and therefore carrying an unnecessarily large supply of stove fuel—many adherents of stove cooking have learned to plan their meals so that a minimum of cooking time is required. It is true that cooked food provides no more calories than cold food does. A few backpackers plan an entire trip with no hot food whatever. However, most prefer some hot food and drink for breakfast and supper, if not for lunch.

The type of activity that is to follow the meal is frequently a consideration in the type and amount of food to be eaten at a particular meal. This especially applies to breakfast and lunch. If heavy exertion is to follow a meal, keep the meal light and avoid excess *fat*, which is not easily digested. Heavy exertion will interfere with digestion of most foods and may actually lead to temporary illness. It should be pointed out, however, that breakfast is an important meal for many backpackers. Most nutritionists would agree with this, from a dietary standpoint. Also, if you cook and eat breakfast soon after you get up in the morning, there will frequently be a time lapse of an hour or more before you are ready to hit the trail. Even after you are on the trail, you can set a relatively easy pace for a while, and this will aid digestion.

There is also the matter of expediency in special situations. If a group is trying to get a very early start on the trail so as to reach a certain destination at a certain hour, then breakfast

88 Backpacking

should be very simple. The larger the group, the more important this becomes. A large group can fritter away hours in preparing a substantial, cooked breakfast, packing up gear, and cleaning up the camp.

You should consider whether you expect to supplement the plan with game or fish. Even if you expect to, you should still take enough food so that you will have enough to eat in the event that you do not get the game or fish you are after.

On trips into many areas you are completely on your own after you leave the roadhead. There is no chance to pick up food along the way. On some trail routes, however, there may be an opportunity to add supplies along the way every few days, and this will affect your plan.

Weather may be a factor. If rain is to be expected, it will be desirable to include more foods that can be eaten cold if you are caught in the rain at mealtime. In general, most people will desire more hot foods and hot beverages in cool and cold weather than in hot weather. However, at least one, and preferably two, hot meals per day are recommended, even in warm weather.

The type of trip and the daily routine will have their effects. If you expect to set up a base camp after you reach a certain destination, the meals will be somewhat different than if you will be hiking most of each day and making camp at a new spot each night. Cooking on layover days will be different than cooking on hiking days.

Regardless of the type of backpack trip, however, a fundamental rule is to count the ounces and keep the pack light. When the sun is bearing down and the pack is starting to feel heavy, you will thank yourself for the extra time you took in planning and packing to enable you to keep your pack weight down. Insofar as possible, leave the cans at home. I have taken many backpack trips where only one can was carried—a container for margarine. Certain meats, also, are sometimes carried in canned form. Other canned goods should be considered very carefully, as to whether they are really necessary. On many backpack trips excess food is carried deep into a remote area, lugged around for a few days, and then packed out again. This is the result of poor planning, and it represents wasted energy.

NUTRITION

Foods consist of varying proportions of carbohydrates, proteins, and fats. Our energy comes from calories, found primarily in carbohydrates and fats, and to a lesser extent in proteins. However, a proper *proportion* of carbohydrates, fats, and proteins is important to the efficient processing of food within the body and to general good health. As a general rule, carbohydrates should make up about 60 percent of the caloric intake; about 20 percent should be proteins, and the remaining 20 percent, fats.

Common sources of carbohydrates are grains, cereals, fruits, vegetables, and candy. Carbohydrates are digested more readily than proteins and fats are. Proteins are important to the rebuilding of muscles and body tissues. They are obtained chiefly from lean meats, fish, milk, cheese, eggs, grains, and legumes. Fats furnish the most energy per unit of weight. They are processed through the digestive system relatively slowly. Therefore, they should be consumed at intervals during the day and in modest amounts. Primary sources of fats are meat, nuts, seeds, margarine, butter, cheese, oils, and chocolate. One of the effects of high altitude on an individual is that fats may become unpalatable. Margarine and butter have very high fat content and are thus high in calories per unit weight. Margarine is often used by backpackers as an addition to cooked cereal, tea, soups, stews, vegetables, main dishes, and so on, as a convenient and tasty way to obtain added calories.

Most backpackers on trips of up to ten days need not be concerned about how the carbohydrates, proteins, and fats balance out. A normally varied diet will provide assurance enough that these food constituents will be consumed in more or less proper proportion. If the diet is a bit lopsided, it would normally cause no problem in such a short period. It is a good idea, however, to consume more fats and somewhat more protein during a backpack trip than would normally be eaten at home.

Vitamins and minerals are also essential to a healthy body. In a varied diet these would probably be obtained in sufficient quantity without any specific planning for that purpose. Here again, if the diet were a bit shy in certain vitamins and minerals for a period of several weeks, that would ordinarily cause no problem. Backpackers on longer trips, or those who *may* be concerned, could add vitamin and mineral capsules to their diet.

For the average backpacker, it is recommended that no concern be given to precise planning of the diet. Simply keep it varied. It is also recommended that you eat to maintain energy and that you not overeat. Scientific diet planning is a herculean task for most people, and it would take much of the fun out of a backpack trip. However, if you are so inclined, two documents that may be of interest can be recommended. One is "Composition of Foods," Handbook #8, USDA. The other is "Nutritive Value of Foods," Home and Garden Bulletin #72, USDA. (See Appendix H for source.)

EATING PATTERNS

There is considerable variation among backpackers as to eating patterns.* Some eat a very light breakfast and little or no lunch, snack constantly on the trail during the day, and then eat a modest supper. Some feel that if they don't keep stuffing food into their bodies, they will suffer a significant loss of energy. Many people who backpack usually work at relatively sedentary occupations, and backpacking represents a greater amount of physical effort, with considerably more strain on the cardiac system, than they are normally accustomed to. If we have a constant food supply entering our bodies, a considerable amount of our cardiac output will be required just to digest that food. The physical effort that we are putting forth in carrying our pack along the trail requires additional cardiac output. Therefore, there is a substantial additional demand placed on our cardiac system if this kind of eating pattern is followed.

Many trail snacks contain large proportions of candy, chocolate, and other goodies. When eaten in moderation, these snacks are satisfactory, but if one snacks on them all day long, it can do harm. First, it is easy to overeat when you are snacking constantly on such items. Filling up on these between meals can make the hiker much less hungry at mealtime. Thus, he may fail to eat enough more nutritious foods at regular meals. This can establish a cycle: because you snacked, you aren't hungry for a good meal; because you didn't eat a good meal, you snacked; and so on. Having candy and other food constantly in the mouth is also bad for the teeth.

For the reasons given above, it is suggested that a meal pattern of medium-to-hearty breakfast, modest lunch, medium-to-hearty supper, and moderate, nutritious morning and afternoon

*In preparing these comments, I have exchanged thoughts with a number of qualified nutritionists, some of whom are into backpacking themselves. Most of them feel that backpackers frequently alter their eating habits too drastically when they take to the backwoods. This particularly applied to type of food eaten (frequently too much starch and sugar), frequency of eating (some eat more or less continuously), and amount eaten (some eat too much).

snacks be followed. Most backpacking foods are concentrated to start with, and stuffing ourselves with them can lead to problems. Therefore, it is best to stop eating before we are completely full. A slight feeling of hunger is better than feeling stuffed. Obesity in this country is very widespread (no pun intended). One of the advantages of backpacking for many is that they can shed a few pounds of fat, improve their stamina, and feel more trim.

The average backpacker on a modestly strenuous trip in moderate weather should do well on 3,600 to 3,800 calories per day. For most people, it will be beneficial if some of these calories come from excess body fat. It is necessary to expend about 3,500 calories in exercise in order to lose one pound of weight. Further, with the gastrointestinal tract that we humans have, it is not necessary for us to eat continuously in order to function at our upper limit. As for other aspects of backpacking, it is recommended that you experiment a bit with various backpack foods, menus, and eating patterns on short backpack trips near your home. Determine the combination of factors that provides maximum energy and a feeling of well-being *before* you make any drastic changes in your food habits on a longer trip into the backwoods.

MINIMUM COOKING TIME

Many backpackers rely entirely on a backpack stove for all their cooking. If you are cooking on a backpack stove, you will want to select foods that require a minimum of cooking time, in order to conserve on the amount of fuel to be carried. You will probably also make up menus to include quite a few foods that require *no* cooking. Supermarkets and specialty food stores now offer foods that are suitable for backpacking. Yet there will probably be some food items that you will want to obtain from a backpack equipment store.

The majority of backpackers do not live within commuting distance of a well-stocked backpack equipment store. Thus, many of their foods will probably be bought by mail. This has disadvantages. One of the major disadvantages is that you cannot read the instructions on the food package prior to buying. Just because a food is labeled as a backpack food does not mean that it is easy to prepare. It may actually be fairly complicated, requiring several items to be mixed, or prepared separately, and so on. Its preparation may require more cooking utensils than you want to carry.

One of the most important aspects is cooking time. There are many backpack foods that require cooking for fifteen or twenty minutes and some that require cooking for thirty minutes or more. If you are cooking over a backpack stove, it is recommended that you carefully eliminate from your menus all foods that require such long cooking periods. This poses a question. How do you know what the instructions and the cooking time are if you can't read the label on the package beforehand? Fortunately, there is a solution to this problem. The book *The Complete Guide to Trail Food Use* by William W. Forgey, M.D., lists many good backpack foods by brand name and gives weights, servings, brief cooking instructions, and cooking time. Thus, you can select lightweight foods with short cooking times without seeing the actual food package. I believe you will find this book quite helpful. It is listed in Appendix H.

It is still recommended, as stressed elsewhere, that you order foods that you think you are interested in and try them out at home before taking them on a full-scale backpack trip. This makes a good spare-time project, and it will pay off in very tangible benefits. By keeping records of your results, you will eventually have a list of foods that suit your appetite and which are easily and quickly prepared. Your records should include a note concerning the quantity of food provided by each package; for example, "two generous servings." This information as stated on the package may be quite misleading.

OTHER FACTORS INFLUENCING MENUS

Some other considerations that should go into your menu planning are listed below.

1. Include in your menus only foods that you have had experience in cooking on previous trips or at home and that you have found that you like. Also, the saying "If all else fails, read the instructions" had best not be applied to cooking of foods on a backpack trip. The cook had better know the recipes—but good—and follow them.

2. Do not include food dishes that are complicated to prepare and those that take a long time to cook. If you use a portable stove for cooking, concentrate on one-dish meals, especially for supper.

3. Foods should ordinarily not require special cooking equipment. Any cooking gear other than two aluminum pans and a skillet is considered special. (Some trips will not require a skillet.) The packing and use of a reflector oven, Dutch oven, or broiler may be justified in a large group, but seldom for the average small group of backpackers.

However, the fact should not be overlooked that some groups particularly *enjoy* cooking on the trail. If they are in an area where wood is plentiful, they may want to carry a reflector oven for making biscuits, cobblers, and "the works." That is their prerogative, and if it adds to the enjoyment of their trip, they should by all means do it.

4. The menus listed in this part of this book are reasonably well balanced, as they should be. However, assuming that you are on a good day-to-day diet before you start the trip and that you will return to the same when the trip is over, then a week or two of a diet that may not be well balanced should not hurt you. Nevertheless, some reasonable balance is desirable if you are to have a maximum feeling of well-being and sufficient energy for the trail (and avoid certain "problems" such as constipation).

5. Lunch is often the meal that is skipped over lightly. Lunch need not be a big meal, but fixing something substantial will help avoid the physical letdown that frequently comes along about midafternoon. It will also eliminate the necessity for an especially big meal at supper, when you may be too tired to fix it or to appreciate it after it is fixed. Further, the body does not digest food well when it is overfatigued.

6. Where unusually strenuous activity is required, such as a climb up a very steep trail for a considerable distance, it is best not to eat just prior to the climb, even though it occurs at mealtime. Delay the meal (or any food) until the worst part of the climb is behind. After the strenuous climbing is accomplished, eat a light, cold snack before continuing the trip.

7. To some degree your cooking gear influences your menus. For example, it is not too convenient to have fried fish and fried potatoes for supper when you only have one skillet, because excessive time would be required. Mashed potatoes, a stew, or similar dish—since they would be cooked in a pan—would be a better choice to have with your fried fish.

8. Don't hesitate to repeat certain foods in day-to-day menus. If you are hungry and the food is good, then the fact that you ate the same thing two days ago (or even yesterday) won't be any problem. It is much better to do this than to start

out with a large variety of foods that you are not familiar with. Also, it generally makes for easier packing if you hold to a reasonable variety.

9. The length of the backpack trip is an important factor. On a trip of more than three or four days, you will want to use the most concentrated, lightweight foods you can find. On a short backpack trip you may prefer locally available foods for most, if not all, of your needs. Some backpackers keep a good stock of dehydrated and freeze-dried foods on hand and use them on every trip, regardless of duration.

10. In some groups, particularly large and formally organized groups, religious practices may influence the menu planning.

EXPERIMENTING WITH FOOD

If the cook likes to experiment with new food dishes, that is fine, but the experimenting should be done at home—not on the trail. Most hikers will not appreciate a cook who experiments with food that has been carried deep into a remote area, over many miles of rugged trails, on their backs. Cooking most food dishes for the first time is an experiment. Neither will hikers appreciate waiting an hour or more for more exotic dishes to cook when adequate, tasty, and nourishing food could have been cooked in much less time, with proper planning and selection of menus.

"FILLER—UPPERS"

One of the important factors in keeping the food load light is eating all, or substantially all, the food that is cooked at any one meal. Food that is thrown out represents wasted energy of the hikers in carrying it. It isn't very convenient to pack a plateful of leftover spaghetti and beef and eat it at the next meal. In fact, it just isn't feasible—from several standpoints—to try to save leftover cooked food from one meal to another. The secret of eliminating the problem of leftover food lies, first, in proper selection of the amount and combinations of food and in careful planning and weighing of food at home and, second, in planning some "filler-uppers" for some menus. A filler-upper is a food that is normally eaten cold and that is conveniently packed and rationed out in individual portions. Candy, sausage sticks, beef jerky, nuts, and cheese are examples of good filler-uppers. A prudent cook will see that any cooked food, or any other food that it is not convenient to save until another

meal, is well on the way to being finished up before the filler-upper for that meal is rationed out. Then if it turns out that some appetites are satisfied without the filler-upper, their rations can be saved for the next meal or later in the day.

BREAKFAST

The starting meal of the day should normally include modest-to-hearty quantities. It might include several of the following items.

Fruit. Dried, dehydrated, or freeze-dried prunes, peaches, pears, or apricots.

Hot drink. Coffee, tea, or cocoa.

Cereal. Oatmeal and Wheatena are suitable hot cereals. If you prefer a cold cereal, granola, Heartland, and Familia Birchermuesli are good. Pancakes with butter and syrup may be a suitable substitute in some instances, particularly on a short backpack trip. A pancake breakfast takes a relatively long time to cook, however.

Meat. Bacon or sausage is a good meat for breakfast. A good way to fix it is mixed with dehydrated eggs.

Hash. This may not appeal to you as a suitable dish for breakfast at home, but your viewpoint (and appetite) will probably change on a backpack trip.

Eggs. An important item on many breakfast menus is eggs. There are relatively few brands that really taste good. Choose your brand carefully and try it out at home before depending upon it on the trail.

LUNCH

The midday meal is usually the lightest and quickest meal of the day. For a layover day in camp, however, you may prefer more food than when on the trail. Normally, lunch is made up of snack food, but this can be varied, if desired.

Hot or cold drink. On cool days a cup or two of hot tea, coffee, or gelatin is good. On a warm day lemonade will probably hit the spot. If it is a bit on the sour side, so much the better. Orange or other fruit drinks may be substituted if you prefer.

Snack foods.   Listed below are some typical snack foods that might be eaten for lunch.

bacon bar	gorp
beef jerky	meat bar
beef stick	milk (dehydrated)
candy	nuts
cheese	pemmican
chocolate	raisins
coconut	sardines
cookies (hard)	sausages (hard)
dates	wafers (RyKrisp,
fruit bar	others)
fruitcake	

Fish.   If you have caught fish, they should normally be eaten within two or three hours after they are caught. If they cannot be eaten while they are fresh, they should be released.

SUPPER

Although supper is usually the big meal of the day, it is best to eat lightly if you are excessively tired. Also, if you are tired, there is no need to further wear yourself out with a lot of complicated cooking. There are many nourishing and satisfying one-pot main dishes that are quickly and easily prepared.

Hot drink.   While you are getting ready to start the rest of the supper, it is easy to heat water for tea, coffee, bouillon, or a hot gelatin drink. It will pick you up and will help to replace the water that you lost during the day through perspiration. It is a good idea, while waiting for the water to boil, to drink a tall cup of cool water with some salt in it.

Soup.   A cup of soup will help whet your appetite. If you don't feel very hungry, choose a thin soup, like onion or tomato.

Meat.   In many remote areas you will be able to catch some trout. If you caught some in the afternoon, this is the time to have them. If not, you will probably want some other meat, either in small individual portions or mixed in with the main dish.

Main dish.   A good main dish is a meal in itself. If you do not feel up to tackling a main dish along with fish or other meat, try corn, peas, string beans, or potatoes in its place.

Dessert.   If you feel the need for a dessert, some of the instant puddings are tasty and easily prepared. Candy, nuts, and some of the snack foods are also suitable.

If you plan to have fruit for breakfast, dried or dehydrated fruit can be soaked overnight. If you prefer, they can be cooked for a short time in the evening, then left to soak. If you plan hash for breakfast, the potatoes and onions can be soaked overnight. They can then be quickly cooked (by frying) in the morning.

EVENING SNACK

If you haven't worn yourself out during the day so that you need to hit the sleeping bag soon after supper dishes are washed, you may want something more to eat or drink. Tea or coffee is *not* recommended just before bedtime. If you still feel thirsty, fix a cup of soup or hot chocolate to drink. Popcorn usually goes over well and is easy to fix. It also has substantial food value and is good for you. When you plan to have popcorn in the evening, the evening meal for that day should be a bit lighter than usual.

If the night is cold and you feel you may be a bit cool in your sleeping bag, make it a point to eat something before going to bed. A cup of soup or a bar of candy will help you sleep warmer.

TRAIL SNACKS

In the menus below, trail snacks are not listed separately. Some suitable snack foods are listed above, under Lunch. You will probably be able to add quite a few more that are suitable and that you particularly prefer. As stated previously, it is recommended that a variety of foods be used in your trail snacks—not too much candy.

MENUS

Now that foods and some basic aspects of menu planning have been discussed, let's examine possible menus, which in turn readily provide the food list. This amounts to your food shopping list, except for the items you may already have at home. Without such a list your "menus" will probably be a hodgepodge of foods and will surely be somewhat less than satisfactory. Let me emphasize that these menus are for *example only*. But I believe that you will find them helpful and will get some ideas from them for your own planning.

Obviously there are a great many possible variations on these menus.

It is strongly recommended that you keep your food lists and menus from trip to trip. It is also suggested that you keep notes on the various foods and brands, as to quantities provided, taste, cooking time, and so on. If this is done, you will find that with each trip your food planning, buying, and packaging becomes easier. It can actually be quite a laborious and painful procedure to start with. You can also end up with some real "bummer" food dishes in almost any of the brands. Over the years, I have experienced numerous occasions in camp when, after a food was cooked and sampled, it was a toss-up as to whether to eat it or go hungry for that meal. That is why, for many years now, I have not taken on a trip any "new" food that I have not first cooked at home and proven to myself that I like. You may say that food taste and preference vary from person to person, and this is true. But it has been my experience that most foods that I found poor tasting (some downright obnoxious) received the same reaction from others.

Recipes for various food dishes are given in Chapter 7. In the menus below note particularly the weights for the various food items. These amounts will provide ample portions for three people when used in combination with the other foods listed. (Three people is the minimum recommended for a trip into a remote area, for safety reasons.) Many backpackers take too much food. If you doubt the weights, they can be readily verified in your own experimental cooking at home, between trips.

OVERNIGHT HIKE

Many people carry only the most lightweight foods, regardless of the length of trip. However, for illustration (not as a recommendation), all foods shown in the overnight hike menus are available from local stores. Thus, some are heavier than if they were of the lightweight dehydrated variety. It is assumed that the trip will start after breakfast and that each hiker will take a bag lunch.

Total food weight. All the food adds up to a total of about 102 ounces, or about 34 ounces per person. This weight could be cut down. By using dehydrated beef in item 3, 11 ounces could be saved; vacuum-dried apricots in item 6, 3 ounces; and canned bacon or bacon bar in item 8, 5 to 8 ounces. Pancakes are also a fairly heavy food item, compared, for example, to dehydrated eggs or cooked cereal. Planning this fine is not considered essential for an overnight trip where the food load is not a major item. However, on extended backpack trips, in particular, it becomes very important.

SUPPER

Item Number	Food		Requirement for Three People
1.	Tea	1/2 oz.	(3 tea bags; makes 6 cups)
2.	Pea soup	4 oz.	(dehydrated)
3.	Spaghetti and hamburger	14 oz.	hamburger (canned or fresh-frozen)
		7 oz.	elbow spaghetti
		2 1/2 oz.	spaghetti sauce
4.	Candy	3 oz.	
		31 oz.	

Note: Prepare fruit for breakfast (cook, or soak, or both).

BREAKFAST

5.	Coffee	½ oz.	(6 tsp. instant; makes 6 cups)
6.	Stewed apricots	6 oz.	(dried; local store variety)
7.	Pancakes	10 oz.	prepared pancake flour
	Syrup	6 oz.	syrup mix or brown sugar
8.	Bacon	12 oz.	(fresh; local store variety)
		34½ oz.	

LUNCH

9.	Hot gelatin or cold fruit drink	3 oz.
10.	Salami or cheese	8 oz.
11.	Hard crackers or cookies	6 oz.
12.	Raisins or nuts	6 oz.
		23 oz.

TRAIL SNACKS

13.	Cheese, cookies, dried fruit, etc.	6 oz.

OTHER FOOD ITEMS

In addition to the foods given above, you will need the following items for preparing the food dishes listed:

Food	Amount	Needed for Item No.
Sugar	3 oz.	1, 6
Salt	¼ oz.	3
Cream substitute	½ oz.	7
Margarine	3 oz.	5
	6¾ oz.	

THREE-DAY BACKPACK TRIP

For a three-day backpack trip, the food weight will be a larger portion of the total pack load, and more attention to the weight of the individual food items is necessary. However, some people will not plan a three-day trip sufficiently far in advance to allow time to obtain such special foods as dehydrated meat, vacuum- or freeze-dried fruits and vegetables, dehydrated eggs, and so forth. Therefore, the menus for this three-day trip have also been planned around foods available in most local stores. If you want minimum weight in your pack, plan your trips far enough in advance that you will have time to obtain some dehydrated foods. Or simply keep a supply of such foods on hand. For minimum weight, select your menus even for short trips from types of foods given in the menus for the week-long trip that follow those for the three-day trip.

Total food weight. All the food adds up to a total of about 177 ounces. This amounts to about 29½ ounces per person per day. Compare these menus with those for the overnight hike and note where the differences occur. Note the weight for the second meal (Breakfast, second day) and penalty in weight for carrying store bacon and fresh eggs (19 ounces) compared with the weight for a bacon bar and dehydrated eggs (6 ounces).

SUPPER   (First day)

Item Number	Food		Requirement for Three People
1.	Tea	½ oz.	(3 tea bags; makes 6 cups)
2.	Vegetable soup	2½ oz.	(dehydrated)
3.	Potatoes and gravy	4 oz.	instant mashed potatoes
		4 oz.	dried beef (for gravy)
4.	Raisins or candy	6 oz.	
		17 oz.	

Note: Prepare fruit for breakfast (cook, or soak, or both).

BREAKFAST (Second day)

5.	Coffee	½ oz.	(instant; makes 6 cups)
6.	Stewed prunes	7½ oz.	(dried; local store variety)
7.	Oatmeal	4½ oz.	
8.	Bacon and eggs	12 oz.	bacon (fresh; local store variety)
		7 oz.	eggs (3 fresh eggs)
		31½ oz.	

LUNCH (Second day)

9.	Cold fruit drink	3 oz.	(makes 1 quart)
10.	Summer sausage or cheese	8 oz.	
11.	RyKrisp or Triscuits	6 oz.	
12.	Candy or nuts	6 oz.	
		23 oz.	

SUPPER (Second day)

13.	Hot gelatin	3	oz.	(makes 3 cups)
14.	Onion soup	2	oz.	(dehydrated)
15.	Chicken and noodles	5	oz.	noodles
		3	oz.	noodle soup (dehydrated)
		7	oz.	boned chicken (canned)
16.	Instant pudding	4	oz.	
		24	oz.	

Note: Prepare fruit and soak potatoes and onions for breakfast.

BREAKFAST (Third day)

17.	Cocoa	3	oz.	(instant; makes 3 cups)
18.	Stewed apricots	6	oz.	(dried; local store variety)
19.	Grape-Nuts	5	oz.	
20.	Hash	2½	oz.	potatoes (dehydrated)
		1	oz.	onions (dehydrated)
		10	oz.	pork sausages (canned)
		27½	oz.	

LUNCH (Third day)

21.	Cold fruit drink	3	oz.	(makes 1 quart)
22.	Sardines	7	oz.	
23.	Hard crackers or cookies	6	oz.	
24.	Granola bars	6	oz.	
		22	oz.	

TRAIL SNACKS

25.	Nuts, coconut, cheese, etc.	12	oz.

OTHER FOOD ITEMS

In addition to the foods given above, you will need the following items for preparing the food dishes listed:

Food	Amount	Needed for Item No.
Sugar	9 oz.	1, 6, 7, 18, 19
Flour	½ oz.	3
Dehydrated milk or Cream substitute	4 oz.	3, 5, 7, 19
Salt	1 ¼ oz.	3, 7, 8, 15, 20
Margarine	5 oz.	3, 7, 15, 20
Pepper	¼ oz.	8, 20
	20 oz.	

ONE‑WEEK BACKPACK TRIP

For a one-week backpack trip, the food weight will be a very significant part of the total pack load, and some skillful planning is required to keep it from getting out of hand. Some of the foods listed may need to be mail ordered. In general, you should allow a minimum of several weeks from the time you send in your order until the order is received. We will again assume that the trip starts in the morning (after breakfast) and that the first lunch will be a bag lunch, each hiker providing his or her own. Many people will prefer a cold lunch, but on a cool day, or a layover day, some hot drink or other hot food may be desired. Therefore, some lunches include hot food.

Total food weight. All the food adds up to a total of 432 ounces. There are eighteen meals, two evening snacks, and 72 ounces of trail snacks.

This food weight amounts to 24 ounces, or 1½ pounds, per person per day. Compare these menus with those for the overnight hike and for the three-day hike and note where the differences occur. These meals provide generous portions, and in a large group there will be some food wasted. Experienced backpackers who have learned to plan food menus and cook without waste will be able to cut quantities on some items so as to reduce the overall food weight by about 10 to 15 percent. This particularly applies to small groups of experienced adult backpackers. In general, the larger the group and the more teen-agers in the group, the more wasted food. Fish have been omitted from these menus. However, on many trips into wilderness areas and other remote regions, trout would be caught, and this would make some further reduction in the food weight.

SUPPER (First day)

Item Number	Food	Requirement for Three People	
1.	Tea	¼ oz.	(instant; makes 6 cups)
2.	Onion soup	2 oz.	(dehydrated; makes 3 cups)
3.	Spaghetti and beef	7 oz.	elbow spaghetti
		3½ oz.	ground beef (dehydrated)
		2½ oz.	spaghetti sauce
4.	RyKrisp or Triscuits	3 oz.	
5.	Candy or raisins	3 oz.	
		21¼ oz.	

Note: Prepare fruit for breakfast.

BREAKFAST (Second day)

6.	Coffee	½ oz.	(instant; makes 6 cups)
7.	Peaches	2 oz.	(freeze-dried)
8.	Oatmeal	4½ oz.	
9.	Eggs and bacon	3 oz.	eggs (dehydrated)
		3 oz.	bacon bar (to mix with eggs)
		13 oz.	

LUNCH (Second day)

10.	Lemonade	2	oz.	lemon powder (makes 6 cups)
11.	Chicken salad	5½	oz.	(freeze-dried)
12.	RyKrisp or Triscuits	4	oz.	
13.	Pineapple chunks	4	oz.	(freeze-dried)
		15½	oz.	

Note: Soak salad for supper.

SUPPER (Second day)

14.	Hot gelatin	3	oz.	(makes 3 cups)
15.	Tomato soup	2	oz.	(dehydrated)
16.	Macaroni and cheese	7	oz.	macaroni
		4	oz.	cheese
17.	Vegetable salad	1	oz.	salad (dehydrated)
		1	oz.	salad dressing
18.	Peanuts or other nuts	3	oz.	
		21	oz.	

Note: Soak potatoes and onions for breakfast.

BREAKFAST (Third day)

19.	Coffee	½	oz.	(instant; makes 6 cups)
20.	Peaches	2	oz.	(freeze-dried)
21.	Wheatena	4	oz.	
22.	Hash	2½	oz.	potatoes (dehydrated)
		1	oz.	onions (dehydrated)
		3	oz.	bacon bar
		13	oz.	

LUNCH (Third day)

23.	Noodle soup	3	oz.	(dehydrated)
24.	Beef stick	8	oz.	
25.	RyKrisp or Triscuits	5	oz.	
26.	Candy	3	oz.	
		19	oz.	

SUPPER (Third day)

27.	Tea	¼	oz.	(instant; makes 6 cups)
28.	Pea soup	4	oz.	(dehydrated)
29.	Rice and gravy	5	oz.	Minute rice
		1½	oz.	French's Gravy Makins
30.	Instant pudding	4	oz.	
		14¾ oz.		

EVENING SNACK (Third day)

31.	Popcorn	4	oz.

Note: Prepare fruit for breakfast.

BREAKFAST (Fourth day)

32.	Coffee	½	oz.	(instant; makes 6 cups)
33.	Stewed prunes	3	oz.	(vacuum-dried)
34.	Oatmeal	4½	oz.	
35.	Eggs and bacon	3	oz.	eggs (dehydrated)
		3	oz.	bacon bar (to mix with eggs)
		14	oz.	

LUNCH (Fourth day)

36.	Lemonade	2	oz.	lemon powder (makes 6 cups)
37.	Apple slices	2	oz.	(freeze-dried)
38.	Granola bars	3	oz.	
39.	Beef jerky	6	oz.	
40.	Candy	3	oz.	
		16	oz.	

SUPPER (Fourth day)

41.	Coffee	½	oz.	(instant; makes 6 cups)
42.	Beef bouillon	½	oz.	(makes 3 cups)
43.	Noodles and sausage	7	oz.	fine noodles
		3	oz.	sausage (freeze-dried)
44.	Vegetable salad	1	oz.	salad (dehydrated)
		1	oz.	salad dressing
45.	Raisins	3	oz.	
		16	oz.	

Note: Prepare fruit for breakfast.

BREAKFAST (Fifth day)

46.	Cocoa	3 oz.	(makes 3 cups)
47.	Apricots	3 oz.	(vacuum-dried)
48.	Oatmeal	4½ oz.	
49.	Scrambled eggs	6 oz.	(dehydrated)
		16½ oz.	

LUNCH (Fifth day)

50.	Beef noodle soup	2½ oz.	(dehydrated)
51.	Fruit bars	3 oz.	
52.	Gouda cheese	4 oz.	
53.	Nuts	6 oz.	
		15½ oz.	

SUPPER (Fifth day)

54.	Tea	¼ oz.	(instant; makes 6 cups)
55.	Tomato soup	2 oz.	(dehydrated)
56.	Franks and beans (Mountain House)	13½ oz.	(freeze-dried)
57.	Instant pudding	4 oz.	
		19¾ oz.	

Note: Soak potatoes and onions for breakfast.

BREAKFAST (Sixth day)

58.	Coffee	½ oz.	(instant; makes 6 cups)
59.	Peaches	2 oz.	(freeze-dried)
60.	Wheatena	4 oz.	
61.	Hash	2½ oz.	potatoes (dehydrated)
		1 oz.	onions (dehydrated)
		3 oz.	bacon bar
		13 oz.	

LUNCH (Sixth day)

62.	Lemonade	2 oz.	lemon powder (makes 6 cups)
63.	Banana chips	4 oz.	
64.	Breakfast bars	6½ oz.	(6 bars)
65.	Candy or nuts	3 oz.	
		15½ oz.	

Note: Soak salad for supper.

SUPPER (Sixth day)

66.	Coffee	½ oz.	(instant; makes 6 cups)
67.	Chicken bouillon	½ oz.	(makes 3 cups)
68.	Beef chop suey (Mountain House)	7 oz.	(freeze-dried)
69.	RyKrisp or Triscuits	4 oz.	
70.	Vegetable salad	1 oz.	salad (dehydrated)
		1 oz.	salad dressing
		14 oz.	

EVENING SNACK (Sixth day)

71.	Popcorn	4 oz.	

Note: Prepare fruit for breakfast.

BREAKFAST (Seventh day)

72.	Coffee	½ oz.	(instant; makes 6 cups)
73.	Prunes	3 oz.	(vacuum-dried)
74.	Wheatena	4 oz.	
75.	Scrambled eggs	6 oz.	(dehydrated)
		13½ oz.	

LUNCH (Seventh day)

76.	Lemonade	1 oz.	lemon powder (makes 6 cups)
77.	Beef jerky	4 oz.	
78.	Fruit bars	6 oz.	
79.	Nuts	6 oz.	
		17 oz.	

TRAIL SNACKS

80.	Jerky, nuts, candy, cheese, etc.	72 oz.	

OTHER FOOD ITEMS

In addition to the foods given above, you will need the following items for preparing the food dishes listed:

Food	Amount		Needed for Item No.
Sugar	20	oz.	1, 8, 10, 21, 27, 33, 34, 36, 47, 48, 54, 60, 62, 73, 76
Shortening (including at least 16 oz. margarine)	22	oz.	2, 3, 4, 8, 9, 15, 16, 21, 22, 23, 25, 28, 29, 31, 34, 35, 42, 43, 48, 49, 50, 55, 60, 61, 67, 68, 69, 71, 74, 75
Salt	4	oz.	3, 8, 9, 16, 21, 22, 29, 31, 34, 35, 43, 48, 49, 60, 61, 71, 74, 75
Cream substitute	12	oz.	6, 8, 16, 19, 21, 30, 32, 34, 41, 48, 57, 58, 60, 66, 72, 74
Pepper	½	oz.	9, 22, 35, 49, 61, 75
Mustard	3	oz.	24, 39, 77
Vegalene	2	oz.	(use on cook pans)
	63½ oz.		

FOOD LIST

The total food list and total weight of the separate food items is easily arrived at. Simply go through the menus, writing down the name and weight of the food the first time it occurs on the menu, and adding the necessary weight for each repetition of the item.

9
Cooking

PLANNING

It is recommended that one member of your backpack group be designated the cook. This does not mean that he will be doing all the cooking. He will simply be in charge of the food, the food preparation, dishwashing, and so on. He should have the full cooperation and assistance of every member of the party in all of these operations.

One of the most important jobs to be done on any backpack trip is the meal planning and the cooking. Equally important is the job of keeping the camp "kitchen" in reasonable order, finding certain foods when needed, and assuring equitable distribution of the food and cooking gear for travel each day. Being somewhat systematic is nearly as important as having cooking ability.

Choose your cook carefully. He should not only be interested in outdoor cooking (on the trail) but should have had significant experience in cooking trail foods on actual backpack trips. Prior to the trip the cook will be responsible for preparing the menu, getting the food and cooking gear together, ensuring that it is properly packed, and distributing an equal load to each hiker. He should call on the other members for their input and help in these preparations, but it is important that some one individual, a leader, have the overall supervision of the job. The cook should know how to properly prepare every item of food on the menu. He should have note cards, or a small notebook, showing each menu and the recipe for each food

item on the menu, if it is not already on or with the food package. Then there will be no need for guessing on the amount of food, seasoning, cooking time, and so forth.

Many of the foods listed in Chapter 7 may be purchased from local food stores or perhaps sporting goods stores. Depending on the length of the backpack trip, a few will probably need to be ordered by mail. In mail ordering, it is desirable that the order be sent at least one month prior to the takeoff date. Allowing two weeks until mail-order foods are received, an additional two weeks is available prior to takeoff; this is none too long when the packing is done in your spare time. An alternative is to keep a supply of certain dehydrated foods (those not available from local stores) on hand at all times.

PACKING FOOD

Most of the individual foods carried on a backpack trip are suitable for packing in plastic (polyethylene) bags and should be so packed. Most of the plastic bags (pint and quart sizes) sold by local stores for use in packing foods for home freezers are not suitable for this purpose. They are too lightweight and will not stand up under trail usage. Some of the suppliers listed in Appendix A carry plastic bags for the packaging of trail foods. Recreational Equipment has a good variety. Some of the plastic bags listed in the Sears Roebuck catalog are also satisfactory. A common bag is of 2-mil thickness. Depending upon the size of the party, the pint or the quart size will be more appropriate. When the food is used, the bag is burned if an open fire is permissible. Otherwise the food bag is added to the litterbag. It is recommended that all dry foods be repackaged in these bags, except certain dehydrated foods that should not be opened until ready for use. Double bags, one inside the other, should be used for fine-particle foods such as flour and sugar. When repackaging food that comes in boxes, cut the recipe from the box and put it in the bag with the food (or copy it onto a small note card and put that in the bag).

Small rubber bands can be used for closing the bags at the top, after they are filled with food. These are not as readily installed and removed, however, as a wire "twister" type of closure. The wire twists with paper cover, which are furnished with the plastic bags sold in most local stores, are generally unsatisfactory for trail usage. The paper cover is not sufficient protection for the wire. Some of the wire ends will poke into adjacent bags and puncture them, and you then have spilled food (and a mess). A good solution is to use ordinary pipe cleaners cut in half. After the pipe cleaner has been cut in half with pliers, the ends should be doubled back and crimped so that no sharp ends protrude to puncture other bags. These pieces of pipe cleaner are simply twisted around the top of the bag after the food is put in.

It is particularly recommended that such twisters be used on bags that hold sugar, tea, coffee, dehydrated milk, and other food items whose bags are opened and closed repeatedly during the trip. A rubber-band closure is usually adequate for bags that hold one-meal portions of such foods as macaroni, spaghetti, and noodles and which are destroyed after one use. (When I use rubber bands, I generally use bands of ½-inch diameter, purchased at an office supply store.)

In addition to being lightweight, the poly bags have other advantages when used for packaging food. Compared to boxes or other stiff containers, they are flexible and will thus fit better into "corners" of the large food-carrying bags, which will contain a number of the smaller bags. In filling the individual food bags, it is recommended that the bag not be filled full, but that a small space be left at the top. All possible air should be squeezed from this space before sealing or fastening the bag at the top. When the bags are filled in this manner, they will "flow" into corners better, when being packed, than if they are filled completely full.

For packaging of certain foods, you may want some durable plastic or lightweight metal containers. Such containers should be kept to a minimum. I have made many trips where only one such container, a lightweight aluminum can for margarine, was taken. Some of the suppliers listed in Appendix A carry suitable containers. Glass containers should not be carried on a backpack trip. They are not needed, and they are not suitable. They are too heavy, and they are subject to breakage. If you want to take some food that comes packaged in a glass container, you should repackage it. If for some unusual reason a glass container is carried on a backpack trip, it should be carried home again after the contents are used (just as all metal containers should be carried out). For all practical purposes glass containers are indestructible. Wherever you leave them, they will be there for the next hundred years. Under certain circumstances sunlight shining through glass may start a forest fire.

Experienced backpackers will be on the lookout throughout the year for various plastic and lightweight metal containers that will serve their needs when it comes time to go backpacking. A baking powder can may make a suitable container for margarine. A better container for margarine is one of the round plastic containers about 2 to 3 inches high and 4 to 5 inches in diameter that are available from many backpack equipment supply firms. A large plastic pill bottle with a screw top is suitable for carrying such things as lemon powder.

Shortening, store bacon, sausage sticks, and other foods that tend to be greasy should be packaged with particular care. Don't depend on the thin cellophane wrapper on store bacon to provide adequate protection in a packbag. Repackage the bacon in a heavy plastic bag, tightly sealed. The plastic or metal container in which shortening is carried should, in turn, be carried inside a heavy plastic bag also. In warm weather the outside of the container will become greasy and soil other articles if it is not properly protected.

Poly squeeze tubes, which are shaped very much like a toothpaste tube, are good containers for some items. Foods such as honey, jams, peanut butter, and so on, are loaded into the large end, which is open, and it is then closed with a clip provided with the tube.

Salt-and-pepper shakers are generally small plastic cylinders with a divider in the center; one end holds salt; the other, pepper. Each end unscrews from the center. Those who do not use pepper may wish to fill one end of such a container with garlic salt, to add a spicy flavor to individual

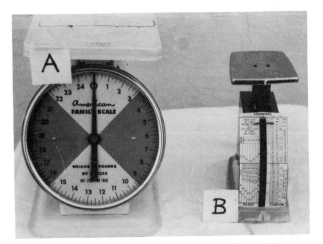

Weighing scales. The kitchen scale (A) will weigh quantities up to 25 pounds, by one ounce increments. It is useful for weighing large food items and some items of equipment. The postage scale (B) will weigh items up to two pounds, by fractional increments. It is particularly useful for weighing small quantities of food and small equipment items.

portions of soups, stews, or main dishes. Salt purchased in small cardboard containers about 3¾ inches high can be carried in those containers, with perhaps the added protection of a small plastic bag in case the cardboard containers should be crushed or leak.

WEIGH OR MEASURE FOOD

All foods should be weighed with a scale reading in ounces or measured (in measuring cups) before being put into the individual plastic bags. An ordinary kitchen scale, which measures in ounces, is good for this purpose. Do not guess at the amounts. This can be disastrous.

A postage scale calibrated in ½-ounce increments is particularly useful for weighing food items. When you are on the trail, a small spring scale can be used for weighing equal loads of food, cooking gear, and other common equipment for distribution to hikers at the start of each day. Most hikers will be satisfied, however, to have the cook simply divide up food and cooking gear into apparently equal loads. These loads are arranged in small piles on the ground. Each hiker then selects one of the loads and packs it into the packsack with his or her personal gear.

LABEL THE FOOD BAGS

It is recommended that all bags be labeled before the food is put into them. A felt-tip marker can be used for this purpose. You can write directly on the bag. It is desirable to mark each bag with the name of the food and its weight. Specifying the weight will be of help when the foods are checked against the food list for the last time, prior to packing. As the trip progresses, the original weight marking will also assist the cook in determining how much of certain foods, such as sugar, milk, flour, cocoa, and tea, remains.

A tired backpacker may easily mistake an unlabeled bag of sugar for dehydrated milk. (Many years ago I had the "privilege" of eating chocolate pudding that was made with soap granules that were mistaken for dehydrated milk.)

On those bags that are used repeatedly during a trip, such as bags for sugar, tea, coffee, and dehydrated milk, an ink marking on a polyethylene bag will gradually wear and become faint. The marking can be protected by an overlay of transparent tape. Or white adhesive paper labels can be used for those bags.

FINAL FOOD PACKING

For final packing of the individual food bags, it is recommended that large heavy plastic (polyethylene) bags be used. Bags measuring roughly 8 by 4 by 20 inches, with a thickness of 2 or 3 mils, are normally suitable for this purpose.

There are several approaches to packing food so that you can find the particular foods for a given meal when you want them. Rummaging through all the food bags looking for one or two items can be quite exasperating and time consuming. You can package foods so that all meat, cheese, shortening, and so on, is together in one large bag; products such as macaroni, noodles, and soups in another; sugar, salt, tea, and coffee in another; and so forth. You can also put all foods for a given day in one bag, with three bags within that bag being labeled BREAKFAST, LUNCH, and SUPPER.

It has been my experience that a good arrangement at the onset of the packaging process is to package the main foods for each meal of each day in separate bags. Thus, there will be a bag labeled MONDAY BREAKFAST, another labeled MONDAY LUNCH, and still another labeled MONDAY SUPPER—and other bags, similarly labeled, for other days. (Items common to many of the meals, such as shortening, sugar, margarine, milk, coffee, tea, soup, salt, and so on, are not placed in the individual meal bags. Instead they are placed in a large bag labeled EXTRA.) Then all the packaged breakfasts are placed in a large bag or bags labeled BREAKFASTS. The same is done with lunches and suppers. Once you are on the trail, if

Food ready for trail. Four 2-mil plastic bags, each 8 by 4 by 19 inches, contain all the food for three adults for a week-long backpack trip, except for some of the trail snacks.

these bags repeatedly during the trip and a "twister" will be least time consuming and most effective.

Ten plastic food bags of 1-pint capacity, suitable for packaging of many of the individual foods, weigh about 1 ounce. Plastic bags (about 8 by 4 by 20 inches) suitable for holding a number of the smaller bags, bacon bars, and other food items weigh about ½ ounce each. Use only plastic bags that are absolutely new.

COOKING UTENSILS

Most people are familiar with cook kits. A kit generally contains two or more nesting aluminum pots with lids and heavy wire bails, a cover which is intended to serve as a frying pan, and occasionally a few other items. Some are complete with metal cups and plates, and a few even contain eating utensils. Most such cook kits are heavier than is desirable for backpacking, the "frying pan" doesn't do a very good job of frying, and the kit usually contains items that the backpacker does not require. For these reasons, experienced backpackers generally assemble their own cooking and eating utensils.

Many backpackers plan their food and menus so that only cooking pans are required. They either eliminate all frying or confine their frying to a few simply prepared items, such as scrambled eggs, that can be adequately cooked in a pan. Fish, if desired, can be cooked in foil or on a rock, as described in Chapter 7, if a wood cooking fire is available.

the weather or other factors indicate that Wednesday's breakfast should be eaten on Monday, that is no problem. It's all together, "in the bag." Also, if your appetite or the terrain ahead indicates that only part of Tuesday's breakfast should be eaten at one sitting, no problem. You eat what you want, and the remainder is still in the breakfast bag, ready to be eaten at another breakfast or another time. After you are on the trail, various factors may cause you to vary your menus from what was originally planned. That is no problem; you can quickly ascertain at any time what alternate food choices are available for a particular meal. You can also quickly take stock of your food supply, so that you are not likely to run out of food.

A pipe cleaner type of "twister," as described earlier, is also recommended as a closure for these large food bags. You will be opening and closing

Cooking pans. Suitable cooking pans for backpacking are often found in variety stores or department stores. Lightweight aluminum pans are usually favored. It is important when shopping for such a pan to keep in mind the characteristics of the backpack stove you intend to use it on. On some stoves too large a pan will cause the stove to overheat; this presents a safety problem. Regardless, there is a reasonable limit to the size pan that you will want to set over the burner area of a backpack stove. An important feature of the pan is that the bottom be flat, so that the pan will sit firmly on the burner and be reasonably level.

A desirable pan will frequently be found that has a handle but no bail. That is usually no problem. The handle can readily be sawed off with a hacksaw. A bail on a pan to be used on a backpack stove is of questionable value. The bail will get too hot to be useful for lifting the pan. Regardless, most backpackers use a pot gripper to grip the rim of the pan when setting it on or taking it off the burner. Therefore, it is a good idea to take along your pot gripper when you go pan shopping, just to be sure you can get a good grip with it on the rim of the particular pan that appeals to you. The inside of the pan where the side of the pan meets the bottom should have rounded edges rather than sharp corners. Otherwise, food will stick in the corners, and the pan will be difficult to clean. A lid for the pan is a desirable feature, although in a lot of cooking the lid is off the pan as much as it is on. If the pan does not come with a lid, you may be able to find among the kitchenware at home a little-used one that will serve the purpose. Some backpackers use a piece of heavy foil when a lid is needed. In using aluminum foil as a lid, a piece of stove wire around the rim of the pan, just below the top, will hold the foil in place with a single twist of the ends of the wire. After the pan is hot, a pair of pliers will be useful in untwisting the wire when you want to inspect or stir the contents of the pan.

I have some lightweight aluminum pans that were purchased in a variety store that have been used for cooking both on a backpack stove and over a wood fire. A pan of 1½-quart capacity weighs 5½ ounces. For a party of three or four persons, I like to carry two lightweight aluminum pans, one of 1½-quart capacity and one of 1-quart capacity. For a larger group, you can use pans of greater capacity, or more pans and an additional stove.

The size of your stove and whether any wood-fire cooking is planned are important factors.

If your pans may be used for cooking over a wood fire as well as on a backpack stove, it is recommended that a wire bail be provided. This will make them adaptable for hanging from a dingle stick (a stick propped off the ground so as to suspend the pans over the fire). I prefer a flexible wire bail, and I install it myself. The first step is to drill three small holes (about 1/16 inch in diameter) equal distances apart on the circumference of the rim of the pan, just below the top edge. Through each of these holes I run a flexible wire, twisting the three wires together at the top to form a bail. I find that pans suspended from a pole by a three-wire bail (using light-gauge, easily bent wire) are much more stable than those using a conventional bail (one heavy wire running from one side of the pan to the opposite side).

These lightweight, inexpensive (mine cost about $1.50 each) pans purchased in the store frequently have handles. I cut off the handles of the pans with a hacksaw, so that only about a 2-inch stub remains. In cooking, I frequently grip this stub with needle-nosed pliers to lift the pan on and off the fire. The stub also makes it easy, using a stick picked up off the ground at the cook site, to install an extension handle "on the spot" for certain types of cooking. Cutting off most of the handle of the pan also serves a purpose from a safety standpoint. If there is no handle, you are not likely to grab the pan with your hand and possibly get a good burn in the process.

In packing the cooking pans, I simply push the wire bails down into the pan. Unless a very sharp kink is put in the wire (bending it back on itself), it can be repeatedly bent and will not break. I replace the bails at the start of each trip, a very simple procedure, and I carry about 2 feet of spare stove wire with which to replace a bail during a trip if it becomes necessary.

If you are certain that all your cooking on a particular trip will be done on a backpack stove, then the wire bails are not necessary. However, don't overlook the fact that you may have an opportunity for *some* wood-fire cooking.

In washing dishes, some people scrub the outside of the pans to keep them clean. This is a lot of work and a messy job. Others cover the outside of the pans with soap or shaving cream before cooking, to make the cleaning job easier. I never do this. I *prefer* that my pans get good and black. They will do a much better job of cooking when they are thoroughly soot coated and black on the outside than they did when they were new and shiny. Cooking pots should be carried in a stout cloth bag, to keep them from blackening other equipment in your pack.

Instead of store-bought pans, some people use "billie cans," which are generally discarded fruit, coffee, or juice cans. I find such cans generally unsatisfactory. They are usually not the right shape for obtaining maximum heat from a backpack stove or open flame. They have sharp corners where the side of the can connects to the bottom, which makes them difficult to clean. They usually rust easily. Also, the average pot tongs will not grip the rim of such cans securely. I frankly cannot understand a philosophy wherein someone would spend several hundred dollars for good backpack equipment and try to save a couple of dollars by using a discarded tin can to cook in.

Skillet or fry pan. As stated previously, even for a backpack trip of a week or more, it is not difficult to plan menus that do not require use of a skillet. Simple frying jobs can be done in a pan. Thus, for some trips, depending upon your menus and planning, a skillet may be an *optional* item of equipment. Also, on most backpack stoves, cooking with a skillet is somewhat difficult because the flame and heat are concentrated in a small area. Food in a skillet is easily burned.

For those trips where a skillet is desired, a Teflon-coated skillet is recommended. There is a wide variety of shapes, sizes, and weights of Teflon skillets available. Some have detachable handles or folding handles. This provides some convenience in packing, but I have not found it to be really essential. A wire or metal handle is preferable. An optimum size is about 9 or 10 inches in diameter. With some searching, you can find a 10-inch diameter Teflon skillet, weighing about 12 ounces, that will be suitable for backpacking. A Teflon skillet is recommended rather than uncoated aluminum or plain steel because it will fry your food more evenly with less shortening and the result will be more tasty. Aluminum skillets may be used, but the food will burn quite easily and much more shortening will be required. There are certain procedures that should be observed in using a Teflon skillet. Those who are helping with the cooking operation should be instructed rather carefully by the cook in regard to the following precautions.

1. Although the instructions for many Teflon skillets say it is not necessary to use shortening after the skillet is once broken in, it is recommended in cooking over an open fire that you use a small amount of shortening each time. Coat the entire inside surface with shortening, right up to the rim of the skillet. Put a small spoonful of additional shortening in the bottom.

2. Don't thrust a cold Teflon skillet into a hot flame and hold it there. Heat it up gradually.

3. Use only a wood or plastic turner for handling food in the skillet—*never* a metal utensil. A metal turner will mar the inside Teflon surface, and the skillet will soon become burnt and useless.

4. A Teflon skillet can usually be satisfactorily cleaned with cold water. Use warm water or warm soapy water if necessary. Rinse in water that has been boiled.

5. Never use a metal cleaning pad or pot scratcher to clean a Teflon skillet. Use only a rag or a plastic scrub pad.

6. In packing the skillet, be sure that metal objects that may rub the inside surface and mar

it are not next to it. A separate lightweight bag is recommended as a cover.

If you have somehow gained the impression that I am a bit fussy about how my Teflon skillet is used and handled, you are right. It is a pleasure to cook with a good skillet and a real pain to use a poor one. The precautions listed are recommended for both Teflon I and Teflon II skillets. Those made of Teflon II are not supposed to require such careful handling. However, in using Teflon II skillets and other Teflon II cookware about the home, my wife and I have both concluded that it is best to use the precautions stated with *all* Teflon-coated skillets and pans. It doesn't take any longer, and it pays off.

Soaking jar. If you want to be soaking dehydrated food while you are hiking, then a leak-proof unbreakable plastic jar is recommended. If you are staying at the same camp after you reach a certain destination, then such a jar may not be essential. You can have dehydrated food soaking in camp by placing it in a strong plastic bag and hanging it from a tree limb. It can also be put to soak in an open pan that has been tied to a tree limb by its wire bail. (The purpose of hanging it from a tree limb is to keep the food out of reach of animals.) I usually carry such a jar because I very frequently have food for the next meal soaking as I hike.

Spoons for cooking. For the small cooking pans that I use, I find that tablespoons are very adequate for cooking use. Aluminum tablespoons are lighter than steel ones. For those who use larger cooking pans, it may be desirable to have larger spoons, possibly special metal or wood serving spoons.

Plastic or wood turner. If you are not using a frying pan, you probably won't need a turner or spatula. When I scramble eggs in a pan, I simply use a spoon and stir them more or less continuously.

Can opener. The GI baby can opener, listed by suppliers in Appendix A, will save weight (it weighs about ¼ ounce), and it will do the job. It just takes a little longer than most other can openers. It is so small that it can easily become lost. Use a stout cord or leather thong to tie it to the handle of the turner (drill a hole if there is none there) or other utensil so you will know where to find it.

Pan-gripping tool. If you have a pair of needle-nosed pliers, these will serve adequately to handle the pans mentioned. They will also be useful for other camp and trail jobs. Grip the pans by the stub of the handle, by the wire bail, or by the rim. Aluminum tools that grip the pan edge are available in a variety of styles. Some weigh about 1 ounce.

Other cooking gear. I have made a great many backpack trips on which no cooking gear was carried other than that detailed above. I have had no problems in the "kitchen," and I was fully satisfied with the meals that my companions and I were able to turn out. It has been many years since I used a reflector oven. Yet I recognize that some backpackers may occasionally use a reflector oven, griddle, pressure cooker, or other gear. If conditions and time permit and more elaborate cooking is your cup of tea, so be it.

Carrying bag. All cooking utensils should be carried in a bag that you can easily make at home out of ordinary muslin or percale. This will keep the utensils together and will keep the soot on the pans from getting onto other items in your pack. Make the bag of generous size, with a tie string at the top. You should use new material so that the bag will be strong. *Don't* try to use a paper or plastic bag for this purpose. The bag will split open, and the inside of your good packbag will get coated with soot from the pans. The inside of the carrying bag will be thoroughly blackened during each trip and should be washed at home before the next trip. Plates, cups, eating utensils, and materials for dishwashing can be carried in another cloth bag.

Cook kits. At the beginning of this discussion on cooking utensils, I made some brief re-

Sierra cup. *(Lou Clemmons)*

marks on cook kits. I feel that most experienced backpackers would prefer to assemble their own kits. However, there are always exceptions to the general rule. There are a few good cook kits available, and the good ones are fairly expensive. It's your choice.

It is possible to buy a backpack stove that has a cook kit designed especially for the stove. The Sigg Tourist cook kit and SVEA 123 stove make one such combination. Weight is about 2 pounds for stove, windscreen, two pots, and lid.

EATING UTENSILS

Plates. In general, a plate is not considered necessary in backpacking. The usual procedure, especially with a backpack stove, is to cook and eat one food item at a time. Also, many menus are planned around a main dish or a couple of cooked foods, rather than around a variety of cooked foods at any one meal. Quite a few people manage to do all their eating and drinking (including fish or what have you) from a single *cup*. Others find that a lightweight plastic or aluminum plate, or a plastic bowl, makes for greater convenience in eating and is worth the small additional weight.

Cups. Plastic cups are good. They will take considerable rough treatment, are light in weight, and can be used for either hot or cold liquids. Such cups are available in many local stores. One such cup weighs 1⅓ ounces, holds about 12 fluidounces, stacks easily, and costs about $0.30. Numbering the cups on the outside with a felt-tip marker will help each hiker to know which cup is his or hers when it is set down someplace during a meal. Cereals such as oatmeal, stewed fruit, and soups are most conveniently and efficiently eaten from cups rather than plates.

Some backpackers favor a stainless steel cup with a wire handle. One such cup is the famed Sierra cup. It holds about 10 fluidounces, weighs 3 ounces, and costs about $1.75.

Silverware. Each person needs one large spoon for eating. A lightweight fork is permissible, but most foods can be eaten without difficulty with just the spoon. For the foods that require a knife, you can use your pocketknife. Do not carry the common knives that you use at the table at home. They are much too heavy, and they are not needed. Silverware can be carried in a small lightweight bag with other eating utensils.

Eating utensils: plastic cup and bowl, and large spoon. Weight, 5½ ounces.

COOKING STOVES

More and more backpackers are coming to rely on portable stoves for cooking and are making such stoves a regular part of their backpacking gear. There are a number of reasons for this. First, wood for cooking fires is simply not available in many of the heavily used backwoods areas. Some of the national parks and forests prohibit wood fires. Others allow wood fires, provided that you obtain a permit for such use. At certain seasons high fire hazard conditions may preclude the use of wood fires, even though a wood supply may be available. Possible foul weather, and the time required to gather wood, cook over a wood fire, and clean cooking pans, may also make the use of a backpack stove more attractive to some persons.

A few people cook substantial and even elaborate meals on the trail, over a wood fire where possible. They consider cooking part of the overall "fun package" of backpacking. Others want to spend minimum time in food preparation, cooking, and cleanup.

Some dehydrated foods are now available that require only the addition of boiling water; after a thorough stirring the food is ready to eat. Other foods with short cooking times are also conveniently prepared over a stove. A bowl of hot soup at lunchtime or a cup of hot tea at a rest break are easily and quickly prepared.

On the other hand, only one food can be prepared at one time on a one-burner stove. However, eating food in "courses," rather than "home style" (eating several foods simultaneously), is acceptable to most backpackers. The many one-pot meals that are available or can be concocted make one-burner cooking and meal planning relatively easy. Frying is somewhat difficult on many backpack stoves, since the heat is concentrated in a relatively small area. If you intend to be fishing and want to fry fish for some meals, you may wish to get a fire-building permit, if such is available, in order to supplement your backpack stove for those meals where frying is to be done. If some wood-fire cooking is done, the wood fire may as well be used to heat water for cooking and dishwashing, also, and will thus lessen the weight of stove fuel to be carried.

One-burner stoves are most commonly used for backpacking, and they can be roughly categorized by the type of fuel they use. Gasoline stoves are widely used, and the majority of backpackers use stoves of this kind. Kerosene stoves are also used, but to a lesser extent. A third category comprises the alcohol-burning stoves (which are used by relatively few backpackers). Another type of stove, which is gaining in popularity, is the propane or butane gas stove.

Most of the stoves described in the following paragraphs are dependable if given reasonable care. As with other equipment, it is important to become thoroughly familiar with them in your back yard at home before taking them on a backpack trip.

Over the years the Optimus and Primus brands of stoves have become well known to most backpackers. Both of these brands of stoves were made by the same company. To avoid confusion, as of January 1973, the Optimus Company discontinued using the Primus label on stoves marketed in the United States and Canada.

Gasoline stoves. The one-burner gasoline stoves are very widely used by backpackers. In general, they are intended to burn white gas or other unleaded gasoline. This is sometimes available in bulk form from service stations. (Take your own container.) However, the quality of such gasoline varies considerably, and it is therefore not particularly recommended. If used, it should usually be strained to remove any impurities, which may readily clog burner orifices. Instead of gasoline, it is recommended that Coleman fuel, Blazo, or a similar product, made specifically for gasoline stoves and lanterns, be used. These products are available in gallon cans at most sporting goods stores. They are more expensive than unleaded bulk gasoline, but considering the modest quantities that are used and the increased probability of trouble-free operation of your stove, the higher cost is considered worthwhile.

The Optimus 8R is quite a popular stove among backpackers. It is contained in a box that has dimensions of about 5 by 5 by 3 inches. The weight is 24 ounces. The fuel tank contains ⅓ pint of fuel, which will burn 1¼ hours. It will boil a quart of water in six or seven minutes. No windscreen is provided. It is somewhat difficult to get a simmer heat, which is true of many backpack stoves. It has a built-in cleaning device. The stove burns by self-pressure. A very large pot should not be used on the stove, since it may cause the fuel tank to overheat and blow the safety valve. Since it is only 3 inches high, with a broad base, this stove has good stability. The cost is about $28.

The Optimus 111B is essentially a large version of the 8R. It is used primarily by fairly large groups (five to eight persons). It will boil a quart of water in about four or five minutes. It has a self-cleaning needle and a built-in pump, which make it suitable for cold-weather use. It is 7 inches square and 4 inches high—a very stable stove. The lid serves as a fairly good windscreen. Cost is about $52.

The SVEA 123R (also made by Optimus) is a popular stove. The stove burns by self-pressure. Earlier versions of the SVEA were not self-cleaning; however, this stove is now self-cleaning. The 123R has an integral windscreen, and a small pot is included. It is about 4 inches in diameter, 5 inches high, and weighs 18 ounces. Cost is about $26. A SVEA stove kit referred to as the Sigg Tourist consists of two pans (2½-pint and 3½-pint capacity), a lid that can serve as a pan, and a windscreen. The packed size is 8½ inches in diameter and 4½ inches high; the weight is about 32 ounces. This version sells for about $40.

There are some other good backpack stoves that burn white gas, such as the Optimus 80, the MSR-9, and the Phoebus. If possible, it is recommended that the prospective purchaser visit a backpack equipment shop, inspect the stoves, and discuss their features with a competent salesperson, before making a purchase.

Lighting a gas stove and getting a controlled flame for cooking is one of the more difficult aspects of their use. Most of the small gas stoves have no pumps. Heat from the burning stove causes the volatile fuel to expand and forces it into the burner. The stove must be preheated by some method to force a small amount of fuel into the burner head so that the stove can be lit. If conditions are just right, this can sometimes be done by cupping the fuel bowl with warm hands, or by setting the stove in the sun or on a hot rock. One soon learns that these methods are somewhat unreliable, however.

Most backpackers who regularly use such

Optimus 8R stove.

Spare parts for stove. Clockwise, from left: wick, tank lid, burner plate, cleaning needle. Center: gasket for tank lid. The cleaning needle should always be carried. *(Lou Clemmons)*

SVEA 123R self-cleaning stove with pot and windshield. *(A. B. Optimus, Inc.)*

stoves carry a plastic eyedropper or a short length of transparent plastic tubing as part of their stove kit. Either of these can be dipped into the fuel tank to extract a very small quantity of fuel. This fuel is placed in the bowl at the base of the vaporizing tube, the fuel tank cap is then closed, and the control valve is turned to the closed position. It is necessary to work fairly fast, because the gasoline quickly vaporizes. The fuel in the bowl or spirit cup is then ignited. Within a few seconds, just as the flame in the spirit cup is about to go out, the control valve is opened. The stove should start burning at this point and should soon be burning with a roar. If the stove fails to start on the first try, you will need to repeat the entire procedure.

Instead of using gasoline for priming, some backpackers use a solid fuel, such as heat tabs or fire-starting ribbon, placed in the bowl at the base of the burner. Since these do not vaporize, they generally provide a surer, better-controlled start than gasoline does.

A few gas stoves are provided with built-in pumps. Starting such stoves is comparatively easy. You simply pump until some fuel comes out of the burner jet and trickles down into the depression at the base of the burner. The Optimus Company markets a separate minipump, about 2½ inches long and weighing about 2 ounces, that can be used on the SVEA 123, 8R, 80, and certain other stoves. The pump is made with a pressure cap that replaces the filler cap on the stove while the pump is being used. Still another starting method is to remove the fuel tank cap and blow into the opening to create the necessary pressure.

Some important precautions must be taken in operating these stoves. If they must be operated inside a tent, snow cave, or other closed space, adequate ventilation and other factors require careful consideration, as discussed in Chapter 11 on safety. Better to have a cold meal in your tent than no tent. After the stove has cooled, and before it is packed away, the fuel tank cap should be momentarily loosened to relieve the vacuum in the tank. The fuel supply should be checked before starting to cook. Obviously, the fuel cap should never be opened or loosened during stove operation. If the fuel is used up during the cooking, the stove should be allowed to cool before it is refilled. When the stove is not to be used for some time, it should be drained of fuel. Aluminum fuel bottles with tight-fitting caps (and pouring caps) are available from equipment suppliers and should always be used for carrying gasoline for your stove.

Minipump. This pump can be used with a number of stoves and makes for easier stove operation.

Basic SVEA stove, fuel container, and special pour spout.

Kerosene stoves. Kerosene stoves must be primed prior to lighting, so as to vaporize the fuel, in a manner similar to that used for the gasoline stoves just described. However, alcohol must be used for priming kerosene stoves. Kerosene will not work as a primer, and white gas is dangerous to use for this purpose. A kerosene stove is smellier than most other stoves. However, kerosene is less volatile than gasoline. A kerosene stove is therefore generally safer to use. All kerosene stoves have hand pumps on the fuel tank. The flame height is controlled solely by the amount of pressure in the tank; the more pressure, the hotter the flame. Kerosene stoves are available with both "roarer" and "silent" burners. Since full pressure is maintained by pumping, these stoves are well suited for very cold-weather use, being more reliable in such weather than stoves without pumps. Safety valves are not necessary for kerosene stoves, as they are for gas stoves, since kerosene does not build up dangerous pressure.

A popular model of kerosene stove is the Optimus 00. Its dimensions are about 3½ by 5½ inches, and it is 7 inches high. It weighs about 25 ounces. The stove collapses for easy packing. The cost is about $30.

The Optimus 45 is a fairly large kerosene stove. It has a roarer burner and a wide burner plate. It is 8½ inches in diameter and 8 inches high. Weight is 40 ounces; cost, about $36.

Alcohol stoves. Backpack stoves that burn alcohol for fuel are available, but you may have to look quite a while to find one. Only a relatively few backpack equipment shops carry alcohol stoves. They are not very popular among backpackers. One reason is that alcohol has only about half the BTU rating of white gas and kerosene. (This means that you need to carry twice the amount of alcohol to obtain the same total heat provided by a given amount of gas or kerosene.) The alcohol fuel is also quite expensive, costing about $5 per gallon. On the other hand, alcohol stoves are simple to use, they will not explode, and they are nontoxic. However, cooking time and the extra weight of fuel to be carried are major disadvantages. Those who normally carry canned heat or heat tabs for making an occasional cup of soup or hot tea would probably consider these stoves worthwhile.

Butane stoves. The butane stoves are popular with some backpackers. For simplicity of operation, they are virtually foolproof. Butane fuel is a liquid contained in a thin metal cylinder under low pressure. A control valve allows the fuel to escape from the cylinder to a burner device, and upon contact with the air the fuel vaporizes. A lighted match is applied to the burner, the control valve is opened, and you are in business. By varying the position of the control valve, you can adjust the flame over a considerable range.

Butane does not have the BTU output per unit weight that gasoline or kerosene does. Therefore, butane stoves are best suited for short trips and those where a minimum of cooking is to be done. Cooking time is longer and more fuel must be carried for a given amount of cooking. Another dis-

Optimus 77A alcohol stove with three-piece cookset.

advantage is that as fuel is used from the cartridge, the heat output drops and the cooking time gradually increases until the cartridge empties. The empty cartridges are trash that must go into the litterbag and be carried out of the back country. At temperatures below freezing, operation is less efficient; it stops altogether at 15° F, at which temperature the butane freezes solid. In planning for breakfast on a cold morning, it may be necessary to put the butane cartridge in your sleeping bag at night, to keep it at operating temperature.

The Bleuet S200 is a commonly used butane backpack stove. It weighs 14 ounces by itself and 24 ounces with one fuel cartridge. It is 8½ inches high and 3½ inches in diameter. The butane cartridges are purchased separately, weigh 10 ounces full, and contain about 7 fluidounces of

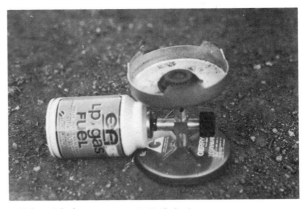

A lightweight butane stove. (J. R. Guinn)

fuel. When in use, the stove tips readily. A base comes with the stove, but a broader improvised base is desirable. The stove costs about $14, with one cartridge. It is important in using this stove to place the cartridge on the stove exactly in accordance with directions. Otherwise it may blow off, and you may end up chasing a burning cartridge through the brush. Once it is correctly attached, the fuel cartridge cannot be removed until it is empty. In a high wind, shielding is required, or the flame may blow out. For summertime use and limited cooking, this stove has proven to be quite popular.

Another stove in this general category is the Gerry Mini Stove. It is 4½ inches high assembled and weighs about 8 ounces without cartridge, thus making it a very lightweight stove. The Gerry cartridges weigh 10 ounces when full and cost about $1.50. The cartridges are special and are not widely found in stores, or even backpack equipment shops. Cost of the stove is about $14. The EFI Mini stove is very similar to the Gerry Mini. Weight is 8 ounces without cartridge. As with the Gerry Mini, there may be some difficulty in locating cartridges. Cost of the stove is about $15.

Propane stoves. Propane is bottled at a somewhat higher pressure than butane is. It is superior to butane for cold-weather use since it

TABLE 11. REPRESENTATIVE BACKPACKING STOVES

Model	Type of Fuel	Capacity of Tank or Cartridge (in pints)	Minutes to Boil 1 Quart Water at Sea Level*	Dimensions (in inches)	Weight Without Fuel (in ounces)	Approx. Cost
Optimus 8R	White gas	⅓	7 to 8	5 × 5 × 3	23	$28
SVEA 123R	White gas	¼	6 to 7	5 × 4	20	26
Optimus 111B	White gas	1	4 to 5	6¾ × 7 × 4	56	52
Optimus 00	Kerosene	1	5 to 6	5½ × 3½ × 7	26	30
Optimus 45	Kerosene	1¾	6 to 7	8 × 8½	39	40
Bleuet S200	Butane	¾	10 to 12	8½ × 3½	14	14
Gerry Mini	Butane	⅔	7 to 9	5 × 4½	7½	15
Primus Grasshopper	Propane	1¾	8 to 10	11 × 3 × 3	11½	11
Optimus 77A	Alcohol	1½	8 to 10	4½ × 8	28	20

*In a wind, heat output will vary considerably and will thus affect the boiling time.

freezes at −50° F. The higher pressure requires heavier cylinders than for butane: weight, about 1 pound each (empty). The Primus Grasshopper (#2361) is a good backpack stove in this category. It has dimensions of 11¼ by 3 by 3 inches and weighs 40 ounces, with fuel cylinder. The cylinders are not reusable. Extra cylinders cost about $2. The stove, without fuel cylinder, costs about $11. The empty cylinders may grow heavy in the pack, but they must be packed out with other litter. If they were packed in full, they can certainly be packed out empty. This applies to absolutely all such canisters.

Using canister stoves. In using butane and propane canister stoves, there are certain precautions that should be taken. They are relatively simple to use compared to the gasoline and kerosene stoves, but they are not foolproof. Some very serious accidents have occurred in the use of these stoves. In using those in which the canister connects to the stove by a screw thread, care should be taken that the threads and point of connection are clean and that a good connection is made. Cross-threading, and leakage, may occur if this operation is performed too hastily. A poor connection between the stove and canister can be a real hazard. In connecting the cartridge to the stove, it is important to do so exactly in accordance with the manufacturer's directions. Otherwise it may blow off. A poor connection may also allow fuel to leak, and the stove may become enveloped in flame. When in use, the fuel canister should be well ventilated. Serious accidents have resulted from piling rocks in such a way that the canister was partially enclosed. This subjects the canister to overheating and possible explosion.

It is difficult to tell just how much fuel remains in the cartridge. For rough estimating, you can record the minutes of operation as the cartridge is used for cooking, and thus have a guesstimate of how much cooking time remains.

Many of the gasoline stoves have built-in windscreens or are furnished with a separate windscreen. Few of the canister stoves do. Regardless, it is important to protect *any* backpack stove from the wind, insofar as possible, when in use. It is a good idea to cook on the lee side of a boulder, log, or other natural wind barrier. Windscreens can be purchased as a separate item, and they can also be made at home.

Fuel supplies. Extra gasoline and kerosene should be carried only in tightly closed metal containers specifically designed for the purpose. In a group where common equipment is being shared, one person should carry the stove and extra fuel in his or her pack for the entire trip. That person should not carry any food items. Food is easily contaminated by fuel fumes and odor when food and stove are carried together.

In those situations where one person *must* carry the stove and fuel as well as food, some special precautions are necessary. It is recommended that the food be carried as high in the pack as possible. The stove and fuel should be carried in a lower compartment and wrapped in double poly bags, or similar precautions should be taken to see that the fuel does not contaminate other items. The conventional quart fuel bottles will fit nicely in the outside pocket of some packbags.

Keep extra gasoline well back from the burning stove while cooking. The burning stove should never be set near an open fire or other intense heat. It may explode. This can happen when pine needles or other material near the stove accidentally catch fire, so keep the stove away from any such material. Plan your cooking operation so that it is not necessary to refill a stove while it is hot. A gasoline stove should be watched just as closely as a wood fire. If the stove goes out, it should be relit at once.

In using canister stoves, it should be noted that fuel in the used cartridge may leak. The fumes not only have a horrible smell but can contaminate food and equipment with their odor. Placing tape over the cartridge orifice will usually take care of this problem. Also, an "empty" cartridge may contain enough fuel to be dangerous in the vicinity of an open flame. Stove cartridges should *not* be changed near an open fire.

WOOD—FIRE COOKING

The use of wood fires for cooking in wilderness areas is becoming less and less common, particularly in the well-used areas. As greater numbers of backpackers take to the woods, areas that once had a sufficient supply of dead wood for cooking are being rapidly depleted of such wood. However, there are still some areas where dead wood is available, and if forest conditions permit, a cooking fire is in order if that is the way you wish to cook. A fire-building permit may be required in some government-controlled areas.

The cooking fire. Sticks lying on the ground should be the source of wood for cooking fires. Limbs, either dead or alive, should not be broken off trees. The same applies to limbs on logs lying on the ground. These are part of the landscape, and to break off such limbs is to mar the natural scenery of the area. If an adequate wood supply cannot be obtained from sticks lying on the ground, then a cold meal, or a meal cooked on a backpack stove, is in order.

If there have been recent rains, it may be necessary to look under cliff overhangs, in hollow trees, under large trees lying on the ground, in rock crevices, and in similar protected places in order to find dry wood for starting the fire. Once a good fire is going, it is possible to dry out fairly wet wood by laying it very near or on the fire and then removing it (for later use) before it starts to burn.

It is important to have a good wood supply *before* starting to cook. Nothing is worse than having the fire die down when the meal is about half cooked and then having to stop everything and go look for more wood.

If the fire is being built near a stream, it is usually possible to find in the stream bed a spot of sand or dirt free from small rocks, or a large, flat solid stone area on which to build the fire. When a fire is laid on shale, porous rock, or wet stones, some of the stones may explode and cause injury.

If the fire is being built in a previously used camping area, it is possible that there will be one or more fire rings where fires were made before. If so, an existing fire ring should be used rather than making a new one. Each new ring further mars the ground surface. The only exception to not using an existing fire ring would be in the case that it had been built in an unsafe place, such as under a low overhanging tree limb, close to a stump, or near a large log.

If the fire is to be built away from a stream, every precaution should be taken to build the fire on sand, dirt, or solid rock. It should be built well away from brush, dead grass, and overhanging tree limbs—and never on the duff of a forest floor. Neither should fires be built against a log or a tree stump, or between two parallel logs. The result will mar the landscape. Even worse, such a fire is next to impossible to put out, if you are to be absolutely sure that it is out. It may require considerable time to find a suitable place for a fire and to exercise the necessary precautions to assure that there is no fire hazard. If the group is not willing to take that time, or if such a place just isn't available, then you must use a backpack stove or eat a cold meal.

It is important to have an ample supply of small twigs, pine needles, or other tinder, as well as kindling, handy before starting to build a fire.

Fire-starting aids.

The contents of the litterbag should not be overlooked for bits of paper and other burnables. Leaves, incidentally, are not usually good fire-starting material. Even though dry, they will often just smoulder and not be very helpful. The less ideal the fire-making conditions, the more tinder and kindling should be gathered. Many people arrange their twigs and other tinder in the form of a small tepee, hold a lighted country match near the bottom until the tinder ignites, and then add larger twigs and sticks. This is generally a satisfactory approach. Frequently, however, the match will go out just when the twigs are about to begin to burn. Oftentimes quite a few matches will be used up in these false starts. That is where fire-starting aids are useful. Fire cubes or pellets, fire-starting jelly, or a candle will save time. The tepee method can be used with these aids. I often use another approach, however. I select a stick 1½ to 3 inches in diameter and prop one end of my twigs, pine needles, and so forth on this stick. This leaves an open space next to the stick, under the tinder. I hold a burning candle in this hollow until the platform of tinder is well ignited, then withdraw the candle for future use. It is important to shield the fire from the wind when it is first started and to add *small* tinder, a little at a time. Oftentimes fire builders are too quick to add large sticks, and their first effort peters out.

If rain is expected, a plastic sheet 6 or 8 feet square can be a big help. Dry twigs, small sticks, pine needles, and whatnot, can be gathered in the evening and placed under the sheet, and the corners weighted with rocks. Then if there is rain, there will be some dry fire-starting materials available in the morning.

For a group of three or four people cooking together, at least one person's job should be to help the cook with the food and to feed the fire so that it burns steadily. Fires should always be small, and a small wood fire will burn down quickly if not constantly attended to. It should be fed a *few* sticks at a time, never building it up into a big fire. A large fire wastes wood and is uncomfortable to cook with.

As soon as the fire is going well, cooking can be started. Cooking over coals may be a bit more romantic (and necessary for some cooking), but heat is heat, and it doesn't matter to food (or water) inside a utensil whether the heat is coming from coals or an open flame. A lot of time will be wasted and there will be some very hungry people getting restless for food if you wait for coals. It is important to have a controlled flame, however. The fire should not be blazing all around the pans one minute and near extinction ten minutes later.

When the cooking and dishwashing are completed, the fire should be put out with water, dirt, or sand, and every precaution should be taken to see that it is completely out. More than one wood fire that was supposed to be out has blazed up again after the campers' departure, especially with the aid of a little wind. This is one way of starting a forest fire. It is important to poke around in the ashes with a stick (or your hand) to be sure that they are thoroughly cool. A cooking fire (or any other fire) should *never* be left unattended in the woods, even for very short periods. When a group goes to bed at night, any fire should be put out just as completely as though they were leaving the area. Any party that "had" to keep a fire going all night for warmth should best keep the story to themselves. Unless the situation was a *real* emergency, this is simply admitting that they were not properly prepared. It is a very poor practice.

The dingle stick.   There are numerous ways of suspending pans over the fire for cooking. They can be set on two parallel stones or suspended from a tripod or from a ridgepole supported by forked stakes. Another way, which can usually be quickly implemented and will not be likely to dump the cooking pots into the fire, is the dingle stick.

The dingle stick is a pole about 8 to 10 feet long, 3 to 4 inches in diameter at the base, and 1 or 2 inches in diameter at the tip.

The dingle stick is rigged so that the large end is on the ground (away from the fire) and the other end is suspended over the fire, about 18 to 20 inches above the ground. Laying the dingle stick, at about its midpoint, over a rock or short

Backpacker grill. This is another method of supporting pans over an open fire.

log will elevate the tip end. The base end is weighted with several rocks to hold it in place.

If a three-wire flexible bail is installed on cooking pans, as discussed earlier, the pans can be easily suspended on a dingle stick so that they will not tip. If the fire is kept small, as it should be, there will be no danger of burning the dingle stick.

Grates.   Some backpack equipment shops stock wire grates that are suitable for supporting cooking pans over an open fire. Some weigh as little as 4 ounces. Many of the available grates have no legs, making it necessary to find two or more good-sized rocks to hold the grate. The rocks must be of roughly equal height, essentially flat on top, and tip proof. Even in an area that has many rocks, it is no easy job to find several just the right size. It should be pointed out that, from an ecology standpoint, a grate without legs is undesirable. The rocks that are used for support are going to get very black from the cooking fire. Unless a fire ring and suitable rocks are found that have been used by previous backpackers, then blackening "new" rocks is going to deface the landscape a bit. I have not yet met backpackers in the wilderness who were scrubbing rocks to remove the soot caused by their cooking fire.

Grates with folding legs are available. A lightweight grate, with legs, having a surface area about 6 by 12 inches, weighs as little as 12 ounces and costs about $4. More rugged versions with slightly larger surfaces will weigh about 32 ounces and cost $5 or $6. The design and strength of attachment of the legs to the grate top frequently leave something to be desired. Many are designed so that there is a "bump" in the grate surface at each point where a leg is attached. This effectively reduces the usable surface area. If a flush mounting is used, one more cooking utensil can be set on the grate than can be set on the same size grate that does not have the legs flush mounted.

Like cooking utensils used over an open fire, a grate will become thoroughly covered with soot after each use. A sturdy cloth carrying bag will be needed to keep the grate from blackening other equipment.

Extension handles.   Even a small wood cooking fire can be uncomfortably hot when a person is continuously close to it while cooking. Since a skillet will often be held while it is being used, it is a good idea to use an extension handle with it. Find a piece of stout wood about 1½ inches in diameter and break it to a length of about 24 to 30 inches. Place one end alongside the skillet handle. Wrap the two handles together at several places with a good cloth tape or with wire. You can also use two automobile radiator hose clamps instead of tape or wire and get a more positive fastening. Use the type of radiator hose clamps that have a screw thread adjustment. For special-purpose cooking (such as for popcorn) an extension handle can also be used with the cooking pans in the same manner, placing the hose clamps very close together on the stub of the pan handle. The handle of a spoon will usually fit the screw head for adjusting the hose clamps. If not, a little modification of the end of the handle with a file before leaving home will make it fit.

When a skillet is being held while cooking, the

Two automobile radiator hose clamps, used as shown here, will hold a skillet securely to an extension handle.

Extension handle for skillet. A handle five or six feet long, supported on a rock, will keep the cook from getting uncomfortably hot during the relatively short period that is required for most frying.

Dingle stick. This is a good method for suspending pans over an open fire and is quickly rigged. Note the three-wire flexible bails on the pans; this is more spillproof than a single heavy-wire bail.

One of the problems of wood-fire cooking is finding lightweight devices for holding or suspending pots, pans, and skillets over the open fire. Shown here are some recommended devices and methods.

least tiring way is to find a log or stone on which to rest the extension handle (at the end nearest the skillet).

Using cooking pans. Dishwashing is frequently a chore, especially the job of washing out the cooking pans. Remains of oatmeal, macaroni, stew, or whatever else you cooked in the pans will cling stubbornly to the sides and bottom. However, this problem can be essentially eliminated. Carry a small bottle of cooking oil and one or two ordinary paper towels. Before you start to cook, use a very small piece of paper towel soaked in cooking oil to thoroughly coat the entire inside surface of each cooking pan. Several special products are also available for this purpose. One goes under the name of Vegalene. After thoroughly coating the inside of your pans with the oil, add water and go ahead with your cooking process in the normal manner. When it is dishwashing time, you will find that pans prepared in this manner clean very easily.

DISHWASHING

Water for dishwashing can be heated in a cooking pan. As soon as a pan has been emptied during a meal, it should be rough-cleaned. Water can then be added and the pan put back on the fire so that the water can heat while the meal is being finished.

Soap or a biodegradable detergent can be used in washing dishes. A scouring pad, nylon netting, or other aid will usually be necessary for removing all bits of food. Before the dishes are washed, each person should rough-clean his or her own eating utensils. It is recommended that all cooking and eating gear be rinsed in clean, very hot water that has been boiled for a few minutes. Utensils can be held for rinsing with needle-nosed pliers or a similar tool. A cup can be used to dip the hot water and pour it over the utensil. The utensils can then be dropped directly into their cloth carrying bag. The use of dishcloths and dishtowels is not recommended. They are not needed, drying them is a problem, and after a few meals they will look as though they had been used to wash the family car.

A Teflon-coated skillet is usually easily cleaned in either cold or warm water, without soap. An aluminum or steel skillet may require special effort to get it clean. Washing in cold water won't help much. Using a small amount of warm water, a pot scratcher, and soap will usually do the job.

After all other items have been washed, the cooking pans can be rinsed. I never try to scour soot off the outside of the pans. I take a quick pass over the outside, however, to remove *loose* dirt or soot. With coordination and cooperation, dishwashing can usually be done in ten minutes.

RESPONSIBILITY

It is again emphasized that the food and all matters pertaining to menus, food packaging, and cooking should be under the overall supervision of one person—the cook. This is one of the most important functions connected with any backpack trip. If the responsibility is divided, or if it is changed from meal to meal or day to day, the results will probably be less than satisfactory.

This does not mean that the cook should not get the advice of others on certain matters pertaining to food. Others *should* be consulted, especially in the planning of food and menus before leaving home. However, after the group is on the trail the cook should have overall responsibility for the food and cooking, even though others will be assisting. In a haphazard operation, with various people getting into the food and being responsible for the cooking, there will be too much or too little of certain foods at some meals, and you will probably run out of some food items before you had planned to. There will probably be some foods that are either underdone or overcooked.

The cook should know or have a record of the recipe of every item of food on the menu. He should give overall supervision to the preparation of every food item at every meal, even though others are preparing it or helping in the preparation. While others are washing dishes, the cook will be repacking the food, getting it ready for the trail again, putting some foods to soak for the next meal, and making up equal loads of food and cooking gear for distribution to each backpacker. The cook has an important job. Give him your full support, and it will pay off in the long run with better food, better dispositions, and a more enjoyable trip in general.

COOKING GEAR SUMMARY

The cooking gear and accessories to be carried on a backpack trip will depend considerably on whether you plan to cook on a backpack stove, over an open fire, or perhaps use a combination of the two. For arriving at a weight for cooking gear, it will be assumed that the cooking is to be done on a backpack stove.

There are a number of good backpack stoves available. I frequently carry the Sigg Tourist Cook Kit, with SVEA stove, which is one of the lightest and most compact stove-cook kits available. With proper choice of menus it will serve adequately for three people. This kit—including stove, stove housing, windscreen, two pans (2½- and 3½-pint), pot gripper, lid fry pan, eyedropper, funnel, and match supply, all in a lightweight cloth carrying bag (handmade)—weighs 39 ounces. (Eyedropper, funnel, and match supply were added to kit.)

A summary of the typical cooking gear for a week-long backpack trip for three is given in Table 12. Some possible additional items are listed in Table 13.

TABLE 12. RECOMMENDED COOKING GEAR

Item	Approximate Weight (in ounces)
Stove and accessories: backpack stove, windscreen, two pans, pan gripper, small frying pan, eyedropper, funnel, match supply, and cloth carrying bag	39
Fuel for stove: 1 qt. in aluminum fuel bottle	30
Dishwashing items: small sponge, pot scratcher, biodegradable soap	4
Other: two tablespoons and G.I. can opener	2
	75

TABLE 13. OPTIONAL COOKING GEAR

Item	Approximate Weight (in ounces)
Frying pan, Teflon	12
Grate (with folding legs)	12
Grill, backpack (no legs)	4½
Jar, pint-size (for soaking food)	2
Reflector oven	42
Spatula	1½

10 The Complete Pack Load

Previous chapters have discussed packs, sleeping gear, shelter, clothing, food, and cooking equipment. Other items that make up the complete pack load are discussed in this chapter. Those who may be beginners in the sport of backpacking will want to proceed cautiously in this area. It is possible to invest a lot of money in nonessential knickknacks. It is likely that many such items will be left at home when the beginner becomes an austere backpacker and starts paring away at the ounces in his or her pack.

ESSENTIAL EQUIPMENT

There are certain items of equipment that are considered to be essential. In general, these are items necessary to assure the person's well-being and safety, or to cope with an unexpected emergency. If the backpacker gets separated from the group, is injured, or meets with some other unusual situation, having these items and knowing how to use them may be important in survival.

Each backpacker should normally carry *all* of the essential items, so that he or she will be self-sufficient. Possible exceptions (for some items) would be a family group that will stay together at all times while on the trail. Those who are traveling only well-marked, heavily populated trails might not consider all items to be essential. Certain qualifying statements are given in the discussion of the individual items in the paragraphs

that follow. In addition to the basic outfit (pack, sleeping gear, shelter, clothing, food, and cooking equipment) the following items are considered essential:

Fire-making equipment	Map and Compass
Canteen with water	Extra clothing
Pocketknife	Sunglasses
Flashlight (with fresh batteries)	Signaling device
First aid kit	Extra food

Fire-making equipment. You may be planning to do all your cooking over a backpack stove. However, if wood fires are allowed, you may want to carry some fire-building equipment for an occasional wood fire. Regardless of whether wood fires are permitted or not, fire-building equipment should be carried for *emergency* use. You may get lost, or soaked in a rainstorm, and require a wood fire for survival. Your stove may break down.

The name *country matches,* or *kitchen matches,* is usually applied to those matches having a "handle" about 2½ inches long. It is recommended that about four or five country matches be carried, in a waterproof container, for every fire that may be required. To save time and to assure that a fire can be started under difficult conditions, a few other fire-making aids are also recommended. A plumber's candle or an ordinary candle stub, flammable pellets, or fire ribbon can be used. Still another fire aid, which is especially good in damp, muggy weather, is a short length of gum rubber hose with metal tubing on the end. With this you can direct a draft to the fire just where you want it. It is usually better than fanning the fire with your hat or a plate, or blowing on it.

In addition to fire-making equipment carried for use by the group, it is suggested that *each member* carry some such equipment for possible survival use in the event that he or she should get lost or separated from the group under adverse conditions. As a minimum it is recommended that each person carry about fifteen or twenty country matches, in a waterproof container, and a candle stub for this purpose (weight about 2 ounces).

If fire permits are required for the area you are going into, it is a good plan to get one even though you may not intend to use it.

Canteen. On most backpack trips you should carry a canteen. Admittedly, there are some areas where good drinking water is so plentiful that a canteen may not seem necessary. However, although water is plentiful, there will frequently be some doubt as to its *purity*. It isn't very convenient to carry a cooking pan of water along the trail while you are waiting for Halazone or iodine tablets placed in the pan to purify the water. A canteen is much better for the purpose. You may also want to mix a quart of fruit punch to drink on the trail. Again, a canteen or water bottle is most convenient.

Even though you drink water frequently during the day, it is not unusual to wake up during the night feeling very thirsty. A canteen of water near your sleeping bag will be very welcome at such times.

It is extremely important to know the availability of drinking water along the route you will be traveling. It should be remembered that the flow of some springs varies from year to year and from season to season. A spring that was good last year may be dry this year. Unless you are thoroughly familiar with the trail and know positively that there will be good drinking water at frequent intervals, then by all means carry a canteen. It can save your life. Running out of water can be one of the most serious problems encountered in wilderness camping.

A quart of water should last from three to five hours, depending on the weather and your level of exertion. If in doubt, carry two quarts.

A good alternative to a conventional canteen is a widemouthed, quart-size bottle of unbreakable plastic. I have found that such a bottle slips in and out of the side pocket on my pack somewhat easier than a canteen. It is also more convenient than a canteen (because of the wide mouth) to use for mixing fruit drinks, powdered milk, and so on.

Knife. A good pocketknife should be carried. Some prefer a fairly large pocketknife. I have one that is 4¾ inches long, weighs 3½ ounces, and has a large blade that locks in open position. I often carry a smaller two-blade pocketknife. I also have a Swiss army knife that I sometimes use. I find that I seldom use all the accessories on the Swiss army knife, however. The boy scout knives are quite popular with some hikers.

A sheath knife should not be carried on a backpack trip. It is too large and heavy and, if carried on the belt, will interfere with the waist strap of your packframe. It is not a good eating tool, and one of the primary purposes of your pocketknife will be to eat with, taking the place of a conventional table knife.

Depending on the anticipated use of your knife (much cleaning of fish for instance), you may want to carry a small whetstone. On the average backpack trip, however, a whetstone is not usually required. Having a good whetstone at home and sharpening your knife just prior to the backpack trip will usually suffice.

A good, serviceable pocketknife can be purchased for as little as $4 or $5. Those with a variety of accessories will cost a minimum of about $10, and some will run as high as $20 to $30.

Flashlight. A large flashlight is not generally required. With few exceptions, camp should be made, the evening meal prepared, and dishes washed before dark. If you start each day at daylight or soon after, you will be ready for your sleeping bag soon after dark. Admittedly, there is usually a bull session at night to review the events of the day and to do some planning for the next day. However, you do not need a flashlight for this. The requirement for a flashlight is therefore simple. You need the light to find your way from the bull session area to your sleeping bag. You can undress and get ready for the sleeping bag in the dark, except for an occasional beam of light to see to untie a shoe or stow your clothes. If you wake up thirsty during the night, you may also need the flashlight to find your canteen (which should be near the head of your sleeping

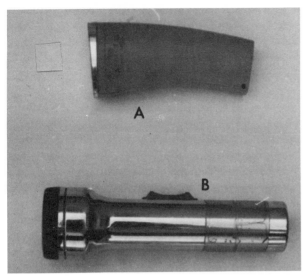

Mallory flashlight. The Mallory flashlight (A) is shown in comparison with an ordinary two-cell C-size flashlight (B).

bag). It all adds up to about three to five minutes of intermittent light required each night.

A standard D-size, two-cell flashlight can be used (weight about 11 ounces with batteries). If for some reason members of a group plan to spend some significant time on the trail at night, they will probably want one or more of these flashlights in the party. The smaller C-size flashlight can also be used and will weigh less (about 5 ounces with batteries). The recommended flashlight for the average backpacker, however, is the Mallory. It throws a good beam, is lightweight (about 3½ ounces with batteries), and is quite durable. It uses two AA penlight batteries and a PR 4 bulb. Long-life alkaline batteries are recommended. The Mallory flashlight is compact in size and can be held in the mouth if you need to work with both hands. The cost is about $2.50.

Ordinary penlights cannot be recommended. Most of them are so cheaply constructed and unreliable as to be worthless to the backpacker.

Most flashlights can be prevented from coming on accidentally while in the pack by reversing *one* of the batteries. (Some flashlights will still work if both batteries are reversed.) With the Mallory flashlight the switch can simply be taped in the Off position during the day to prevent the light from coming on accidentally.

Two new long-life alkaline batteries will usually be adequate for a week-long backpack trip. Depending upon your experience and how much you usually use your flashlight at night, you may wish to carry spare batteries. It is recommended that a spare bulb *always* be carried. Used batteries are trash and should, of course, be packed back

to the trailhead with other trash. Used batteries should never be thrown in a fire. There is a good chance that they will explode.

First aid kit.

INDIVIDUAL KIT.   Except for a family group, it is recommended that each hiker carry a first aid kit. It need not be elaborate but should contain items for treatment of minor difficulties that frequently occur on the trail, as well as provide for certain unexpected emergencies (such as snakebite). The following items are recommended, as a minimum, for an individual first aid kit:

Band-Aids — about 3 to 6.
Sterile gauze pads — 3 pads, 3″ × 3″.
Adhesive tape — 1 small roll, 1″ wide. Can be rerolled on tongue blade or stick.
Aspirin tablets — 6 to 10, depending upon length of trip and past needs.
Salt tablets — 6 to 10, depending upon length of trip and weather. Should be of the coated variety, to avoid nausea.
Needle — for removing splinters and opening blisters.
Razor blade, single-edged — for cutting tape and moleskin and removing hair.
Moleskin or molefoam — for covering sore areas on feet, to avoid blisters.
Antiseptic washcloth — in small foil packet.
Matches — 3 or 4, for sterilizing needle.
Snakebite kit, suction type — depending upon region and season.
Milk of magnesia tablets — 6 to 10, for constipation and upset stomach.
Glycerin suppositories — 2 or 3, for constipation, if individual's past experience indicates need for such.
Small booklet or instruction sheet on first aid. (A small first aid booklet weighing 1 ounce is available from Johnson & Johnson, New Brunswick, New Jersey 08903.)

If a wound occurs on a part of the body thickly covered by hair, it may be desirable to remove some of this hair before dressing the wound. Also, the suction cup on a snakebite kit will not work too well if that part of the skin is covered with hair. Such hair can be readily removed with a sharp single-edged razor blade (no soap or water needed), by holding the blade almost parallel to the skin.

Some people are highly allergic to bee, wasp, and other insect bites. If you are in this category, it is advisable to carry some Benadryl tablets or a similar medication, as advised by your physician. If you are regularly taking some prescription medicine, then this can be either added to the first aid kit or placed elsewhere in the pack.

The items listed above can be easily packed into a small aluminum box. My first aid kit is 1⅜ by 3¾ by 5¼ inches and has a weight of about 7½ ounces when filled. An oval aluminum container of similar capacity, readily available at many backpacking equipment supply stores, can also be used. Some people carry their first aid supplies in a plastic bag.

If the purity of the water in the area is questionable, it is recommended that each hiker carry water purification tablets. Halazone or iodine tablets can be used. Iodine tablets are recommended, because Halazone tablets lose their strength and effectiveness after a period of storage. It is recommended that the water purification tablets be carried in the same pocket of your pack as your canteen or water bottle, so that they will be readily available. They will then be more likely to be used if the occasion arises. If the taste of the purified water is considered objectionable, fruit drink powder or lemon crystals can be used to alter the taste due to the water purification tablets.

GROUP KIT. For a group that plans to stay together at all times while on the trail, the items listed above for the individual first aid kit should be adequate. Some additional items should be carried for the benefit of the group. The following items are recommended:

> Antibiotic ointment—½-oz. tube.
> Pain-killer—Codeine, Darvon, or other tablets for severe pain. Consult your doctor.
> Ophthalmic ointment—⅛ oz., for eye injuries. Consult your doctor.
> Elastic bandage—3″-wide Ace bandage, for sprains.
> Triangle bandage—for sling.
> Inflatable splint—for arm or leg.
> Antidiarrhea medication—Consult your doctor.
> Butterfly Band-Aids—for closing cuts. You can make your own from adhesive tape.
> Scissors—small pair.
> Tweezers—1 pair.
> Gauze pads—6 sterile pads, several sizes.
> Ammonia inhalant—for fainting.
> Antivenin kit—for snakebite, if in snake country.
> Ethyl chloride—1 tube, for use in treating snakebite.

You should get expert pretrip instruction on the use of the antivenin kit and the ethyl chloride. For example, you must know the horse serum sensitivity of the patient before using antivenin. Ethyl chloride, if sprayed directly on the skin, can cause sloughing of the tissue, with very serious results. It should be sprayed on a cloth, which is then carefully applied to the skin. (Ethyl chloride in a metal tube container with a valve and spray nozzle on top is recommended.) The last two items are recommended only if the area has a reputed population of poisonous snakes. I frequently carry these items on my backpack trips. I recognize that they are somewhat controversial, however. I strongly recommend that you seek the advice of your physician, both to satisfy yourself on the desirability of carrying these items and for expert advice on their use, if you do carry them.

An instruction booklet on first aid is also recommended. One such booklet that is very good is *Mountaineering Medicine* by Fred T. Darvill, Jr., M.D. The booklet measures 4¼ by 6⅝ inches and weighs 1½ ounces. It is available for $1 from Skagit Mountain Rescue Unit, Inc., P.O. Box 2, Mount Vernon, WA 98273.

All items listed, excluding the antivenin kit and ethyl chloride, have an approximate weight of 10 ounces. The antivenin kit and ethyl chloride weigh 5 ounces and 6 ounces respectively.

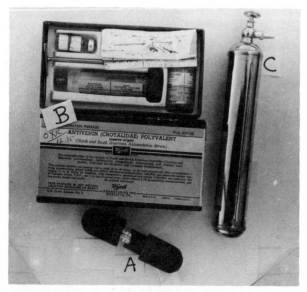

Cutter suction kit (A), Antivenin kit (B), and Ethyl chloride (C). These are good items to have when traveling in a remote area where rattlesnakes are prevalent. The same antivenin is also effective for water moccasin and copperhead snakebite.

Map and compass. In a small group a map and compass for the group will ordinarily be sufficient. However, in remote and unfamiliar regions it is recommended that each hiker have a map and compass. To become proficient in their use, practice is important. It is best to practice using map and compass in familiar areas so that you will be capable and confident in their use when they are really needed. For this reason it is recommended that each individual carry a map and compass and practice using them, even though the group is in familiar territory.

To be oriented means to know where you are. On most trips into wilderness areas or other back country you will be following trails that will be marked. You should stay oriented at all times, following your progress on a map and knowing at all times where you are on the map. In the United States the topographic maps put out by the U.S. Geological Survey will be found most helpful to the average backpacker. These maps show all the important natural features, as well as main trails. Elevations are shown by contour lines, and this is an important feature when traveling in rugged terrain. For the Western states, an index of the maps, as well as the maps themselves (costing about $1.25 each), is available from the U.S. Geological Survey, Denver Federal Center, Denver, Colorado 80225. Some very useful maps of forest and wilderness areas are available from the U.S. Forest Service and are usually free. They can be obtained at ranger stations or requested by mail from headquarters of national forests. Other sources for maps and trail information are listed in Appendix D.

It frequently happens that your route will cover only a relatively small portion of the total map. It is often helpful to outline this portion, including some of the surrounding area (peaks, for example) for orienting purposes, and then have that portion of the map enlarged. A litho printer can make such an enlargement, and it will be much easier to read in the field.

Before going into an unfamiliar area, try to talk with a park ranger, rancher, or other person who is familiar with the area and go over your map with him or her. Make a sketch of your route. Note helpful landmarks, such as abandoned cabins, unusual rock formations, fallen trees across the trail, and other features that will not appear on a topographic map. If water sources are few, ask about water supply and the flow of springs shown on your map.

You should have a good compass, but it need not be expensive. A liquid-filled compass with a clear base and attached base plate is recommended. The base should have a direction-of-travel arrow and grid lines that can be aligned with a map reference line when orienting the map. Satisfactory compasses are available at $5 to $7. If the end of the needle that points north is not unmistakably marked, then you should make a small note as to which end of the compass needle (for example, the red end) points north. Use transparent tape and tape this note to the bottom of the compass.

Extra clothing. The matter of having extra items of protective clothing was discussed in Chapter 5. An individual preparing for a backpack trip will, if experienced, routinely include extra protective clothing. The amount and kind of such clothing will depend upon the season, the expected weather, possible unexpected weather, and the individual's past experience.

A person preparing for a backpack trip of a few days to a week or more will quickly realize that a considerable variety of weather may be encountered over the period and will be most likely to prepare for it. On the other hand, a day hiker starting out on a balmy spring day for a hike of six to eight hours is probably least likely to give serious thought to extra protective clothing that will be required if unexpected bad weather occurs. Also, he or she may become lost or hurt or perhaps become ill, and need to bivouac overnight. Having protective clothing and a simple shelter (plus other essentials) in the day pack may save a day hiker's life.

Sunglasses. Whether sunglasses are to be considered an essential item of equipment depends primarily on the season, your headgear, and the type of country you will be hiking in. Even with a broad-brimmed hat that shades the face and eyes, sunglasses should normally be worn in desert country, open alpine regions, and always where snow is expected. Snow blindness is serious, and you should take no chances with it. If your travel is to be primarily in forested areas and your eyes are protected by a brimmed hat, sunglasses then become an optional, rather than essential, item of equipment.

Some people prefer goggles rather than sunglasses, particularly in open alpine country and where there is snow. Those who wear prescription glasses will need to take extra care to select sunglasses that are compatible with the prescription glasses.

I find that if there is much rough hiking or

scrambling to be done, sunglasses have a habit of getting knocked out of position and need to be continually pushed back into place. The cure for this is to use an adjustable elastic band that passes around the back of the head and slips over the end of each earpiece on the glasses.

Signaling device. Normally, a group going into the backwoods (especially off the beaten path) should carry some sort of signaling device for emergency use. A sturdy high-pitched whistle is a common item in this category. Those who have participated in search-and-rescue operations for lost backpackers would probably state flatly that *every* hiker should carry a whistle. A lost hiker can soon shout himself hoarse. A shrill whistle can be heard much further than a shout, and it takes less effort. In bear country a blast on a whistle when approaching thick cover is a good precaution. Some backpackers carry a bell attached to their pack in bear country. I carry a whistle, and in bear country a good bell, costing about $0.75 and $2.00 respectively.

A metal mirror with a sighting aperture can be seen a long distance by both ground parties and aircraft. It can also be considered a toilet article for use by members of the party who wish to shave, comb their hair, and so on. A 3-by-4-inch metal mirror weighs about 2½ ounces and costs about $1.00.

Some parties will consider a smoke bomb, which produces an instant cloud of dense smoke, to be a good safety device. There are also light-weight pencil-shaped flare guns available for shooting a cartridge that produces a bright flare several hundred feet into the air.

Extra food. I know of many experienced backpackers who do not carry extra food on their trips. They plan their meals carefully, and they intend to eat, during the number of meals that are planned, essentially all the food that they take with them. If an emergency does occur, they have a considerable supply of food that can be rationed so as to make do for a longer period than orginally intended. The type of trip is probably an important factor to be considered. Those venturing into unfamiliar country, hiking far from the beaten path, or traveling in cold weather would be well advised to carry *some* extra food. Those making a "routine" trip into familiar country during mild weather may not consider it necessary.

Here again, the day hiker is one type for whom some extra food may be particularly desirable. If he gets lost or hurt, he does not have the ample

stores of food that can be rationed, as does a group on a week-long backpack trip. Although a person can go for days without food, having extra food for an emergency can provide extra energy and a boost in morale. These are important considerations if you are lost or hurt. If there is a possibility of encountering weather conducive to hypothermia, having extra food can be an important factor in saving a person's life. The extra rations should normally be high-energy, nutritious food that can be eaten cold.

OTHER IMPORTANT EQUIPMENT

Toilet articles.

SOAP.   There are a number of good bar soaps available that will lather well in hard water and can be used for personal bathing as well as washing dishes. The Vel and Zest brands are examples. About 2 ounces of soap per person per week is required for personal use. Germs are not carried by a bar of soap, so the same bar can also be used for dishwashing.

There are also some very good all-purpose biodegradable soaps, packaged in essentially spill-proof plastic bottles or tubes, that are available to backpackers. Some of these are quite good. Biosuds, Coghlan's Plus 50, and Trak are examples. They are available from some of the suppliers of backpack equipment.

Most liquid soaps available in local stores are not suitably packaged for backpacking, even though the soap itself may be suitable. If they are repackaged, it is recommended that a spill-proof container be used. If is downright disheartening when someone accidentally knocks over an unstoppered bottle of liquid soap and you watch the week's supply soak into the ground.

TOWEL, WASHCLOTH.   One small towel and washcloth per person should be sufficient. A large bath towel is too heavy and bulky. If you don't have a small one, make one from a towel remnant. If it should get too dirty, rinse it out and hang it on a line to dry overnight. Or it can be fastened to your pack to dry. Some people get by with just the washcloth and let the air do the drying. A Curity diaper is lightweight and absorbent and makes a good towel. Many experienced backpackers use them. A 16-by-36-inch size weighs 2¼ ounces.

WASHBASIN.   I find that some kind of washbasin is almost indispensable for taking a bath or just washing the hands, face, and upper body. Washing in a stream or spring is "against the rules" in wilderness areas today. I like to heat water, dipped from stream or spring, in one of the cooking pans enough to take the chill off. The washbasin can be a coffee can or one of the commercially available plastic or canvas basins. However, I consider many of the commercial plastic washbasins to be too shallow and flimsy and the canvas ones too heavy.

After much experimenting with various washbasins, I have finally settled on an unbreakable plastic bowl that some frozen foods such as ice cream are now packaged in. (I think my "washbasin" originally contained Cool Whip.) It is flexible and for all practical purposes unbreakable. It weighs 1½ ounces. It is about 3½ inches high and 6 inches in diameter.

I use my washbasin by partially filling it with water from one of the cooking utensils. By repeatedly dipping the washcloth into the basin, I can take a full-fledged "bath." I sometimes splurge and take two such basins (nesting together) — one for soaping and one for rinsing. In addition to its other benefits, I find that on the trail a daily washing is a good morale booster.

TOOTHBRUSH, TOOTHPASTE. Most people will want to carry a toothbrush. Toothpaste is considered optional. Teeth can be satisfactorily brushed with half a teaspoon of salt. Rubbing the bristles of a toothbrush against a cake of unscented soap will also provide a good cleanser for the teeth. This may not sound very appealing, but it works. Try it at home. It will leave your mouth clean and refreshed. If a tube of toothpaste is carried, it should be a very small tube or one that has been mostly used up. A full large-size tube of toothpaste weighs about 8 ounces and represents unnecessary weight.

Stories persist about backpackers sawing off part of the handle of their toothbrush in order to save weight. A full-size toothbrush about 6 inches long weighs only ⅜ to ½ ounce. If half the handle is sawed off, the difference in weight is only about ⅛ ounce, which isn't much — even to a backpacker. Also, with half the handle gone, the toothbrush is much more difficult to use.

The plastic holders (carrying cases) for toothbrushes are something else. The usual plastic toothbrush case will weigh ¾ to 1 ounce. Essentially all this weight can be saved by simply wrapping the bristle end of the toothbrush in a small square of foil or cloth. I have a strong aversion to brushing my teeth with a toothbrush which has damp, soggy bristles. I like to start with a nice dry toothbrush. For this reason I wrap the

Folding plastic washbasin, 10″ diam., 4″ high. Weight 3 oz.

Plastic homemade washbasin, 6″ diam., 3″ deep. Weight 1½ oz.

bristle end of my toothbrush with a small square of cloth and snap a rubber band over it. Utilizing the hole in the handle, I then fasten the toothbrush to one of the D rings on the outside of my pack. Result: a nice dry toothbrush when I am ready to use it.

Folding toothbrushes are available in which the container case unfolds to become part of the handle. (The bristles usually stay damp.) Still others are made so that the handle can be filled with toothpaste. I have had some rather disastrous results with this latter type.

Those who regularly use dental floss may want to take about a yard for a week-long backpack trip. It can be wrapped around a matchstick or a small piece of cardboard, or around the toothbrush handle (secured with a rubber band). Most dental floss is very strong and can double as thread for a sewing job.

TOILET TISSUE. This is best carried in roll form, just as it comes for household use. I make it a point to occasionally "snitch" a partial roll from the bathroom at home after it has been used to the point where its diameter is compatible with the diameter of a plastic bag, in which it is carried. Packaging the tissue in a plastic bag and keeping it out of the rain and away from anything damp is very important. The requirements are about ⅓ ounce of toilet tissue per day for males and roughly twice this amount for females. As bought in the store, a full new roll is about 4½ inches in diameter and weighs about 6 or 7 ounces. In most brands, ⅓ ounce is equivalent to about a 9-foot strip.

COMB.   A comb is advisable, but a hairbrush is not. Most people can get along without brushing their hair for the duration of a backpack trip. Toilet kits should also be left at home.

SHAVING GEAR.   On most backpack trips the usual approach is to "let 'em grow." Shaving gear means added weight. It frequently turns out that even those who carry shaving gear don't use it. If some members of the group decide that they want to carry such gear, it is best to get together on the equipment required, so as to save weight. Battery-operated and spring-wound shavers are available. It's your decision.

Mirror.   A mirror was mentioned earlier as a possible item of survival equipment. After three or four days on the trail many backpackers will prefer not to look at themselves. However, a mirror is useful in combing your hair, shaving (if you shave), and in applying sun protective cream. The same metal mirror that is taken as an item of survival equipment can be used.

Foot care.   Some persons seem to have naturally tough feet that require very little care beyond occasional application of some moleskin to a tender spot and the wearing of clean socks. Others find that their feet need considerably more attention. If you are in the "tender feet" category, daily application of rubbing alcohol and foot powder will probably be helpful while you are on the trail. At home going barefoot for short periods as often as possible will help to toughen the feet.

Skin care.   Your skin needs protection from the elements if you are to feel comfortable. Overexposure also frequently leads to severe illness. Most hikers will get plenty of sun and wind without purposely exposing themselves. Even though they wear a broad-brimmed hat, long-sleeved shirt, and long trousers, most people need some additional protection from the intense sunlight and strong winds that are usually encountered in mountain backpacking. At certain seasons of the

year protection from mosquitoes, black flies, deer flies, and similar insect pests is also needed.

SUN AND WIND PROTECTION.   The degree of protection required varies greatly from person to person. However, almost everyone needs some protection from the sun at high altitudes. Glacier cream, available from most mountaineering shops, gives protection from the sun, wind, and cold. It is used particularly by mountaineers and skiers. It is not a tanning agent. It is packaged in a tube that will not break or split in your pocket or pack. A-Fil cream, made by the Texas Pharmacal Company, of San Antonio, Texas, also prevents sunburn and suntan. It is available from many pharmacies. It too is well packaged in a strong tube. There are a large number of suntan lotions and creams, locally available, that are intended to permit an individual's skin to tan but not burn. For occasional use in everyday activities at home, some of these may do the job, but for backpacking in the mountains, they may not be satisfactory. Individual experience will determine whether they are suitable for backpacking. However, in case of doubt it is better to overprotect your skin than to get burned.

HAND LOTION.   The backs of your hands can get painfully sunburned or very rough and uncomfortable if not protected. Especially if you are fishing and have your hands in and out of the water frequently, they can get so they feel like a coarse grade of sandpaper. One of the face creams mentioned above can be used on your hands. Or you may prefer to use one of the many hand lotions that are available. Some people use light cotton gloves to protect the hands from sunburn.

LIP PROTECTION.   Some people find that a special lip salve is necessary to keep their lips from getting sunburned and chapped. The higher the altitude, the more likely that special protection will be needed. Labiosan lip cream offers good protection and is available from many mountaineering stores. An ordinary ChapStick may also be satisfactory.

Insect repellent.   At certain seasons the only satisfactory protection from insects is a face net, gloves, and long trousers (in other words, complete coverage). At other times a liquid or cream repellent applied to face, neck, and hands will do the job. The most effective repellents have one ingredient in common. That is N, N-diethyl-meta-toluamide. One rather inexpensive product containing this ingredient is a liquid generally known as Jungle Juice, available in some mountaineering stores and war surplus stores. A more expensive but popular repellent also containing diethyl-meta-toluamide is Cutter Insect Repellent. It is in the form of a cream and is considered by some backpackers somewhat more pleasant and longer lasting than Jungle Juice. Another good insect repellent that uses diethyl-meta-toluamide as a base is called Repel. Repellents that come packaged in glass bottles or aerosol cans are generally unsatisfactory for backpacking.

Pliers. A small pair of needle-nosed pliers is a useful camp tool. They should be kept in a leather sheath, preferably having a belt loop so that you can wear them on your belt while working around camp. Or if you put them in your pocket, the sheath will prevent a hole's being torn in the pocket. Needle-nosed pliers are handy in moving pans on and off the fire if you do not have a pan-gripping tool. They can be used in first aid for removing splinters and thorns. In dishwashing they can be used to dunk eating utensils in a pan of hot water for rinsing. If you are fishing, needle nosed pliers are almost a necessity for removing fishhooks (preferably from the fish).

Pliers are also useful in making repairs if you are using wire or in removing a tight knot from rope. The cost is about $3.

In servicing your backpack stove, pliers or a wrench may be required to remove the burner tip from the stove before cleaning (so that loosened soot does not fall into the fuel tank). They are also useful in bending the tabs on the stove burner plate, to hold it in place on the burner head. If the cap on the fuel tank was tightened too much when the stove was last used, pliers may be necessary to remove the cap.

Hiking staff. Whether to carry a hiking staff or not is a very controversial subject. A hiking staff can be useful in negotiating rough terrain or a steep slope and can serve as a "third leg" in helping to steady yourself in some situations. In other places many people consider a staff to be just so much added weight and more of a nuisance than a help in most hiking. A few consider a hiking staff to be a liability and claim that you have to watch your step to keep from stumbling over it.

Some people have a "pet" hiking staff of ash or hickory wood, or bamboo, or even aluminum tubing, that automatically goes along whenever they

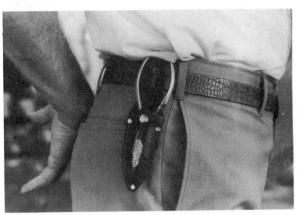

A pair of needle-nosed pliers is one of the most useful camp tools. You cannot grab a pan, or the bail on a pan, with your bare hand after it has been on the fire. I frequently use needle-nosed pliers when working around an open fire, and also in working with my backpack stove.

go on a backpack trip. Others acknowledge the usefulness of the staff in certain terrain but depend upon finding a makeshift staff in the form of a stick or pole in the area where they need it.

I have used a hiking staff at different times during my backpacking career. A photo (see page 5) reminds me that when I hiked the Grand Canyon at age sixteen, I used a wood hiking staff. I have since used other wood staffs and even a rather fancy aluminum one with a few "survival goodies" stuffed inside.

For the last eight or ten years, however, I have not carried a hiking staff. A few years ago I spent the summer hiking in the Canadian Rockies, and some of the trails were fairly crowded. I probably met 200 people on the trail during the summer. I don't believe more than 10 or 12 of these hikers were carrying a staff. I believe most people like to hike with their hands free. However, this is one of those areas that is strictly a matter of personal choice. If a hiker likes to use a walking staff, enjoys carrying it, and it perhaps gives him a sense of security, he should by all means stay with it.

Repair kit. There will be occasions when repairs will need to be made on the trail. You may tear your sleeping bag on a tree branch or a bush. A packframe joint may develop a crack. Perhaps a sharp rock will make a hole in your tent floor. You may rip your shirt or trousers or lose a shirt button. A small repair kit for making repairs on the trail will usually be worthwhile. A single kit to be shared by all members of the group as an item of common equipment is recommended. The amount of the various items to be carried will depend upon the number of people in the party and the length of the trip.

Sewing items—Carry several needles of various sizes, including one curved needle, and several yards of cotton-covered nylon thread.

Awl—Some parties may want an awl for heavy-duty repairs.

Clevis pins and split rings—These may be needed for repairs to packframes.

Safety pins—A few medium-sized safety pins are useful. In addition to their ordinary uses they are smaller than clothespins and equally suitable for hanging socks or towels on a line to dry. They can also be used to pin sweat-soaked socks and other items to your packbag, for drying as you hike along the trail.

Wire—Several yards of light-gauge wire, commonly referred to as stove wire, is frequently useful. This flexible wire can be used for temporary repairs to packframes, spare bails for cooking pots, and so on.

Cloth tape—As much as 4 or 5 yards may be needed in repairing polyethylene tarps (if you are using such a tarp rather than a nylon tarp or tent).

Ripstop tape—This tape is good for repairing clothing, sleeping bags, tents, and similar cloth articles.

Nylon cord or rope. A 50- or 75-foot length of 5/16-inch-diameter nylon rope, weighing 1½ to 2 pounds, will sometimes be useful in negotiating very short stretches of steep trail and possibly river crossings. This depends somewhat on the experience of the hikers. For the young and inexperienced a rope tied around the waist while negotiating perilous places can mean the difference between a pleasant trip and one where they are occasionally scared half to death.

Braided nylon cord of ⅛-inch diameter (550 lb. test), usually referred to as parachute cord, is most commonly used by backpackers for rigging tents and tarps, clotheslines, and the like. It is recommended that the cord required to rig your tent or tarp be packed with that equipment. If you are not in bear country, about 25 to 30 feet of cord should be sufficient to suspend your food bag and other "smellables" from a tree limb so that it is safe from raccoons and other small animals. If you are in bear country, the rigging will be a bit more complicated; a minimum of about 100 feet of nylon cord should be carried for that purpose. In throwing a cord over a high tree limb, you will need to tie the end to a stone about fist size or larger. This is no easy job. The rope frequently comes loose from the stone, and the flying stone may hit someone. An easier approach is to make a very small cloth bag with drawstring at home and keep this with the "bear-rig" rope. Then place the stone in the bag, fasten the rope to the bag, and the job is much more easily accomplished.

It is a good idea to suspend your packframe from a tree limb or high rope line at night so that some irresponsible deer or porcupine doesn't chew away on the sweat-soaked straps. Also, it is important to remember when in bear country that packs are probably tainted with food odors. For night rigging of packframes, about 25 to 50 feet of parachute cord should be sufficient. Such cord can also be used for spare bootlaces, fish stringers, and similar things.

Some thought will need to be given to this item to determine whether rope is required and how much to take. It is hard to conceive of a trip where at least 25 to 50 feet of nylon cord would not be required.

Litterbag. Modern wilderness ethics require that *all* refuse that is not burned must be packed back to the trailhead. There will be some trips where no fires are possible, or where they are not allowed. Thus, plastic food bags and all garbage must be packed out, along with all other trash.

Some people say that they use a stout *plastic* bag for litter. Not me. I use a stout *cloth* litterbag, which I easily made myself and which I recommend. A plastic litterbag is too likely to be punctured by the corner of a small crushed can or some similar object, within the bag, and thus spill the contents and possibly soil your packbag.

My litterbag is about 9 by 12 inches in size, with a zipper across one of the short ends. It has four tie tapes—one sewn to each corner. The litterbag can be carried in the large pocket on the outside back part of the packsack, or inside the pack. I usually carry mine tied into position against the back of my pack, however, using the tie tapes to fasten the bag to D rings on the packbag. I sometimes use a plastic bag as a liner for the cloth bag.

Survival kit.   Some persons make it a habit to *always* carry some sort of survival kit, even for relatively short day hikes. For day hiking, the "kit" is very frequently a small day pack containing most (possibly all) of the essential items listed at the beginning of this chapter.

On a backpack trip many of the essential items listed will be a part of your basic pack load. The few that are not can readily be made into a special kit to be used only under survival conditions. Many backpackers carry a small folding day pack inside their regular backpack. If they are at a camp in the wilderness and leave the camp for any significant length of time, they make it a point to carry the day pack containing survival items. In strange country a person may get lost, and possibly hurt, even a relatively short distance from camp. Carrying some survival equipment is a good precaution.

NONESSENTIAL EQUIPMENT

There are a few other items of equipment frequently carried by backpackers that can generally be considered nonessential equipment. Since it has been stressed that the knowledgeable backpacker takes primarily only essentials plus some emergency gear, it might well be asked why nonessential gear is even mentioned. It is simply that there are a few additional items of equipment that will make your pack trip more enjoyable under certain circumstances, if you feel the added weight is justified.

Camera.   A camera is not an essential item of equipment, but on many trips it will be desirable. There are a number of 35mm single-lens reflex cameras available that are very good for backpacking use. A 35mm camera and case will weigh about 20 to 40 ounces. One way of saving weight on this item is for several hikers to go together; the one with the camera can simply take duplicate or extra shots where desired. The others sharing in the camera shots take a corresponding weight of the "cameraman's" share of the common equipment.

Binoculars.   Unless you are an ardent bird watcher and expect to be doing some serious bird-watching during your backpack trip, give concentrated thought to the matter before you add the weight of a pair of binoculars to your pack. A satisfactory pair of binoculars might weigh 8 to 16 ounces. A monocular may weigh only 4 or 5 ounces. Either may prove interesting, and even useful, in scanning the countryside, watching animal life, and so forth. At any rate, most backpackers manage to get along without these instruments. It's your decision.

Backpacker's trowel made of high-impact plastic. Length, 11''; weight, 2 oz.

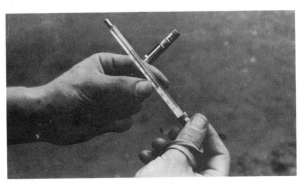

Pocket thermometer. *(Lou Clemmons)*

Fishing equipment.   If you are going into an area where there are lakes or trout streams, you will probably want to take some fishing equipment. This will usually be either a fly rod, spin-cast rod, or spinning rod, with a reel to match, plus a small box of lures and some extra line. Don't go overboard on accessories. A landing net is nice, but it isn't essential. Neither is a creel. If you intend to wade streams, you will want a pair of tennis shoes or lightweight waders. In addition to providing the pleasure of catching fish from wilderness streams or lakes, the weight of the fishing equipment will probably more than make up for itself by the lighter food load (meat) that will need to be carried. This will depend primarily upon your knowledge of the area and your fishing experience.

Pocket thermometer.   Some people carry a pocket thermometer. I have one that I occasionally carry. They weigh only about 1 ounce. It is interesting to wake up on a frosty morning, guess how cold it is, and then look at your thermometer and see what the temperature really is. A thermometer is particularly useful in helping determine what clothing and combinations of clothing, sleeping gear, and so on, keeps you comfortable at a certain temperature. (Wind velocity can be estimated.) If this information is recorded, it will help in selecting suitable protective clothing and similar gear for future trips. The cost of a pocket thermometer, with case, is about $6.

Backpacker's trowel.   A backpacker's trowel, made of high-impact plastic and weighing about 2 ounces, can be useful. It is particularly helpful in digging a small hole about 6 to 8 inches deep for the disposal of human waste. The cost is about $0.75.

Wind meter.   Wind meters weighing about 2 ounces are available from mountaineering equipment shops. You may find it interesting and helpful on a windswept mountain ridge to know just how strong the wind is. Few backpackers carry a wind meter, however. The cost is about $6 to $8.

Altimeter.   Altimeters are available, in a weight range of from 3 to 5 ounces, that will tell you your altitude. Conceivably they could be of some help in route finding. I have an altimeter and have carried it on a few backpack trips, but I seldom used it. The type I have can be readily mounted, by a suction cup, on the dash of your recreational vehicle, and mine most often is in my pickup truck, rather than in my backpack. The cost ranges from about $20 to over $100. Not recommended for the average backpacker.

Pedometer.   Theoretically, a pedometer should be a useful item of equipment in backpacking, since it measures distances. I have owned one for many years. Once it is calibrated to your stride, it is usually reasonably accurate on level terrain. However, it is very inaccurate in the mountains, and that is where I do most of my backpacking. It has been many years since I carried a pedometer on a backpack trip. The cost is about $8 to $10.

Weighing scale.   A lightweight spring scale is useful in measuring out loads of common equipment for distributing to members of your backpack group at the start of each day. I have such a scale. Sometimes I carry it, but more often I do not. Large parties would probably find it more useful than small groups would. My scale weighs 7 ounces and cost $9.50.

Map distance measurer.   This is a small instrument with a tiny wheel that can be traced over an irregular path on a map to find the distance to be traveled. Some people carry these on the trail; others use them only in planning the route at home. I do not carry one on the trail. An important aspect in using these devices is to remember that the map distances that they measure will always be considerably less than the actual trail distances to be traveled. These instruments weigh about 1 ounce and cost about $3 to $5.

Spring scale. This is useful in measuring daily loads of food and common equipment for distribution to hikers.

Map distance measurer. These devices are useful in planning the route during preparations at home. They are not normally carried on the trail.

Watch. In your escape from the schedules of civilization you may feel that a watch has no place on a backpack trip. Normally there is no need to set a rigid itinerary. However, a watch can still be helpful. You should know roughly how far you can travel over mountainous terrain in an hour or a half hour. With this knowledge and a watch, you will know where to look for certain checkpoints on your map. Thus, a watch is an aid to following your progress on your map and staying oriented. You will want to make camp, get supper cooked, and the dishes washed before dark. A watch will give you a good idea of how many hours of daylight are still left to accomplish these activities. If everyone is to meet back in camp at a certain hour after an afternoon of fishing, it will be pretty hard to do this without a watch.

Guidebook. A guidebook can be an aid in the planning of your route at home. If it is accurate and detailed enough (some are neither), it may be of help in staying on the trail in unfamiliar terrain. Some guidebooks give information on points of interest along the trail and this, for some, can make the trip more enjoyable.

Notebook and pencil. A small notebook (or 3-by-5-inch note cards) and a pencil stub will be useful in keeping a log of the trip, noting changes in your checklist for the next trip, leaving a note at a base camp for your companions, and so forth. A wood pencil stub (with a metal protector for the tip) about four inches long is recommended, rather than a ball-point pen. A ball-point pen will not write well on a greasy or slightly soiled surface, which is apt to be the case with note cards or a notebook carried in your pocket and worked on when your hands are sweaty, or covered with sun protection cream or mosquito repellent.

Playing cards. Many people will say that a deck of playing cards has no place on a backpack trip. However, if you have ever been tightly cooped up with two or three companions for a day or two, waiting out a severe rainstorm or snowstorm, you may change your mind. A deck of miniature playing cards weighs about 1½ ounces. If your companions are chess fans, you might consider a miniature chess set.

Paperback book. It may be desirable to take a paperback book for essentially the same reasons you would carry a deck of miniature cards. Or maybe you simply like to read a bit in the evening. A paperback book will usually weigh about 5 to 7 ounces.

Wallet. Most backpackers leave their wallets in their vehicle at the trailhead. There are several items that may be in your wallet, however, that you may need in the backwoods. These are camping permit (if required), fishing license (if you are to be fishing), and fire permit (if required, and if you may want a fire). I have found that a good way to carry these items is in a plastic bag with a small piece of cardboard for a stiffener, and with a rubber band around the whole business.

SUMMARY OF RECOMMENDED EQUIPMENT

Now that packs, sleeping gear, clothing, cooking equipment, general equipment, and so on, have been discussed, they will be summarized to show what it adds up to for an actual backpack trip. First, only that equipment, clothing, and so forth, will be listed that is considered necessary to do the job, provide reasonable comfort, and assure the well-being of the hikers. Recommended items in this category, generally adequate for a backpack trip of up to one week, are used in making up Tables 14 and 15. Equipment and other items are considered in two categories. First, the *personal items*, which are those items taken for the personal use and benefit of the particular member. Each person will need to make his or her own decisions as to what to carry in this category. Secondly, the *common equipment*, consisting of those items shared by the group as a whole. Some hikers will not have all the items recommended in these lists. When a different or substitute item, or one that weighs more or less than the one given, is used, proper allowance will need to be made for weight.

SUMMARY OF OPTIONAL EQUIPMENT

This is the point where many backpackers get carried away. They take too many things (often just gadgets) that they think they might need and then never use them. With such an enticing array of backpacking equipment currently available, it is not at all difficult to be an equipment freak. With each trip into the backwoods most backpackers will become more adept at distinguishing the essential from the nonessential equipment. From trip to trip, keeping checklists and notes on how equipment performed, what equipment was not used, what modifications should be made, and so on, will be a big help in selecting proper equipment—and minimum equipment—for subsequent trips.

As with recommended equipment, the optional equipment items are divided into two categories—personal equipment and common equipment. Tables 16 and 17 list optional personal equipment and optional common equipment, respectively. These are simply suggestions of some items you may want to consider.

TABLE 14. RECOMMENDED PERSONAL EQUIPMENT

Item	Approximate Weight (in ounces)
Packframe and packbag	66
Sleeping gear	
Sleeping bag	72
Sleeping pad, 3/8″ closed-cell foam, 21″ x 56″	14
Ground cloth, coated nylon, 3′ x 7′ (not needed if tent is used)	11*
Shelter gear	
Tent, one-person: tent, fly, pole, and stakes	44*
OR	
Tent, two-person: tent, fly, poles, stakes, small whisk broom, and sponge	48†
Equipment	
Eating utensils: plastic cup, spoon, and bowl	6
First aid kit, personal	7½
Flashlight and spare bulb, Mallory type	3½
Litterbag, cloth, about 9″ x 12″	1
Map and compass	3½
Matches in waterproof container, and candle stub	2
Parachute cord, 1/8″-diam. nylon, 30 ft.	2
Pocketknife	3
Sunglasses	2
Water bottle, plastic, quart-size (filled)	35
Water purification tablets	½
Toilet articles	
Comb	½
Insect repellent	1½
Soap	2
Sun protective lotion	1¼
Toilet tissue	2
Toothbrush	½
Towel and washcloth	3½
Washbasin (plastic bowl)	1½
	275
Watch (carried on person)	

*One-person tent assumed in arriving at total weight.
†Half of total weight.

TOTAL PACK WEIGHT

In arriving at the total weight of the individual packs, a week-long backpack trip for three persons will be assumed. The weight will obviously be dependent upon a number of factors. However, the following is an approximate breakdown of the main categories of equipment, clothing, and so forth.

Recommended personal equipment. As outlined in Table 14, the weight of the recommended personal equipment is 275 ounces, including packframe and fitted packbag.

Recommended common equipment. The recommended common equipment is outlined in Table 15 and amounts to 44 ounces per person.

Optional personal equipment. Some items of optional personal equipment that may be desired are outlined in Table 16. A total of 55 ounces of optional personal equipment is assumed.

Optional common equipment. Optional common equipment is listed in Table 17. A weight of 20 ounces of optional common equipment per person is assumed. This would provide 60 ounces of this equipment for a group of three people.

Duplicate and extra clothing. As shown in Chapter 5, Table 5, the only recommended duplicate clothing is socks—duplicates of the combination of socks that you use for hiking (about 5 ounces). For extra clothing (protection), a medium-weight wool shirt, insulated vest and windshell jacket is a typical combination and will provide protection down to about 20° F. A nylon poncho large enough to go over both hiker and pack is frequently used for rain protection. These items total 56 ounces.

Optional clothing. Some people may want to take hiking shorts, gloves, knit cap, or other items. A total of 35 ounces of optional clothing is assumed.

Food. As discussed in Chapter 8, the total food weight was 432 ounces, or 144 ounces per hiker.

Total pack weight. A summary of the foregoing items is contained in Table 18. The total pack weight is about 39 pounds. For a group larger than three persons, the weight would be slightly less, because of additional sharing of common equipment. Also, as the food is eaten, the food load per person is reduced by about 1½ pounds per day.

TABLE 15. RECOMMENDED COMMON EQUIPMENT

Item	Approximate Weight (in ounces)
First aid kit, group	10
Camera, 35mm	30
Film, photographic, 3 rolls	3
Repair kit	6
Parachute cord, ⅛"-diam. nylon, 75 ft.	6
Mirror, metal	2½
Cooking gear	
Stove and accessories: backpack stove, windscreen, two pans, pan gripper, eyedropper, funnel, match supply, and cloth carrying bag	39
Fuel for stove: 1 qt. in aluminum fuel bottle	30
Dishwashing items: small sponge, pot scratcher, biodegradable soap	4
Other: two tablespoons and G.I. can opener	2
	132½

Some people may want to take a tarp for rain protection or to depend upon their poncho for both rain protection on the trail and emergency protection from rain at night. This depends largely upon the season and the experience of the backpackers. If you are doing all cooking over a wood fire, the weight of the backpack stove and fuel is eliminated. A small party of experienced backpackers will normally be willing to make more sacrifices than a larger group that includes novices. If you have a group of "bottomless pit" teenagers, about 2 pounds of food per person per day may be required, instead of 1½ pounds.

By sacrificing some comfort and convenience and by eliminating most nonessentials, the total pack weight can be safely reduced to 30 pounds, or a bit under, for one week. Most backpackers will not want to be quite this austere, however.

TABLE 16. OPTIONAL PERSONAL EQUIPMENT

Item	Approximate Weight (in ounces)
Bear bell	2
Batteries, flashlight (spares)	1 (each)
Binoculars	9
Book, paperback	5
Camera, 35mm	30
Drinking cup, folding	1
Eyeglasses	2½
Film, photographic	1 (per roll)
Fishing equipment: rod, reel, small box of lures	19
Monocular	4
Notebook and pencil stub	1
Pliers, small needle-nosed	4
Rubber bands (assorted sizes)	¼
Safety pins and plastic clothespins (assorted)	¼
Shelter gear	
Groundsheet, coated nylon (for under floor of one-person tent)	6
OR	
Groundsheet, polyethylene (for under floor of two-person tent)	20
Sleeping gear	
Air mattress	20
Pajamas	11
Snakebite kit, suction type	1½
Toilet articles	
Feminine hygiene items	—
Foot powder	4
Hand lotion	1
Lip salve	½
Razor and blades	1½
Rubbing alcohol	3
Waders, lightweight plastic	22
Whistle	½

TABLE 17. OPTIONAL COMMON EQUIPMENT

Item	Approximate Weight (in ounces)
Altimeter	4
Bags, plastic (extra)	1 to 3
Bucket, folding, plastic-coated cloth, 2-gal. size	6
Cooking gear	
Frying pan, Teflon	12
Grill (with folding legs)	28
Jar, pint-size (for soaking food)	2
Reflector oven	42
Guidebook	6 to 12
Nail file	1/4
Plastic sheet, 6' x 8' (for covering woodpile)	6
Playing cards, miniature	1½
Pliers, small needle-nosed	4
Rope, 5/16"-diam. nylon, 50 to 75 ft.	24 to 36
Scale, weighing	7
Shaving gear: shaving cream and plastic washbasin	9
Snakebite kit: antivenin and ethyl chloride	11
Survival kit	5 to 20
Tennis shoes, canvas, large	32
Tent, two-person or larger: tent, fly, poles, stakes, small whisk broom, and sponge	96*
Thermometer	1
Trowel	2
Whetstone, Carborundum	2
Wind meter	2

*Two-person tent; larger tents will weigh more.

TABLE 18. WEIGHT SUMMARY

Item	Approximate Weight (in ounces)
Recommended Personal Equipment	275
Recommended Common Equipment	44
Optional Personal Equipment	55
Optional Common Equipment	20
Recommended Duplicate and Extra Clothing	56
Optional Duplicate and Extra Clothing	35
Food	144
Total	629
	(39 lbs. 5 oz.)

11
Safety

CAUSES OF ACCIDENTS

It takes considerable know-how to plan a backpack trip and a daily route that will take a group safely from place to place in a wilderness or other remote area. The main contributing causes of accidents on a backpack trip are lack of preparation, exposure, being in a hurry, and getting too tired.

Lack of preparation. There are many areas of preparation. There are the matters of food and equipment preparation. These may be relatively simple, depending upon how often you backpack and the state of readiness of your food and equipment. Other important aspects of preparation are to be mentally and physically prepared. If you are just recovering from a deep emotional experience, to go on a backpack trip may be unwise. You may think that a backpack trip will aid in your emotional recovery. If there is any doubt, you should seek the advice of your physician or another qualified counselor. The activity and mental stimulation of tasks at home may be better for your recovery than the exertion, fatigue, and routine of a backpack trip. Especially on a backpack trip where many miles are to be covered, an individual sometimes hungers for mental activity. On long, routine paths or on steep switchbacks in the hot sun, the mind can become dull and bored. It is not uncommon to do a certain amount of daydreaming in such instances,

and thinking about a recent bad emotional experience may do considerable harm.

There is also the matter of body conditioning. If you have kept yourself in good physical condition throughout the year, then a minimum of special exercising and hiking may be sufficient. However, practically everyone needs some special physical conditioning before a backpack trip. Perhaps you have been so unfortunate as to acquire a cold, toothache, or some other minor illness just recently and have not fully recovered. You need to be honest with yourself as to your true physical condition, and if you are not up to par, you should probably cancel out. This requires a lot of courage, after having prepared and looked forward to the trip for perhaps many weeks.

Other important considerations include a careful study and evaluation of the route, probable weather, stream crossings, and so on. These may be fairly routine and simple, or they may be quite complex. An important consideration is whether one or more members of the party are acquainted with the area and have backpacked into it at that particular time of year.

Still another phase of preparation is to become familiar with the experience, equipment, and physical condition of any newcomers to the group. This may present little or no difficulty, or it could develop into a serious matter. If problems develop on the trail because of a newcomer's lack of preparation or experience, it is then too late to do anything about it except take emergency or make-shift measures.

Exposure. Regardless of the anticipated weather, backpackers should always be prepared for the unexpected. This particularly applies to backpacking in the spring and fall, when extreme changes in weather and temperature may occur over a relatively short span of time, and to hiking in the high mountains at any time of year. (*Exposure* in this discussion is intended to mean that type of exposure that may lead to hypothermia.) Low temperature, wind, wetness, and fatigue are important contributing factors to hypothermia. Hikers should carry protective clothing even though they don't expect to need it. Each hiker should take every precaution to keep the clothing that he or she is wearing dry, through control of exertion (and perspiration), removal or addition of clothing as needed, and protection from wind and rain. In other words, hikers should learn to keep themselves comfortable in the out-of-doors. They should carry protective clothing for warmth and rain, even on short day hikes.

Being in a hurry. If a trip is properly planned, there should be no need for getting in a hurry. Normally, ten to fourteen miles is a good day's travel in mountainous areas where reasonably good trails are available. If hikers are going to be rock hunting, fishing, or engaging in some other activity during the day besides hiking, this distance must be scaled way down. Unless there is a very special reason for going cross-country, it is best to stay on or near the trail, or stick to suitable terrain that someone in the party is familiar with. This should preclude such mishaps as running out of water, coming up against blind cliffs or precipices and having to backtrack, or falling and breaking a leg by trying to hike through terrain that should not have been attempted.

Even with these precautions it is still possible to have an accident because the party got in a hurry. Let's assume there is a stream to be crossed. The stream could be waded at a certain point, but to save time, it is decided to use a tree that happens to bridge the stream. It is not a very good bridge and it is dangerously high above the water, but the decision is to risk it. On the way over, one hiker's pack throws him off balance and he goes into the river, breaking a leg in the process. This accident was caused because the party got in a hurry (and failed to use good judgment).

On a rough trail containing loose rock, tree roots, mud, steep grades, and so on, some very bad falls (and injuries) can result from simply trying to hike too fast.

Getting too tired. A backpack trip should not be an endurance contest. The number of miles to be covered in a day of hiking should normally be relatively unimportant. It is always better to underestimate a group's ability to cover miles than to overestimate. It is extremely difficult to judge distances and traveling time in mountainous terrain from a map. Where it is necessary to do this, if scaled distances are multiplied by a factor of two or three, they will probably be about right. However, there are still some unknown aspects. Unless some member of the party has been over the trail before, you don't know for certain how good the trail is. Foul weather can also change the *condition* of a trail very quickly. You also never know how many times the group may temporarily lose the trail and have to spend time to pick it up again.

Five or six hours of hiking (with a full pack) for the first day or two will be enough, unless you are a seasoned hiker. Seldom should you plan to hike more than eight hours per day. When you get too tired, you are a safety hazard to yourself and others. You will stumble, and you may fall when ordinarily you would not. Your reactions are slower. You can easily hurt yourself doing simple camp jobs or other things that normally would not be dangerous at all. For example, I once witnessed a very tired hiker breaking wood by laying sticks on a log and stomping on them with his foot. One of the pieces flew up at an odd angle and caught him just above the eye, making a bad cut that bled profusely. Had this person not been dog tired, he would probably have easily dodged the flying stick. If you push yourself to the point of exhaustion, you are inviting trouble. Why not settle for fewer miles and a more leisurely pace and enjoy yourself?

When you get too tired, your judgment and thinking are also impaired. You may find yourself doing things—or planning to do things—that ordinarily you would not do. Extreme fatigue acts in much the same way as a tranquilizing drug.

ACCLIMATIZATION

Those who live at an altitude considerably lower than that of the area where they plan to backpack should give serious thought to the matter of acclimatization. There is less oxygen in the air at high altitudes, and the blood has to make certain adjustments in order to supply enough oxygen to the body. However, even after acclimatization, there is always less oxygen in the blood at high altitudes than at sea level. Some people are much more seriously affected by high altitudes than others are. However, it is recommended that *all* persons who plan to backpack in the high mountains allow time in their schedule for acclimatization.

A good way to acclimatize to high altitudes is to drive to the area a day or more before you start to backpack. The time required for acclimatization depends upon the specific altitude, the degree of exertion, and the speed at which you ascend to higher altitude. The ability to acclimatize to high altitudes also varies considerably from individual to individual. However, if you go too high at too fast a pace, you are very apt to suffer from mountain sickness. The symptoms are queasy stomach (possibly vomiting), drowsiness, headache, loss of appetite, irritability, lack of mental alertness, and chills. Sleep patterns are usually affected, with much awakening at night and weird dreams.

As a *minimum* precaution it is recommended that hikers drive to the trailhead the day before they intend to start hiking in the mountains. A good night's sleep at the trailhead will help the body acclimatize to the higher elevation. If it is necessary to start hiking the next day, it is important to set an easy pace, particularly for the first day or two. A route that rises rapidly to higher elevations should be avoided, if possible. The appetite, particularly for certain foods, is often dulled at high altitudes. However, an adequate diet with generous consumption of liquids is important.

If you find the symptoms of mountain sickness coming on, slow down in your exertion, or lay over for a day. Avoid heavy eating, alcoholic beverages, and smoking. Limit your physical activity. Aspirin may be helpful in relieving the symptoms. If these measures are not effective, you should descend to a lower elevation.

Major serious symptoms may occur at elevations of 9,000 to 10,000 feet and above. Some of the advanced major symptoms are unusual fatigue (possibly complete collapse), shortness of breath, a racking cough, bubbling noises in the chest, and bloody sputum. *These symptoms are serious.* The victim should be moved to a much lower altitude *immediately*, or death may occur within hours. If oxygen is available, it should be administered to the victim.

WEATHER

A very important contributing factor to accidents and tragedies in the wilderness is weather. For example, after a few weeks of early balmy spring weather a party of hikers takes to the mountains. The days are bright; the weather is warm. Wildflowers have started to appear. Temperatures at night may be barely freezing. Off goes the party of backpackers, wearing normal mild-weather hiking clothes with light jackets and carrying corresponding equipment. But after they are on the trail a few hours, or perhaps a day or two, a storm front may move in suddenly. Within several hours temperatures may plunge to far below freezing. Heavy snowfall causes the party to lose its way. Panic sets in. The matches are quickly used up in trying to start a fire under adverse conditions. Within a few hours the group is hopelessly lost. One or more members perish. Over the years, I have observed that such accidents happen in the state of New Mexico and neighboring states with a fair degree of regularity.

This type of tragedy is fairly frequent in the spring of the year. It also happens to parties of hunters in the fall. It sometimes happens to day hikers (often hiking solo), who take to the mountains on a nice, early spring day with the intention of taking a short hike of just a few hours and returning the same day. Hikers should never underestimate the fury of the wilderness and its harshness on the unprepared under adverse weather conditions.

Unseasonably warm weather can cause snow runoff at a much more rapid rate than normal. Mountain streams that were easily waded a year ago are now a foot or more higher. Don't take lightly the tremendous force of ten or twelve added inches in depth of a fast-moving mountain stream. It can cost you your life.

So be prepared for sudden changes in weather when you enter the mountains, particularly in the spring or fall of the year, when sudden deep snowfalls can make trails impassable and easily lost to hikers. At these seasons temperatures can change fifty degrees within a few hours. Have the necessary clothing and equipment for such an eventuality. Don't depend upon matches alone for starting a fire under such conditions. When you are in a semipanicked state of mind, you are not going to want to whittle sticks of wood into shavings or "fuzz sticks" or take the necessary time to gather good fire-starting materials, as you would in a normal situation. Have a long-burning, hot-flame plumber's candle, fire-starting jelly, or a similar material in your fire-starting kit. Remember, it is one thing to sit in your easy chair at home and halfheartedly plan what you would do in such an emergency situation in the woods and quite another thing to be in the woods, trying to cope with that situation, unprepared, and with time running out.

Anyone who hikes into the mountains should routinely carry a pack, even for a short day hike. The pack should contain protective clothing, fire-starting materials, first aid kit, drinking water, a few items of emergency food, knife, and so on. (See page 121 for a list of essential equipment.) This practice should always be followed, regardless of how brightly the sun may be shining or how warm the day may be. Those who come from some distance away for their hiking or backpacking adventure should make advance inquiry of

weather conditions in general and possible very recent changes in weather. They should not hesitate to cancel or alter their plans if weather conditions so dictate. The dollar they save by not making a last-minute long distance phone call to inquire about the weather may look pretty small later on.

Backpackers who venture forth in the early spring or late fall (or winter), or who go into the very high mountains at any season, should study Table 19 (Wind Chill Factor) and note the effect that wind has on the effective temperature. Anyone who has ridden in the back end of a pickup truck at thirty miles an hour on a cold morning will quickly realize how important it is to consider not only the temperature but the temperature-wind combination. As will be seen from the chart, if the outside air temperature is 30° F and the truck is traveling twenty-five miles per hour, the *effective* air temperature is 0° F.

TABLE 19. WIND CHILL FACTOR

When the temperature/wind speed factor falls in the area shaded below, frostbite, especially of the face, is a serious hazard.

When thermometer reads (°F)	When the wind blows at the speed below, it reduces temperature to (°F)								
	Calm	5 mph	10 mph	15 mph	20 mph	25 mph	30 mph	35 mph	40 mph
+50	50	48	40	36	32	30	28	27	26
+40	40	37	28	22	18	16	13	11	11
+30	30	27	16	9	4	0	−2	−4	−6
+20	20	16	4	−5	−10	−15	−18	−20	−21
+10	10	6	−9	−18	−25	−29	−33	−35	−37
0	0	−5	−21	−36	−39	−44	−48	−49	−53
−10	−10	−15	−33	−45	−53	−59	−63	−67	−69
−20	−20	−26	−46	−58	−67	−74	−79	−82	−85
−30	−30	−36	−58	−72	−82	−88	−94	−98	−100
−40	−40	−47	−70	−88	−96	−104	−109	−113	−116
−50	−50	−57	−85	−99	−110	−118	−125	−129	−132
−60	−60	−68	−95	−112	−124	−133	−140	−145	−148

To measure speed of wind without instruments: Calm (smoke rises vertically); 1–12 mph (just feel wind on face, leaves in motion); 13–24 (raises dust or loose paper, snow drifts, branches move); 25–30 (large branches move, wires whistle); 30–40 (whole trees in motion, hard to walk against).

For the properly clothed, there is little danger down to −20° F, but caution should be used with regard to all exposed flesh. At below −20° F, take no unnecessary chances.

(Great World, West Simsbury, Conn.)

Hypothermia. Exposure to the elements, leading to hypothermia, is one of the most common tragedies in the out-of-doors. Hypothermia is loss of body heat. The victim does not need to be exposed either to extreme cold or high altitude in order to suffer fatal hypothermia. The exposure temperature is often above freezing, frequently between 40° and 50° F. The altitude may be relatively low, even near sea level. He may be wearing normal and adequate clothing for protection on a 40° day. However, there are other factors present. Perhaps the victim has been hurrying to reach a certain objective and has perspired extensively. He probably failed to remove unneeded clothing when he started to perspire and his clothing is now wet with perspiration. Wetness of clothing may also have been caused by rain or snow and failure to put on rain gear in time. Another factor that is commonly present is wind. Wet clothes are actually refrigerated by wind, because it evaporates moisture from the surface.

If a group is proceeding toward an objective and any member's clothing gets soaked, or he or she becomes chilled, a halt should be called and immediate steps taken to remedy the situation. Specific precautions should be taken whether or not the person shows any signs that hypothermia is present. The party should give up its particular objective for the day, or at least until the person has been made comfortable and feels normal. Select the best spot that is immediately available and get out of the wind or rain. Try to get on the lee side of a ridge, or behind rocks, trees, or other natural barriers from the wind. Use a tent, tarp, poncho, natural shelter, or whatever is necessary and available. Build a fire if possible and make your bivouac reasonably comfortable. Anyone whose clothing is wet should change at once into dry clothing (if available) or remove clothing and get into a dry sleeping bag. If you have been able to build a fire, dry the wet clothes by the fire if conditions permit. Drink hot liquids of any kind (even hot water) and eat some food.

Any member who does show symptoms of hypothermia should be given immediate and continuous attention. He or she should not be allowed to go to sleep as long as the symptoms of hypothermia are present. The symptoms are these:

Incoherent, slurred speech
Violent fits of shivering
Fumbling hands, stumbling gait
Drowsiness
Exhaustion
Shallow breathing

When the above symptoms are present, hypothermia has already set in. The temperature of the inner core of the body is no longer a normal 98° F. It is lower than this; how much lower depends on how long hypothermia has been present. It could be as low as 85° F. If it drops to 80°, the victim will be unconscious, and if it falls several degrees lower, death will occur.

When the signs of hypothermia first appear, treatment should start without delay. Make the best shelter that surroundings and your equipment will provide, but start to work on the victim immediately. Don't place the victim in a cold sleeping bag. Have one of the well members of the party, wearing only underclothes, prewarm a dry sleeping bag (under which as much insulation as possible has been placed). The victim should then be placed in the sleeping bag with the well person, to warm the victim by skin-to-skin contact.

Warm stones or canteens filled with hot water, properly wrapped, can be placed in the sleeping bag. If the patient is able to drink, give hot soup, hot coffee, or other hot drinks. This can be followed by small amounts of high-energy food, depending upon the patient's reaction. Try to keep the victim awake. Do not leave the victim alone, even for short periods.

Continue the treatment until the patient shows definite improvement and the symptoms have disappeared. The patient can then move around a bit, properly clothed, to determine his reaction to mild exertion. The next step is to try to evacuate the patient to civilization, but only if he is well rested and ready for it.

A most important aspect of hypothermia is that the victim will often not be aware of his condition. Added to this is the fact that all members of the party may feel warm and snug except one — the victim. The well members may fail to notice that the one person is not up to par. If they do notice him at all, they may think he is a bit tired, or even a little lazy, if they are not well acquainted with him. By the time it is apparent that the victim is ill, damage may already have been done. Hypothermia may have set in. Therefore, it is important that the leader, as well as other members of the party, be fully aware of the conditions that can lead to hypothermia. When the group is hiking under such conditions, the leader should stop occasionally and chat with other members to see that they are responsive, to inquire about their comfort, and so on. If a hiker *says* he is all right, but doesn't look so good, and doesn't talk and respond normally, you had best take some definite steps *right then* to assure yourself of his condition. Other members should also communicate with each other, for the same reason, being careful not to overlook some one member who may be suffering in silence. Play it safe!

Hyperthermia. Much backpacking is done under conditions which are not ideal. Many people find that their only real vacation has to be taken in the summer. In some areas the summer daytime temperatures are very hot, and often combined with a high humidity, which makes ordinary labor difficult and uncomfortable. Even at high altitudes in the mountains, the hot sun on a clear day can make backpacking very hot work. I have hiked near glaciers or ice fields on a clear summer day and had to exercise caution not to overexert and perspire too much.

When backpacking on a hot summer day, hikers need to take certain precautions against hyperthermia, the opposite of hypothermia. Perhaps a hiker is wearing heavy protective clothing and fails to remove it as the day warms. He may fail to drink adequate water or other cool liquids. Heavy exertion under these conditions can bring on hyperthermia. In hyperthermia the body does not get rid of heat fast enough. Symptoms such as headache, nausea, chills, and dizziness may appear.

As for potential hyperthermia, the leader, as well as other members of the party, need to be on the alert for a member who may exhibit initial symptoms of illness. Profuse sweating (or no sweating), flushed skin, and inability to maintain a moderate pace may be initial symptoms of hyperthermia. In hot, humid weather it is important to set a reasonable pace and try to schedule the most difficult hiking for the coolest part of the day. Frequent rests in the shade may be necessary. A do-or-die attitude can get the group into trouble. Some goals may need to be given up.

Lightweight, loose-fitting clothing is important to the prevention of hyperthermia. A shirt that can be opened up for ventilation is preferable to a pullover sweater that must be either all on or all off. Drinking at regular intervals, preferably cool water with *some* salt, is very important. Excess salt should be avoided. Good physical condition and preconditioning, which includes hiking or working in hot weather, will also make a person less susceptible to hyperthermia.

RAINSTORMS

A little wetting on a warm day won't hurt you, but don't try to continue hiking in a bad storm.

Seek the best shelter you can find, make yourself comfortable, and wait it out. If there is a hard rain, put up a plastic sheet or a tarp on a ridgeline and keep yourself and your equipment dry. If your pack is not waterproof, or you are not sure whether it is or not, by all means take extra precautions to keep it and its contents dry. If your pack gets thoroughly soaked, it will be so heavy that you can hardly lift it, let alone carry it. Besides, if everything in it is wet or damp, you will have a mess. If you are wearing a poncho or other good rain gear and there are trees in the area, you can huddle under a tree. It is surprising how much protection is afforded by a good-size tree with thick branches and foliage.

LIGHTNING

In many mountainous regions, sudden electrical storms are very common at certain seasons of the year. Your chances of being struck by lightning are small, but it does pay to have some basic knowledge of how to protect yourself.

Mountain peaks. Stay off mountain peaks, especially those which are relatively sharp and prominent. At a good distance downhill from the peak, say several hundred yards, you should be quite safe. A mountain with a broad ridge or rounded top is less dangerous than those with sharp, prominent peaks. In any case, in the event of an electrical storm, get off the top of the mountain as fast as possible.

Cliffs, caves. The overhang of a cliff should be avoided. It is a very risky place to be in an electrical storm. If you are under the overhang, a bolt of lightning coming down the cliff is likely to jump across the edge of the overhang and pass through your body. Likewise, do not seek shelter in a small, shallow cave. It is better to get wet (and stay alive). Only fairly large caves are safe. If you do seek shelter in a cave, or under a very large overhang, do not stand but sit. Stay back from the cave entrance and avoid the walls of the cave. A sitting position near the center is best.

Crevices. Avoid a crack or crevice that leads up the slope of a hill or mountain. This may be a good attractor of lightning, especially if filled with damp earth or if there is a trickle of water flowing.

Prominent objects. Lightning may be attracted to a prominent object on the landscape, such as isolated or very tall trees, buildings, large boulders, and so on. If you yourself are the most prominent object on the landscape, you should assume a crouching position. You can also move into the general area of some other more prominent object, but keep a distance away from it equal to about twice its height. Never get directly under it.

Other precautions. Wherever you seek shelter, the best body position is a crouch. Both feet should be together, without other parts of the body touching the ground. It is important to remove packframe, cooking utensils, knife, and any other metal objects from the place where you are crouched, since they are attractors of lightning. You should also be separated from your companions by about eight feet or more. Outcroppings of rock should be avoided. Solid earth, or a forest floor, with as few rocks as possible, is preferable.

SOLO TRAVEL

Backpacking by yourself in remote areas is not recommended. If you should break a leg or get sick, you have a serious situation that could cost you your life. Having a companion will provide a very significant added margin of safety. If one person gets sick or injured, the other person can take care of him or her or go for help. A minimum of three persons is actually recommended. One person can then stay with the sick or injured hiker while the other goes for help. Another good reason for having a companion or two is that pack loads will be lighter because of the sharing of cooking utensils, general camp equipment, and other common gear. Additionally, for most of us

(even though we may shun large hiking groups) a companion or two to share our adventures makes a backpack trip more enjoyable.

On some of the well-known, regularly maintained, and frequently traveled trail systems, such as some sections of the Appalachian Trail, a few hikers will be found traveling alone. If it is a section of the trail that is known to be frequently traveled, the risk in traveling alone is certainly not as great as in solo travel in some of the wilderness areas or other remote regions. However, it should be recognized that there is risk involved in any solo travel away from civilization. Important factors to consider are your experience, your knowledge of the area and trails, and the time of year and probable weather. Each year, many hundreds of dollars are spent in locating lost or injured hikers, and the searchers are subjected to additional risk and possible accident in doing so.

Forest Service personnel and other professional outdoorsmen sometimes go into remote areas alone. It is part of their job. However, not only are they usually expert woodsmen, but their headquarters knows where they are and will soon be looking for them if they do not show up or check in according to a prearranged plan. Further, such persons usually travel by horseback, and having a well-trained horse provides an added margin of safety. Also, they are usually well acquainted with the area in which they are traveling, which is an important aspect.

Regardless of the size of the party, it is important to let some responsible person know when and where you are going and your itinerary. A relative or close friend back home should have this information. He or she should also have the license number and general description of the

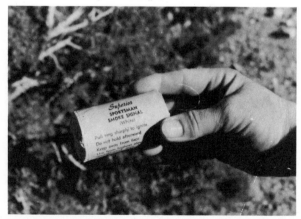

Sportsman smoke signal. This device, made by the Superior Signal Co. of Spotswood, N.J., provides a dense cloud of smoke instantaneously. Since it is often very difficult to quickly produce a dense cloud of smoke from materials at hand, it may be a worthwhile item to some backpackers.

vehicle in which you will be traveling to the take-off point. If an emergency at home requires that someone get in touch with you while you are traveling on the highway, this information will be of utmost importance to state police or others who are attempting to find you. If you have left your itinerary and return date with a responsible person, emergency action can be initiated if you have not returned by a certain cutoff time. (See page 198.)

CROSSING STREAMS

A considerable number of accidents occur in crossing unbridged streams. Some result in broken bones. In others, people have lost their lives. Crossing streams is one of the greatest hazards of backwoods travel. It takes time to remove shoes, socks, and possibly trousers, in preparation for wading a stream. It takes additional time to put these items back on after the stream is crossed. Therefore, most hikers look for a quicker way to cross the stream. Before crossing a stream by any means other than a bridge, you should unbuckle the waist strap of your backpack, and preferably loosen the shoulder straps. Then you can slip out of your pack quickly if a mishap occurs.

Sometimes, with some reconnoitering upstream and down, rocks will be found that will serve as suitable stepping stones for crossing the stream. If they are properly placed and reasonably large and stable, fine. You have your "bridge." However, beware of making long hops from one rock to another with a fully loaded pack. You are not nearly as nimble with a large pack on your back as without, and it can easily throw you off balance. Also beware, in early morning or cool weather, of stepping on ice-covered rocks. Your lug soles won't help a bit.

Another possibility is a log or tree trunk that bridges the stream. A log so close to the water that it gets wet from spray can be extremely slippery. It may be better to pass it up.

If you can find a stick or pole of sufficient length, it can be of some help in crossing a stream on a log. It is generally best to place the pole in the water on the downstream side of the log and lean into it a bit as you cross. Then, if you should fall into the river, you will not be swept into the log and maybe trapped against or under it by the fast-moving water.

If it is a tree trunk that bridges the crossing and there are projecting branches or stubs on it, the branches may be of some assistance in helping you to steady yourself as you cross. But be-

ware. Such projecting branches may catch on a corner of your pack and throw you off balance.

Before you cross any stream on a log or tree trunk, you should carefully consider the character of the stream below. How far down will you fall if you should slip? Will you fall onto jagged rocks or boulders? Study all such crossings deliberately and critically before you start across. Even though it takes longer, wading the stream may be best.

Generally a mountain stream will be swiftest at its narrowest point. It will often be deeper there also. Therefore, you should usually select the widest part of a river for wading. Instead of wading directly across swift streams, you should cross at a downstream angle to the bank.

Streams that originate in glaciers can be especially tricky to wade. The gray-colored, silted water often makes it impossible to see the bottom in water only six inches deep. Using a stick or pole as a probe in such water and as a "third leg" will aid in crossing.

The experience and physical ability of the hiker must always be considered when a hazardous stream crossing is to be attempted. No one (especially a novice) should be goaded into attempting a dangerous stream crossing that he feels is beyond his experience and capability. The stronger, most experienced members of the party should try the crossing first, if the decision is made to attempt it. It may be a good idea for those persons to carry across the packs of the less experienced. Also, a rope tied around the waist (with a bowline knot) of each member during his or her crossing and held by persons on the bank is a good safety precaution. If there are hikers on both shores, some members may feel more secure with two ropes around their waist, one being held by

Author crossing stream in British Columbia. My pack was heavy and I was not sure of my footing, so I chose the safe way. *(Bill Lee)*

persons on the far shore and the other, by persons on the near shore.

If you need to wade streams knee deep or deeper, a pair of hiking shorts will prove useful. Depending upon the company you are in, underclothes may also be satisfactory.

As you cross a stream, each step should be made carefully and deliberately. Be sure the forward foot is firmly positioned before taking the next step. Hurrying across may lead to a broken arm or leg or some other disaster. If you are crossing on a log and it is wet, or if you are fatigued, play it safe. Sit astraddle the log and ease yourself across by bumping along on the seat of your trousers, using your hands for leverage. This may be a little embarrassing, but a broken leg that could have been prevented is also embarrassing.

Wading streams in bare feet is not recommended. Your footing will be unsure, and there is always the risk of cutting or bruising your foot on a sharp rock or other material in the stream bed. Where there are streams along your route that will require wading, it is recommended that tennis shoes be carried for the purpose. One large pair may suffice for all members of the party and they can be retrieved, with a hand line, as each hiker completes the crossing. Where there are many crossings along the route, each person may prefer to carry his or her own tennis shoes. Where crossings are close together, the tennis shoes can then be left on for walking between crossings. Tennis shoes dry out quickly and can be worn around camp as a welcome change from hiking boots. If there are only a few "mild" stream crossings, a pair of rubber-soled shower slippers may give adequate protection to the feet. Some people, in wading a stream, remove their hiking boots and socks, put the hiking boots (minus socks) back on, and wade across in their boots. The water can then be dumped from the boots and the dry socks and wet boots put on again. A disadvantage of this method is that it is difficult to keep the feet dry if there are very many stream crossings. Damp feet are a discomfort, and they tend to make the skin tender and promote blisters. Also, the wet boots will frequently pick up dirt on the trail, which then becomes mud. The repeated cycle of wetting the boot, having the caked mud dry on the boot, wetting the boot again, and so on, is not good for the leather.

Stream crossings that lie along your route should be considered, insofar as possible, before you leave home. Get all the information you can on depth and nature of crossings, possible recent floods, and so forth. When you are out on the trail, you may find some crossings more hazardous than anticipated. A fast-moving mountain stream a foot deep requires careful evaluation. A depth of sixteen or eighteen inches may dictate that the party turn back. If the risk is great, give up the particular objective for this trip.

ABANDONED BUILDINGS

As you hike through the wilderness or other remote areas, you may come across an abandoned building. In foul weather it may appear desirable to seek shelter in such a building, if there is enough of the building left to offer some shelter. However, there may be some problems if you should decide to move in. Vermin and rodents such as bedbugs, fleas, and mice may be unusually plentiful in such a place. If you move in, you may decide to move out again and into a tarp shelter or whatever other shelter you are carrying. When walking about such a building, inside or outside, be very careful of boards with nails lying about. They may penetrate your boot, cause a puncture wound, and give serious trouble.

COOKING IN TENTS

During foul weather it may appear desirable to do your cooking inside your tent. This practice can present several serious safety hazards, however.

First, you are liable to set your tent on fire. The hazard is especially great when your cook stove is first started, before the fire is under control and regulated. With the flame out of control and possibly some spilled gasoline, you have a perfect setup for burning your tent, the occupants, and any equipment in the tent. If you feel you must cook in your tent, light your stove *outside* the tent and get it well under control before moving it into the tent. Have your escape route planned in case you need to get out of the tent in a hurry. (For example, have a sharp knife ready to cut through the back side of the tent, if the back of the tent is your position during the meal.) Extra care should be taken to see that the stove is sitting level inside the tent. While it is being used, the stove should also be watched constantly. In the event that it gets out of control, you need to be prepared to throw the flaming stove out the door of the tent. A good point to remember is that a backpack stove that explodes can have the destructive force of a dozen sticks of dynamite. Most stoves have a pressure relief valve or plug that will rupture when excessive pressure is built up in the fuel tank.

When it ruptures, however, a relief valve may spew out a real fireball of flame. If backpack gear, clothing, or a person is in the path of this fireball, the consequences can be serious.

Second, in a good tent all zippered up because of the weather, there can be danger from lack of oxygen. If it is windy outside, it is more likely that the tent will be tightly zippered so that there will be minimum wind disturbance to the burning stove. Drifting snow can also act to effectively seal off all fresh air from the tent occupants. A stove being used inside a tent not only uses up oxygen but it gives off carbon monoxide gas. This gas is odorless and very poisonous. It gives no warning of its presence. Your stove, a candle, or other flame will continue to burn even though there is a high concentration of carbon monoxide present. Being aware of the potential danger and providing adequate ventilation is the only way to prevent carbon monoxide poisoning.

Consider the possibility of doing your cooking under a separate fly, away from your tent, if cooking under a shelter is necessary. This will be much safer than cooking in a closed tent. Also, some tents have a vestibule where cooking can be done with less danger than by bringing the stove into the main tent. In bear country, cooking in or near a tent may result in food odors that will attract bears to the site.

Also, seriously consider a cold meal if the alternatives do not seem satisfactory. Better to eat a cold meal than to cook a hot meal and not be alive to eat it.

Ventilation. It is possible to have a ventilation problem in a tent even though you are not cooking in the tent. In foul weather the tendency is to close the tent up tight and consequently shut off the fresh air supply. Depending upon the number of occupants and the size of the tent, the oxygen in the air may be used up. Thus, it is important that at least some ventilation be provided in all weather. If snowfall occurs, the tent may be sealed by the snow. It then becomes necessary to make periodic inspections outside the tent and remove snow that may be sealing the tent (and may also cause it to collapse). Some indication of oxygen supply can be obtained by lighting a candle. If it burns with less than a normal flame, the oxygen supply is probably somewhat diminished.

You may have occasion to spend some time in a snow cave, either by plan or from necessity. The size of the cave should be ample to assure an oxygen supply for the number of occupants. It is im-portant to make a vent in the roof, using a ski pole, branch, or similar object. Snowfall may completely cover the vent as well as seal the entrance to the cave, however. Routine inspections should be made to assure ventilation. Again, lighting a candle will give an indication of the adequacy of the oxygen supply. If a stove is used inside the cave, much more ventilation will be necessary than would otherwise be required.

HATCHETS, SHEATH KNIVES

A hatchet is a useful item of equipment in some types of camping. So is an ax. It is a good idea to know how to use them safely, pack them properly, and keep them sharp. They are not necessary items of equipment on most backpack trips, however. When a wood fire is desired and permitted, wood can usually be had by simply picking it up off the ground. A sheath knife may be taken, but a good pocketknife will do the essential jobs that a sheath knife would be used for. Also, speaking of sheath knives, it is a good idea to keep your belt free of equipment. Modern packframes usually have a hip belt, and this cannot be properly used when there is equipment on your trouser belt.

Hatchets and sheath knives are common sources of accidents in camping. They represent a hazard when used by those who have not had good instruction and experience in their use. Firearms are in the same category.

INSECTS

Except in unusual circumstances, insects are simply a nuisance, rather than a threat to safety. At certain times of the year, in some areas, insects such as mosquitoes or flies may be so thick as to require the use of a head net that fits over a broad-brimmed hat and ties around the neck. Long-sleeved shirts and trousers are also important. Use reasonable precautions, and you will probably avoid being bitten by spiders, scorpions, and the few other insects that do represent some degree of hazard. Before you put your shoes on in the morning, shake them hard to get rid of any insects that might have crawled inside during the night. Or you can carry a very lightweight plastic or cloth bag and put your shoes in this at night. In areas where there may be scorpions, do not pick up loose rocks on the ground without first turning them over with your foot. There may be a scorpion underneath, and you could get a bite on the hand. Avoid thrusting your hands into thick vegetation, cracks in rocks, holes in stumps, and other places where you cannot see well. In other words, if reasonable precautions are taken, insects should present no threat to your safety.

Ticks are found in many sections of the United States, frequently in mountain valleys and forests. They cling to the underside of leaves and brush, or to grass, usually along trails used by animals. When an animal or person comes along the trail, the ticks fasten onto the unsuspecting traveler. They then dig in and suck blood. Their prevalence in a given area often varies from year to year. An area having few ticks one year may have many the next time you visit there. Ticks vary in size from about 1/4 to 1/2 inch in length. They are usually dark brown in color and always have eight legs. They attach themselves to the skin and bite by burrowing their entire heads into the flesh. If they have not started to dig in, they can be brushed off easily (but carefully). Once they have fastened themselves, special measures are necessary. Light a match, blow it out, and apply the hot end to the exposed part of the tick. It will back out. Or cover the entire tick with grease or oil. When in tick country, hikers should frequently inspect one another during the day for ticks that may be on outer clothing or on exposed skin areas (such as head, neck, chest, and back of legs) that are more easily seen by another person. In tick country take time to shake out clothing frequently. Inspect underclothing occasionally. Look carefully for ticks around your waist, on the skin under your belt. Ticks may inflict a painful bite and, in addition, sometimes spread certain serious diseases. Only a very small percentage of ticks carry such diseases, however.

POISONOUS PLANTS

Poison ivy, as well as poison oak and poison sumac, is a widespread plant that everyone should learn to recognize. If you realize that some part of your body has touched a poisonous plant, immediately wash the affected part with water and soap. Chances are that a rash or blisters will not develop. If you are particularly allergic to poisonous plants, you should carry a lotion, such as calamine lotion, that you have found to be effective in treatment.

On a well-planned backpack trip it should not be necessary to eat wild plants to supplement the food that you carry. About 1/3 ounce of prepared dehydrated salad provides a generous serving for one person, and there are some tasty dehydrated salads available. The energy spent in carrying

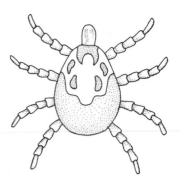

Tick (enlarged). Many varieties of ticks are found in the United States. All have the same general shape and eight legs. A well-fed female tick will be about half an inch long, others much smaller. Examine your skin and clothing frequently when in a tick area.

several ounces of dehydrated salad in your pack will probably be far less than the energy required to search for, find, and clean some wild-growing salad substitute at mealtime. In well-traveled areas, the ecological effect of persons gathering wild plants for food is also to be considered. Further, unless you are an expert, there is always the possibility of wrong identification of wild plants, and this can lead to severe illness—or worse. Water hemlock grows along many mountain streams and is very poisonous. Other common poisonous plants are wild cherry, poison oak, elderberry, and black locust.

SNAKES

Some people have a morbid fear of snakes. To avoid going into the mountains or desert because of that fear is very foolish, but not to have some knowledge of snakes and take a few reasonable precautions is equally foolish. Rattlesnakes are the most widely distributed of all our poisonous snakes. You may hike hundreds of miles without seeing a rattlesnake. Then, probably when you least expect it, there is one in your path. Rattlesnakes are found over most of the United States. They do not travel much in the daytime since they do their hunting for food mostly at night. In hot weather they will never be very far from shade. Unless you step on a rattlesnake or get very close to it, it will move out of your way if you give it a chance. Following are a few precautions you should take when traveling in country where there may be rattlesnakes.

Wear long-sleeved shirts and trousers. A rattlesnake may penetrate these when it strikes, but compared to bare skin, they offer significant additional protection.

When bushes are in or near your path, walk several feet out around them, rather than brushing up against them. Then, if there is a rattlesnake coiled there, it won't matter. Otherwise it may strike. Stay out of dense grass, brush, and foliage, insofar as possible.

In climbing either up or down hillsides, don't put your hands or feet down in places that you cannot see completely. Putting your hand over the edge of a blind cliff is asking for trouble.

If a stone or log is in your path, just assume that there is a rattlesnake coiled on the blind side and act accordingly. If you cannot see over the object, step up on it, then down, or go around.

If the trail goes along cliffs, walk several feet out from the face of the cliff. Then if a rattlesnake is coiled on a ledge of the cliff, you will probably avoid being bitten. A bite on the face or on the trunk of the body is much more serious than one on an arm or leg.

The treatment of poisonous snakebite has been the subject of considerable controversy in recent years. Some advise packing the bitten area with ice or snow and getting the victim to a hospital as soon as possible. The effectiveness of this treatment in itself is subject to question. Also, you may be deep into a wilderness or other remote area without ice or snow, and it may be several days or more before the victim can be moved to a hospital. A common accepted treatment for snakebite is to make a single incision over each fang mark, parallel to the muscle and avoiding any tendons. Mouth suction or a suction kit is then used to extract as much venom as possible—and as quickly as possible. A constriction band (not a tourniquet) is placed above the bite and is loosened every ten or fifteen minutes. In combination with the suction treatment, antivenin is usually administered if available, and if the victim is not allergic to horse serum. A tube of ethyl chloride may be helpful if you have had expert instruction in its use. The same applies to antivenin kits. Treatment of snakebite is a very serious matter. The foregoing remarks are not intended to be a complete description of the treatment for snakebite. You may want to seek the advice of your physician and prepare yourself accordingly.

It may be of some comfort to know that most people in good health (except the very young or very old) would recover from the average rattlesnake bite even if it were not treated, but don't count on it. It is recommended that you determine the course of treatment that you wish to use if it becomes necessary, carry the required equipment, and use it if the occasion arises. If you are interested in statistics, in the United States about 3,900 persons are bitten each year by poisonous snakes. Of this number about 60 persons die. It is believed that intense fear on the part of the victim is an important factor in most of these deaths.

ANIMALS

Normally there are no animals in our wilderness areas that will cause you any harm if you leave them alone and do not get too close to them. They will usually go out of their way to avoid you. Surprise encounters at close range, however, can frequently lead to trouble. Also, hikers should particularly avoid getting close to large animals during the rutting season. Further, they should take special precautions to avoid getting close to deer fawns, bear cubs, and the young of other large animals. The mother will usually be close by, and a serious encounter may result. Obviously a person should never try to corner or capture any wild animal, of any size.

Most people are aware of the potential dangers involved in getting close to *large* animals. On the other hand, many people are careless when it comes to *small* animals and rodents. Skunks are frequent visitors to backwoods camps. Like most other animals, they are looking for tidbits or scraps of food that may be lying about, usually around the cooking area. They usually appear tame, sometimes visiting camp in daylight. However, consider this: if you should agitate a skunk into spraying you, your clothes, or your equipment, you have a real mess. It requires special measures and plenty of time to clean up yourself and your equipment when you are close to home. In the backwoods it is next to impossible. Also consider the fact that the skunk may be rabid. This very real possibility also exists with chipmunks, ground squirrels, and other playful little animals. It is not too unusual for an overly friendly small animal in the wilds to also be rabid. Now, suppose you should get bitten by getting too close to such animals, or possibly in trying to feed them. It may only be a scratch, but you are now faced with a real dilemma. You can either consider the wound as just another small scratch, or you may consider the possibility of the animal's being rabid. In the latter case you can pack up your gear and head back for civilization and the uncomfortable consequences of a series of rabies shots. Hikers should keep a reasonable distance away from all wild animals, large or small! It should also be noted that bubonic plague may be contracted by handling of small animals and rodents. This serious, but not common, disease is transmitted by the bite of an infected flea. All animals should be observed from a respectful distance. Those who want a close-up photograph should use a telephoto lens.

When in camp, keep food stored out of reach of animals, preferably in bags suspended by ropes from trees or on a very high rope line. Keep food out of tents and away from where you sleep. Most animals have a keen sense of smell, and they will sometimes enter a camp area in search of food. Food stored in your tent may encourage the animals to come in. On rare occasions a bear or other animal may enter a tent during the night, even though there are people sleeping there, if you have food stored in the tent with you. A candy bar in your pocket is food, and the smell is readily picked up by some wild animals.

Bears. The most dangerous wild animals are not the completely wild ones, but rather those that are partially tame. Normally, wild animals are more afraid of you than you are of them. The bears in some of our national parks are examples of partly tame wild animals. In some areas of the parks, the bears become so accustomed to people that they are no longer afraid of them. In fact, they may become quite aggressive about coming into camp, stealing food or begging for it, and getting into mischief. As long as you leave these animals completely alone and keep food and other attractions out of their reach, there is normally nothing to fear from them. When you start feeding them by hand, teasing them, and so forth, it is a different story. You may end up without a hand—or worse.

As you hike along a mountain trail, if you see many good-sized rocks that have been freshly turned over, a bear has probably been along that trail recently. A bear will often do this in looking for beetles, grubs, ants, and other insect "tidbits." It will also tear apart stumps and rotten logs. The presence of fresh bear dung will indicate that a bear is, or has recently been, in the area. Most bears have a keen sense of smell but poor eyesight. You may see a bear coming toward you before it sees you. If you do, ease away and go around. Don't run unless you are sure the bear is chasing you. It may be coming toward you only in order to get a closer look and identify the "intruder." If you run, a bear is more likely to chase after you, whether or not that was its original intention. You can't outrun a bear.

A particular danger when traveling in bear country is to come upon a bear unexpectedly at

Bear bell on pack. These are commonly seen and used in bear country.

close range. Their reaction when surprised is generally unpredictable. If you are traveling where thick vegetation, brush, or terrain may lead to a surprise encounter with a bear, carry a whistle or bell. (If you don't have these, loud conversation or other noise will help.) Blow on the whistle frequently when you are in or near thick brush. The bell can be fastened to your pack where it will provide a continuous sound as you hike. Bears hearing the noise will take off in the opposite direction.

I have backpacked in the Canadian Rockies, and some of the areas had a good population of both grizzly bears and black bears. Certain precautions must always be taken in bear country. Wardens and other knowledgeable personnel in such areas generally advise selecting a sleeping area not closer than 300 feet to the area where you have been cooking, or where food is stored. Not only food but also the odors of such items as insect repellent, sunburn lotion, shaving cream, toothpaste, and cosmetics may attract bears. When you leave the area during the day or go to bed at night, put all such items in a bag with your food. Suspend the bag at least 15 feet off the ground. The best suspension system is to string a rope between two trees and tie your food bag at about the center of the rope. An alternate method, somewhat less desirable, is to suspend the bag from an isolated branch of a single tree. The tree should be of small diameter (8 to 10 inches) and relatively free of good-sized branches near the ground. It is desirable that the food bag be hung at least 6 feet out from the tree trunk and, again, a minimum of 15 feet above the ground.

Cooking inside a tent is dangerous at any time. In bear country such a practice may be an invitation to disaster. There will then be strong food odors in and about the tent—a perfect invitation for a bear. The tent, your clothes, and other articles will all have the food odor.

It has been stated by a number of sources that female personnel should not camp out in known bear country during their menstrual periods. It is claimed that the odor associated with menstruation may be attractive to bears. Some knowledgeable persons disagree with this. Based on the information that I have been able to obtain, I believe that there is no particular risk associated with camping in bear country during menstruation.

Before going to bed, wash from your body any insect repellent, sunburn lotion, or other substance that has an odor that may be attractive to bears.

Do not leave unwashed utensils and dishes near your sleeping area during the night. All garbage, food scraps, food wrappers, and so forth, should be meticulously burned in a fire if you have an open fire. If not, they should be stored and handled as food, away from animals, until you come to an area during your trip where it can be burned. Do not bury garbage. You might bury it where it is a safe distance from your sleeping area, but the next backpacker who comes along may unknowingly make camp near where you have buried garbage, a serious situation.

Bears like to follow streams or the shore of a lake. Keep your camp back a good distance from such places. Bears also follow trails—the same trails that you follow during the daytime. Again: Keep your campsite away from the trail.

Bears very seldom attack sleeping campers, but it has happened. If it happens to you, play dead. You can't fight a bear and win. Campers who have played dead have proven that with this technique you are likely to get by with the fewest possible injuries. If you are on the trail and are charged by a bear in an area where there are no climbable trees, throw off your pack, and again, play dead. Assume a fetal position. Clasp your hands over the back of your neck. The legs should be drawn up to the chest. It is entirely possible that the bear may be satisfied to simply rummage through and tear up your pack. Regardless, the perfectly still form of a human is least subject to

attack, as proven by many persons who have encountered bears and used this method.

These are the "rules" for bear country. Those who are not willing to take such precautions had best do their backpacking in a region that is free from bears.

HUNTERS

In many areas of the country the fall of the year is one of the ideal times to go backpacking. The daytime temperatures are invigorating, the woods are colorful, and there is usually less "competition" from other backpackers.

There is one aspect that should be carefully considered in planning a fall backpack trip, however. That is the hunting season. In some areas there are too many hunters in the woods during the hunting season, particularly during deer and elk seasons. Most backpackers would prefer to plan their trips around these hunting seasons so as not to be in the woods at the same time as the hunters. This can be easily done by consulting the state fish and game department and obtaining a copy of the hunting regulations and seasons. These vary from state to state, and often from area to area within a state. Thus, specific information on hunting seasons for that particular area is necessary.

The risk during hunting seasons other than those for deer and elk should be evaluated on an individual basis, from knowledge of practices in that particular area. A "hunter" sitting on a tree platform near the carcass of a dead horse, waiting for a bear to visit the carcass so he can collect a "trophy," isn't much of a risk. Most bird hunting is usually done in open areas, away from the woods, with short-range shotguns and would not usually be considered a risk to the backpacker in the woods. But heaven help and protect the backpacker who goes into an area that is saturated with hunters (from experts to raw novices) armed with high-powered rifles and hunting for deer or elk.

PREDATOR TRAPS

A possible source of danger, particularly to backwoods travelers in the Western states, is predator traps. These take a variety of forms, which normally are of no consequence if you are reasonably alert, but they are not to be fooled with. The U.S. Fish and Wildlife Service is one branch of the government that engages in predator control. An example of one predator device is the

Coyote gun. This is the "business end" of a coyote gun, with a wad of scented bait projecting a few inches above ground. The remainder of the gun is buried. A coyote, tugging on the bait, discharges the gun and gets a shot of cyanide (and certain death). If you come across such a device, leave it alone.

cyanide gun. A cyanide gun takes a special cartridge and discharges a load of cyanide. It is sometimes used in controlling coyotes in an overpopulated area. The gun mechanism is usually buried below the surface of the ground except for one small projecting part. This is the "business end," which is baited with food or a scent attractive to coyotes. When it finds the bait and tugs at it, the coyote gets a shot of cyanide in the mouth, which results in quick death. Poison meat and poison grain are sometimes used in predator control also, but a hiker should have no occasion to expose himself to these hazards.

Still other devices used in animal control are game traps. These generally take the form of a cage, which is baited so as to cause the door of the cage to close when the animal tugs at the bait. Bears are frequently live-trapped by such devices in order to transfer them to another locality.

There are rather strict procedures pertaining to the use of devices such as those mentioned. One of the procedures is to place conspicuous signs at all places where these controls are employed, warning persons that such a device is close by and not to tamper with it. Obviously, such warnings should be rigidly observed. As you travel in remote areas, if you should come across any piece of mechanical equipment or other man-made item, leave it strictly alone. Blasting caps are an example of such equipment frequently found in remote areas. They have turned more than one hiking and camping trip into a tragedy. If you

should discover a blasting cap, *don't touch it!* Note its location carefully, and report it to the nearest Forest Service office or similar agency.

WATER SUPPLY

When planning your day-to-day route, it is very important to keep in mind the location of all sources of water. In some regions this may be no problem at all. In other areas it will require serious consideration. If potable water sources are more than four or five hours apart, perhaps an alternate route should be considered. Or make certain that you have ample water for every member of the party, plus some to spare.

The water from most springs will be cool. If it is warm, it may simply be ground seepage rather than a spring. In determining whether a spring or other water source is safe for drinking, observe the plants and aquatic life in and about the water. The water may be crystal clear, but if it is completely free of small aquatic insects and other life, it is highly suspect. The water in many high mountain streams and from most springs in the mountains will usually be safe to drink without treatment of any kind, but not always. If there is any doubt, boil it or treat it with iodine or other water purification tablets.

Dishwashing should be done away from the stream, lake, or other water source. Dirty dishwater should be thrown on the ground away from the campsite, and not into the stream.

You should not swim or bathe in lakes and streams unless they have been approved for such by the responsible authorities. Not only can this damage the ecology, but swimming in some high mountain lakes can be quite dangerous.

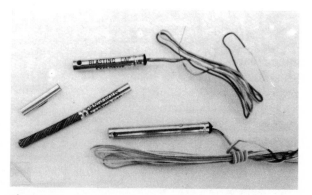

Blasting caps. Two types of caps are shown. Those with wires are electric caps. Such caps are often found in an area where there has been construction work or mining. They are very dangerous. If found, leave them alone and report their location to the nearest authorities.

WATCH YOUR STEP

When hiking on a wilderness trail, don't walk along with your head in the clouds. Watch your step! Few wilderness trails are level like city sidewalks. There will be holes, loose stones, tree roots, and other things in the trail over which you may stumble and fall. When you stumble, it is much more difficult to recover your balance with a full pack (or if you are tired) than it is without a pack. Stepping at an odd angle on a loose stone may give you a wrenched ankle, which will be very unpleasant to say the least. It can even mean the end of the trip.

Keep your eye on the trail. This doesn't mean you can't glance up once in a while as you hike along, but govern the length of your glances according to the difficulty of the trail. If it is really rugged, you had best watch where you "pick 'em up and set 'em down." If you like to admire the scenery under such circumstances (and who doesn't?), stop frequently on your feet for a few seconds in order to do so.

Remember when hiking through rugged country or through brush that your pack projects beyond your body outline and that places where your body may squeeze through, or just slip by, may not allow your pack to do so too. When you are going along at a good clip and your pack suddenly catches on a tree limb or other projection, it can be a rude awakening, and it can mean a spill. If you are crossing a "bridge" provided by a fallen tree and your pack catches on a limb, it can tumble you into the creek or whatever else is below.

In going up a short steep slope that has loose rock on it, go up one hiker at a time. Those standing below should be out of the way where they will not be struck by rocks dislodged by the person on the way up.

SCRAMBLING

Most backpacking for pleasure is done on trails or over terrain where, for the most part, you will be walking essentially upright. Yet there are occasions, particularly when one ventures onto little-used trails, or perhaps during brief off-trail travel, when rock scrambling is called for. Even a short section of the trail itself may be so rough, strewn with loose rocks, or otherwise "challenging" as to call for special measures and precautions if it is to be safely negotiated.

If you are on a trail, it is unlikely that the going will be so rough that there is any real danger of a serious fall, but don't take too much for granted. No one is nearly so nimble with a pack on his back as without it. It is not difficult to be thrown off balance. A slip on loose stone, mud, snow, or ice on the trail can cause a bad tumble. The patch of mud or ice need only be large enough for a single footstep to cause trouble.

Bad weather may cause a trail that is normally easily negotiated to become dangerous. In such a case the members should swallow their pride, suppress their egos, or whatever, and either turn back or seek a safer route. A radical change in trip plan may be called for, but where life and limb are at stake, the sacrifice must be made. Failure to do so may very well result in members of a rescue party having to risk their own necks to remove injured hikers or bodies from the backwoods.

Especially in off-trail travel, it is very important to remember that it may be fairly easy to go *up* a relatively steep hillside or cliff and quite difficult to come *down* the same route. It is not unusual for a novice to get high up on a wall in such a place and then find that he cannot proceed further. So he attempts to retrace his route and finds that he can't get down either. Thus he is trapped, an uncomfortable position to be in, to say the least. Some other party member must now undertake considerable risk to go after him and lead him to safety.

In negotiating steep terrain, there are several fundamental aspects that should be kept constantly in mind. The body should be kept essentially erect, with the weight directly over the feet. The hands should not be used for pulling the body up in such places. Rather they should only be used as a safety hold in the event a foot slips. A difficult place should not be negotiated hurriedly with the thought that if a foot slips, your momentum will hopefully carry you forward to safer footing. Each foot should be firmly planted, backed up by a good handhold, before the next foot is moved to a safe position. At all times the body should be supported on the slope at three body points: either two feet and a hand, or two hands and a foot. It is important to move slowly, "testing" each hand grip or foothold as you go. As for many other aspects of backpacking, practice near home is important. If you have not had such practice, a steep slope in the backwoods is a poor place to learn.

Normally there will be some hikers in a party who are more experienced and adept at negotiating steep and potentially dangerous terrain than others. It will frequently be a good approach to the problem for at least one of these hikers to make his way up the slope ahead of the lesser experienced. When he has reached a safe position, he can then belay another up the stretch, by a rope tied around that person's waist. The rope should be used only as a safety measure. The hiker should make his way independently up the slope, using the rope only in case of a slip or fall.

CAVES, MINE SHAFTS

Unless the trip is specifically planned to include the exploration of caves (under expert guidance), they should be avoided. Special equipment and clothing is required in the science of cave exploration (speleology). Abandoned mine shafts will be found in some remote areas. Avoid them like you would the plague.

YOUR GENERAL WELL–BEING

Although not exactly in the category of accident prevention, there are certain things you can do on a backpack trip that will benefit your general well-being and thus help you to get more enjoyment out of the trip. Here are a few of them:

Drink water freely. You will frequently be so engrossed in what you are doing that you will actually forget or neglect to drink enough water. You will probably be perspiring considerably, and your body will lose water as well as salt. Make a point of taking a drink of water at least once each hour. If you are perspiring freely or have been exerting strenuously, it is a good idea to take a bit of salt with the water, or to take a salt tablet one to three times a day. If salt tablets are used, it is important to drink plenty of water when the salt is taken. Also, the coated, slow-acting tablets are recommended, to avoid nausea. In hot weather you will probably want to salt your food more heavily than you normally would. The extra salt is important.

It is easier to remember to drink water freely in warm or hot weather than it is in cool or cold weather. However, it is equally important to maintain a frequent intake of water in cold weather. Some hikers may go for several hours in cold weather without drinking water or other beverage. This is dangerous. Your body will not be so quick to alert you to the need for liquid intake in cold weather; thus, drinking should be made a conscious habit. Drink *some* liquid every hour. In cold weather you may want to take time to heat some water for a drink of hot gelatin, hot chocolate, or other hot beverage, during a morning or afternoon rest break. In some situations it may be desirable to carry a thermos to be filled at breakfast or lunch time with hot water for preparing a hot drink at a rest break. More attention should also be given to nutritious between-meal snacks containing protein, fat, *and* carbohydrates, in cold-weather hiking.

The color of urine is some indication as to whether your intake of liquid is adequate. If it is a bit darker than usual, you probably are not taking in enough liquid. It is a good idea for the group leader to stress fluid intake, particularly to new or inexperienced members.

In warm weather it may occur to you to add fruit flavoring or other powdered drink preparation to the water in your canteen. Especially in hot weather this may not be a good idea. Under trail conditions it is not easy to clean a canteen thoroughly. Particles of sugar, flavoring, and whatnot may cause bacteria to grow within the canteen and may cause a digestive upset. It is recommended that, particularly in warm weather, the powdered drink preparation be carried in a separate container, kept in a handy compartment of your packsack. A tasty drink can then be mixed, in one-drink portions, directly in your drinking cup.

Avoid overfatigue. Don't push yourself to exhaustion. Especially go slow for the first day or two until you see how much you can take. Get at least eight hours of sleep each night, and preferably nine or ten.

In addition to inadequate sleep, fatigue can also be caused by concern and worry. If you have never carried a forty-pound pack for twelve miles through the mountains on a hot day, you will have some apprehension the first time you try it. While you are on the trail, this apprehension is going to increase the fatigue that you would normally experience from such physical effort. After the hike is accomplished, this apprehension is going to give way to a sense of elation because of your accomplishment, and some of your fatigue will disappear. It is not unusual for beginning backpackers to become so fatigued during the last few miles of hiking into a remote area that they can "hardly take another step." Upon reaching camp, they are so elated that they then want to go for another hike around the area. The cure for fatigue due to apprehension is practice. When you are confident of your ability and you keep your efforts within the bounds of that ability, this kind of mental fatigue is no problem.

If you have been so unfortunate as to acquire a blister or sprained ankle, concentrating on the

Careless backpackers in one of our large national parks built a fire here against the large log, which was almost completely burned through. An afternoon shower probably put out the fire after it was abandoned. There was other burnable material in the immediate vicinity, and a forest fire could have resulted. There were also designated campsites in the general area for use by backpackers; this was not one of them.

pain will cause fatigue in a hurry. If you have properly treated the blister or other problem, take your mind off it. Think about a recent pleasant activity or a contemplated one, but don't allow yourself the luxury of concentrating on the pain or other negative thoughts. Your mind and your attitude have a real and important bearing on how well you feel and how fatigued you become. Carry on a conversation, hum a tune, or joke with the others to avoid monotony. The miles and the hours will pass much faster and at the same time be more enjoyable.

Keep regular. Your daily routine will be changed quite a bit from your normal habits when you go on a backpack trip. Individuals who have very regular bowel habits at home may find themselves having difficulty on a backpack trip. Dehydrated foods can readily contribute to constipation. The inclusion in the diet of foods such as fruit and certain cereals and the regular intake of adequate fluids will do much to alleviate or prevent constipation. Taking two to four milk of magnesia tablets at bedtime is often effective in relieving constipation. Some tablets are mint flavored. Regardless, they are easy to take. More stubborn cases may require the use of glycerin suppositories, and a few of these may prove useful. They too are harmless. Never resist the urge for a bowel movement. Even though it may not be an opportune time, or the particular circumstances may cause some embarrassment, to delay for any significant length of time is foolish. Delay

of defecation may result in stool impaction, which can be very unpleasant, to say the least.

Avoid sunburn. It is strongly recommended that you not try to acquire a suntan on a backpacking trip. Most of the hikers who do so end up wishing they hadn't. You will get plenty of sun without purposely exposing yourself. Even though they wear a hat, long-sleeved shirt, and so on, most people need the help of a protective cream or lotion on their hands and face to keep the skin from getting too dry and uncomfortable. The back of the neck is particularly susceptible to sunburn. Your pack may offer some protection, depending upon how high it is and the angle of the sun. A broad-brimmed hat will help. A bandana worn as a neckerchief is good. Don't overlook the backs of your hands when applying sun protective cream. They are very susceptible. If your nose gets dry and crusty inside, put a bit of cream on a paper tissue and coat the inside of your nose with it.

Take care of your feet. They must get you where you are going and bring you back again. Carry some moleskin patches in your pocket. At the first sign (don't wait for a rest stop, meal stop, or until camp at night) of a tender spot on your foot or toe, stop and put a moleskin patch over it. In this way you will probably avoid a blister. If you do not have moleskin, put plain adhesive tape (not a Band-Aid) over the tender spot and leave it there. When you have a chance during the day, wash your feet. Use clean socks and change them daily even if they do not appear very dirty. If your feet sweat considerably, you will want to change your socks more often. In this case have a pair of extra socks handy and change them as necessary. Hang the sweat-soaked socks on the outside of your pack, so that they will dry as you hike along. The use of a good foot powder may also be desirable.

Avoid overeating. For most people, it is best to eat regularly (but not too much at one time) even though they may not feel particularly hungry. It is recommended that you try to make between-meal snacks as nutritious as possible, rather than primarily candy. Before starting a really hard climb, eat very lightly, if at all. When the climb is finished, eat a bit more—to hold you until time for the next regular meal. Some people eat less on a backpack trip than they do at home; others eat more. Regardless, being on a backpack trip should not be reason for you to stuff yourself with food. You will feel better and enjoy yourself more if you keep this in mind. Large quantities of food should not be eaten in an attempt to combat fatigue. For true physical fatigue, rest or a change in pace is needed. A moderate quantity of food, if any, may be eaten after the rest.

Practice sanitation. On the trail, hikers' clothes will become dirty, most hikers go unshaven, and after a few days a group may begin to look a little tacky. This is expected, but it is no reason for the group to let down when it comes to exercising ordinary good rules of cleanliness and sanitation. Washing hands after toilet functions and before meal preparation is just as important in the backwoods as it is at home. This should be especially borne in mind by those who are handling food and engaged in meal preparation. A cook sticking an unwashed finger in a pot of food, or handling food with unwashed hands, may very well give dysentery to the entire group.

One of the most common illnesses in backpacking is dysentery. This is often picked up from dishes that are not completely clean or from soap left on dishes during the dishwashing operation. Prevention is not difficult. You may rough-clean your dirty dishes, and they may look satisfactory. Regardless of how clean they may appear, however, rough-cleaning should always be followed by washing all dishes and cooking utensils thoroughly in hot soapy water, followed by a good rinsing in very hot water that has been boiled for a few minutes. An important camp rule is that each person drinks only from his or her own canteen and that eating utensils are never shared.

Keep clean. Hikers should not try to look like fashion plates in the backwoods. If they do try to, they will only wear themselves out and will be a pain to their companions. Clothes are going to get dirty, but good.

Even though your general appearance may suffer a bit, good body cleanliness can and should be maintained. Certain body areas, in particular, should be washed daily, if possible, to avoid discomfort, rashes, itching, or worse. It is important to keep the feet clean. Cleanliness in the crotch and anal areas is vital. As stated before, washing hands regularly is important. Other areas of your body might go for days without washing, with no adverse results. If your face, shoulders, legs, or another area is sunburned, it is recommended that you wash those areas with water only; use no soap. Using soap will only add to the discomfort of the sunburn. The same applies to windburn on the face, which can be almost as painful as sunburn.

In warm weather a complete sponge bath every day will add much to your feeling of well-being. With a few changes of water, plus some skill and dexterity, a full-fledged sponge bath can be taken with a small plastic washbowl. Or a plastic washbasin might be carried for the purpose. It isn't necessary to remove all clothes at once when taking a sponge bath. Shirts can be removed to wash the upper body and put on again while washing the lower body. The shadows of the night will provide the necessary privacy.

With reference to clothes, they are going to get dirty, but a few reasonable precautions will slow the process a bit. After cleaning fish, hands should not be wiped on the trousers. A clean rock or log to sit on is better than sitting in the dirt on the ground. Hands that get black from cooking utensils should be washed instead of wiped on clothes.

For washing socks, underclothes, and other items, a washbasin can be used, or a large billie can might be carried for that particular purpose. When the ground is soft, such as on a forest floor covered with pine needles, it is also possible to "make" a basin. A depression can be scooped in the ground and lined with a section of a poncho or a piece of plastic, thus providing a container for wash water. The depression should be restored to its original appearance after you have finished. If a wood fire is not permitted or available, you will probably not want to use the fuel required to warm water on your backpack stove. In that event it is suggested that you carry Woolite or a similar soap that will satisfactorily wash socks and other woolen materials in cold water. Socks, in particular, should usually be washed daily.

It is important to emphasize that the temperature of the body is greatly affected by the temperature of the extremities. Therefore, bathing of face, hands, and arms frequently on a hot day will help in keeping cool. A piece of thin toweling in your hip pocket or fastened to the outside of the pack will come in handy when you want to sponge off. Or in the dry climate of some of our states, you may prefer to remain wet and let the air do the drying.

FIRST AID

It is possible to make trip after trip into the backwoods and never need to use any first aid

Aftermath of a forest fire. This photo was taken soon after a fire had ravished many acres of good forest land, not far from the author's home. Within one to three years insects will move in and finish off the charred trees that remain standing.

beyond putting a bandage on a cut finger. The nature of first aid, however, requires that the supplies and techniques be available for use at a moment's notice. All hikers should know their first aid well and have the essential first aid supplies and knowledge at their fingertips, ready for action if and when an emergency occurs. It has probably been a good while since some hikers have thoroughly reviewed a first aid book. Refresher first aid courses are periodically given in many communities and are a good investment. There are probably many hikers on the trail today who would be hard pressed to define the difference between sunstroke and heat exhaustion. The symptoms and treatment are very different. Many hikers would probably panic if the need occurred to really put their first aid knowledge to a good test. Giving an injured or sick person the *wrong* first aid treatment is frequently worse than giving no treatment at all. In addition to knowing what to do, it is important to look through the contents of first aid kits occasionally, replacing or adding certain items and making certain that the kit is in good shape, ready for use.

This point cannot be emphasized too much: It is far better to *practice safety*, on the trail and in camp, than to have to use first aid.

12
On the Trail

HOISTING PACK

There are several ways of getting a loaded pack onto your back. If there is a rock ledge or fallen tree nearby, about waist high, you have a ready-made loading platform. Lift the pack off the ground and onto the loading platform, preferably by grasping the packframe members. Jerking the full weight of the pack off the ground by the shoulder straps alone puts considerable strain on the straps and their points of attachment. Balance your pack in an upright position on the platform, and face the shoulder straps. Slip one arm through its shoulder strap (usually the left arm first) and move the shoulder into the strap. Then thrust the other arm and shoulder through the other shoulder strap, and the pack is on your back.

When there is no convenient "loading platform" nearby—the usual case—a different approach must be used. The usual procedure is to first lift the pack onto the bent left knee, which is extended forward a bit. The pack is momentarily balanced on the left knee while the left arm is placed through the left shoulder strap. The body is then bent well forward, bending at the waist, at the same time rolling the pack onto the back and slipping the right arm through its shoulder strap. Then straighten up and adjust the pack. If it comes easier, balance the pack on bent right knee and slip the right arm through its shoulder strap

first. I am right-handed, and it comes most naturally to me to balance the pack on my left knee and get it onto my left shoulder first. I suggest you try it both ways, to see which way is more natural for you. Regardless, the whole process should be done in one essentially continuous motion.

Getting out of the pack is essentially the reverse of getting into it. From a standing position, to remove your pack, lower it to the ground in one continuous motion, but be careful not to drop the pack so that it hits the ground hard. You can very easily damage a packframe by "dumping" a heavy load onto the ground. If you are tired and your pack is heavy, the "safest" way to get out of it is to kneel on the ground and then "turn over" into a sitting position.

With a good rock or tree trunk to lean your pack against, you can also get it on while you are in a sitting position on the ground. (You could also prop your pack in some other manner.) Back up to your pack, in a sitting position, and slip your arms through the shoulder straps. In getting up from the sitting position with a full pack, first turn your body and move to a kneeling position on the ground. Then push up from the ground with your arms and your legs into an upright position. Getting a pack off by using this method is essentially the reverse of the foregoing procedure. You first unbuckle your hip belt. Then kneel on the ground, using your arms and hands to brace yourself as you lower your body into a kneeling position. Next, turn your body so that you end up in a sitting position. You are then ready to slip your arms out of the shoulder straps and free yourself from your pack. This method of getting into and out of a backpack is particularly useful if you are carrying a heavy load, or if you are very tired, or both.

Still another method of getting your pack on is to simply have someone else hold it in position while you slip into it. However, most backpackers prefer to get into their packs without help.

After the pack is on your back, push it up by the bottom ends of the two vertical frame members and adjust its position on your back. Then tighten your waist belt. The waist belt must be very tight if it is to serve its purpose of transferring a major part of the pack load to the hips. The shoulder straps should be quite snug. The pack should ride high, and the shoulder straps should serve primarily to hold the pack in place, rather than to support the load. The pack should not "hang" from your shoulders when you are carrying it. The top end of the shoulder straps should be positioned so that they pass close to the neck, never far out on the shoulders. This is an adjustment that should be made at home.

Most rest stops should be made with pack on and should be about thirty seconds to one or two minutes in duration. It should be emphasized that the process of removing your pack and putting it back on requires coordination and energy. When you are fatigued, it gets to be a real chore. Even though you may not be fatigued, you are using up energy that could better be spent in hiking. Also, less frequent rest stops with pack removed are not as helpful as the frequent short rest periods with pack on.

If a trail stop is going to be more than three or four minutes long, it is usually best to remove your pack. For more than a few minutes, it is much more tiring to stand still with a full pack on your back than it is to walk with it. For rest stops of three or four minutes or a bit longer, it is helpful if you can find a smooth rock or log of the right height on which you can rest the bottom of your pack without removing it. This is easier said than done.

FINDING THE TRAIL

Most people are alert to the possibility of losing the trail after you are on it. Taking a wrong turn, or getting off onto a game trail, or taking a trail that leads to the wrong destination are possible

Shoulder straps here are holding the load in place, but the load is not "hanging" by the straps. The hip belt is properly supporting most of the load.

Shoulder straps here are riding too low and are supporting much of the pack load. The hip belt should be carrying more of the load.

hazards under certain conditions. The matter of getting on the wrong trail *to start with* is not so obvious and deserves a bit of thought. It is rather disconcerting to discover, perhaps two or three hours after you have left the trailhead, that you are on the wrong trail.

Getting started on the right trail may be no problem at all. There may be a well-defined trailhead with a prominent sign clearly marking the trail as the one you wish to take. Or there may be several main trails leading out from that trailhead. Again, they may be clearly marked, and there may be no problem. However, if more than one trail starts off in the same general direction, there may be some confusion as to which is the desired one. Also, shortly after it leaves the trailhead, there may be one or more unmarked trails leading off from it. These might have been made by day hikers taking short hikes near the trailhead and not staying on any particular trail. There are also the remote areas, with rather obscure, poorly maintained trails that may be vaguely marked or perhaps not marked at all. Cattle trails near the perimeter of a wilderness can be a problem. Thus, in your anxiety to get going, it is not difficult to find yourself on the wrong trail—perhaps only after an hour or two of hiking.

To prevent getting started on the wrong trail, take a little extra time at the trailhead to assure yourself that the trail that appears to be the correct one is, in fact, the one you want. Make local inquiry if there are knowledgeable persons in the area who can help you. Study your map carefully. After you have started up the trail, keep referring to your map often, if necessary, to assure that the direction, landmarks, and other features shown by the map coincide with those of the trail you are on.

In general, the same procedure applies to picking up the trail out of a camp, after you are in the backwoods. There may be only one trail; there may be a junction of several trails near the camp. It gets the day off to a bad start to hike an hour or more along the wrong trail and then have to retrace your steps and start over again.

SETTING THE PACE

Most backpack trips are made for pleasure, and most backpackers are not too much concerned with how many miles they cover in a day. In fact, most backpackers could care less. However, a day on the trail is usually started with some goal in mind, even though it may not be far in distance.

Also, depending on the terrain, there are certain fundamentals in hiking to be adhered to if the miles that are covered are to be in relative comfort and with the least expenditure of energy.

In hot weather try to get an early start on the trail. You can hike more miles on a cool morning, with less expenditure of energy, than in a hot afternoon when the sun is bearing down. Usually the larger the group, the more difficult it is to get an early start in the morning. It may be well to sacrifice a hot breakfast for a cold one just to get an early start. Even if you call a halt by midafternoon, the early morning start will usually pay off if there is a specific distance to be covered and the weather is hot.

The natural inclination of many hikers is to start off in a burst of energy, while they are fresh, and then taper off or perhaps give out relatively soon. This is a poor approach. A steady, even pace can be maintained for more hours, and more miles will be covered in greater comfort, than with a fast pace that will require prolonged rest stops and may even lead to collapse and illness.

During the first hour some halts may be required for adjusting pack loads, relacing boots and similar tasks. After that, the frequency of stops will usually depend on the nature of the terrain and whether the hiking is on essentially level ground, uphill, or downhill. A set rule of taking a break of so many minutes out of each hour will seldom be beneficial in the ever-changing terrain of mountain travel. In general, the longer the rest break, the harder it is to get started again.

On reasonably level ground, walk with a determined pace, never hurried, but as though you were going someplace. Feet should be planted flat on the ground. If most of the weight is put on the toes, the leg muscles will soon tire. Never trot, or even walk extremely fast, with a pack on your back. Keep hands out of pockets and don't carry gear in your hands. (Usually, if there is gear left over that you have to carry in your hands, you are not properly packed.) Although your pack will interfere somewhat, swing your arms a bit rather than letting them hang like dead weights. Don't saunter or stroll. Too slow a pace is just as tiring as one that is too fast. Anyone who has ever led a slow-moving, stubborn, one-speed pack animal along a wilderness trail knows how tiring an unnaturally slow pace can be. If possible, settle into a *rhythmic* stride, which is not hard to do on a good smooth trail. However, on an uneven trail and in rough terrain it is very difficult, if not impossible, to maintain rhythm.

If you are climbing an uphill slope, use a slow

but steady pace and stop on your feet for a few seconds as necessary, rather than push yourself to the point of giving out and then stopping for a much longer period. The steeper the grade, the shorter your stride will be. On very steep grades the *rest step* should be used. The rest step allows a short period of rest between each step: (1) One foot advances to a new position. (2) The knee of the rear leg is locked and that leg momentarily supports the entire body weight. The unweighted advance leg rests. (3) The rear foot advances to rest. There is an alternative to this method: (1) Transfer all weight to the forward leg and lock the knee; (2) Let the trailing leg go limp; (3) Advance the trailing leg to the forward position. Since the grade is steep, the steps will be short. If you are at high altitude (8,000 feet or more) make a conscious effort to breathe deeply with each step. Deep breathing will help to make up for less oxygen at high altitudes and is helpful in preventing altitude sickness.

As you travel uphill, you will from time to time be able to see the top of the ridge, and as the top draws near, the spirit soars. However, when you finally reach the ridge top, you find that there is another ridge beyond that, and the spirit falls. This process will probably be repeated many times during the day. Just when you think you have it made, another long, steep grade comes into view. This can be very damaging to the enthusiasm. The cure is to forget about the ridges ahead, maintain a slow but steady pace, and let your mind drift to more pleasant thoughts.

Traveling downhill is not as difficult as uphill hiking, but it is not as easy as it appears it should be. Your feet and knees can take a real beating in downhill travel. Before you start downhill, it may be desirable to add a pair of socks to reduce the motion of the foot within the boot. Boots should be laced up snugly. Your stride will be increased, but resist the temptation to walk fast. With each downward step there will be a certain jar or shock. This should be cushioned by bending the knees slightly. Downhill travel is tiring, and rest stops are just as important as in uphill travel.

Traveling cross-country, off the trail, can be very difficult. In wooded and rugged terrain it can be essentially impossible. Your trip should normally be planned so that trails are followed. Thick brush, boulder fields, and blind canyons can quickly take the fun out of cross-country travel in rough terrain. Traveling with a heavy pack in such areas can also be dangerous. It is easy to lose your balance and take a tumble.

If you should feel a bit light-headed while hiking, stop and prop one foot up on a rock or log (with your arm resting on your thigh). Then lean over (keeping your pack on) so that your head is at about the level of your hips. If this doesn't help, call a rest stop and take off your pack. Then lie down on your back and prop your feet higher than your head. In a few minutes you should feel well again. Before continuing on your way, take a drink of water with a little salt in it and eat some candy or other trail snack. Never neglect your water intake. Take a good drink at least once an hour, but not huge amounts at any one time. Never ration yourself to see how long you can go without water. When the weather is hot (and even on a cool day when you are exerting heavily), you need to replace the salt that is lost through perspiration. Don't take too much salt at one time, however, and always take it with plenty of water.

Do not cut across switchbacks. They are there for a reason. The switchback represents the easiest, most energy-conserving route up (or down) the slope. Further, cutting across switchbacks leads to erosion.

Take every precaution to avoid sweating when the weather is cool. On a cool morning you may start hiking while wearing an extra shirt, sweater, or other heavy clothing. In your desire to keep moving down the trail, you may forget or neglect to stop and remove unneeded outer layers of clothing when you warm up. This is a serious mistake. Heavy exertion can take the place of a lot of clothing insofar as keeping you warm is concerned. Slow your pace and open up or remove some of your outer clothing, but don't sweat. It is far better to be a bit cool when you are exerting than to be perspiring. On a cool day, if you allow your shirt to become wet with perspiration, your body is going to cool down rapidly as soon as you stop or slow down in your exertion. Wet clothing quickly loses its insulating value. Also, the evaporation of the water from your perspiration-soaked shirt or jacket will cool your body too suddenly. This is why several layers of clothing are better in cool weather than a single heavy layer is. You have a better range of adjustment to suit the outside temperature.

KEEP TOGETHER

A small backpacking group of several persons will generally keep together. They will have chosen one another as backpacking companions because they are acquainted and socially compatible. Their attitude and capability on pace, as well as other basic aspects, will probably also be similar. In all probability, no member will consciously consider any other member to be the leader, in the usual sense of the word. The group will keep together by instinct and preference. With larger groups the matter of staying together, or at least in contact, will usually take on a different aspect, and may develop into a very real problem.

When on the trail, hikers should generally walk in single file and should not follow one another too closely. It is very annoying to have a hiker follow so closely that each time you stop or change pace a bit, he has to do likewise to keep from running over you. On the other hand, hikers should keep in contact as a group, unless they specifically plan to break up into more than one group. The leader should not need to make frequent checks to determine where certain members are. Stragglers should be eliminated at home, before the trip starts—not on the trail. In general, the pace of a group must be governed by that of its slowest member. Some leaders like to have the slow hikers at the front of the group, so that the whereabouts of those persons is known at all times.

Walking in a tight group, in close formation, can be very tiring and is unnecessary. Variations in natural pace and personalities will soon be in conflict. In a fairly large group, the individuals will gradually seek out others whose pace is similar to theirs and who have some appeal in sociability. In order to maintain contact and not "lose" any members, the leader will need to request caution by the members in keeping in touch with the "group." This will particularly apply where the trail may be a bit obscure, where the possibility of taking a wrong turn in the trail exists, or where safety aspects require experienced leadership in negotiating a particular stretch of trail.

For fairly large groups, depending upon the experience of the members, the leader may want to appoint an "assistant" to bring up the rear. If it is a very large group, assistants should be placed at intervals along the line of hikers. By their experience they will know when the pace should be slowed or speeded up and when to take breathers. By visual contact with the assistants, hikers will in turn know when to change their pace. For most of the short stops (of a few seconds to one or two minutes in duration) that hikers will make during the day, they will be stopping in their individual places, not as a group. When stops are made as a group, an accordion effect results. When the leader stops, it takes from a few seconds to a few minutes for the nearest and farthest hiker, in turn, to catch up. By the time those farthest away have caught up (or before), the leader is ready to move on again. This can be pretty exasperating, particularly to those farthest from the leader. One of the reasons you came on this trip was to "get away from it all," including crowds of people (remember?). Your backpack trip will give you more of a feeling of a wilderness adventure as an individual if your trail pace and stops are patterned along the lines described.

There may be times when you will *want* to walk quite close together. You may want to carry on a brief conversation with one or more other members of the group. It is better to move in close to them rather than to shout. At other times you may simply want close companionship for a while. Some sections of trail through easy terrain may even allow you to walk abreast of another person, if there is a mutual desire to do this.

In steep and rough terrain, some distance between hikers is necessary for reasons of safety. Loose rock may be dislodged which can be dangerous to a person following too closely. Occasionally a tree limb may project across the trail, perhaps at shoulder level. When a hiker in front temporarily pushes the limb out of his way, it may spring back and whip the following hiker in the face. This is unpleasant, to say the least. It could bruise the hiker, it could hit him in the eye, or it could throw him off balance.

Hikers following one another too closely can be safety hazards to each other. I know of a situation where a small group was following very closely on one another's heels on a downhill stretch of trail. They were going a bit fast. The hiker in the lead stumbled badly and fell. Those following fell over him and each other, in turn, in an accordion effect. A reasonable distance between hikers is essential.

Dust is a factor that will sometimes govern the distance between hikers. If there is much dirt in the trail, it will often become ground to a powder-like consistency. This is particularly true on trails that are heavily traveled and those frequented by animal packtrains. Each hiker will stir up a little dust cloud in hiking along such a trail. Walking in someone else's dust is not only unpleasant, but it is actually harmful to your lungs and to your health in general. Therefore, it is recommended that on dusty trails the distance between hikers be such that walking in dust clouds is not necessary.

In a large group there will always be certain

"eager beavers" who find the pace of the main group to be too slow and who will want to dash ahead. Rather than drawing away from those in the main group gradually, and perhaps being out of touch with them for hours, they should consult with the leader. They should get permission to plunge ahead, if that is their desire. They should arrange to keep in contact with the main party by stopping at a designated place further along the trail. Or they can be told to stop along the trail at a certain hour wherever they may be. If there is any danger of their getting off the trail and losing it, they had best be told to stay close to the main group.

Animal packtrains may be encountered on some of the main trails of our national forests and parks. These animals and their handlers have the right of way over foot travelers. When you see such a packtrain approaching, step well off the trail (on the outside edge) and stand quietly while it passes. Any sudden movements you may make can readily cause some animals to shy and give their handlers real trouble. You should remain quiet or talk very softly. Practice courtesy.

TRAIL STOPS

It makes the trip more interesting if some thought is given to choosing places for rest stops. One of the major reasons for making most backpack trips should be to enjoy the beauty of each day and whatever natural features the area has to offer. In fact, within reason, a brief stop should be made at all interesting places, whether a rest stop is needed or not. Those who set a grueling pace, with the objective of reaching some final "goal" as soon as possible, will miss much. There should be more to a backpack trip than watching the heels of the hiker in front of you—much more.

When you make stops along the trail during which you remove your pack (whether they are rest stops, lunch stops, or whatever else), keep your equipment together. Don't set your pack in one place, lean your fishing rod against a tree in another place, and put your camera or canteen on a rock in still another place. It is recommended that in such temporary stops you set your pack on the ground and set camera, binoculars, canteen, or anything else that is not in the pack on the ground beside it. In this way you will probably avoid such problems as getting two or three miles down the trail and suddenly remembering that you left your camera hanging from a convenient limb on a nearby tree at the last rest stop. In stopping for lunch, set your pack and gear back far enough from the work area (where you are getting lunch) that other hikers do not have to stumble over it and possibly step on some piece of gear in the process. Such stepped-on (and possibly broken) gear is usually considered to be the responsibility of the hiker who left it there, not the person who stepped on it. It is best to lean your pack against a tree trunk, bush, or rock, away from the work area, and to put any other items of equipment right beside it. Fishing rods not fastened to the pack should be propped against the pack or something else so that they are off the ground. More than one backpack trip has been seriously affected by, and bruised feelings have resulted from, leaving fishing rods lying on the ground and having them stepped on. The same general idea applies in camp also. Stow your gear in one place, insofar as possible, and keep it away from the general work area where others are working and walking about.

Most hikers are well aware of the necessity for suspending packs off the ground at night. Even though you may not be in bear country, which calls for more elaborate procedures, it is desirable to suspend the pack in order to keep it out of reach of small nocturnal animals. They can readily be attracted to your pack by food odors and may not only steal some food but damage the pack by gnawing on it (or through it) in trying to reach the food. Actually, similar precautions also need to be exercised for certain trail stops that are made during the day. During a lunch stop, or other lengthy stop, it is best to stay very close to your pack so that you can keep an eye open for possible marauders. If this is not convenient, it is best to suspend the pack from a tree limb. Otherwise, a pack rat, ground squirrel, or other creature may "help himself" and damage your pack.

HAZARDOUS TRAVEL

Well-traveled main trails in the mountains will normally present minimum hazard. However, there are exceptions. Foul weather, heavy snow or ice, and sudden changes in weather can change a normally safe trail into a hazardous one. There is also the matter of off-trail travel, which may be quite safe or may present a few problems.

A rock slide or rock falls may occur on nearly any steep, rocky slope. Gullies and chutes that lead up a steep mountainside are particularly vulnerable areas, and are to be avoided. Talus is rock that usually accumulates near the base of cliffs. It is composed chiefly of rock fragments that have weathered and broken off from peaks and cliffs higher up the mountain. The fragments are usually sharp-edged and fairly large, the size of cobblestones and larger, with perhaps boulders here and there. *Scree slopes* consist of small rocks and gravel that frequently collect under cliffs. The slope itself is usually at an angle of about 30° to 40°. The size of the rock particles that make up a scree slope may vary from sand to pieces the size of a fist. Occasionally a scree slope will contain larger particles, but in general they will be fairly uniform in size. A scree slope may slide fairly easily, depending upon the slope and amount of vegetation and boulders that may be interspersed among the scree. When one is ascending, a scree slope should generally be avoided, if possible. In trying to climb such a slope, each foot will slip a bit before it holds and offers a firm platform for the next step. Therefore, there is some wasted energy with each step. For descending, depending on the nature of the particular slope, scree may offer a satisfactory way down, and it may even be fun. In descending, coming down the slope essentially in a straight line is usually the best method. Generally the back should be kept straight and the knees bent. The feet need to be shuffled to keep them from sinking into the slide. Running down scree should be avoided. You can easily get up too much speed and lose control. It is best to lean the body slightly out and downhill. If you slip, the body will then be forced into nearly an upright position. If you stand straight, a slip will throw the body backward, out of balance, and you may take a tumble. A scree slope may contain some grass and other vegetation. However, if you are ascending, you should take hold of such vegetation only to maintain balance, rather than to pull yourself up. One of the consequences of traversing a scree slope is that some small stones will usually find their way into your boots. Gaiters will be helpful in preventing this problem.

In a *talus slope* the fragments are larger and have sharp edges. There is greater friction between the individual rock particles making up the slope. The angle of such a slope may be 45° or greater. A talus slope is somewhat more difficult than a scree slope to descend, and it can also be more dangerous. It should be remembered that a loose and rolling rock no larger than your head could kill a person below. The danger of falling rock can never be overemphasized. A hiker should not cross, or ascend or descend, a talus slope when he is in a position directly above other persons who may be hit by falling rock. In going

up, down, or across a talus slope, the steps are generally quite short and fairly rapid. The foot contacts the rock, preferably the topmost part, but the next step is taken before the full weight is placed on the foot. Some of the rocks stepped on will not be stable. Balance and rhythm are required, and you need to be on the alert to take the next step quickly if the rock should start tipping or sliding. Brief pauses for rest can be made when you come to a large rock or boulder that is obviously stable. Large boulders can generally be depended upon to be more stable than smaller ones. Boulders will have less tendency to overturn or shift if you step on the uphill side.

It is best to get acquainted with rock and to practice your technique on short slopes, where mistakes will be less dangerous, before attempting high slopes. Practice near home, or near a trailhead, is again preferable to practice on a slope deep in the backwoods.

If you have snow or an ice field to cross, it is desirable to do so before noon, if that is feasible. Snow and ice become more stable overnight, because of moisture draining out of the snow and cooler temperatures solidifying it. A clear night is normally a cold night. In contrast, rain during the night could make the snow unstable for crossing. Shadows and light are also most favorable in the morning. If the sun is shining, the snow will be melting away from the edge of any rock outcrop. This is because light-colored objects reflect light (and thereby reflect heat also), while dark objects absorb light and heat. For that reason, a rock protruding through the snow absorbs more heat than does the snow around it. As the rock warms, it melts the nearby snow. The larger the rock, the more heat it generates and the greater the distance from the rock the snow will be "rotten." The snow pack may thus be undermined there, and walking within even a few yards of the rock may cause you to break through the surface. If you must pass near rocks when the sun is out, go along the least melted side.

Snow blindness is an ever-present danger when traversing snow-covered terrain. Dark glasses or goggles are important. Tying a large handkerchief around the head, just below the eyes, will help reduce the sun's reflection off the snow.

Avalanche terrain should be avoided when possible. Slopes of 25° or less do not usually slide. At angles greater than 35° the possibility of a slide is greatly increased. Steep gullies are natural avalanche paths. Heavily timbered slopes seldom avalanche. However, slopes with only scattered timber are essentially no safer than those that are completely open. Changes in weather are the major cause of avalanches. In an electrical storm, thunder can cause a rock slide.

The study of snow avalanches is a science in itself. For some layman's information on this subject, read E. R. LaChapelle's *The ABC of Avalanche Safety*. (See Appendix H.)

STAY ORIENTED

To be oriented means to know where you are. Unless you have been over a trail before and know it well, you probably cannot stay oriented without a map and compass. Before starting out on a new trail, especially one in a remote area, make every reasonable effort to find and talk to some person who is familiar with that trail. Ask about *checkpoints* and *prominent landmarks* that will help you stay on the trail. Inquire about those places where you are likely to miss a turn and lose the trail.

From the time you leave the roadhead, follow your progress on the map. A stream crossing, a swamp, a spring, and a mountain peak in the distance (that will provide a compass bearing) are all good checkpoints that will appear on a topographic map and help you stay oriented. A fallen tree across the trail, an abandoned cabin, and a prominent rock formation are possible checkpoints (and good ones), but they will not appear on a map. These are the types of checkpoints that you should inquire about before starting on the trail.

In some terrain, especially if good trails are being followed, it is relatively easy to stay oriented. An occasional reference to a map is all that is required to assure yourself that you are where you think you are. However, it is recommended that the compass be kept handy and used regularly, though not necessarily often, simply to retain familiarity with it and to bolster your confidence when in a situation where you *must* rely on it.

Keep in mind where the trail is going. The purpose of a trail is to get from one point to another. It will usually be the shortest route consistent with the terrain. Many trails in the West, as well as those in some other regions, are laid out to accommodate horses and pack animals. If you find yourself scrambling among boulders, confronted by very many logs in the trail, going through thick brush, or using your hands to negotiate a steep slope, then you are probably on a deer trail and *off* your chosen trail. Trails having very

many of the obstacles mentioned would not normally be used for horse travel.

You may be following one of the trail systems that has its own distinctive markings. In a national forest it may be a blazed trail laid out by the Forest Service. In some of the national parks the trail markers will be orange-colored, rectangular pieces of metal, about 3 by 5 inches, nailed to a tree at a height of about 6 to 8 feet above the ground.

Depending on the wilderness, national forest, or other area that you may be in, and the frequency of usage of the trail, its general condition may be very good, fair, or pretty rough. A main trail will usually have small, neat signs at the takeoff from the roadhead, showing the trail name or number and the distance to the major objectives. Along the trail, at points of intersection with other trails, there will frequently be additional signs showing where those trails go and the distance, as well as the remaining distance of your trail to its objective. Where the trail cuts into the mountainside, the outside edge will frequently be reinforced with logs or stones to prevent erosion. On steep slopes, more stones or log formations will often be laid across the trail for the same purpose. Such trails are usually very easy to follow. Except for reading the signs along the trail and an occasional reference to your map, no significant effort is required to stay on the right trail.

Obviously not all trails in our national parks and wilderness areas are prominently marked and easy to follow. On most government trails there will still be the sign at the roadhead, but that may be the last one you will see for a good while if you are in a remote area. Availability of personnel for maintaining the trail and infrequency of usage simply make it impractical to accomplish any more maintenance than perhaps the occasional removal of a large tree that falls across the trail and makes it impassable for horses. The blazes may be very old and faint or obscured from sight by growing limbs.

Deer paths that intersect with your desired trail may be more used than the trail itself and can easily lead hikers to follow them and get off the main trail. The trail that appears as a good solid line on the map you are holding in your hand may be faint indeed in actuality, and overgrown with weeds and brush. I well remember one trail turnoff that has been marked for many years only by a rusted horseshoe and a more rusted condensed milk can hanging by a rope from a low bush.

Is all of this bad? Not by a long shot. Few of us who have frequented such areas would want it any other way. We do not particularly look forward to "progress" and improvements dictated by advancement of civilization into such areas. This will call for replacement of such markings by small neat signs and "brushing up" the trail, and the area will then be frequented by more people.

This is simply mentioned so that hikers won't take too much for granted in their pretrip planning when they study that nice, pretty map, with its very distinct lines marking the trails. What may appear as a very easy problem in pathfinding when the map is spread out on the living room table at home may be much more of a problem when you are out there in the mountains with the sun boiling down, perhaps a bit fatigued, and trying to figure out "where the heck the trail went to."

As you progress along the trail, keep a mental or written record of important checkpoints that you pass and the time of day that you pass them. Fix in your mind the approximate time that you should arrive at the next checkpoint. When you arrive at a checkpoint, make sure that it is the particular checkpoint that you think it is. (There may be lots of stream crossings, more than one spring, and more than one fallen tree in the area where you are looking for such a checkpoint.)

Keep a mental note of your general direction of travel. The trail will continue in a given general direction as shown on the map except where it is necessary to temporarily deviate to avoid difficult or impassable terrain. These deviations may not be apparent on a map and at times they may amount to a complete change in general direction. In some unusual situations it is possible to get so turned around that you may start back down the trail in the direction you just came from. In foggy or stormy weather, where there is no sun to aid you in determining general directions, it is a good idea to take a look at your compass occasionally.

Your trail may top out on a windswept, rocky ridge where there are no trees to be blazed. You may assume that it goes on down the other side of the ridge, but when you look there you don't find it. The heat of the noonday sun, fatigue, and your eagerness to keep going ahead may impair your judgment. You finally pick up a trail on the other side of the ridge and follow it. However, you may have picked up a deer trail, and after a while you decide it's the wrong one. Backtrack! Don't go cross-country, even for a short distance, in the hope of picking up the right trail. Chances are that going cross-country will require more time

and energy than backtracking. There is a good chance that you may cross your desired trail at a place where it is a bit obscure, not recognize it, and keep right on going. You may soon become thoroughly lost.

Your trail may lead down into a dry arroyo. You assume that the trail crosses it and continues on up the other side. However, when you look for the trail on the other side, it is not there. In all probability the trail has gone right up (or down) the middle of the arroyo in order to pick up a better section of terrain for climbing out. There may not be any trees lining the arroyo that are suitable for blazing; hence, the trail is not marked there (and right when you most needed the marking). Water rushing down the arroyo after an occasional rain has obliterated any sign of the path on the ground. These little problems add to the difficulty (and pleasure) of backpacking. They are most apt to occur in remote areas, off the beaten path. That ten dollars per day and food that the ranch boy wanted for guiding your party may start to look rather insignificant about this time. Before you go into remote areas, be sure that your technique, your knowledge of the area, and your general preparedness are a match for the job at hand.

MAP AND COMPASS

The maps most commonly used by backpackers are the topographic (or topo) maps, available from the U.S. Geological Survey and some equipment supply firms. They show the topography, or surface configuration, of the land. Contour lines, brown in color, show elevation above sea level. All points on a given contour line are at the same elevation. Differences in elevation can be seen by comparing adjacent contour lines. Where contour lines are close together, the lay of the land is steep. The farther apart the lines are, the more level the land is. The line for every fifth contour is heavier than the others, and the elevation is printed in brown. Natural features on a topo map include lakes, streams, springs, swamps, and forested areas. Trails, roads, and buildings are also shown.

Backpackers most commonly use the 7½- and 15-minute quadrangle maps. On the 7½-minute series, an inch on the map represents about 2,000 feet on the ground. In the 15-minute series, one inch on the map represents approximately one mile on the ground.

When a topo map is held in reading position (right side up), true north is toward the top of the map. This will be verified by a small diagram at the bottom of the map, which shows not only the direction of true north but also the declination (or variation) and the direction of magnetic north, and the difference in degrees between the two.

To orient a map means to place it in such position in front of you that north on the map is the same as north on the ground. This can frequently be done by lining up known features in the terrain, such as mountain peaks, lakes, and streams, with the same features on the map. To do this, you must find on the map the position where you are located and be able to recognize prominent features in the surrounding area.

A map is easily oriented by use of a compass. The compass is set at 360° and is placed near the declination diagram at the bottom of the map. The direction-of-travel arrow should point north, toward the top of the map. The side edge of the base plate of the compass is positioned so that it is parallel to the magnetic-north line of the declination diagram. The map is then turned, with the compass on it, until the North end of the compass needle points to N on the compass housing. The map is now oriented.

Because of the magnetic declination it is possible to make errors in going from map to compass bearing and vice versa. When the declination is east of true north and you are going from map to compass bearing, the declination is *subtracted* from the bearing. When the declination is west of true north and you are going from map to compass bearing, the declination is *added* to the reading. When the declination is east of true north and you are going from compass bearing to map, the reading is *increased* by the amount of declination. When the declination is west of true north and you are going from compass bearing to map, the reading is *decreased* by the amount of declination. It is easier to work with a map, and avoid the possibility of errors in going from map to compass bearing and vice versa, by drawing a series of magnetic-north lines across the face of the map. If the declination is 15° east of north, draw a series of parallel lines one inch apart across the map, parallel to the magnetic-north index arrow at the bottom of the map. Thus, all these superimposed lines will be 15° east of the true north-south meridian lines on the map.

With the magnetic-north lines drawn in on the face of your map, it is much easier to use. Place your compass on the map with the direction-of-travel arrow pointing toward your desired direction on the map. (One edge of the compass base plate should touch both starting point and desti-

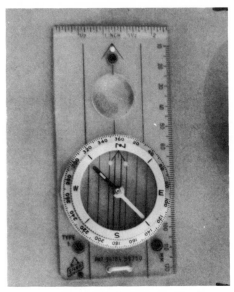

Compass. With attached base plate, direction-of-travel arrow, and straight edge, this type is most useful for orienting a map, taking a field bearing, and following that bearing.

nation.) Then hold the base plate of the compass firmly on the map in that position with one hand. With your other hand, turn the compass housing until the orienting arrow on the bottom of the housing is parallel to the nearest magnetic-north line drawn on the map. (You should disregard the compass needle.) The compass is now set for the correct bearing, and you are ready to travel. In traveling, the North end of the compass needle should cover the North arrow on the compass housing. You follow the direction-of-travel arrow on the compass. Select a prominent landmark in line with that arrow, travel to it, select another landmark, and so on.

In some situations a hiker will know that he is on a certain trail, or along the bank of a stream, as shown on a map but not know just where along the trail or stream he is located. To determine his position, he will need to look around at the terrain and locate at least one identifiable landmark that is also shown on the map. Perhaps in the area that he just came from, he can identify a mountain peak that is also on his map. He then takes a back-reading on the peak. This is done by sighting with the compass with the direction-of-travel arrow pointed *toward* him instead of away from him. The bearing is transferred to the map, compensating for magnetic declination in doing so. The bearing line passes through the landmark on the map and will intersect the trail that he is on. The point of intersection is his approximate location on the trail.

Maybe you will know the general area you are in but not your particular location in the area. This problem is similar to the above example except that *two* landmarks will need to be known. It is preferable that they be located so that your line of sight to each will intersect at approximately a 90° angle, or as near to 90° as possible. Take back-readings to each landmark and transfer the reading to your map. Draw the bearing lines through each landmark and project them until they intersect. The point of intersection is your approximate location. If you can get a similar bearing on a third landmark that you recognize, that bearing line should intersect at the same point as the other two and will further verify the location of your position.

Perhaps you do not recognize *any* landmarks in the area, either from where you have come or ahead. You are now *lost*. It is time to backtrack if you can. If you do not know your way back, it is time to bivouac and initiate survival procedures.

You should practice using your map, compass, and orienting procedures when you are in familiar country. Such practice can also be done close to home during a day hike. Then you will have more confidence in your efforts when you are in relatively unfamiliar country and trying to get your bearings. In your training and practice, use a good reference book such as *Be Expert with Map and Compass* by Bjorn Kjellstrom. This book is available from many mountaineering and back-packing equipment supply firms.

MAPS AND TRAIL INFORMATION

On most backpack trips you should provide yourself with some maps of the area, as well as sketches and notes that you make yourself. Depending upon the area that you choose for your backpacking adventure, the following are sources of maps that will usually be found helpful.

U.S. Forest Service. The U.S. Forest Service has maps of the national forests and wilderness areas. These maps are available to the public free of charge and may be obtained by writing to the supervisor of the national forest or wilderness area that you are interested in. The Forest Service maps will generally show trails, roads, streams, springs, prominent mountains, fences, and buildings (if any). They do not have contour lines. These maps are very useful to have and to

use in conjunction with the U.S. Geological Survey maps. I use them regularly.

If you have some questions concerning the area you plan to pack into, write to the nearest Forest Service office. I have always found members of the Forest Service to be very helpful in furnishing information on trails and forest and stream conditions, and in supplying similar data important to the planning of a backpack trip.

U.S. Geological Survey. The maps published by the U.S. Geological Survey will be found very helpful in most backpacking. These maps show all important natural features, as well as trails, roads, and isolated buildings. Elevations are shown by contour lines, and this is an important feature when traveling in rugged terrain. These are called quadrangle maps. An index (free), as well as the maps themselves, is available from the U.S. Geological Survey. (See Appendix D for address.)

Trail organizations. Detailed maps and information on the Pacific Crest Trail are available from the Sierra Club. Information on the Appalachian Trail is available from the Appalachian Trail Conference. Helpful information on the Long Trail, which winds along the Green Mountains in Vermont, can be obtained from the Green Mountain Club. (See Appendix D.)

Other sources. The chamber of commerce of a city in the general vicinity of the area of interest will frequently be able to furnish some maps and information that may be of value. Large cities often have local hiking clubs, and the city chamber of commerce can furnish names and addresses of these clubs, if you are interested. Some states have a state chamber of commerce, usually located in the capital city. Practically all states have a state fish and game department, or its equivalent, that can furnish information that will frequently be helpful in your planning. Some of the suppliers listed in Appendix A have maps and books available giving detailed information on areas of particular interest to mountaineers and backpackers. Guidebooks vary greatly in their accuracy and general usefulness. A guidebook may be a good supplement to map and compass, but it is never a substitute for these items.

CARE OF MAPS

In the field, maps will be subject to wear and will be exposed to moisture and dirt. Too much

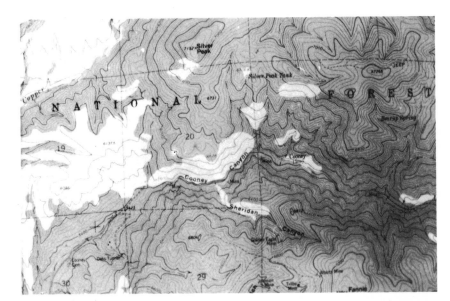

This is a section of a U.S. Geological Survey map. This is the type of map most frequently carried by backpackers.

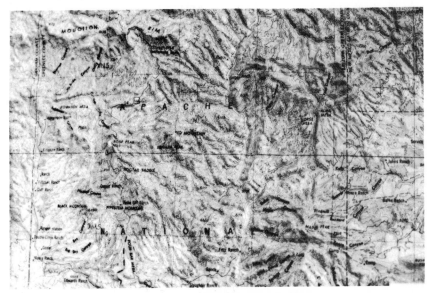

This is a plastic relief map. These maps are not suitable for carrying in the field. They are very useful in getting a bird's eye view of the area you are packing into and studying it over before the trip. These maps are available from Hubbard, P.O. Box 105, Northbrook, Ill. 60062 or from the Army Map Service, Fort Sam Houston, Texas 78234.

This is a close-up view of a small section of the map shown above. A framed map of this type, of your favorite backpacking area, makes a nice wall decoration for your den or study.

moisture, in particular, can soon render a map worthless. It is a good idea to take some precautions to protect your maps.

A substance known as artist's fixative is sold in most art supply stores. It is usually available in spray cans. Applying two coats of artist's fixative to each side of a map, in accordance with directions, will provide very significant protection from moisture, although they will not make it waterproof.

Another material that can be used to protect maps is transparent plastic sheeting. This is frequently available from local stationery stores. When the paper backing is removed from one side of the transparent plastic, an adhesive surface is exposed onto which your map or map section is placed to accomplish a bond.

Some backpack trips will only be concerned with a small area of a map. Instead of carrying the complete map, you can use a razor blade to cut out that area of the map that is of interest. It can be reinserted after the trip, using transparent tape. In cutting out the area that is of interest, ample adjacent area should be included for orienting purposes. The less familiar a party is with a particular area, and the more remote it is, the greater the map area that should be left intact. There is always the possibility of getting lost and wandering away from the planned route.

Transparent map cases (some have grid lines) with a zipper opening are available from some of the suppliers listed in Appendix A and from some office supply stores. These are convenient for use in wind and rain and will keep your map clean. I sometimes carry my map in a plastic bag tucked inside my shirt at the front.

On a wind-swept mountain ledge it is relatively easy to lose your map. In a windy area it is best to seek some protection from the wind before getting out your map to study your position. A sudden gust of wind may tear the map from your grasp and carry it to a point beyond retrieval. This could be a serious situation.

Large maps can be folded with an accordion-style fold, which is easy to do. With the map face up, draw an imaginary horizontal line from west to east, dividing the map into two halves. Now fold the map along this horizontal line, back surface to back surface, with the printed side of the map on the outside. Then, starting at the northwest corner of the map, fold it accordion style, into sections about 4 to 6 inches wide. With this type of fold, you can read your map in the field without unfolding the entire map.

LEAVING THE TRAIL

There will probably be some occasions during a backpack trip when the group will want to temporarily leave the trail it is following. This may be for the purpose of exploring a particular area, taking pictures, or pursuing some similar objective. Or it may be decided to make an overnight hike to a particular point of interest. In some mountainous areas the terrain may be open, and there may be no difficulty in finding the way back to the trail again. In other areas the trail may traverse such rugged country that you might not readily find your way back to the trail even if you were only several hundred yards away. Thus, depending on the terrain and the distance to be traveled off-trail, it may be desirable to take some special precautions to assure that the group can find its way back to the trail again.

It should be emphasized that trees should *not* be blazed, bushes bent over, or rocks piled so as to mark a trail. Such practices not only mar the landscape but require considerably more energy than other methods that can be used. First, there is the matter of simply making mental notes of your position and prominent features in the terrain and following your progress on a map or sketch of the area. Stop and look backward frequently. It is surprising how different the same area can look when viewed from various angles. When you come to a particular spot where you think you may have trouble staying on course on the way out, make a note of it on a 3-by-5-inch card or in a small notebook, take a compass read-

A map case will protect your map from wind and rain. It will also keep it clean. *(Lou Clemmons)*

ing on the back route and prominent objects, and record them.

If you desire to mark your route over some particularly rough stretches, a grease pencil or chalk can be used to make a small marking on rocks. The marking will soon deteriorate, and you will not have marred the landscape. You can also use 8- or 10-inch lengths of crepe paper and tie them to tree limbs or bushes with a single overhand knot. They too will deteriorate, and in rainy weather may not stay in place long enough to be helpful. A somewhat more permanent marking, but one that will also deteriorate in time, is 10-inch lengths (about 1 or 2 inches wide) of lightweight cloth. It is recommended that the cloth strips be cut at home and that a number be put on each strip with a felt-tip marker. Twenty or thirty such markers, made of lightweight cloth, will weigh about an ounce. When a route is marked with such a cloth marker, a description of the back trail should be entered in a notebook, identifying the note with the number on the cloth strip. The purpose of using such markers, as suggested before, is for the group to find its way back, along the same route, to the trail. The cloth or paper markers can therefore be retrieved on the way out. A conscientious effort should be made to pick up all such markers. In the event a few are missed, however, they will deteriorate. The colored plastic ribbons used by surveyors should not be used for marking routes. They will not deteriorate.

Occasionally during a backpack trip it may be desirable for trip members to be temporarily separated. This may occur during a period of fishing, wildlife observation, and so forth. It is recommended in such a case that all persons travel with one or more companions, rather than alone. Sometimes it happens that you don't know whether a group or certain individuals are ahead on the trail or behind. This can cause some anxiety, as well as wasted effort in locating them. For example, some hikers by prearrangement may be traveling parallel to the trail but a hundred yards or more to one side. This sometimes happens when some members of the group are fishing a section of mountain stream that parallels a trail. Engrossed in what they are doing, they fail to notice whether certain companions have moved on ahead. They finally make their way back to the trail, but they don't know whether to hurry and catch up or sit down and wait.

This problem can be solved in several ways. If it is a small group, persons traveling along the trail can use a stick and make a distinctive mark (such as X, −, or O) where there is soft dirt in the trail, doing so each several hundred yards or so. Other companions coming along the trail will see the marks and will know that the person or group assigned that particular mark is somewhere ahead on the trail. Distinctive colors of crepe paper, tied on tree limbs or bushes, or small cards bearing initials or a name (and hour) and impaled or tied to twigs, can be used in the same manner. The last person coming down the trail can pick up the pieces of paper or cards and burn them at the next campsite or carry them out as trash.

Agreement to meet back at camp, or at a prominent place on the trail, at a certain hour, is a good safety precaution. It can save a lot of anxiety on the part of all members of the group.

13
In Camp

GIVE YOURSELF TIME

As you hike along your trail, you will probably see many "picture book" campsites. Quite frequently, however, you may not find such a campsite when you need it most (when it's time to make camp). Once you have agreed on a time to make camp, you should usually take the first acceptable campsite that you reach within a half hour after that time, unless you are familiar with the area and know absolutely that a better campsite is only a short distance away. If you do this, you will probably avoid being caught in the darkness on the trail, still faced with finding a campsite, making camp, cooking your supper, and washing dishes. It takes the "fun" out of these activities if you have to do them after dark. It is also hard on flashlight batteries and dispositions.

If you are traveling in the vicinity of a stream in late afternoon, don't leave that stream and go chugging off up the mountainside unless you know that there will be a water supply when it's time to camp. Better to camp early and have some leisure time than to be caught in an unfamiliar area, away from any water supply, and have to make a dry camp.

Give yourself time to properly prepare your chosen campsite for the night and to cook your evening meal. This usually means making camp a minimum of two hours before darkness, preferably longer. Some backpackers look upon the job of setting up camp as a real chore. It need not be. If, however, you spend too many hours on the trail, get yourself too tired, and then have to race against time to get camp set up, supper cooked and eaten, and so on, it *can* be a chore. Think back over some of your previous backpack trips. You will probably recall that many of the most pleasurable moments were spent in a well-chosen backwoods camp where you were able to go about setting up camp in a leisurely manner and had time left over to enjoy the area, explore the vicinity, and so forth.

CHOOSING A CAMPSITE

Many of the considerations pertaining to the selection of a camp in general camping also apply to campsites for backpacking. However, some deserve special emphasis. Water is one of the prime requirements of a good backpack campsite. In planning your trip, the length of travel each day should be gauged so that you will have a stream, spring, or lake available as a water supply when it comes time to make camp. It is far better to underestimate how far you will travel in a day than to overestimate. It is possible to make a "dry camp" away from any water supply, but this should be avoided if possible. You do not need to camp in the immediate area of your water supply, however. Instead of camping along a lakeshore, close to a stream, or near a spring, you should camp some distance from these places, for several important reasons. First, there is the matter of ecological impact. Most people instinctively want to camp very near the water. Well-worn paths, trampled vegetation, and debris cluttering the area soon result. By camping back away from such places, you will not only be doing your part environmentally but will have much more privacy from other campers in the area. It should be no big problem to walk three to five minutes to get to your water supply. Bears have some tendency to follow the shores of lakes and the banks of streams. If you are in bear country, that is another good reason for camping back from such places.

If wood fires are permitted and you want to do some or all of your cooking over a wood fire, you will also want to select an area where there is a supply of wood within reasonable walking distance. If you are doing all your cooking over a portable stove, then wood is no problem.

In some of our national parks and forests you must camp at designated campsites. However, even in those areas, there is some leeway in selecting the particular spot for your camp. In many areas you will be able to choose your campsite at will. Camps should never be made in meadows. They are too fragile from an ecology standpoint, and are very likely to be permanently damaged when used for camping.

It is best to make your camp well off the trail. At night, bears and other animals often follow the trails that hikers use during the daytime. Selecting an area away from the trail lessens the possibility of having such animals enter your camp. If the trail is well used by hikers, you will have more privacy if you are some distance from it. Camping away from the trail and being out of sight and earshot of other camps is an important factor to many backpackers.

Avoid making camp near bogs, marshes, or any other areas that contain stagnant water. These are natural breeding places for mosquitoes. Meadows with poor drainage are also likely areas for mosquitoes. During insect season, a campsite should be chosen that is on relatively high ground that will be exposed to any breeze. In the western mountains, depending upon the elevation, mosquitoes are usually quite prevalent during June and July. Gathering some advance information on the mosquito aspect, prior to your trip, will be time well spent.

In cool weather you will want to pick your campsite so as to be protected from the wind. If you are in a canyon, you can depend upon the wind blowing up the canyon during the day and down the canyon at night. A campsite on the lee side of boulders or a grove of trees is a good choice if you want to avoid the wind. Also, large boulders soak up heat during the day and dissipate heat during the night.

In cool weather you may also want your campsite to be exposed to the sun as early as possible in the morning. You can use your compass to determine where the sunny spots (or the shady spots, if you prefer) will be in the morning.

Anticipate the course of temporary streams or flash floods if it should rain. Don't have your bed site in such an area. Pick out a spot that looks like it would drain well and also soak up moisture in the event of rain. Bed sites or tent sites should not be ditched. Ditching leads to erosion and leaves ugly ground scars.

Near the bottom of a rock slide is a poor place to camp. The rocks may slide some more. Directly under a high cliff or near the bottom of a steep slope is a dangerous place to camp. Animals moving about, or changes in weather, may dislodge stones or boulders and send them down into your camp area.

The natural inclination of a group when entering an area that they have chosen for a campsite is to select the biggest tree in the area and drop their duffel there. Soon after, they will be laying out their beds in the same spot and otherwise preparing the camp for the night. The dead wood that you find lying on a forest floor comes largely from live trees, and it has to come off the tree sometime. It might come loose during the night while you are under it. Avoid picking out the biggest tree in the area and making your bed under it. (That tree may also attract lightning.) If you are camping where there are trees, pick out a cluster or grove of medium-sized trees and look them over carefully for dead limbs before you decide to make your bed there.

Hikers have been known to make their beds right in the middle of ant colonies. Not only look the ground over, but look as well for nearby dead trees or dead limbs. Ants can be quite a nuisance, even though there does not appear to be a typical ant colony in the area. I recall that several years ago I had selected a promising area for my tent at the end of a day on the trail. I had the tent about half set up when I first noticed that the ground seemed to be "crawling" with ants. They were also starting to crawl over and into my partly erected tent. I decided very quickly to move my tent site. About 100 feet away was a good site, and I made camp there. A few ants were on the ground — as there are in many places — but not the hordes that were in the spot I had just left. Ants may also follow certain trails, or "ant paths," in getting from one place to another. There may be hundreds or thousands of ants on one of these trails, perhaps only an inch wide, with ants crawling in both directions. Putting your bed down on one of these ant trails can lead to problems that you really don't need.

When a group first enters a prospective camp area, a few minutes should be spent walking around and looking it over. Hikers are frequently in too much of a hurry to set up camp. Then when it is about set up, they discover one or more features that make them wish they had chosen another spot. The first thing to do in looking over a likely campsite is to take off your pack. Walking around with your pack on is more likely to make you want to hurry and get the job over with.

You should try to select an area that is generally level and that also has enough fairly level places of sleeping bag size or appropriate tent size to accommodate the number of persons in the party. However, no area will be absolutely level. A few inches in elevation where you choose to sleep may mean the difference between whether you stay dry in the event of rain and whether water runs into your sleeping bag area. Observe which way water is likely to flow over the ground in case of a hard rain. The nature of the ground surface is also an important consideration. Rain will not soak into hard-packed, bare ground as it will into a forest floor or ground that has a covering of pine needles, grass, and so forth. Bare ground also means more difficulty in keeping your bedding and other gear clean. The individual sleeping sites should be spread out, rather than clustered too close together. Again, one reason you probably had for making this trip was to get away from crowds. Most people like some privacy. This applies on a backpack trip as well as at home.

Some people feel that they need to cook and eat in the immediate area of their tent sites or bed sites. It is not necessary to do this; further, it may not be desirable for several reasons. First, a good tent site or bed site will not be on rocky or bare ground. It will be on forest duff or pine needles. A wood fire should not be built on such a surface, nor a camp stove used there. There seems to be a psychological feeling among some backpackers that having their bed site close to a fire offers some "protection." The opposite is true. In the first place, any fire should be out — dead out — when you go to bed. Secondly, any animals that enter the general camp area during the night will

Water bag. A water bag is a useful item in camp, particularly when the water supply is not close by. It can also be used for occasional carrying of emergency water on the trail. This bag, made by Adventure 16, is plastic (replaceable), with a nylon cover. Weight, about 3 ounces; capacity, 2½ gallons.

go either to the cooking site, where bits of food and food odors persist, or to where you have your food stored, or both.

Near a stream may be a good place to cook, especially with a wood fire. There will probably be gravelly areas or rock slabs on which to build the fire, water for cooking, and plenty of water to put the fire out. However, a knoll or other higher ground may be much more preferable as a sleeping area. That should be no problem. You can take a three-to-five-minute hike — if it is that far — to the stream bed at mealtime, carrying cooking gear and food.

A good view from your campsite is nice, but it should normally be one of the lesser considerations. Unless it is a base camp or layover camp, you will be asleep most of the time you are there.

On some backpack trips you will be packing into a base camp, working out from there each day and returning to the same camp at night. In setting up such a base camp, give some consideration to locating it near prominent features in the terrain that will help you find it when returning at the end of a day's activities. For example, in a dense forest where the view is limited and many areas look pretty much alike, finding your way back to camp can turn out to be quite a chore. On returning to camp in a dense woods, you may pass within a hundred yards of it, never see it, and go right on by. (You then have a problem.) Try to set up such a base camp near a prominent tree, an unusual rock formation, the fork of a river, or some other irregular feature in the terrain that will be of assistance in locating it.

TRAIL SHELTERS

Trail shelters will be found on some of the large trail systems. These are frequently three-sided shelters with a roof and dirt floor. I have had occasion to use such shelters only a very few times. The areas that I generally backpack in do not have such shelters. Regardless, I do *not* recommend them, except possibly in an emergency situation where you doubt the capability of your tent or other gear to keep you comfortable in a bad storm. The idea of trail shelters may be a good one. As with many things constructed for the good of the public, however, there are always those who do not use them properly and make no effort to keep them clean.

Some trail shelters that I have seen have been absolutely filthy, with garbage, cans, and trash thoroughly cluttering the area. I wouldn't want to take a short rest in such a shelter, let alone spend the night there. Assuming you could tolerate the trash and mess that seems indigenous to many such shelters, it should not be overlooked that bears and other animals may visit the shelter during the night in search of scraps of food that may be lying about. Mice will frequently inhabit such shelters in large numbers. Listening to mice running around the shelter and having them scrambling over your sleeping bag can make for a poor night's sleep.

So in the planning of your trip, I would recommend that you not depend on the protection of trail shelters, though there may be some on your planned route. If it happens to be a good shelter, and clean, there is also the possibility that it may be occupied by other persons. It is better to be properly prepared by having good foul-weather gear and using it as required.

SETTING UP CAMP

One of the first things to do in setting up camp is to decide where the cooking area will be. If you are cooking with a backpack stove, this may be a rather minor problem. However, it is usually desirable to have a boulder, log, large tree, or some other type of windbreak when using a stove, even though the stove has a windscreen. A breeze can greatly decrease the efficiency of a stove. A suitable place within a short distance of the cooking area, in the form of a rock slab, clean grass, pine needles, or something similar, on which to spread out food and cooking and eating utensils is also desirable.

As was mentioned in Chapter 9, if you are using a wood fire for cooking and the campsite has been previously used, you can probably find a fire ring or place where an open fire was built by previous backpackers. This is the place you should usually build your fire, so as not to make new scars on the ground. The only exceptions would normally be where the original firesite was improperly selected. It might possibly have been built under low-hanging tree branches, near other burnable materials that cannot be moved, against a large log, or so close to a boulder that it blackened it.

When you are appraising a possible campsite, it is actually a good idea to consider the cooking area and sleeping areas simultaneously. Each has specific requirements, if it is to be satisfactory and safe. In some cases, particularly if you are not in bear country, the two areas may be fairly close together. However, even though there are no bears in the vicinity, you would probably prefer not to have skunks, raccoons, and other small scavenger animals moving through your sleeping area.

Tents and sleeping bags should usually be upwind from a wood fire, and a reasonable distance away, irrespective of any consideration of bears and other animals. Flying sparks can easily damage a nylon tent and similar gear. When using a tent, it will be more stable and warmer if the front end is faced downwind. Normally, a tent should not be erected broadside to the prevailing wind.

In unpacking their packs, hikers should take their share of the food, cooking gear, and any items of common equipment that they have been carrying, over to the cooking site, or to some other designated suitable spot. Food should normally be hung in bags off the ground, even for very short periods and even though hikers are in the area. With everyone engrossed in setting up sleeping sites, it is quite possible that small animals will get into the food supply—in the daytime—without being noticed. After the evening meal, more elaborate measures for protecting the food for the night should be taken, usually by hanging a bear bag high off the ground (if you are in bear country). Remember that leaving food within the reach of animals is inviting them to a treat—and they may accept the invitation. Even birds can at times be a nuisance. Jays, crows, and other birds can be real camp robbers. Food that is left unsupervised for only a short time may be raided and damaged or lost.

If your packbag is waterproof, or if you have a waterproof cover for it, there should be no need to put it inside a tent or to have it at your bed site. After you have removed the items that you will need for the night, it is recommended that the pack be suspended off the ground. It can be hung from a tree limb or a high rope stretched between two trees, away from your bed site. Packs should not be left on or near the ground during the night. Some "irresponsible" porcupine or deer may feast on pack straps, or other sweat-soaked equipment, for the salt that is in them. Since you have probably carried food in your pack, there will be some food odors remaining in it even after the food has

been removed. Those food odors may bring a bear or other animals into camp during the night. The same food odors may cause small rodents to get into your pack. They may gnaw a hole in your packbag and possibly do serious damage. Incidentally, in some well-traveled areas, bears and other animals learn to associate the *sight* of hikers' packs with food, even before they can smell the food odor.

Parachute cord or other stout cord can be used to put up a short rope line. Towels and damp articles of clothing, or freshly washed socks and other items, can be hung on such a line. Try to place such lines away from the main area of camp and out of the way of people who will be moving about the camp area. If a white rag or article of clothing is left on the line at all times, it will be clearly seen and hikers will not walk into it and possibly hurt themselves.

Extra clothing can be stowed in the packbag, or in your tent if you are using one. In cool weather, dry clothes placed under the sleeping bag will provide additional insulation from the ground.

Hoisting the "bear bag."

The pack should be suspended for the night, out of the reach of animals. All pockets should be closed. Either a rope line between two trees or a line far out on the limb of a small-diameter tree is recommended. *(Lou Clemmons)*

BED AND SHELTER

If the spot you select for your bed is not absolutely level (the usual case), you will be most comfortable if you put the head end of your sleeping bag at the higher end. Go over the ground carefully (on your hands and knees), and remove pine cones, rocks, and sharp twigs before putting down your groundsheet. Spend a good five minutes in doing this—more if the spot is not fairly smooth—and it will pay off. Try lying down on your prospective bed site; you may discover some features that were not apparent before. The site may have a sideways slope, or there may be a tree root just below the surface. When your sleeping bag is on the ground and not in use, keep it rolled up, at least loosely, with the head end in the middle of the roll. This will keep ants and other insects out of the bag.

If you are using a tent, it is recommended that you go over the tent site on your hands and knees and remove sharp objects just as you would before putting down a groundsheet for your sleeping bag. The floor of a backpacking tent is not rugged. It can readily be punctured or torn by irregular objects on the ground. A grove of medium-sized trees with spaces for tents, and soft duff or pine needles covering the forest floor, usually makes ideal tent sites. In using a tent, it is a good idea to remove hiking boots before entering the tent, or to crawl around on hands and knees inside the tent. Otherwise, unnecessary dirt will be tracked into the tent. Heavy lug soles are also hard on tent floors.

The tent should be pitched so that the walls and fly are not so close to tree limbs, rock projections, and so on, that they may be blown against them and damaged. Any guy lines for tent or fly should be anchored by stakes or tied to tree trunks or very stout limbs. Ropes that are tied to limbs that may whip about in a wind will place unnecessary strain on the tent fabric and can easily damage it. Peg loops around the ground edge of the tent should not be driven into the ground with the stake. This also strains the fabric. Short lengths of nylon cord can be tied to the tent loops, if necessary.

A small square of plastic, packed with your tent, is handy in keeping the tent floor clean. Before entering the tent, you can sit or kneel on the plastic, unlace your boots and remove them. You can then knock them together, to remove excess dirt, mud, or snow. A heavy plastic bag is convenient for storing boots while they are in the tent or in your sleeping bag (in cool weather).

Perhaps you are not using a tent. If a poncho or rain fly of some kind is pitched over your sleeping bag, make sure that the outer edges of any ground cloth you may be using are well *within* the area covered by the rain fly. Otherwise any rain running off the fly will fall on the exposed edge of the ground cloth, be unable to soak into the ground, and will run under your sleeping bag. You will become much wetter than if you used no ground cloth at all. If you use a ground cloth, mark one side of it (using a felt-tip marker) with the word UP, in large letters, before leaving home. When you use the ground cloth, lay it on the ground so that the side marked UP is always the top side and the opposite side is next to the ground. The ground side will collect dirt over a period of usage, and there is no point in having this dirt next to your good sleeping bag. In using a clear plastic ground cloth, in particular, it is not always obvious which side was next to the ground the last time it was used.

If you use a tarp, hopefully it will have grommets along the edges. A plastic tarp may not have grommets. In that case you can use round, smooth rocks for anchoring the sides. A one-foot length of ⅛-inch-diameter shock cord inserted in the ridgeline will provide give and will help avoid tearing the plastic. Rocks, preferably flat and smooth on one side, can be used to anchor the tarp securely so that it will not flap during the night. A little breeze can make a loose tarp flap loudly, and it sounds even louder when you are trying to sleep. You can also tie down corners or edges of plastic tarp with heavy cord and small, smooth stones about an inch in diameter. Push the stone into the plastic and tie your cord around the bulge in the plastic on the opposite side.

Since it is the loft, or thickness, of a sleeping bag that determines its warmth, it should be fluffed up well before you go to bed. A down-insulated sleeping bag, in particular, has good resiliency. It will compress into a small bundle when pressure is applied and will spring back into a large volume when the pressure is removed. It will therefore compress under your body while you sleep.

In using a down bag, if you wake up cold during the night, reach your arms outside of your sleeping bag and fluff up the sides and top with your hands. Now roll over, moving the sleeping bag with your body, so that the fluffed-up side is next to the ground and the compressed side is skyward. You are now lying on your stomach and you will need to roll over on your back carefully, without turning the sleeping bag with you. Do this and then fluff up the sides and top again with your hands and you are in business. By this time the sleeping bag hood is probably not where you want it, so you may need to do a little more twisting and organizing. However, the sleeping bag has now been fluffed up on all sides, and you should sleep warmer for a while. If you have a liner in your sleeping bag, there is not much point in trying this trick unless the liner is made of very smooth material, and also firmly anchored to the inside of the sleeping bag at several points with tie tapes, because it will get hopelessly twisted. If you are brave enough, you can, of course, step out into the night air and fluff up your sleeping bag the "easy" way.

Walk around the area before dark and note the location of any large stones or logs that you may walk into or trip over after dark. Dead limbs at eye level are dangerous. Break them off or hang white rags, a towel, or paper on them, to avoid injury after dark. This precaution applies to the camp area in general as well as to the area immediately around your sleeping site.

BEFORE YOU GO TO SLEEP

Before you retire for the night, make sure you have certain items within reach of your sleeping bag. You may want your flashlight during the

Sleeping bag hung up to dry. (Lou Clemmons)

night. Once you have it, you should be able to find other items within reach without too much groping around. After a hard day of hiking, regardless of how much water you drank during the day or in the early evening, it is not uncommon to wake up thirsty during the night. Have your canteen handy (within reach), with water in it. Just before you go to sleep, it may be a good idea to take one or two aspirin. You may not have a headache, but you will probably have a few muscles that are a bit tired and achy. A couple of aspirin will help you relax, ease those aches, and let you get a good night's sleep. If you are not under an insect screen, have your insect lotion within reach in case you have to do battle during the night. Do you have the habit of thinking about the next day's activities just before falling asleep? Several 3-by-5-inch note cards and a pencil stub within reach will be useful for jotting down certain reminders for the next day.

If the temperature is at freezing or below, it is best to put your flashlight (and canteen) *inside* your sleeping bag. It shortens the life of batteries if they are exposed to freezing temperatures.

THE FIRE

Where it is safe and permissible to build a fire in the camp area, the place where the fire is built will usually be the center of camp activity. Hikers will frequently be found there, whether to cook, to eat, to talk, or just to sit and stare at the fire. Because of the heavy traffic around the fire, the soil there will frequently become ground to a fine dust from the passage of many feet. It is therefore recommended that you plan your camp layout so that the place for the fire is at one end or one corner of the camp rather than near the geometric center. This will cut down on unnecessary "by-traffic" of those who are simply going from one point in the camp to another.

Open containers of food may have dirt kicked into them if they are set on the ground or on low stones around the cooking fire. Bags of food may be stepped on and split open. It is therefore recommended that your "worktable" for meal preparation be somewhat removed from the immediate vicinity of the cooking site. Choose a spot about 15 or 20 feet away. It should be grassy, covered with pine needles, or provide a flat rock or otherwise nondusty area. This is the place to lay out eating utensils, food, and condiments for that particular meal. It will usually be a cleaner and better spot to wash the dishes also, rather than doing this in the immediate area of the cooking site.

The cook needs still another work space. He needs a small, clean area, away from foot traffic, where he can sort through food bags and equipment after the meal is over, while others are washing dishes. Find a small, clean spot about 20 to 30 feet in some other direction. Here the cook will have the room and the necessary solitude to concentrate on what he is doing as he sorts through food bags, finding the right bags for the particular meal, getting the individual bags back into the larger carrying bags, and so forth. Here he will make up equitable loads for each hiker to carry or, following the supper meal, will put the food into suitable bags for hoisting off the ground.

When fire-starting conditions are difficult (just after a hard rain, for instance), take more than the usual amount of time to gather a good supply of dry wood before you try to start a fire. Damp hikers are frequently somewhat impatient to get a fire started, and this impatience may lead to more delay in the long run. An inadequate supply of dry twigs will be quickly used up, perhaps before larger pieces of wood start burning. Then you must take time and go look for more fire-starting material, and the time spent in gathering the supply for the first attempt has been wasted. Pos-

sible sources of good fire-starting materials on a rainy day are the underside of downed timber that is partially propped off the ground by limbs, the overhang of a cliff, the underside of a pile of driftwood near a stream, hollow tree trunks, and on the ground under trees having dense foliage. Don't overlook used paper tissue, candy wrappers, and other burnables that you may have in your pocket. Pine needles are excellent fire starters, and where they form a thick carpet on the forest floor, some dry needles can usually be found, even after a good rain.

When you go to bed at night, the fire should be thoroughly extinguished by dousing it with water. Be just as careful to ensure that it is completely out as you would be if you were leaving the area. There should be no need for having a fire going at night. However, if for some reason a fire is desired during the night, it should be watched continuously. Hikers can take turns doing this. An unattended fire is potentially very dangerous. It is unsafe if everyone is asleep, even though only a few feet away.

LOSING GEAR

It is easy to mislay eating utensils, knives, and other small items of camp gear and leave them behind when you leave camp. There are several things that can be done to minimize the possibility of losing such items. First, do not set such items down in out-of-the-way places. Immediately after using such items as knives and matches, put them in an assigned place. Very small items, like a can opener, can be tied to a larger piece of equipment. Second, small items such as silverware can have the handles or other surfaces coated with a bright-colored, nonlead paint, which is nonpoisonous and which will make them easy to locate. A small piece of bright-colored rag can also be tied to the item. Third, spend the last five minutes before leaving camp in walking around the area and making a last check to see that some item of equipment has not been left behind. Specific individuals should be in charge of specific items of all common equipment. Those individuals should have a checklist and should use it to check off all items for which they are responsible before the group leaves each campsite and lunch site and moves on down the trail.

SANITATION

It is very important in choosing a toilet area that it be in a spot that is not likely to be chosen

A pair of moccasins provides a welcome change from hiking boots after a hard day on the trail.

by some future party as a campsite. Few things are more disgusting than to find a good potential campsite and then to discover exposed human feces nearby, complete with toilet paper littering the ground or impaled on the branches of bushes and fluttering in the breeze.

Toilet areas should be well off the trail and away from potential campsites. A thicket or brushy slope in uneven terrain is usually a good location. It is important to be well away from streams, brooks, or potential stream beds, such as a gully. Whether the soil is loose enough to permit the digging of a shallow hole or whether loose rock, bark, or other debris is available for covering all "evidence" should also be considered.

"Cat sanitation methods" should normally be used and a hole 6 to 8 inches deep dug with a trowel, rock, stick, or the heel of your boot. A suitable plastic trowel weighs only about two ounces (see page 132). Hikers should be considerate of those who will come after them. It is a good idea to carry matches to the toilet area and to burn used toilet tissue. However, if you are in a thicket, or if there is much burnable material lying about, this may be unsafe. In such a case, toilet tissue also should be thoroughly covered—never left above ground to blow about. It is a good idea to have a washbasin, soap, and water available back at camp, for use upon your return.

Large backpacking groups should carry a small shovel for the digging of a latrine. It is again important that the chosen site be on high ground, away from any water source or potential watercourse. An area that may be chosen as a campsite by some future party should never be used. Depth of the latrine should be about 8 to 12 inches, to stay within the biological disposal layer of the soil. A greater depth will retard bacterial action and decomposition. The shovel should be left at the latrine so that waste may be covered each time the latrine is used. It is a good idea for a large group to carry lime, or a similar substance, that can be used to aid decomposition, control odor, and keep flies away. Obviously, all such holes should be carefully filled in when the group prepares to leave the area.

Urination does not require such "cover up" effort, but the same rules and precautions should be taken to select an area away from any potential campsite and away from watercourses.

Fish heads and entrails lying about on the ground and swarming with flies where someone has cleaned fish are not a pretty sight. Some people clean fish in a lake or stream and leave the viscera lying in the water. Either practice is un-acceptable. Fish, as well as cooking and eating utensils, should be cleaned far back from the shore of any lake or stream. The resulting garbage should be burned in a hot fire, if a fire is available. Otherwise it should be packed in a plastic-lined cloth litterbag to the next site where a fire is available. If no such fire is forthcoming, the garbage should be packed all the way out to the roadhead, along with aluminum foil, cans, and similar trash.

CAMP SPIRIT

A proper camp spirit has a lot to do with making the trip an enjoyable experience for everyone concerned. When you take to the woods on a backpack trip, seldom does everything work out exactly as it was planned at home. There are always some unknowns. If you knew precisely what experiences and problems you were going to have, what the weather would be, and so forth, it would no longer be an adventure. Each individual should be mentally and physically prepared to make the most of the situations that are encountered, whether they are good or bad. You will probably plan your next backpack trip by "including out" those hikers that display "camp spirit" along the following lines:

1. They did not check out their hiking boots, nor did they take the time to make a few conditioning hikes before the trip. After a few hours on the trail, they start to complain of sore feet, an uncomfortable pack, and so forth.

2. They did not check out their equipment before leaving home. They have trouble with some of their gear and frequently ask to borrow some items (not common equipment) from other hikers.

3. They "surprise" the other hikers by hauling out transistor radios the first night in camp, and play them long and loud, even though it was specifically agreed that such equipment would be left at home.

4. They always manage to stay in their sleeping bags until someone else gets up in the morning and has the fire going. When breakfast is about half-cooked, they straggle out and finish dressing.

5. They take needless risks that are a threat to their individual safety and to the welfare of trip in general.

6. When meals are being prepared, they always seem to have some item of personal equipment that needs attention at that particular time,

or they may simply wander off and go fishing or exploring.

7. They frequently hold up the group from starting their next activity, as planned and agreed to by the majority.

8. They are chronic complainers about the weather, the trail, the food, the fishing, or a dozen other things.

9. They brag about their equipment. If some hiker is getting along with a "cheapie" sleeping bag, it isn't necessary to call his attention to the luxury of a superior sleeping bag. A single glance on his part at a good sleeping bag will do the job very nicely. If he wants details, he will probably ask for them.

10. They raid the food supply. They may also take more than their share of a certain food without first asking others if they have had all they want. (The cook is in charge of the food supply, and he is responsible for seeing that everyone gets enough to eat and shares alike in the "goodies." Getting into the food supply without the cook's permission is strictly against the rules.)

11. They fail to keep litter picked up around their tent sites and do not assist in keeping the general camp area clean. "Leave no trace" means nothing to them.

12. When others are ready to sack out for the night, they can be depended upon to remain up long afterward, filling the night air with loud talk, tramping around camp, rummaging through gear, and so forth.

13. They are incessant talkers. From the time they leave the trailhead, until they return, they seem to be talking constantly. Most people enjoy some conversation, at the proper time and place, in camp as well as on the trail. However, one reason for taking a backpack trip is to enjoy the quiet and serenity of the backwoods. An incessant talker can have a most detrimental effect on this aspect.

Loud talk and noise, and racket in general, is not commensurate with backwoods camping. A reasonable degree of quiet and solitude is to be expected. In the well-traveled areas of some of our national parks and forests, there will often be more than one group sharing a general camping area. A few individuals "hootin' and hollerin'" and otherwise disturbing the peace can make a hiker wish he were back in the "quiet" of the city. Campers need to be considerate of others in the area.

On a backpack trip, you will be with your companions for twelve to fourteen hours each day. This is more hours per day than you usually spend with members of your immediate family. All personalities have certain idiosyncrasies (except yours and mine). Sooner or later one of your companions is going to say something or do something that you do not like. To avoid spoiling a good trip, hold your temper. Take a walk, bite your fingernails, or go kick a big boulder, but don't "spout off." Make an extra effort to get along with other members of the group and to be considerate. Give someone else the first cup of coffee, the first plate of food, the first drink at the spring, the first cast at a trout pool, and show other kindnesses. It will pay big dividends in the long run and assure maximum enjoyment from the trip for the time and effort you have invested. The rule "Do a good turn daily" is a good plan to follow.

When the trail is long and hard, the weather foul, and the food burned (how bad can things get?), dispositions have a way of getting "on edge." Thorough planning and preparation at home and setting reasonable schedules on the trail will do much to counteract this. Be kind to one another. Punctuality, helpfulness, and cheerfulness all have an important place in backpacking. If you are to meet with individuals or a group at a certain place on the trail at a specified time, be a few minutes early rather than a few minutes late. When the time for meals is established, all members should report promptly to the scene of action. Everyone should help with the operation from the time cooking is started until the last dish is washed and packed. Be considerate of the group's welfare. That piece of cheese that someone decides to snitch from the food supply for a private snack may be just what the cook was planning to flavor a pot of macaroni with at the next meal. The old sleeping bag feels mighty snug on a frosty morning, but someone has to get up, start the fire, and put the coffee on. Hikers should be ready and willing to take their turn in performing such chores.

BACKWOODS THEFT

Unfortunately, a few of the problems of the city have begun to invade the backwoods. One of these is theft. Apparently there are a few people taking to the trails for the specific purpose of stealing some of the property of others. It appears that the closer to the trailhead a group may be camped, the more prevalent the problem. Expensive cameras, other equipment, and clothing items seem to be prime targets. If you are camped at the trailhead or within a day's hike of same, it is recommended that you give this matter some thought, particularly if you are in a popular area well-used by other backpackers.

If you are camped at the trailhead just prior to taking off for a backpack trip, all excess duffel can probably be locked in vehicles. If you are already a day's travel into the woods, you can put extra equipment and clothing in your tent, or very near your sleeping site. When you are in the back country and others are in the area, it is recommended that you carry cameras and other items of expensive gear with you, insofar as possible, if you leave camp for a day of fishing or a similar purpose. It is also possible to rig a small padlock on a tent so as to lock the tent entrance. This will probably be *some* deterrent to would-be thieves.

If you were in the backwoods in cold weather and returned to camp to find that your sleeping bags and protective clothing had been stolen, this could be a very serious situation. Depending particularly on the area where you are camped, its proximity to main trails, and so on, this potential problem deserves some careful thought.

GARBAGE AND LITTER

The wilderness and national forest areas belong to all of us. We should take care of them as we would any other prized possession. We should be thoughtful of those who come after us. We should not leave a trail of debris, garbage, and litter as we travel through the backwoods. All campsites should be policed carefully before leaving them and traveling on down the trail. While we are making a last-minute check of our campsite to determine if any small items of gear have been overlooked, we can pick up small bits of string, foil, paper, a can lid, or other items of refuse and put them in our litterbag.

If a fire is safe and permissible, many items of refuse can be burned. All refuse that is not completely burned *must be packed out*. There should be no exceptions. This includes all cans, bottles, and metal foil. It also includes empty metal fuel cartridges for those who use propane or butane stoves. They may be a bit heavy, but if they were packed in full, they can be packed out empty.

In getting the equipment together at home, before starting the trip, too little attention is often given to providing for a good, stout litterbag. Too many people rely upon a makeshift litterbag after they are on the trail, often using a cast-off poly bag that was carried for some other purpose. This is the wrong approach. Even a relatively stout poly bag can develop holes and tears after a

few days on the trail. Then the contents spill out and soil your good packbag. I have not seen cloth litterbags listed as an item of supply in any of the backpacking and mountaineering equipment catalogs. I consider such a bag to be a very important item of equipment. Regardless, such a bag is easily made. Denim or muslin makes a good, stout bag. It is not so likely as nylon to be abraded and to develop holes or tears from irregular-shaped debris that is carried. A good addition is a poly-bag liner or cover for the cloth litterbag, to prevent any moist garbage from seeping out. If the poly bag is used as a cover for the cloth litterbag, odd-shaped debris in the cloth bag will not be likely to puncture the cloth bag and make a hole in the poly bag, therefore keeping it liquid proof against any moist garbage that may be carried.

When on the trail, hikers should not throw candy and gum wrappers, bits of string, plastic, tape, and other litter on the ground. Such material should be put in the pocket and burned at the next camp—or packed out. Although single, uncrumpled layers of foil will often appear to burn if thrown in a hot fire, most frequently there will be very small flakes of the "burned" foil left in the fireplace after the fire is out. These hundreds of minute particles of "burned" foil are then beyond recovery. They will continue their ugly glitter among the ashes for years to come, and will seriously detract from the natural appearance of the fire site.

There was a time, when the backwoods was not so heavily used, when it was permissible to carry and use an ax or hatchet. Campers frequently cut trees and branches—often live trees—for the purpose of lashing together chairs, tables, and various other items of camp furniture. Oftentimes they did not even bother to unlash and disassemble such items when they broke camp. It was also common practice to chop off the lower branches of pine, fir, and spruce trees to obtain material for bough beds. That time is past! Hatchets and axes should be left at home. Lashing chairs or other items, and the making of bough beds can no longer be condoned. If there is not sufficient firewood lying on the ground that can simply be gathered by hand, it is inappropriate to build a fire.

Before you leave a campsite, it should be restored to its natural appearance, insofar as possible. If more wood was gathered than was used, the elements of the woodpile should be scattered so as to blend in with the surroundings. Stones or logs that were hauled to a certain area of the campsite to make seats should be returned to more natural settings. Incidentally, the foam pads that many backpackers now carry make good seats or back-rests (propped against a tree) when the group is gathered for the nightly bull session.

PRESERVING THE WILDERNESS

It is recommended that you take an interest in wilderness legislation and in other legislation that seeks to preserve a part of the natural beauty of this country for generations to come. Developers and private interests are constantly and relentlessly at work making further and further inroads into unprotected back country. You may visit a region one year and find it to be a good camping area, with trees and natural vegetation contributing to its beauty. Another year and you may find that the same area has been taken over by developers, with streets, a shopping center, golf course, and all the other luxuries of "civilization" starting to take shape. Mining is now permitted in some wilderness areas, and miners frequently leave a real mess. "Controlled lumbering" in some of our public forests is not nearly as controlled as it should be. For those who are in doubt as to how to proceed, Appendix E is a partial list of some well-known organizations that are fighting the battle to ensure that your children and mine will have *some* clean air to breathe, *some* clean and natural rivers, and *some* wilderness and forest areas for wholesome recreation. These organizations need your support. Please give it to them!

14
Backpacking with Children

Some parents may want to try a family backpacking trip. I have taken many backpack trips with my family — some when the children were quite young — and most of them were thoroughly enjoyable. Family relationships can grow stronger in doing things together, and backpacking is no exception.

Of major importance to the success of a family backpack trip is the experience of the parents. They should not attempt taking the children on a backpack trip until they have had extensive experience themselves. Parents can tolerate such misfortunes as losing the trail, overextending themselves (with resultant aching feet and bodies), getting gear wet, spending sleepless nights, and so on. Such events take on different proportions from a child's viewpoint and may be sufficient to thoroughly discourage them from wanting to undertake any more backwoods adventures. One or both parents should be able to act with confidence in planning and accomplishing the many activities and tasks inherent in a backpack trip. This will do much to bolster the children's confidence and add to their enjoyment of the trip.

AGE OF CHILDREN

With young children an age difference of a year or two makes a big difference in the type of trip to be undertaken, the length of trip, the terrain to be attempted, and the planned activities. The physi-

cal growth and stamina of the particular child is an important consideration. The hiking ability of a *few* children at three years of age may be superior to that of most children four or five years of age.

Babies can be carried in a child-carrier pack, and some children have had their first backpack trip by the time they are four months old. Since parents must not only carry the baby but also all of the usual backpack gear plus special equipment and foods for the baby, such trips seldom get more than two or three miles into the backwoods. Some parents might not consider such a minimal distance worthwhile. However, it is surprising how much of the usual car-campground atmosphere, crowded conditions, noise, and so on can be left behind in even this short distance. On backpack trips with babies one parent may need to make a trip back to the trailhead for gear that could not be hauled in one trip. Thus, the distance obviously needs to be kept short. With a little planning, searching, and inquiry, however, an attractive, quiet, backwoods camping spot may be found (in some areas) within a couple of miles of the trailhead. With babies, there is also comfort in knowing that a quick retreat back to the trailhead can be made in the case of unexpected bad weather, illness, or other emergency.

When children are at the toddler stage — roughly two or three years old — backpacking with them takes on different aspects. They are then too heavy to be carried any significant distance. Neither are they able to walk enough or are they sufficiently sure footed to get very far on their own two feet. They can get far enough on their own to get into trouble, however. It's an "awkward age" for backpacking families. Toddlers can often keep a couple of adults busy just looking after them. Waiting until the toddler is subject to some degree of verbal guidance and able to walk the trails may be best for parents and child alike. If you get the urge to take a toddler on a backpack trip—even on a very, very short one—it is strongly recommended that you first take a number of day hikes to get a feel for just what the problems are going to be.

As is the case for other endeavors, the age at which a child may be able to undertake an elementary type of backpack trip varies somewhat with the individual child and his or her ability. However, at about four or five years of age most children can undertake a short-distance trip over good terrain. A stretch of ocean beach in an interesting area may be suitable for a first backpack trip with small children. Lacking an ocean beach, parents should be careful to select a trail in terrain that is commensurate with the child's ability. Steep climbs are generally not for four- or five-year-olds. Yet there are always parents who feel that *their* children are above average. These parents often urge a child into hiking over terrain and distances that are actually beyond capacity. The child may be able to accomplish the trip but won't *enjoy* it, and that is very important. The parents may even brag a little about their child's ability in this regard. However, such parents may find themselves having difficulty later on. The child may achieve the "goals" that the parents have set. However, a few years later, just when the parents think their child is about to develop into a full-fledged mountain climber, the child may rebel and want nothing further to do with the sport. It is very important that children have fun and enjoy the backpack trips that are planned for them.

TYPE OF TRIP

In planning a backpack trip with young children, it is very important that it be planned *for* the children. Adult objectives in backpacking simply do not coincide with, and can seldom be satisfactorily combined with, a trip that is suitable for children. The pace while on the trail must be slower. A group of adult backpackers may, at times, average two or three miles per hour on the trail. With small children one mile per hour may be too fast.

On most backpack trips, even for an all-adult party, an important consideration should be to enjoy whatever the time and place have to offer, rather than to hurry from one major goal to another. On trips with small children this consideration assumes major importance. A small mountain brook may simply be a minor obstacle to an adult backpacker—something to be quickly crossed before hurrying on down the trail. To a child that same small brook may be one of the major attractions of the trip. The child may want to spend half an hour there, or perhaps more, tossing pebbles, looking for minnows or frogs, and so on.

Thus, in planning and conducting a backpack trip with children, it is important to look at the trip and its attractions from the children's viewpoint. Not an easy task!

Beautiful scenery that may intrigue adults for hours may be good for only five or ten minutes of a child's attention. Long, monotonous stretches of trail, which an adult can tolerate because of known attractions further ahead, may cause a child to essentially give up. He or she may not want to go any further, and the psychological effect may result in lack of energy and in physical inability to continue. If the child were in a more interesting environment, he or she might suddenly be possessed with boundless energy.

Backpack trips with small children should therefore normally cover only short distances. Although a child may be able to hike five miles in a day, if he doesn't enjoy it, three miles would probably be more realistic. A trip on which a family hikes into an attractive area and makes a base camp is generally a good approach, especially on initial trips with children. Daily excursions, carrying light day packs, can then be made from the base camp. Even for adult backpackers the changing of camps daily can often be quite a chore. With small children it can be a disaster, and the entire family may suffer.

A type of wilderness trip that some parents with small children may want to consider is the conducted family trip. Some organizations, such as the Sierra Club, sponsor such trips. Family trips are generally made with burros or donkeys carrying most of the gear. Some animals that can be ridden by small children, or even by a child *and* parent, are usually available. The animals themselves are an attraction to many children, and such a trip can be thoroughly enjoyable for the entire family.

Yet another possibility for backwoods trips with small children is to hire an outfitter to transport your gear into a base camp on pack horses or mules. The family walks in, ahead of the outfitter, to a base camp location that has been scouted by the parents prior to the trip. By prearrangement the outfitter returns to the camp on a certain day (and hour) to transport the family's gear back to the trailhead. There are many places, particularly in the Western states, where such a trip can be arranged.

On the day hikes it is important to try to choose routes that will be interesting to the children. If the day hikes are too monotonous, it may so discourage the children that they won't want to take *any* backpack trip. On the day hikes note the type of terrain and other aspects that seem to be of interest to the children. A day hike along a stream will usually appeal to children. Rugged trails and close proximity to high cliffs and similar dangers should be avoided. Many stretches of ocean beaches are good places for day hikes, as well as for overnight trips.

Hiking boots should be carefully checked out. If the trails for your initial backpack trips are good (and they should be), some children may be able to get by satisfactorily with canvas (tennis) shoes. Almost any rubber- or composition-soled boot, above-the-ankle type, will serve adequately for the first few short backpack trips, provided they fit properly.

In general, it is a good idea for children to wear two pair of socks with their hiking boots, just as is recommended for adults. A thin inner sock should be worn next to the foot, and a thicker outer sock (usually wool) over that. The outer sock (in particular) is frequently a bit difficult for a child to get on properly over the inner sock. It is a good idea to help the children with this operation for a few times (possibly each time, for a while) to assure that the outer sock is on straight, not wrinkled, free of burrs, and so on, which could cause problems later on.

During the preconditioning hikes, children's feet should be checked periodically. Children frequently will not inform a parent at the onset of a tender spot on the foot or toe. They may wait until a blister has already started to form and they are in trouble.

If the children are of such age that they can carry small packs, it will bolster their morale and enthusiasm if they are allowed to do so. When on a backpack trip, it will also take part of the bulk and weight out of the parents packs. A light load

of extra clothing, rain gear, food items, drinking water, and so on, can be added to the child's pack. It is important to check regularly to assure that the packs fit properly. If the children complain of sore shoulders or other discomfort with a light load, the pack may be too large, too small, or improperly adjusted, or there may be some other problem. Better to remedy the difficulty now than to wait until the group is on a backwoods trail.

It is important to remind children to add or shed outer clothing as necessary to stay comfortable. They will usually not be as conscientious about this as an adult will. If they are not comfortable, they probably will not enjoy themselves.

Some photos taken of the children on day hikes, as well as on backpack trips, will probably heighten their interest. The best photos can be enlarged and placed on the walls of their rooms at home. They will provide daily reminders of the highlights of their adventures.

It is important to keep the children interested as they hike. Various animals and birds, unusual rock formations, clouds, and so on, can be pointed out to them. It is important to try to get a feel for their best pace and for things along the way that keep them amused and in good spirits. It is essentially impossible, however, to set a pace and stay with it in the way that an adult backpack group does. The most unlikely attractions along the route may interest children, and they may want to stop for ten or fifteen minutes at such places. If it is really something that interests them and they are not just "goofing off," it is best to let the children have their way. Setting "goals" of so many miles to be covered each day must be done very carefully when there are children in the group.

Children often want to start down the trail in a burst of energy at the beginning of the day, but then they quickly slow down. It is best to keep them in check a bit. At fairly frequent intervals brief rest stops should be made, to observe interesting surroundings, adjust equipment, check clothing and feet, or perhaps to have a refreshing drink and a snack. Telling the children stories about the area, or on almost any subject, will break the monotony for them.

EQUIPMENT

Good-quality backpack equipment is fairly expensive. When you are attempting to outfit an entire family with packs, sleeping bags, hiking boots, and so on, the price tag may appear quite formidable. One consolation is that backpacking in itself is a comparatively inexpensive type of recreation. That is, for example, compared to a vacation where a family spends day after day on the highway and must pay for gasoline for the family vehicle, meals in restaurants, motels, entertainment, and so on. Another consideration is that the special clothing and backpack equipment can be used for trip after trip once the initial investment has been made. One (dreadful) thought is that the members may not take enthusiastically to this new type of family activity. However, unless clothing and equipment are reasonably appropriate and suitable for the adventure, there may be too many problems, and this may *assure* that the family will not enjoy their adventure. But don't despair! There are several means that can be used to keep the initial outfitting cost to a minimum.

Initial trips with young children should be planned for mild weather, when temperatures will be warm. Insofar as possible, trips should also be planned when the likelihood of heavy rains and severe storms will be minimal. Another matter to seriously consider is the insect season. A few weeks one way or the other can make a big difference. With these considerations taken into account, some of the clothing and equipment required will be relatively inexpensive (in contrast to that required in other seasons). The initial trips to the wilderness will probably also be much more enjoyable for the children if done in mild weather.

In some areas it is possible to rent all kinds of equipment used in backpacking, and this may be a good approach. Especially for the first few trips, until the parents can see how the children are going to take to this new family sport, it might be wise to rent or possibly borrow much of the special equipment needed.

As was discussed in Chapter 5, very little special clothing is needed for mild-weather backpacking. Where wool clothing is called for, if it is not already available at home, satisfactory used items might be obtained at bargain prices at rummage sales. Another possible source of special clothing and equipment is an ad in the local newspaper or in one of the trail magazines or newsletters. (See Appendix H.) Other families before you have tried backpacking and given it up, graduated to more sophisticated equipment, or outgrown certain items.

Making certain items of clothing and equipment is still another way to economize in outfitting your family for backpacking. There are now quite a number of firms that market kits for making many items of clothing and some equipment (tents, sleeping bags, and so on) for backpacking. Many kits are not difficult for a person experienced in sewing to use, and the savings compared to ready-made items can be considerable.

Depending on the age and sex of the children, a tent (or tents) of their own can increase their enjoyment of the outing. Very young children may feel more comfortable sleeping in the same tent with Mom and Dad, however. This is a factor to be carefully considered in purchasing (or making) tents for your family adventures.

Finding suitable sleeping bags for young children is frequently a problem. They can be made with some of the do-it-yourself kits. Also, "elephant-foot" bivouac bags, which are readily available, often make good sleeping bags for young children.

PRECONDITIONING

Thorough preparation and conditioning is of the utmost importance. Camping with car and tent is a good way to initially introduce children to living out-of-doors. The family should also make a number of day hikes, of perhaps three to five miles, in preparation for an overnight backpack trip, which in turn can be extended to longer trips.

Guidebooks to flowers and trees, birds, and/or animal tracks will probably increase the children's enjoyment in hiking. With some help and encouragement from Mom and Dad they may become quite knowledgeable and interested in these aspects of nature, depending upon their ages.

There are hazards in the woods, and the children should become acquainted with some of them. Point out poison ivy and poison oak to them, if there is any. Teach them to exercise caution in stream crossings so that they do not slip on a wet log or hurt themselves in wading a stream. If there may be poisonous snakes in the area, tell the children to avoid thick terrain, to watch where they step, and not to put either hands or feet into places where they cannot see well. It takes some tact and diplomacy to point out such hazards without alarming a child unnecessarily. Don't dwell on hazards too much. Spend at least an equal amount of time in showing them the beauty of the outdoors and stressing that with reasonable precautions they are completely safe.

Tents are recommended when backpacking with children. *(Owen Thero)*

PREPARATION

Thorough advance preparation is especially important in planning trips with young children. It is strongly recommended that the route and area be limited to that which the parents (or at least one parent) have been over before. This will assure that the trail and terrain will be within the capabilities of the children and will be interesting to them. An open, parklike area near a stream or lake is much more preferable for camp than thick, brushy terrain. Children never cease to love water, and if there are shallow areas where they can wade, it will heighten their enjoyment tremendously.

Although poisonous snakes have a very wide distribution, certain local areas may have a particularly high density. These areas should be carefully avoided. Snakebite is always dangerous, but it is apt to be much more serious, and possibly fatal, in the case of young children.

The length of the trip, and whether a base camp is used or camps are changed, will depend primarily on the age and abilities of the children. In hot-weather camping, if camps are changed, it is recommended that hiking be confined to the cool, morning hours. Distances between camps should be short. The children may *tolerate* hiking in the heat of the afternoon and going considerable distances, but in all probability they won't *like* it. Again, adult objectives should be forgotten and every reasonable attempt made to satisfy the children and keep them happy.

Although trips should not be planned at the peak of the insect season, there will usually be *some* insects. Liquid insect repellents are useful to adults but only to a limited extent to children. Depending upon their ages, it may be best to take

along mosquito netting for children and to rely upon that more than upon liquid repellents. Young children have a tendency to rub the repellent into their eyes, and it may thus be harmful.

In planning the food list, it is important to include foods that your children particularly enjoy, including lots of snack foods. A variety of easily prepared drinks that they like is also important. When the group slows to a halt on the trail and all else fails to motivate the children, a favorite snack or drink will often do the job. If your food list includes typical dehydrated foods, it is best to try them out at home to see how the children are going to take to them. Try having the children drink various brands of dehydrated milk at home to see which they like best, before taking one on a backpack trip. Also, children who refuse dehydrated milk may relish it if chocolate flavor is added, or they may prefer drinking it as hot chocolate. Even if you intend to cook on a portable stove, it is recommended that a fire permit be obtained (if required) if wood fires are allowed in the area. Children always enjoy a fire, even if it is only a small one. They may be able to toast marshmallows over the fire. Possibly you can make them some popcorn.

For small children, one or several of their favorite items from home may help considerably in their introduction to backpacking and aid in their emotional well-being. A toy or two (not too heavy or bulky), or a favorite blanket, would be an example.

If you have a family dog and dogs are permitted in the area you are packing into, it may be a good idea to take the dog along. Although dogs are not generally recommended on backpack trips, on a short trip with children it may heighten their enjoyment considerably to have their favorite pet along.

Sunburn and dehydration are potential problems with children on a backpack trip. Although children may not be accustomed to wearing long-sleeved shirts, long trousers, and a hat at home, such clothing is recommended for a backpack trip, for all members.

In planning the trip, some of the plans should be discussed with the children, so that they feel they have a real and important part in it. During actual preparation, children can perform some minor tasks in getting food and equipment ready.

Checklists are as important in backpacking with children as they are with a group of adults. In addition, it will give older children an added sense of responsibility if they are made accountable for certain items on the checklist. Certainly

Backpacking family on the trail. (Owen Thero)

they can be responsible for their own clothing and equipment. (This will also save time and work for the parents.) Let them assist in planning the checklist and impress upon them the necessity of assuring that all items on the checklist are accounted for, both before leaving home and after the group is on the trail. Depending upon the ages of the children, let them also be responsible for certain items of common equipment that are for the benefit of the entire group.

ON THE TRAIL

Small children will usually stop and rest when they are tired, but older children may not. The older children may set goals for themselves that are beyond their capabilities and may experience bodily harm from overexertion. Some restraint may need to be placed on them, particularly if there is rivalry with other children in the group.

A harness with a leash can be an aid and comfort to parents in controlling very young children. This is especially true of sections of trail which may border fast-moving streams, cliffs, and so on. In such places very young children can get themselves into dangerous situations in a matter of seconds, if not carefully controlled.

Generally, the slowest member of the group should be in the lead or between the leader and another adult who brings up the rear. In order to keep the group together, you will have to gear your pace to that of the slowest member. Sometimes slowness of the children's pace will be directly related to the monotony they are experiencing. Talking, singing, pointing out items of interest, will help relieve the monotony. Depending on the age and physical stature of the child, don't be too hasty to relieve him or her of part of the load

at the first complaint about a heavy pack. Promise a rest stop and a snack within the next ten minutes at an interesting place. The child who complains of being too tired may explode in a burst of energy once you reach camp.

Watch carefully for sunburn and dehydration in children. They cannot be expected to take the preventive measures against sunburn that an adult would take. A good case of sunburn can spoil their trip and be a burden to the adults. Apply protective lotion to children regularly. Encourage the children to drink water and other liquids frequently. They are apt to neglect this unless reminded. Have plenty of fruit flavoring, cocoa, malted milk, and so on, along as a help in getting the children to keep their liquid intake at a high level.

Side trips off the main trail to points of interest will increase the children's interest if the side trips are not too long and do not take away too much energy needed for the main trip. A whistle on a cord around each child's neck will help in locating them if they get out of sight and will also give them a sense of security. It is a good precaution.

Children are prone to throw gum and candy wrappers, tissues, and so on, along the trail. Teach them from the beginning the importance of using a litterbag and burning all burnables when (and if) a fire is available. Impress upon them that nature is sensitive and cannot fight back against man. The motto "Take nothing but photographs; leave nothing but footprints" should be stressed to children from the beginning of their first backpack trip.

Teach children to keep a respectful distance away from all wild animals, even very small ones. The animals should not be disturbed in their natural environment, and if they are regularly fed by people, they may get so accustomed to this that they will die when no one is around to feed them and they must scrounge their own food. There is always the possibility of animals being rabid, particularly the overly friendly ones. If your child should get bitten by an animal, this poses a real problem and the vacation may end right there.

IN CAMP

Don't be too anxious to set up camp when you first reach your destination. Let the children goof off a bit. Depending upon their age and experience, let them have a part in choosing the area where they are going to sleep and pitch "their" tent. Instruct them in proper storage of their bedrolls and other camp articles during the daytimes. Explain how and why many articles of gear and clothing should be kept off the ground and how they should be stored.

It is never too early to teach children backwoods manners and wilderness preservation. Designate a toilet area and instruct the children in digging a "cat" hole and covering all "evidence," including toilet paper. When it is time to wash up or do dishes, impress upon them that these tasks are accomplished well back from any water supply and explain the reason.

Some parents with very young children will be using disposable diapers during their stay in the backwoods. If open fires are permitted, soiled diapers can be burned after being dried in the sun. If they are not burned, they should be carried back to the trailhead, along with other trash.

If there is some fishing to be had, let the children have a try. Don't expect them to stay at it very long, however, if the fish are not biting. Be prepared to exercise a lot of patience and restraint. Remember, the trip was planned for the children. Try to view it from their standpoint. If your child catches a fish, makes a "discovery" on his or her own, comes up with a good suggestion, and so on, applaud or commend the child properly.

As the children grow older, there will be quite a few changes in the type of activity that they will enjoy. They may develop into "serious" trout fishermen, or if their indoctrination to fishing has not been up to par, they may want nothing to do with it. Perhaps rock hunting, bird watching, or photography will spark their interest. At a fairly early age there will be times when they will want to take a friend along on their backwoods trips. Encourage them! The time will come all too soon when your children will be taking trips on their own — and probably into areas and terrain that Mom and Dad wouldn't even want to attempt. Enjoy your family while you can!

LOST CHILDREN

Your child can get lost within just a short distance of camp. More than one parent has suffered the fear and panic of suddenly discovering that his child was missing in the backwoods. Also, if it happens, the parent will probably chastise himself for not having taken more careful precautions, and thus add to the misery. The type of terrain is a factor in children's getting lost, but it can readily happen even in fairly open terrain.

A carrier of this type for children of "toddler age," is a good investment. *(Lou Clemmons)*

A small child alone can easily get lost if he or she wanders even a short distance from camp. Using the buddy system, where small children stay with older children at all times when out of sight of camp, is a good approach. If the children dress in brightly colored clothes — especially bright shirts and brightly colored protective garments — it will be of help in keeping track of them.

When a camp is established, it is a good idea for the parents to acquaint the children with the lay of the land. A simple freehand map can be drawn to show the relationship of trails or paths, streams, hills, cliffs, and other prominent features in the terrain, with respect to camp. It is a good idea to mark on the map some boundaries beyond which the child is not to go alone. As was stated earlier, a good precaution is for children to carry a whistle and to be instructed on when to use it.

Older children can be taught how to use a compass in connection with a map and to read a topographic map. A simple version of orienting will probably boost their enthusiasm while they learn to use a compass. If done in short sessions, such lessons will be fun as well as beneficial.

Children should also be taught what to do in case they do get lost. Older children going any significant distance from camp should carry a day pack containing some survival items and water. Even quite young children can carry a canteen and will probably be quite happy to do so. At a fairly early age they can carry a pocketknife and matches whenever they are in the backwoods. Day hikes near home are a good time to teach children fire building, orienting with map and compass, and certain other survival techniques. This will add greatly to their resourcefulness and will provide much peace of mind for the parents when they take to the backwoods with the children. There is a good possibility that such training may prevent the children from getting lost. Or if they do get lost, their knowledge on how to handle the situation may save their lives.

A FAMILY VACATION — BACKPACKING

Every year thousands of families in all types of recreational vehicles take to the highways for their vacations. Many of them spend much of their time in crowded campgrounds, often with much less privacy and feeling for the outdoors than they would have in their backyard at home. They "visit" the national parks (more crowds), spend time in the souvenir shops and main points of interest, then speed to the next national park (to repeat the process). If a family has the proper

equipment and some backpacking experience, it can vary this routine, get away from the crowds, and make the vacation one which all members will thoroughly enjoy.

The next time your family plans to visit a national park or similar scenic area, take along backpack equipment and supplies. Get information in advance on the hiking trails and backpack campsites in the park by writing to the superintendent of the particular park. Order topographic maps of areas that have trails that are of possible interest. When you arrive at the park, get more information on the particular trail you have in mind, type of terrain, campsites available, fire permits required, and so forth. Then select the trail that is commensurate with the experience and age of all members of the family. Take off for a few days into the backwoods and really enjoy a wilderness vacation. Admittedly, some of the trails in the national parks, and the backwoods campsites, will be fairly crowded, but nothing like the recreational-vehicle campgrounds and points of interest that you can drive to in an automobile. It is amazing what a complete change in atmosphere can be accomplished by hiking just a few miles into the backwoods. If your experience is up to it, avoid the popular trails and areas of the park in favor of a more remote and little-used area. It can be a truly enjoyable vacation — one which all members of the family will enjoy and fondly remember for years to come.

Children enjoy helping with the cooking. (Fred Mulholland)

15
Preparing for a Backpack Trip

SETTING A DATE

One of the first things that needs to be done in planning for a backpack trip is to set a date for the trip. This may seem like a simple thing, but it does require some thought. Most backpackers do their backpacking in relatively mild weather. If in midsummer the area thay have in mind is hot and humid, or subject to daily heavy rainfall, they would probably prefer another season. They would probably also prefer to avoid the extreme cold and deep snow of winter, unless they particularly enjoy winter backpacking and have the equipment and knowledge to safely undertake such a trip. Insects are also something to be reckoned with in your planning. If you go into an area at the height of the mosquito or black fly season, your trip probably won't be very enjoyable.

Late spring and early fall are favorite backpacking seasons with many backpackers. Daytime temperatures are usually invigorating, insects are seldom a problem, and the "tourist traffic" of the summer months is avoided. However, most backpackers work for a living, and the season for their desired trip may be dictated by work schedules and company policy, rather than by personal preference.

For a full-scale backpack trip, the date should usually be set at least a month in advance, and preferably somewhat longer. If you are going into an area that no member of the party is acquainted

with, it may require more than a month of intermittent correspondence and other preparation just to obtain maps and other information on the area. Some dehydrated foods may be ordered through the mail, and about a month from the time you send in your order should be allowed for delivery. It is desirable to package the food at least a week in advance, because there are usually some unexpected matters that come up during the last week before a trip, and you will want to get as much of the routine preparation out of the way as possible.

For those who may be going on paid, formally conducted trips, it may be necessary to make reservations as much as three to six months in advance. It will also probably be necessary to furnish to the trip leader advance information in regard to your past experience, physical condition, backpack equipment, and so on.

Trying to get three or more people to agree on a date for a trip can be quite a job in itself. At the same time, you should reach agreement on an alternative date, in the event that you have unexpected bad weather move in just prior to the takeoff date, someone gets sick, or there is some other emergency. With the planning and preparation that is required for such a trip, when someone backs out for reasons of "personal convenience" just a few days before takeoff, this is usually reason for "exclusion from the club" as far as future trips are concerned. At the minimum, it means repackaging of practically every food item (which is no small job). If only three persons were going and someone backs out, it possibly means cancellation of the trip. In remote areas a group of three is considered a minimum from a safety standpoint.

Once a date has been set, every member of the group should work conscientiously toward that date. At the same time, trip members need to condition their thinking to the fact that if a real emergency occurs, or definite bad weather moves in, the trip will be delayed to the alternative date. There are types of people who, after setting a date and telling their friends, neighbors, and others about the proposed trip, feel that it almost amounts to a bad mark on their reputation if they do not take off as planned, regardless of what comes up in the meantime. That is why agreement on such matters and on an alternative date is important.

It is usually desirable to take care of as many of the trip preparation details as far in advance of the trip date as possible. Few things are more frustrating than working right up to the time of takeoff in repairing or locating equipment or doing numerous other jobs that could have been done weeks in advance. It will be a much more enjoyable trip if you can spend the week or two prior to takeoff in making daily conditioning hikes and so forth, without being bothered by a lot of last-minute details.

BE PREPARED

If possible, store the equipment that you use in backpacking in a special place. Since it all goes in or on your pack, it doesn't take up much room. A few medium-sized cardboard boxes will usually hold all of it. The best time to make repairs or changes in your equipment is as soon as possible after a trip, while the events and problems are still fresh in mind. It is poor practice to wait until just before another trip to get gear in order. If something needs repair, repair it; if it needs sharpening, sharpen it. If it is planned to try out a new item of equipment or a new food, it should be done well in advance of another trip. In other words, "Be Prepared." Many of these preparations should be made right after each trip, and most of them can be done weeks before the next trip. Following are recommendations on a few jobs in this category.

1. Immediately after each trip, thoroughly air and sun sleeping gear and any items of cloth-

ing that are not washed. Sleeping bags should be stored in a fluffed condition, rather than in a tight roll. The ideal way to store is to suspend them vertically from a hanger and not roll them at all. A sleeping bag should never be stored in its stuff bag.

2. Immediately after each trip, some notes should be made on how menus and food quantities worked out. Was there too much or too little of some foods? Were some foods unsatisfactory in taste, preparation time, or otherwise? Good records on foods used in your backpack trips, kept from trip to trip, can save a lot of time when it comes to preparing for subsequent trips.

3. There were probably some mistakes made in general planning, detailed preparations, amount and kind of gear taken, techniques, and other areas. Admitting mistakes and planning how they will be corrected on the next trip will make that trip more enjoyable.

4. Checklists should be reviewed after each trip. You will probably want to make a few changes or additions. Checklists and notes should be kept from trip to trip.

5. Soon after each trip, wash pan bags, utensil bags, cloth food bags, and so on. Any worn drawstrings or tie strings on such bags should be replaced. All cooking and eating gear should be washed thoroughly. Soap, pot scratchers, sponges, and so on, should be replaced. After cleaning such gear, store it in large plastic bags.

6. Repair or replace any equipment or clothing that is torn or broken. Lubricate zippers on packs and clothing. A soft lead pencil or a candle will work well, as will the special zipper lubricants available.

7. Clean hiking boots and the lugs on the boots. Use a waterproofing material, after cleaning, if the need is indicated. Did you have any trouble with your boots on the last backpack trip? Do they need repairs? New insoles? This is the time to check them over, have any necessary repairs made, and then try them out on some practice hikes.

8. Did all items of clothing perform their intended function on your last trip? Do you want to try out a different item of clothing in place of one that did not perform satisfactorily? Now is the time to do it.

9. Do any items of rain gear or equipment need a new coat of waterproofing compound? Waterproof now and then check it out under a shower or garden hose.

10. Did your backpack stove perform satisfactorily? Do you need to mail order any new

stove parts? Regardless, it is a good idea to get out your stove and check it over, just to be sure it is in good operating condition.

11. Sharpen knives, fishhooks, and so forth.

12. Try out a new trail food. The place to first try it out is at home.

13. Review your first aid technique. Check over the contents of your first aid kit. Replace aspirin, moleskin, and other items that may have been used up. Check the rubber suction cups on snakebite kits. After several years the rubber frequently becomes hard and brittle, and the suction cup may be worthless for the purpose intended, even though it has never been used.

14. Check over fishing equipment, rock hunting equipment, cameras, and other special gear.

15. Replace "old" matches in match containers. Matches that are more than six to nine months old do not work as well as "fresh" matches. Only wood stick matches are recommended.

SELECTING NEW EQUIPMENT

One advantage in belonging to a hiking or backpacking club is that you can talk to others about their backpacking gear and see the equipment in use. You can get firsthand information on the virtues and deficiencies of various items of equipment; you cannot get this from reading retail catalogs. Even though you may still do most of your backpacking with a small group, belonging to a club can provide these and other benefits that you could not obtain otherwise.

From time to time some of your equipment will need to be replaced. With most gear there must always be some compromise between weight and ruggedness. A cast iron skillet will last a lifetime, but that doesn't make it a good piece of backpacking gear. You will enjoy carrying a lightweight Teflon or aluminum skillet much more, and it will serve the purpose even though it needs to be replaced periodically. You may buy a pair of hiking boots that will last five years or more, and with each step you take you may have to pay for that durability by lifting an extra pound of weight. A lighter boot may need to be replaced every one or two seasons, but that is of no consequence if you have enjoyed many miles of extra comfort in hiking as a result of less durability. If you are buying a fishing rod for backpacking, buy one with a detachable handle and with sections nearly equal in length. Avoid heavy, overdesigned equipment and clothing. This particularly applies to war surplus items.

When you order equipment from catalogs, be sure to note the difference between weight of the item and its shipping weight. If in doubt, write to the supplier and ask for a clarification of weight before placing an order. When ordering hiking boots, ask what the weight of the boot is in your size. The catalog weight given for some of the hiking boots can be quite misleading.

DO-IT-YOURSELF KITS

There is now a large variety of kits on the market from which you can make your own parka, vest, rain pants, and other items of clothing. There are also kits available for tents, sleeping bags, and similar, more complex gear. A list of some of the firms that sell such kits is given in Appendix A. Making some of your own gear by using these kits can be interesting and profitable. For some items, however, the benefits may be marginal. If you should decide to do-it-yourself, it is suggested that you start with one of the simpler items, such as a vest or rain chaps, and progress gradually from there. Unless you or a member of your household is fairly accomplished at using a sewing machine, you may find that the results do not compare very well with the store-bought version. Your endeavor may also be less interesting and more time-consuming than you had planned.

TYPES OF BACKPACK TRIPS

There are many types of backpack trips. They can vary greatly in objectives, itinerary, length, degree of physical endurance required, and other factors. It is important to consider your personal desires and objectives, your previous backpacking experience, your physical stamina, and other aspects carefully before deciding on the kind of trip you would like to participate in. Otherwise you may find yourself on the trail with a group whose objectives, daily itinerary, pace, and other features are different from what you had in mind. The daily activity may be a bore. You may have essentially wasted your time, money, and energy. Following are outlined some of the various types of backpack trips.

1. A small group backpacks into an interesting wild area for a period of from several days to a week or more. They may spend most of each day hiking, or they may establish a base camp in a desired location and travel out from there each day. Compared to many other backpack trips, the actual distance covered may be very minimal. The group will probably return to its takeoff point

at the end of the trip (in contrast to a group that hikes a one-way route and has prearranged for transportation at the end of the one-way trip). The majority of backpack trips probably fall in this general category.

2. A fairly large group, perhaps ten to fifteen persons, takes to the trails. Typical groups would be boy scout, girl scout, or church groups. (Hiking clubs or trail clubs could be included, although short small-group trips are often planned by such clubs.) The pace must be geared to that of the slowest and least prepared member. The quality and amount of experience of the leaders are important factors in making the trip interesting and safe, and in order to have minimum impact on the ecology of the region. Such groups do not normally have the flexibility in itinerary and other aspects that is inherent in a smaller, informal group, but they can be worthwhile if you are fortunate to participate in a well-planned trip that is properly managed and conducted.

3. Medium-to-large groups, perhaps eight to twenty persons, are taken on an organized backpack trip for a fee. Trips conducted by the Wilderness Society, the Sierra Club, and many private organizations are examples. The leaders of such groups are paid and are generally well experienced. The rates for participation usually seem fairly high. However, there are some compensations. You do not normally need to have any concern about lost trails, or running out of water or food. The leaders will have been over the same route and into the same area before, perhaps many times. On most such trips you must carry, in addition to your personal gear, a share of the common equipment that is used by the group as a whole. A variation of this type of trip uses burros or other pack stock for carrying the common equipment and food.

Although you may normally shun large groups in your backpacking activity, joining such a group may be the most feasible way of becoming acquainted with a new area that you have a potential interest in. Not all areas of a wilderness or other backwoods region are equally interesting. Conducted trips will generally concentrate on those areas that are most appealing from scenic and other standpoints. The leaders will generally select the most feasible and interesting route through the area. Since the leaders are usually very familiar with the area, you can learn much from them that would take a lot of time and effort if you were to simply start exploring the entire area through numerous trips made according to your own plan and initiative.

4. A group, possibly a family group with children, arranges for most of its gear to be packed into a scenic area by a professional packer, using pack stock. The group, with very light packs, hikes in ahead of the packer, to an area that is easily reached in a day of hiking. There is a single base camp for the entire trip. When the trip is over, the packer, by prearrangement, returns to pack the group's gear back to the roadhead. Most trips of this type are made in the Western states.

THE CONDUCTED TRIP

Many backpackers will shun a "formal" backpack trip, where you pay a fee to a firm or organization for a conducted trip into a wilderness or other backwoods area. Such trips are rather expensive, compared to one that you organize and undertake yourself, with perhaps several friends. The flexibility of itinerary inherent in a small group of backpackers is essentially nonexistent in most formally conducted trips. It should be recognized, however, that there are a few outfitters that will take small groups into the wilderness and will tailor the trip pretty much to your desires. As mentioned, a conducted trip is one way of becoming initially acquainted with a large wilderness area. Provided you are in good physical condition and select a trip with an itinerary commensurate with your abilities, a conducted trip is comparatively safe for the neophyte backpacker, depending largely upon the particular leadership. The beginning backpacker will usually learn quite a bit from such trips.

I took my first conducted backpack trip after I had been doing "serious" backpacking for well over twenty years. I have taken several such trips. I did this primarily out of curiosity and a desire to have some familiarity with that type of trip. In particular, I wanted to get some firsthand information that might be helpful to others who might be contemplating such a trip.

From my experience with this type of backpack trip, I would emphasize the following aspects to anyone who is considering such a trip.

1. The sponsor should provide a good description of the trip. This should include information on major points of interest, typical daily activities, off-trail travel (if any), layover days (if any), opportunity for wildlife observation and fishing, and so on. In other words, there should be sufficient information for you to evaluate the trip in terms of your particular interests.

2. There should be some very definite information as to the physical demands on the backpacker. Average number of miles to be traveled per day is important, as well as whether there will be layover days. What altitudes will be involved? Very important information is the altitude to be gained, lost, and regained in any one day. This is generally the most important aspect to consider from a physical standpoint and to compare with your past experience and your general health and stamina. It can very well be the deciding factor in whether you should undertake the trip. In addition to specifying altitudes involved and mountain passes to be traversed, the sponsor should rate the trip as moderate, moderately strenuous, or strenuous, or use similar descriptive terminology. If the sponsor does not provide this information, you should ask for it (and also be a bit wary because it was not provided in the first place).

3. The sponsor should specify the maximum weight of pack to be carried. Two weights should actually be provided. First, the maximum weight of your pack, including all of your personal equipment, should be stated. Secondly, you should be informed of the weight of food and common equipment (provided by the sponsor) that you will be expected to carry for the benefit of the group.

4. The sponsor should request your age and inquire about your present physical condition, including any physical deficiencies. Information about your past and recent backpacking experience should also be requested. There will probably be some questions in regard to your major items of equipment, that is, what type of pack, sleeping bag, protective clothing, and so on, that you have. This general information will usually be provided to the sponsor on a form that you are required to fill out, sign, and return.

5. The sponsor should provide information on expected weather—in particular, rain, snow, and maximum and minimum temperatures. This will be of the utmost importance to you in planning protective clothing to be taken.

6. The rendezvous point should be stated. This will generally be a motel, cafe, or some such place in a small town near the trailhead. Does the sponsor provide transportation to and from the rendezvous point to the trailhead? If not, you will need some detailed information on the distance and the type of road (the road may not be passable by cars in all weather). A license is generally required by a firm to haul "business" passengers in an automotive vehicle. Does the firm have such a license, or are you traveling at your own risk?

A few years ago I found myself at a rendezvous point (a motel) in Colorado about to participate in a week-long conducted tour with eight or ten other persons. We were leaving for the trailhead early the next morning. Just hours prior to take-off "problems" developed with the firm in regard to their ability to furnish transportation to the trailhead. On the spur of the moment I volunteered my pick-up truck to transport myself and some other trip members (and our gear) to the trailhead. The developments that took place during the next few hours after I volunteered were incredible. They would fill another chapter in this book. But I learned something. Have all of the basic arrangements concerning the trip well understood beforehand. If just prior to takeoff the outfitter changes some basic aspect or is unable to provide certain services previously agreed to, ask for your money back. If you make compromises, do so with extreme caution. In your natural eagerness to get the "show on the road," it is all too easy to make hasty decisions that you may deeply regret later.

Individual preparation. On a conducted trip there may be some tendency toward laxity in preparation by the individual participants. After all, the leader is responsible for preparing the itinerary, getting together food and cooking gear, general camp equipment, and so forth. Admittedly, this does relieve the individual members of considerable work. However, you must still carry your own pack. The shelter you choose must provide adequate protection and the clothing you take must keep you warm. There may be safety in numbers. Certainly you aren't likely to get lost with a leader who has been over the trail before, and there are other compensations. But there are certain preparations for which you alone are responsible, and the other members cannot and should not be depended upon to help if you get into trouble after you are in the backwoods.

Courtesy. I would like to leave another thought about conducted trips. When hikers arrive back at the trailhead after the trip is over, they are usually eager to be off to their individual destinations, or headed home. I have seen some depart from the group without even saying goodbye to the leader. If you had a good trip, you should take a moment to thank the leader for his or her effort, say that you enjoyed the trip, and wish the leader well. It only takes a few moments, and your thoughtfulness will most certainly be appreciated.

ORGANIZING YOUR OWN TRIP

As was stated previously, the majority of backpack trips are probably made by small groups of three or more people who are well acquainted with each other. Some members have probably backpacked together before, perhaps many times. It is not uncommon for such a group to invite on the trip one or two other persons, who although they are acquainted with the group, have not backpacked with them before. Perhaps the newcomers have done very little previous backpacking and this will be their first "real" backpack trip. The "regular" members of the group had best take some very special measures to obtain some information about the newcomers' general backpacking experience, their equipment, physical stamina, and so on. Failure to do so may get the trip off to a bad start.

The objective of such a group is frequently to explore a backwoods area that is new to them, perhaps one recommended by other backpacking friends. Or perhaps it is to explore a new part of a general area that they have been into before. In any case, some planning and organization is essential if the participants are to get "full value" for the time and money they have invested in the trip.

Why organize?   Would you like to participate in a backpack trip that is a comedy of confusion, frustration, wasted effort, and hurt feelings? It's very simple. Just take any group of reasonably well qualified hikers and backpackers, and assume that because of their experience you don't need to do any significant amount of planning or have any definite organization in preparing for the trip you have in mind. You will end up with too much of certain equipment (unnecessary duplication), not enough of other items, a conglomeration of food and menus, an itinerary that was supposedly satisfactory to everyone but that actually doesn't please anyone, and other problems. Certainly in a small group of experienced backpackers the role of the leader is not as distinct or as involved as in a large group with varied and less experience, but someone still needs to spearhead the preparations.

Intermittent preparation and coordination over a period of six weeks or longer, prior to takeoff, is not unusual. The more complex the trip, the more lead time should be allowed. A few meetings of the group concerned, to plan your trip and to determine who is going to do what in getting ready for it, are recommended. Following are some of the things that should be discussed and decided upon.

Choosing a leader.   A small, informal group of backpackers may hesitate to choose a leader. Yet, for the reasons given above, it is best to have someone in the party who will have overall responsibility for trip preparations and the conduct of the trip. If the individuals in the backpack group are well experienced, the leader s responsibilities will simply be lesser in scope and difficulty than with an inexperienced group. After the group is on the trail, most matters requiring decision will probably be discussed and decisions made as a group.

Setting goals.   In discussing the proposed trip, it is well to give some thought to the possibility that you may not reach your desired goal or goals. Determination is a good virtue, but if it is not tempered with good judgment, it can result in disaster. The goals that the group has in mind for the trip may be well within their capabilities for accomplishment. However, adverse weather, illness of some trip members, or other factors may require a change in plans, and some goals may need to be postponed for a future trip. Most people are capable of exercising good judgment in not jeopardizing the safety and welfare of trip members under such conditions. However, there are some whose determination to reach a goal outweighs even good judgment.

Stay together.   During the pretrip discussions, it is well to emphasize that the group will keep together, once it is on the trail. With a small group of people who are used to backpacking together, this may be no problem at all. The larger the group, the greater the possibility that some hiker may tend to wander off alone at some time during the trip. Considerable time may then be wasted in locating that person. The trip may even be ruined. The tendency to separate is probably greatest after the climax of the trip has been reached and the group starts the return trip to the roadhead. Some members may be so anxious to return home that it is almost impossible to keep them with the group. They may dash ahead and, in their haste, expose themselves and others to unnecessary dangers and accidents. This can lead to problems. That is why the matter deserves emphasis during the pretrip planning at home.

Food, cooking gear.   One person, hopefully someone skilled in cooking on the trail, should be in charge of menu planning, buying and packaging food, getting together cooking gear, and distributing equal loads among the hikers in time for them to pack it with the rest of their equipment. In a small group the leader may also be the cook, but not necessarily. Someone in the group may be allergic to certain common foods or may have a strong dislike for some foods. It is best to find this out when the menus are being made up at home, rather than when the group is cooking in camp.

Other common equipment. Someone will need to assemble other items of common equipment, such as repair kit, group first aid kit, rope, and so forth, and distribute an equal load to each hiker. If it is agreed that one person will carry a camera (or other item) for the benefit of all, then that person should be compensated accordingly in the weight of other common equipment that he or she is given to carry.

Choosing a route. Hopefully some member of the party is familiar with the area that the group plans to pack into, and also with a route into the area. If the area is new to all members, more effort will need to be expended in obtaining maps, literature, outlining an itinerary, and providing all possible information on the route. For some trips into particularly remote regions, this aspect of your planning can, and should, amount to a major effort.

Transportation. You will need transportation to the takeoff point. One approach is that some hikers furnish vehicles and the others pay for the gas and oil. However, gas and oil represent only a fraction of the cost of operating a vehicle. An alternative is for riders to jointly pay the driver at the end of the trip for car or truck expenses, based on mileage driven (say 12 cents per mile for passenger cars). Those furnishing vehicles should take special precautions to ensure that the vehicles are in good operating condition and not likely to break down on the way to the takeoff point. If a vehicle breaks down en route and the group has to wait at some remote crossroads while a fan belt or ignition coil is being brought out from the nearest town, it gets the trip off to a bad start. Preventive maintenance costs money, and a generous mileage allowance to the vehicle owner is essential.

Do the drivers have the full name and address of each hiker that they are to pick up? (There are a lot of Johns in the phone book.) Searching out street names and house numbers with a flashlight at four o'clock in the morning can be quite a chore, and phoning people at that hour to ask them how to get to their home can lead to a certain amount of difficulty.

Funds. You will need to purchase foods and certain common supplies well in advance of the trip. If you are hiring a guide or arranging for special transportation at the roadhead, a deposit is usually made toward this service. Each member should make an advance deposit toward these costs. There also needs to be a clear understanding as to whether any of this advance payment is to be returned to a trip member who later cancels out. Generally such advance payments are not refunded, either in whole or in part. When supplies are purchased for the trip, or deposits made for a necessary service, the planning is already too far along to permit any refunds.

Uninvited participants. A person who is planning to go on an informal group trip should never on his or her own initiative ask a companion or other person to go on the trip. The matter should first be cleared with the trip leader. This should be done far enough in advance for the other members to give the matter adequate consideration and to possibly rearrange transportation and repack the food. If a space is available and there is adequate lead time, the leader will probably want some information on the prospective member's backpacking experience, physical condition, and state of equipment before making a commitment.

GENERAL PLANNING OF YOUR OWN TRIP

There should be a trip plan, and every participant should understand it thoroughly. It is amazing how even very fundamental aspects, such as the length of a trip, can be misunderstood by some. It is not unusual to be far into the woods and then have an argument arise between some trip members as to whether the group was to return to the roadhead on a Saturday or on a Sunday. The date and the exact hour of the takeoff from home and the date and approximate hour of return to the roadhead are very important. There should also be a return date and hour, left with a responsible person back home, that will be a "cutoff" time. If you have not returned home by that time, it is to be understood that you have encountered a serious emergency or accident and that the responsible person at home is to take action accordingly. This is a very important and serious matter, and it should be treated as such.

An itinerary. There should be an itinerary for the trip, starting with the hour that the group leaves the trailhead, outlining the expected travel for each day and camping place for that night. After the group is on the trail, the itinerary can be as flexible or as rigid as you want to make it, but there should be a plan. On a well-conducted backpack trip a group does not go into a remote area and simply wander aimlessly about for a week. Be careful, however, not to try to crowd too many miles or too many activities into one day. Be particularly careful in your planning so that you will have a suitable campsite, especially with respect to water, when it comes late afternoon and it is time to camp.

A guide. Are you going to hire a guide? If you are going into a remote area, away from marked trails, and no one in the group is familiar with the area, a guide can save a lot of headaches. He or she need not be a professional guide. A teenager from a local ranch may be an entirely satisfactory guide. Anyone who knows where the trail is and can stay on it will be of more service to you than a Ph.D. who can speak seven languages (and doesn't know where the trail is).

Road to trailhead. Is there an automobile road all the way to the trailhead, or will special transportation need to be arranged for the last few miles of travel? If there is a road all the way to the trailhead, is it good in all seasons? Is a four-wheel-drive vehicle required? If the road is dirt and an unexpected heavy rain makes it impassable, what alternate transportation is available? There has been more than one backpack trip that never got off the ground because the planners failed to recognize the possible need for special transportation for the last few miles of travel to the trailhead.

Photography. As you discuss and think through the proposed trip, you will find that there are many questions to be answered and some "rules' to be made. Some snapshots or color slides are an important feature of most backpack trips. However, if some trip member insists on a commercial quality shot every time he or she takes a photograph, it is going to mean some delays. There are types who would like the entire "safari"

to trip by a certain spot two or three times so they can get just the right shot. Unless the trip is planned for this type of photography, most members will not want to go along with it. It is best to talk these things out beforehand. For example, you can make a rule that photographs can be taken freely as long as the photographer doesn't hold up the group. Those who need tripods and too much other paraphernalia every time they click the shutter may find that the rest of the group is a quarter mile down the trail by the time they get set up.

Weather. Have you carefully investigated the weather and minimum temperature that can be expected for the area (and altitude) that you will be in? Is rain expected at that time of year? At high altitudes don't overlook the possibility of snow and severe winds. These factors are important in planning your sleeping gear, clothing, and possibly the itinerary. A long-distance phone call to a weather bureau, chamber of commerce, Forest Service office, or rancher in the area, just prior to leaving for the trip, is a good idea. This will serve to determine whether there has been a sudden change in weather, floods, forest fires, or similar conditions that may call for postponement or a change in trip plans. State police in some states maintain radio contact with units in other parts of the state and will be glad to furnish information on local road conditions.

Insects. Try to get some reliable information on the prevalence of flies, mosquitoes, ticks, and other insects in the area where you are planning your trip. At certain seasons insects can be such a nuisance as to call for unusual protective measures or perhaps postponement of the trip. A few weeks earlier (or later), there may be no problem at all. Get advice on locally used insect repellents and protective measures, such as head nets, gloves, bug dopes, sulfur, and kerosene.

Water supply. Some trip member may be acquainted with the area where the group will be backpacking and may know the trails. This person may recall where certain streams and springs are located and think that there is adequate water along the trail. Remember in such planning, however, that the flow of streams and springs may vary with the season of the year and that a spring that was flowing one year may be dried up the following year. If you write to the Forest Service or to another knowledgeable organization for maps, this is a good time to inquire about the flow of certain streams and springs and other possible water sources along the trail. Never underestimate the seriousness of running out of water on a backpack trip. In some areas there may be no problem whatever. In other areas, and at certain seasons, some careful planning may be required.

Stream crossings. One item of preparation is to determine what stream crossings are to be encountered on the trails you will be hiking. Some of these crossings may have natural "bridges" in the form of stepping stones or a log. Others will need to be waded. The probable depth of crossings is important.

Permits. In some areas a fire permit will be required for building a wood fire. Even though you may plan to do all your cooking on a backpack stove, it is recommended that a fire permit be obtained, if they are available. You may want a wood fire to do some "special" cooking for a meal or two, or for other purposes, such as heating water for personal bathing. A camping permit may be required in some areas. If it is necessary to cross private property in order to get to the area where you plan to do your backpacking, it is recommended that you get permission in advance.

Takeoff time. If the takeoff point is more than a two- or three-hour drive from your home, it may be desirable to drive there the evening before and camp at the roadhead. In this way you won't need to start hiking right after being fatigued by a long drive, and you can get an early start on the trail. When this is done, your breakfast at the roadhead should be planned with foods, utensils, and cooking gear that are carried separately for the purpose. The only items you should need to unpack from your trip gear are your sleeping bag and mattress. Keep the breakfast simple. Otherwise it will take too long, and you will probably start up the trail on too full a stomach, which is not good.

Another reason for early arrival at the trailhead may be to allow time for acclimatization to the altitude. If some members live at a much lower altitude than that in which they will be hiking, even an overnight stay at the takeoff point will be beneficial. In some cases a longer time may be required.

Dogs. The matter of taking dogs on a backpack trip is a controversial subject. Even though dogs may not be forbidden in the area you are planning to pack into, having a dog along may be objectionable to other members of the party. That is why the matter should be discussed early in the trip planning. When a member shows up ready for the trip with a favorite dog in tow, it is then too late.

All national parks, by regulation, require that pets be on a leash or otherwise restrained. Dogs are prohibited on the back-country trails of most national parks. The superintendent of a park has the authority to prohibit dogs in specific areas of the park. In general, the national forests have far fewer restrictions on dogs than do the national parks.

Dogs are sometimes a threat to other hikers and to small children. They sometimes spook horses on a trail. Obviously, the degree of restraint exercised by the dog owner is important.

Very often a dog owner will start out with a dog on a leash, but once they are in the backwoods, the leash comes off. Free-roving dogs harass wildlife and may kill small animals such as ground squirrels, deer fawns, and elk calves. The presence of dogs sometimes leads to encounters between campers and bears that would not have occurred if the dogs had been left at home.

Taking fish home. Some people (including myself) object to taking home (or attempting to take home) fish that have been caught in wilderness lakes and streams. I am an avid trout fisherman, but while fishing in the wilderness, I have never kept more fish than I needed for the next meal. Further, I don't ever intend to. There are several reasons for this.

First, it is very difficult to stock most wilderness lakes and streams; the majority of them are *not* stocked. Trout and other fish are part of the wilderness environment. It is a source of great pleasure to many backpackers to catch trout in unstocked waters and then release them, keeping only enough to eat for the next meal. Those who attempt to carry fish out of the wilderness are depleting the supply and eradicating a source of enjoyment for future backpackers.

Further, trout and most other fish taste really good only when they are freshly caught. Often those who attempt to carry fish out of a wilderness area will end up throwing them away later. Where icing facilities are available, fish can be preserved for a time, if you want to do it, but this does not apply to wilderness backpacking.

It is therefore strongly recommended that if you fish on a backpack trip, you keep only enough fish for the next meal. All others should be carefully released. As for other aspects of the wilderness environment, hikers should give some consideration to those who will come after them. Many people would not want to be members of a party that carried fish out from a wilderness lake or stream. That is why it is recommended that the matter be discussed in the planning that takes place at home.

Stops en route.   Are you going to allow any stops on the way to the trailhead, except for food and gas? Most hikers who have gotten up at three o'clock in the morning to meet an early takeoff hour will not appreciate sitting in a vehicle while some other member trips gaily from store to store, shopping for camera film, suntan lotion, a fishing license, or some other item that should have been obtained weeks before. Are you going to allow shopping or sight-seeing stops on the return trip home? Once they are back at the roadhead, most hikers are anxious to return home. It's up to you, but it's best to have these things well understood beforehand.

Insurance.   The subject of insurance is primarily a matter for your individual consideration, rather than for group planning. However, to some it will be very important. The general increase in theft of valuable items from backwoods camps was discussed earlier (see page 181). Some people will want to obtain insurance to cover such possible losses. Term insurance for this type of coverage is generally available. It is recommended that you first check with your insurance agent, however, inasmuch as some of the insurance that you already have may be applicable and may provide coverage. In addition to insurance coverage of valuable equipment, term insurance is available to cover backwoods accidents and the medical expenses resulting therefrom, if your present insurance does not provide adequate coverage.

Other items.   Should each hiker take a bag lunch for the first meal on the trail? Are floods a possibility? If you are hiking along one of the big trail systems that "touches base" with civilization every few days, are certain supplies to be replenished along the trail? Will smoking be allowed along the trail? Are you going to permit firearms to be carried? Are typhoid or tetanus shots recommended for trip members?

After you have discussed all these factors and made your decisions, it is a good idea to have the basic trip plan typed, and a copy made for each member. Then there can be no misunderstandings. This particularly applies to groups of six persons or more. The trip plan should outline the itinerary. It should also list common equipment that will be taken for the benefit of all members. It should list the basic "rules" that you have agreed to for the conduct of your trip.

THE TRAIL

If no member of your party has been over the trail before, this item requires very careful consideration. This particularly applies to trails that are off the beaten path. There are a number of possible sources for obtaining trail information. Guidebooks, if they are reliable, are one source. In general, the best source for obtaining information on the trail is to talk with someone who has been over the trail before and knows it thoroughly. That person will be able to point out landmarks to watch for so that you can stay on the trail with minimum difficulty. From talking with such a person, it is possible to obtain much information that will not be available from a guidebook or a map.

There are certain precautions to be taken in obtaining information from a person who has been over the trail before. Some individuals do not like to admit that a trail is difficult. In fact, it apparently bolsters their ego to describe a trail as "ten easy miles," or "nothing to it," when in reality the trail may be fairly difficult or even downright tough. Also, some people may not intentionally understate the difficulty of a trail. It may simply be that, having been over a trail a number of times, it really does seem relatively easy to them. Particularly in regard to staying on a trail that may be faint or obscure in places, there is no doubt that just having been over it once makes it many times easier to follow thereafter.

The general condition of the trail is important. A moderately strenuous trip might cover from 40 to 60 miles in a week. A strenuous trip might cover 50 to 80 miles in the same time. However, the number of miles hiked per day or per week is only one factor in determining the difficulty of the trip. Even more important is the altitude to be gained, lost, and regained in a day of travel. Extremes in number of ups and downs can make a relatively few miles of travel much more difficult than longer distances in more gentle terrain. If there is some off-trail travel to be done, it may be fairly easy or it may require hours to go only a short distance. Exertion at high altitudes can cause difficulty, although the average backpack trip is made at modest altitudes except for an occasional mountain peak or ridge. However, the specific altitude may be important to hikers who live at low altitudes and are not accustomed to the mountains. The change in altitude may result in discomfort or illness to such persons.

THE LEADER'S JOB

The leader does not have an easy job. Except in large and formally organized groups, the leader will be paying his or her way, along with other trip members, and the time that he or she has spent in planning and organizing the trip will be donated. Everyone should keep in mind that the leader is entitled to a share of fun from the trip and full participation in all activities.

One of the most important tasks of the leader is to determine the hiking and backpacking capability of each member of the group, early in the trip planning that takes place at home. Probably most and perhaps all of the members will be well known to the leader and this may be no problem at all, but don't take too much for granted. A single newcomer to the group or an individual whose capabilities are not well known to other members can ruin a trip for the entire group. The newcomer to the group may overestimate his ability in the discussions and planning that take place in the living room at home. After a couple of hours on the trail he may throw off his pack, spread-eagle on the ground, and not want or not be able to go on. Mr. or Ms. Leader, you now have a problem — and a very serious one. The other members will see many weeks of their own planning and careful preparation going down the drain, and they probably will not take kindly to you as a leader from now on.

Early in the planning at home, if there is any reasonable doubt about a trip member's capability, particularly hiking ability and general stamina, you had best take some very specific steps to find out for yourself. If there are some mountain trails near your home, you can designate a particular trail and ask this individual to make a few hikes over it with a full pack. Or the two of you can spend an afternoon hiking together over some rugged terrain. A few hours of reasonably strenuous hiking, with a full pack, should be sufficient to tell the story, and it will be a good investment for everyone concerned.

It will probably be a good precaution for the leader to specify a maximum weight of pack to be carried, especially for newcomers to the group. I once backpacked into a wilderness area with an individual who represented himself as an experienced backpacker. During the first hour on the trail, he consistently lagged behind the group and was not keeping a reasonable pace. I then had a talk with him, and during the discussion I lifted his pack. It was immediately apparent that he was way overloaded. We discussed some of the equipment in his pack, and it was obvious that he had many unnecessary and heavy items. We spent the next half hour hiding various items of equipment and clothing behind rocks, to be picked up on the way out. From then on he did better in maintaining the pace of the group, but it was very evident that he was not the experienced hiker he had considered himself to be. I climbed one long hill twice — once to carry my pack up and the second time to carry his. One experience like this and you soon learn not to take too much for granted in evaluating newcomers.

When the group is on the trail, there will be various times when decisions have to be made and one of several possible courses of action decided upon. In a small, closely-knit group of backpackers, such decisions will usually be arrived at by group discussion and mutual agreement. The role of the leader may be very minimal. However, someone may need to tell a newcomer to the group that he or she is doing something wrong, is holding up the party, or is otherwise having an adverse effect on the group's activities — a rather distasteful job. This unpleasant task usually falls to the leader.

If the group is "honored" with a daredevil type of individual, it is a good idea to remind that person early in the planning phase at home that the leader reserves the right to restrict any activities on the trail insofar as they may affect the welfare and safety of the individual and the group.

If your group has found a leader who has had a lot of backpacking experience, and has good leadership and management capabilities, take good care of him or her. There aren't too many of these types around.

PHYSICAL CONDITIONING

If you normally do considerable hiking and walking, you may be able to start a backpack trip with no special preconditioning and make out all right. For most people, however, some special preconditioning is desirable to harden muscles, toughen feet, and check out pack and pack load. Books or magazines wrapped in towels or blankets are good for simulating a loaded pack. Rocks do not provide a good simulation because the weight is concentrated in a small area. Carrying a load of rocks is also very hard on a packsack.

Pretrip hikes. There is a lot of difference between hiking over level terrain and hiking through mountains, where normally there will be a lot of uphill and downhill travel. Try to arrange your preconditioning hikes in hilly country if there are no mountains nearby. Wear the same boots and combination of socks that you will be wearing for your backpack trip, and the same clothes, insofar as possible. This preliminary hiking should take place at least a month before your backpack trip, and preferably longer. The situation is somewhat like studying for an exam in school. If you don't know the lesson thoroughly a week before, then you aren't going to be able to prepare yourself in a day or two. In preconditioning, you should occasionally push yourself to where you are thoroughly fatigued, to increase your endurance and to find out just what your limitations are. This will also give you confidence when on a real backpack trip you are faced with a situation that calls for unusual exertion. For about a week before takeoff, however, take only moderate (but regular) daily hikes and exercise, never pushing yourself to the point of fatigue. Never prepare yourself for a backpack trip by taking another backpack trip just before "the big one." After any such trip, you need a week of limited activity before you will be back to normal. For a week or more prior to a trip, get plenty of sleep. Avoid late hours, as well as the exertion and concern that comes from waiting too long before getting your gear, clothing, and food ready and packed. Take extra precautions to avoid contact with people who have colds or other communicable diseases. Give more than usual attention to good personal hygiene.

Other exercise. Backpackers who live in large cities may find it difficult to make regular hikes in preparation for a backpack trip. Some people condition themselves by carrying a loaded pack up and down the stairs in an apartment building. Jogging is a good way to get in condition for backpacking. It builds up endurance and also toughens the feet. Alternating jogging with walking trips, where a pack is carried, is good. When walking for pretrip exercise, always wear the boots and combination of socks that you will be wearing on your backpack trip. It is recommended that the walking and jogging exercises be done four or five days a week, interspersed with a couple of rest days.

If you resort to calisthenics to get into shape, skipping rope and running in place are good exercises. Also, doing partial knee bends (not deep knee bends) in a standing position is good. Fatigue in the knees is a common discomfort in backpacking.

The main objective of a physical conditioning program to prepare a person for backpacking is to build endurance, or stamina. Bulging muscles are not needed and they may even be a disadvantage. Exercise should be rhythmical, such as that provided by jogging, swimming, or bike riding. Isometric exercises and weight lifting are not recommended. A "Cadillac heart" is desirable, but "Ford muscles" will suffice very nicely. Anyone who has not previously exercised regularly should start out slowly and increase the length of exercise periods gradually. It is amazing, however, how quickly a healthy body adapts to regular exercise and how quickly the endurance increases.

If possible, try to acquire some suntan in the few weeks prior to a backpack trip. This is not for the purpose of being able to hike unprotected from the sun while backpacking. A hat, long-sleeved shirt, and long trousers are still recommended. In the high altitude sunlight of the mountains you will simply be less prone to severe burn if you have some suntan prior to the trip. If you plan to backpack part of the time in shorts, rather than long trousers, it is very important that the legs be included in this preliminary tanning process.

Physical examination. If you have not recently had a physical examination, it may be desirable to have one well in advance of taking a backpack trip. The necessity of such an examination will depend somewhat on your age, how often you backpack, your general physical condition, and similar factors. If you have recently had an illness and have not fully recovered, don't start a backpack trip with the thought that it will cure your illness. Backpacking is a strenuous activity, and you need to be in good physical shape when you start.

Some backwoods areas are frequented by livestock, especially near the perimeter. Also, the main trails in the backwoods are frequently used by animal pack trains. If this is true of the area you plan to travel in, it may be advisable to have a tetanus shot. It is suggested that you consult your physician about this. If your party is going deep into an area that is frequented by poisonous snakes, an antivenin kit may be carried. I recommend such a kit; others do not. You may want to seek your physician's advice on this matter also. If such a kit is carried and you plan to use it if the need arises, it is recommended that you obtain a horse serum sensitivity test from your physician prior to the trip.

Altitude conditioning. For those who are going on a backpack trip in the high mountains and who are not accustomed to exerting at high altitudes, it is very desirable for them to take a number of hikes in mountainous country prior to tackling a full-scale backpack trip. No person functions as well at high altitudes as at lower ones, but some are much more seriously affected than others. They should not wait until they are on a backpack trip to find this out. (See Chapter 11 and comments on acclimatization.)

Feet. It makes a sorry situation when a hiker develops blisters on the feet, usually (if at all) in the first few hours of a backpack trip. Besides taking preconditioning hikes, soaking the feet in tannic acid about fifteen minutes daily (for seven to ten days) just before a backpack trip will toughen them significantly. Use 1 ounce of tannic acid (available from drug stores) to 2 quarts of water. You can use the same mixture over and over for any one trip. It will turn very dark, but that doesn't matter. Wipe your feet on paper towels after soaking. Tannic acid will permanently stain a cloth towel.

Hours of walking over rugged trails can bring about sore spots and problems with your feet that will never show up in normal daily activity. A particularly vulnerable area is the toes. Trim your toenails straight across. If you round the outer corners, the nails will dig into the skin, causing irritation and possibly infection.

A good way to toughen feet is to go barefoot. Walking barefoot on city sidewalks and streets will build up calluses, toughen the skin, and will result in fewer foot problems when hikers are ready to hit the trail. As the feet toughen, you may want to do some barefoot walking on footpaths or backroads near your home.

For persons who experience foot problems, it may be desirable to carry a small bottle of rubbing alcohol. Apply this to your feet each morning and at night while on the trip. Foot powder may also be a help.

From previous experience you will know which areas of your feet develop tender spots or blisters. Perhaps you have a bunion problem. Protect all such areas with moleskin before leaving home and leave the moleskin in place for the entire trip. A small polyfoam pad placed between the big toe and the next toe will usually be an aid to those who have a bunion.

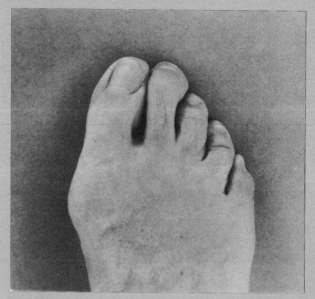

The big toe of a hiker's foot folding under the second toe (a mild case). This is quite a common condition, often hereditary.

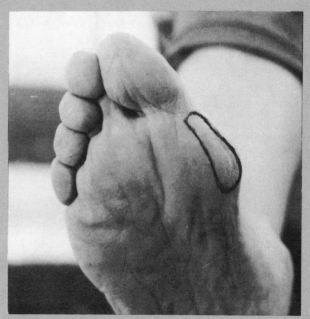

Although the folding under of the big toe as shown above is not severe enough to cause trouble in normal walking, when you are hiking, a large painful bunion will usually form in the area outlined in this photo.

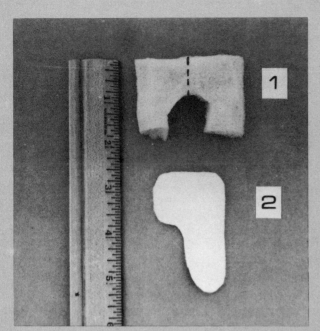

These items will alleviate the bunion and soreness caused by the above foot condition on a long hike. Item 1 is polyurethane foam, cut to about ½-inch thickness at center (half-moon) and tapered to about ¼-inch thickness at the outer edges. It is folded along the dotted line and wedged between the big toe and second toe as shown in the next photo below. Item 2 is moleskin adhesive, placed over the potential bunion area as shown at right.

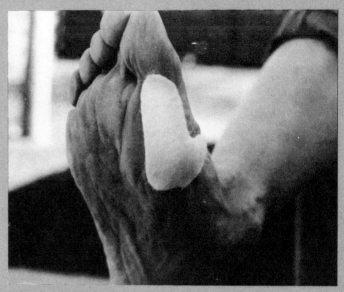

Moleskin adhesive in place. Use moleskin also on the top surface of certain toes or any other places on the foot where you have experienced soreness or chafing on past hikes.

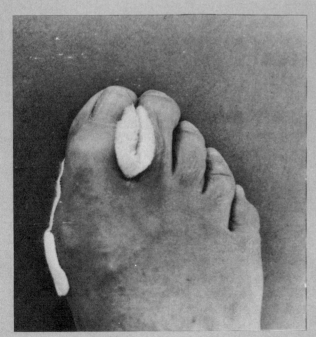

The polyurethane foam (after folding) is placed as shown. It is so light that you will soon forget it is there; yet it does the desired job of holding the big toe in a more normal position. The moleskin adhesive can be left in place for the entire trip. When you wash your feet just wash over it — no problem.

Devices such as this — a firm rubber form — for doing the job shown for the polyurethane foam are not recommended. They are generally uncomfortable, and you will usually end up not using the device even though you have carried it with you.

Eating. Serious and experienced backpackers will train and condition themselves for backpacking, just as an athlete trains. They will keep themselves in condition throughout the year by a continuing exercise program. Just prior to a backpack trip they will exercise regularly, but not excessively. The matter of when to eat, how much to eat, and what to eat is one of the aspects of physical training, and therefore of backpacking, that is subject to much discussion. On a backpack trip it is recommended that hikers eat to sustain energy, rather than try to digest the particular number of calories needed to sustain body weight.

When undertaking heavy exercise that is not a part of your daily pattern of living, you will probably have more energy and feel better if you eat a bit less than necessary to maintain body weight. Prolonged strenuous activity brings on fatigue. The prime remedy for physical fatigue is rest, or a change in pace, and a good night's sleep. Eating large quantities of food is not the cure for physical fatigue. When the body is fatigued, it does not readily digest food. A person can actually become ill by overeating at such times. In general, it is best to stop eating well before you acquire a stuffed feeling.

The body needs to burn, primarily through exercise, roughly 3,500 calories in order to lose about a pound of weight. If you start a backpack trip with a few pounds of body fat, this represents stored energy. This does not refer to being obese — far from it. Obese persons should undertake a program of exercise and regulated eating far in advance of a backpack trip, in order to get excess fat down to a reasonable level.

If you lose a few pounds of body weight on a backpack trip, you have done yourself no harm. In fact, you will probably feel more trim and fit than you did before the trip. When you get back to the daily routine at home, your weight will probably soon return to normal.

There are several eating patterns that seem to predominate among backpackers. One approach is to eat a light breakfast, light lunch, and modest supper, and to snack more or less constantly on the trail during the day. Another approach is to eat a modest-to-hearty breakfast, light lunch, and modest-to-hearty supper, and to have a snack stop at midmorning and midafternoon. It is recommended that you experiment a bit with eating patterns and different foods in your local hiking and on short backpack trips, to see which results in the most energy and sense of well-being. Snacking constantly on the trail can lead to problems. Many trail snacks are not particularly nu-tritious. Also, constant eating requires energy for digestion, which detracts from the total energy available for physical exertion.

It is recommended that hikers not go overboard on sugar intake during a backpack trip. Some backpacking literature advises that you not only eat more sugar at mealtime than you normally do, but that you eat a lot of candy between meals. This is not recommended. Your body does not need that much sugar, and it may be harmful. Some increase in sugar over the quantity normally eaten at home is suggested, but certainly not the huge amounts that some literature indicates. It is recommended that you increase your intake of a variety of nutritious carbohydrates and also add to the quantity of fat and protein foods normally consumed. Fats are a good source of sustained energy, with the energy being more slowly and continuously released than with sugar. Fats should be consumed regularly but not too many at one time, since they do not digest easily, particularly at high altitudes. Proteins, also, are best eaten in modest portions at any one time.

Glycogen stores. Glycogen is a limited but essential supply of energy that is stored in the muscles and liver. In recent years there has been considerable interest and experimentation in special diet and exercise procedures for the purpose of ridding the body of old glycogen stores and then building up a fresh supply just prior to a period of intensive exercise or exertion.

The procedure that is usually followed is to deplete the glycogen stores of energy about four days prior to the planned period of exertion. Depletion is accomplished by a day of prolonged, heavy exercise, to near exhaustion. After the glycogen stores have been initially depleted, the individual then undertakes, for several days, a special diet rich in carbohydrates but low in protein and fat. During the three days of this special diet, exercise should be kept light. By the fourth day the glycogen stores have been replenished, and the individual is theoretically ready for a period of intense, strenuous exercise on the following day.

There are several aspects concerning this special exercise-diet procedure for depleting and renewing glycogen stores that should be emphasized. First, it is intended as a preliminary measure to increase energy stores for a planned, relatively short period of intensive exertion. Secondly, it is not recommended that the average person undertake either this or any other very special diet regime without medical supervision.

Thirdly, even for planned activities that are short and strenuous in duration, there is some difference of opinion among medical authorities as to whether or not it is a desirable procedure.

Therefore, it is recommended that the average backpacker not undertake a special program of depleting and renewing glycogen stores prior to a backpack trip. A backpack trip does not consist of a short period of intense, heavy exertion. Rather it involves periods of a few days to several weeks of prolonged exercise in which the exertion varies from moderate to fairly strenuous. Certainly it is not, or should not be, an endurance contest. It is recommended that no special diet-exercise regimes be undertaken prior to a trip. A normal balanced diet should be adhered to, and for approximately a week prior to the trip, exercise should be regular but modest in quantity and severity, never strenuous.

Practice.   There is no substitute for practice if one is to become proficient, and this certainly applies to backpacking. Day hikes and short backpack trips are an ideal way to try out various items of equipment, clothing, and food. They also serve to increase your endurance and to help you become familiar with your limitations.

Such practice will probably disclose some deficiencies in your gear or technique that can be changed before you undertake a prolonged backpack trip. It will also increase your confidence in your ability to negotiate varying terrain with a loaded pack and to keep yourself comfortable while on the trail. This element of confidence is very important. Starting a full-scale backpack trip with certain untried gear, and perhaps some doubts about your technique, can cause concern that will increase fatigue and detract from your enjoyment of the trip. As with many other endeavors, advancement in backpacking techniques and added enjoyment comes largely from experience and persistent effort to improve.

WEATHER PROTECTION

A major decision in the planning of any backpack trip is to decide what is needed in the way of clothing and shelter for protection against the elements. This will largely depend upon the season, the particular area, and the altitude. Don't take this matter too lightly. To a lesser degree, the planning will depend upon the individuals making up the party. For a mixed group, or a group of young persons, more protection would probably be planned under the same anticipated weather conditions than for a group of experienced backpackers. The latter would normally be willing to take certain calculated risks that might not be advisable for some other group.

The difference of a few weeks in the time of the trip may dictate a difference in protective clothing and shelter. For example, the mountains of New Mexico are normally very dry in the spring of the year, through the month of June. Starting in early July, however, and extending through August, daily heavy rains can be expected in the afternoon. Therefore, a backpack trip in this area from April through June requires minimum rain protection. The same trip, taken in July or August, requires good personal rain gear and a good rain shelter at night.

Obtaining advance information on probable weather conditions for the area you plan to pack into is a very important factor in the planning of a backpack trip. It should not be underestimated.

USE A CHECKLIST

How many automobile trips have you been on where someone asked soon after the trip got under way, "Well, I wonder what we have forgotten?" When you are traveling by automobile, forgetting needed equipment may not be too serious. You can stop in some town and buy the forgotten item, if it is important enough. When you are in a wilderness or other remote area and find that you have forgotten something, it is a different story. Your money won't help there. If you think it isn't serious, try getting along without matches, toilet paper, soap, shortening, or some other essential item on a week-long backpack trip. It will make you a firm believer in checklists. Presumably, practically every item that you take on a backpack trip is essential; otherwise you would have left it at home.

Prior to doing any packing, make out a list of equipment, clothing, and other gear that you plan to take. If planning and packing the food and cooking equipment is assigned to another member of the party, you won't have to worry about that, but you will need to leave room in your pack for your share of this and other common equipment. As you make out the list of items that you intend to take, put down the weight of each one. Review the list a number of times, and be sure that you are not taking too many items of nonessential equipment or that there isn't some substitute item available that will do the job just as well and weigh less.

Checklists serve another important function in

addition to serving as a means of reviewing every item of equipment that is to go in your pack and its weight. Hikers have left home on pack trips forgetting cameras, canteens, fishing gear, food in the refrigerator, and other items that they planned to take. When you finally pack your gear for the last time, check off every item of equipment, as it goes in or on your pack, against your checklist. Then you will know absolutely that you have everything you planned for. If some items are to be carried separately (in the car) from your pack until you get to the takeoff point, make a special note of this and fasten the note to the outside of your pack, where you won't overlook it.

At the takeoff point.   After arriving at the takeoff point, you should review the checklist carefully for items (if any) that were not put in the pack or fastened to it when you left home. Few hikers forget their packs. However, in their haste to hit the trail they sometimes leave canteens, fishing rods, and other gear "safely" in the trunk of an automobile at the roadhead. To discover this after they are a few hours distant from the roadhead is very disconcerting, to say the least. Admittedly, it saves a certain amount of wear and tear on equipment to leave it in the car, but that is beside the point.

There are a few items that should be left at the roadhead. For example, billfold, car keys, loose change, and similar items are normally of no use on the trail. If you should lose your car keys while on the trail, you have a problem over and above the nuisance of carrying them and keeping track of them while hiking. It is a good idea to have at least a spare ignition key hidden inside the car. One way of storing keys is to wrap them in foil and hide them under a rock near the car at the roadhead. (Don't forget which rock.) If your fishing license is in your billfold, and you store your billfold in the vehicle at the roadhead, remember to remove the license and take it with you.

PACKING

Many people wait too long before they start to pack. With some minor exceptions, most items can be packed a week or more in advance. After the checklist has been reviewed a number of times and the decision made that those items are what is needed, you are ready to pack.

Rather than having the pack contents a jumble of gear, it is convenient and time saving to pack most items in heavy plastic bags. Plastic bags are available in a variety of sizes from some of the suppliers of backpacking and mountaineering equipment. Bags which are roughly 9 by 18 inches in size are suitable for packing shirts, underclothing, socks, and many other items. In general, it is best to pack related items in the same bag. Pint- and quart-sized bags can be used for small items. Thus, except for very large items, the main contents of the pack should consist of a number of plastic bags. The plastic bags are very light in weight and the contents can be immediately seen without opening the bag. If it rains hard and some water gets into the packbag, the plastic bags will help keep your gear dry. It is recommended that only new plastic bags be used.

If there is so much gear that the packsack bulges at every corner when it is packed, some gear should probably be eliminated. It was recommended in Chapter 2 that a reasonably large packframe and packsack be selected, commensurate with body build. This is not for the purpose of carrying an extra heavy load, but rather because any normal load that is carried will be more comfortable using a large frame and large packsack. It will also be easier to pack and unpack a packsack, and to find certain items later on when they are needed, if every nook and cranny of the packsack is not stuffed with gear.

In packing gear, the usual tendency is to put heavy items in the bottom of the pack. This is wrong. The heavy items should be as high in the pack (without making it top-heavy) and as close to the hiker's back as possible.

Do not tie canteens, cooking pans, and similar gear to the outside of your pack or packframe. Usually the only items that should be lashed to the packframe are the sleeping bag, tent (if you carry one), and sleeping pad. (In a large packbag there may be room inside the bag for the tent.) The sleeping pad roll is quite frequently lashed to the frame above the top of the packbag. The sleeping bag should always be carried in a high-tear-strength, waterproof stuff bag. Cooking pans, canteens, and so on, if hung on the outside of the pack, will usually swing with each step you take, and this is enough to drive most people crazy. If your gear is properly planned, there should be room inside the pack for such equipment.

Some hikers who carry fishing equipment will not have the special backpack fishing rods, with short sections of equal length, and this deserves special mention. The individual sections of most fishing rods are too long to go inside the average packsack. Some backpackers carry their rod sections in an aluminum case and lash or tape the

Plastic bags. The heavy poly bags (1- to 3-mil thickness) make excellent containers for certain foods, various items of clothing, and other gear. A rubber-band closure or pipe cleaner twister can be used to close the opening.

case on one side of their packframe. This case represents added weight and length, however, and is not usually necessary. Instead, it is recommended that you start by taping the rod sections together, simply lining up the sections in a parallel position, and then wrapping tape completely around the sections at several points. In addition, tie an 8- or 10-inch length of stout cord to one of the line guides of each section. Now lay the taped sections alongside one of the vertical outside frame members of your pack so that the bottom of the rod sections is slightly higher than the bottom end of the packframe member. Then wind some more tape completely around the sections and the frame member, at several points, taping them fast. The short length of cord fastened to the line guide of each rod section is a safety cord and should be tied to the frame member also. Then if the tape should come loose, you will not lose the rod section. Some rod sections will protrude up to 6 inches or more above the topmost part of the packframe, but if you are careful in passing under overhanging limbs, this should not be a problem. Fishing reels and detachable handles go inside the pack.

First aid kits, pocketknife, eyeglasses (if not worn), trail snacks, and other items that will probably be needed during the day should go in the outside pockets of the packbag. Then they will be readily accessible. This includes your canteen (or water bottle) and water purification tablets. The aluminum fuel bottle containing fuel for the backpack stove is also generally carried in an outside pocket. On many packbags one of the large outside pockets is just the right size for a typical

quart fuel bottle. If your packbag has a separate lower compartment, with outside access, this is a good place to carry rain gear, tennis shoes for wading streams, and other large items that may be needed during the day. If your packbag does not have such a compartment, then such items should be placed near the top of the load in the main compartment.

Care should be taken in packing food bags to keep them away from items that may tear or rub holes in the bags. Wrapping a towel or an item of clothing around food bags will help protect them. In packing a flashlight, one of the batteries should be reversed so that the light does not accidentally come on while you are hiking. *Both* batteries should *not* be reversed, because some flashlights will still work when this is done. The On-Off switch on Mallory flashlights can be taped in place; this will usually prevent them from coming on accidentally.

Some items like matches, soap, and so forth, are best packed by dividing the total supply into two or more parts and packing in separate packs. Keep one supply as a spare until the other is totally used up. Then if the one supply is misplaced or lost, you will have the spare. This is another reason for taking a few minutes to police each campsite and lunch site before you leave it. A supply of matches or soap left at the last campsite isn't going to help when you are ten miles down the trail.

Avoid the use of brittle plastic boxes in packaging small items of equipment. With a little shopping you will find a good variety of unbreakable plastic and aluminum containers. I well remember a trip long ago where I carried a small, neat, brittle plastic box in my hip pocket. It contained fishing lures and supplies, including some small, very sharp treble hooks. The first inkling that all was not well, and that my hip pocket was a mess of broken plastic and balled-up lures, was a "pointed reminder" from some of those sharp treble hooks.

In a group that is using a backpack stove, it is best for one person to carry the stove and fuel but no food. In this way there can be no contamination of food on the trail from the fuel.

Specific items of common equipment should be assigned to the various members of a group on a permanent basis (for the trip). That is, they should be responsible for carrying those particular items for the entire trip and knowing at all times where the items are.

In packing camera film, place it in the packbag where it will be reasonably cool. On a hot day the heat from the sun may affect the exposure time of the film. Color characteristics may also be affected. Wrapping spare film in insulated paper bags and placing it near the center of the load in the main packbag compartment is a good precaution to take.

If you plan to come out of a remote area the same way you go in, you may want to leave a cache of food along the way. A cache or two of food set aside for the last few meals will save you from carrying that food all the way in and most of the way out again. If you plan to do this, put the food for the cache in a separate bag (or bags) when you are doing your packing at home. A cache (temporary) can simply be a heavy plastic bag containing the food for a particular meal or two, hung from a tree limb about 15 feet off the ground. Select a tree that will not be readily visible from the trail and mark the trail at that spot, so that you will not pass by it on the way out. Pick a small-diameter tree with no limbs close to the ground, so that a bear will not be so likely to climb it. Such caches are recommended *only* for very remote areas.

It is a good idea to keep sketches and notes from trip to trip as to how certain items of gear were packed. You may find that you changed some items from one outside pocket to another or changed the grouping or location of certain gear within the packbag. Keeping such records, as well as checklists, from trip to trip will make for more systematic and easier packing on subsequent trips.

PACK WEIGHT

In Chapter 10 it was determined that the weight of the full pack for a week-long trip would be about 39 pounds. This was for a group of three persons. This weight can be reduced somewhat by eliminating all nonessentials. Also, the food load is reduced by about 1½ pounds per day as the food is eaten.

In general, a person of average physical strength and stamina can carry about 30 percent of his or her weight. This would mean about 48 pounds for a 160-pound man or 36 pounds for a 120-pound woman. Obviously persons in poor physical condition cannot carry this much. Neither does the rule apply to growing children. Also, there is a big difference in laboring up steep switchbacks with a 40-pound load and hiking over relatively easy terrain. Hiking in the cool of the morning will not sap your strength as will midday hiking in the heat of the sun. The length

An unbreakable-plastic quart bottle makes a good water bottle and fits nicely in an outside pocket of many packbags.

of hike each day and the frequency of layover days are also factors.

Another major factor in pack weight is the weather, or possible weather. If your backpacking is done in mild weather, you will not need the clothing and other protective gear that you do for backpacking in the rainy season or when it is cold. It should also be emphasized that a good packframe and packbag, properly loaded, and good hiking boots, are major factors in determining the load that you can comfortably carry.

I know of persons of relatively small body build who make their living as guides and regularly pack 50- and 60-pound loads for long distances. For most people, however, backpacking is a sport to which they turn in order to escape the routine of a sedentary job. Most of their backpack trips are from several days to a week in duration. They are not interested in setting endurance records, and they couldn't care less how far they hike in a day as long as they are in scenic country and enjoying themselves. For the average man a 40-pound load is near maximum for optimum comfort. For most women a load of 25 to 30 pounds should be the limit.

Quite a few groups hike into a base camp and then make daily hikes from there. Others may change camps only once or twice during a trip. It should be recognized that changing camps (setting up and taking down) in itself requires considerable energy and that a backpack trip in which camp is changed daily can, for some, be a real grind.

For those who are planning to backpack with a formally organized group, it is quite possible that the group leader will specify a maximum weight for packs. This is done for a good reason. The leader knows the trail and the terrain that lies ahead and also the size pack that an average person in good health can carry over that trail, at a moderate pace, without undue fatigue. The weight of common equipment and food that will need to be added to each hiker's pack, to be carried for the benefit of the group, will probably be specified also. If the leader says the maximum pack weight is 30 pounds, this means that no one should show up with a 35-pound pack. If there is any doubt, hikers should get clarification from the leader before the trip.

TAKE THE INITIATIVE

Well, that's about it. Three or more people, each carrying a 30- to 40-pound pack, can go into a wilderness or other remote area and live comfortably for a week, shut off from all outside communication. Backpacking is a sport with many challenges and many rewards. One of the challenges is to reduce the weight of the pack by a few ounces and still live comfortably and eat well. Each ounce becomes a little harder than the one before, but it's fun trying.

Like a lot of other endeavors, it is one thing to talk about backpacking and another thing to do it. It is recommended that your first few backpack trips be short ones, primarily for the purpose of checking out and getting acquainted with your gear and to test your own capabilities. As your technique improves, you can lengthen the trip and get further from the roadhead. A good winter project is to make complete plans and preparations for a spring or summer backpack trip, getting packs and all equipment checked over, taking preliminary hikes to check out gear, and so forth.

If you like the out-of-doors, a well-planned backpack trip can be one of the outstanding experiences of a lifetime. So let's get going. We aren't getting any younger. The mountains were never more beautiful, and it would be a shame to let all of those trout die of old age. There are mountain summits to be climbed, intriguing canyons to be explored, winding trails to be pursued through pine forests, and meandering paths to be followed across mountain meadows and along rushing white-water streams. As with any other sport, there will come a time in your life when you will be unable to participate because of physical limitations. Backpacking can provide some mighty fine memories for your old age. (It will also help to put off that old age.) *Take the initiative!* Use your ingenuity (and, hopefully, this book). Good luck. May the good Lord smile upon you, may you have many campfires ahead, and may you have a light pack and a light heart as you go tramping along the mountain trails. *Adios!*

Appendixes

SUPPLIERS SPECIALIZING IN BACKPACKING AND MOUNTAINEERING EQUIPMENT

Adventure 16
656 Front Street
El Cajon, California 92020

Camp Trails
4111 West Clarendon Avenue
Phoenix, Arizona 85019

Early Winters Ltd.
110 Prefontaine Place South
Seattle, Washington 98104

Eastern Mountain Sports
1041 Commonwealth Avenue
Boston, Massachusetts 02215

Great World
250 Farms Village Road
West Simsbury, Connecticut 06092

Holubar Mountaineering
Box 7
Boulder, Colorado 80301

Indiana Camp Supply
P.O. Box 344
Pittsboro, Indiana 46167

Margesson's Sports Ltd.
17 Adelaide Street East
Toronto, Ontario M5C 1H4
Canada

Moor and Mountain
14 Main Street
Concord, Massachusetts 01742

Mountain Safety Research
South 96th Street at 8th Avenue South
Seattle, Washington 98108

The North Face
P.O. Box 2399, Station A
Berkeley, California 94702

Paul Petzoldt Wilderness Equipment
Box 78
Lander, Wyoming 82520

Recreational Equipment Company
1525 11th Avenue
Seattle, Washington 98122

Sierra Designs
Fourth and Addison Streets
Berkeley, California 94710

The Ski Hut
1615 University Avenue
Berkeley, California 94703

The Smilie Company
575 Howard Street
San Francisco, California 94105

Thomas Black & Sons
930 Ford Street
Ogdensburg, New York 13669

SOURCES OF DO-IT-YOURSELF KITS FOR BACKPACKERS

Altra, Inc.
5441 Western Avenue
Boulder, Colorado 80301

Eastern Mountain Sports
1041 Commonwealth Avenue
Boston, Massachusetts 02215

Frostline Kits
452 Burbank
Broomfield, Colorado 80020

Holubar Mountaineering
Box 7
Boulder, Colorado 80301

Mountain Adventure Kits
P.O. Box 571 W
Whittier, California 90608

Plain Brown Wrapper Kits
(various local stores)

SOME SUPPLIERS OF GENERAL CAMPING EQUIPMENT WHO CARRY SOME BACKPACKING EQUIPMENT

Eddie Bauer
P.O. Box 3700
Seattle, Washington 98124

L. L. Bean, Inc.
Freeport, Maine 04032

The Camp & Hike Shop
4674 Knight Arnold
Memphis, Tennessee 38118

Don Gleason's Campers Supply, Inc.
9 Pearl Street
Northampton, Massachusetts 01060

I. Goldberg
902 Chestnut Street
Philadelphia, Pennsylvania 19107

Herter's, Inc.
Waseca, Minnesota 56093

Morsan
#810, Route 17
Paramus, New Jersey 07652

Waters, Inc.
111 East Sheridan Street
Ely, Minnesota 55731

Note: Many of the large mail order firms such as J.C. Penney, Sears Roebuck, and Montgomery Ward also carry backpacking equipment in their catalogs and in some of their retail stores.

APPENDIX B

SOME SOURCES OF SPECIAL FOODS FOR BACKPACKING

Chuck Wagon Foods
176 Oak Street
Newton, Massachusetts 02164

Freeze Dry Foods Ltd.
579 Speers Road
Oakville, Ontario L6K 2G4
Canada

Indiana Camp Supply
P.O. Box 344
Pittsboro, Indiana 46167

Oregon Freeze Dry Foods, Inc.
  (Mountain House brand)
P.O. Box 1048
Albany, Oregon 97321

Perma-Pak
  (Pantri-Pak brand)
40 East Robert Avenue
Salt Lake City, Utah 84115

Rich-Moor
P.O. Box 2728
Van Nuys, California 91404

Ad Seidel & Son, Inc.
2323 Pratt Boulevard
Elk Grove Village, Illinois 60007

Stow-A-Way Products Company
103 Ripley Road
Cohasset, Massachusetts 02025

Trail Chef
1109 South Wall Street
Los Angeles, California 90015

Wilson & Company, Inc.
Chicago, Illinois 60601

Note: Many of the suppliers of backpacking and mountaineering equipment listed in Appendix A, and many other firms that carry backpack equipment, stock dehydrated foods (including the brands of the companies listed above).

APPENDIX C

ONE-PERSON BACKPACK TENT

One primary reason for going backpacking is to be out-of-doors; that is, to live, cook, eat, and sleep in the open. We are really not getting maximum benefit from our backpacking experience if we coop ourselves up in a tent each night. Admittedly, a conventional mountaineering tent is very desirable and even necessary for some backpack trips. However, in mild-weather backpacking, at normal elevations, the tent described in the following paragraphs will serve adequately.

Sleeping in the open, with nothing but the sky for a roof, is one of the great pleasures of backpacking. To lie in your sleeping bag and watch the starlit skies overhead before falling asleep is an exhilarating experience. Yet there are occasions when flies, mosquitoes, ants, and other "peskies" can definitely detract from the pleasure of such a night. There may also be times when you want to be away from camp for brief periods but would like to leave your bed and some items of clothing or gear on the ground without having them accessible to bugs, rodents, snakes, and birds.

The "tent" described here is lightweight and will provide protection from the nuisances mentioned above. Yet you will still retain that pleasurable feeling of sleeping in the open and won't feel cooped up when using this tent. It is made essentially of nylon mosquito netting, which is a rather strong but lightweight material. For rain protection, you simply cover the nylon netting "tent" with a fly sheet of plastic or waterproof coated nylon. It is not very difficult to make a tent of nylon netting. The sketch shown below shows dimensions of the finished tent, and the paragraphs that follow describe the process of fabricating the tent.

Materials

1. Nylon mosquito netting (about 5 square yards) is required for the top and ends of the tent. The netting is sold in varying widths, so note the width as listed in the catalog and figure your requirements accordingly before ordering.

2. It is recommended that a waterproof floor of coated nylon be used. A "bathtub" construction is recommended, which will extend the floor up the sides and ends of the tent from 6 to 8 inches. You can use a cheaper material and then treat it with a waterproofing compound, but it will not be as satisfactory as coated nylon. As with the nylon netting, the nylon is sold in varying widths, so you will need to consider the width of the material in figuring your requirements. Recreational Equipment Company, The Ski Hut, and some of the other suppliers listed in Appendix A sell such materials by the yard.

3. The waterproof rain fly for the tent may be either polyethylene sheeting or coated nylon. Waterproof coated nylon is recommended as being more durable, lighter in weight, and easier to use. The fly should be about 10 feet 6 inches long, 6 feet 10 inches wide at the head end, and 4 feet 6 inches wide at the foot end.

Cutting

SIDES. The netting for the sides of the inner tent need not be one solid piece. Odd-shaped pieces of netting may be cut and sewn together to made up the required area. If you don't do a perfect job of sewing, no problem. The only requirement is to keep out insects. Unlike that of a commercial tent that must have "sales appeal," the appearance of your sewing job is not important.

TOP. For the top you will need a piece of netting about 44 inches wide at one end, 64 inches wide at the other end, and 98 inches long.

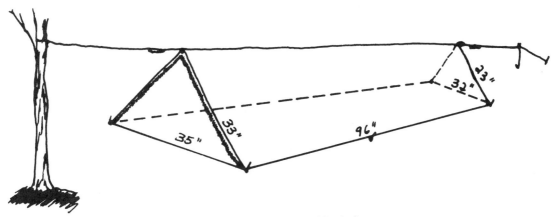

Sketch showing dimensions of finished tent.

ENDS. Cut a triangular piece of netting that is 36 inches along the base (ground) edge and 34 inches along each of the other edges (about 29 inches high). Sew the two zippers onto this front end piece so that the open ends of the zippers meet about one inch down from the peak of the triangle. One zipper should be sewn to open from the outside, the other from the inside. The foot end (before sewing) is a triangle 33 inches along the base and 24 inches along each of the other edges (about 17 inches high).

A small hole, about 1/8 inch in diameter, is needed at the peak of each end. The tent ridgeline is installed inside the tent, passes through this small hole at each end, and is tied to cloth loops at the front and foot end of the tent.

FLOOR. The floor of the tent should be about 35 inches wide at the head end, 32 inches wide at the foot end, and 96 inches long. To each of these dimensions add 12 to 16 inches, to allow the floor to extend up the sides of the tent from 6 to 8 inches. Do not cut into the cloth at the corners of the tent where the floor extends up the sides. Simply overlap the cloth at these points and sew it in place. It will then be more waterproof than if you make a cut at the corners for a somewhat neater appearance.

FLY. In making the fly, sew the strips of cloth together so that the seams run vertically down from the peak, rather than parallel to the long edges. The fly will then shed water more readily. Provide cloth loops at the front peak and rear peak of the fly, for attaching a ridgeline. Reinforce these points of attachment with 4-inch squares of cloth. Use similar squares of reinforcing cloth at the four corners of the fly and at two intermediate points along each ground edge, for attaching grommets.

Sewing. All the sewing on this tent can be done on an ordinary household sewing machine. Sew a piece of cloth about 4 inches square to the netting at the top front of the tent and at the top foot end. The sew small loops of cloth to these points for securing the ridgeline. Sew three small loops for stakes, about 1 inch in diameter, along each side of the floor (head end, foot end, and center). Before sewing the loops, sew on 4-inch squares of cloth at these points, for reinforcement. Next, using straight pins or a basting stitch, fasten the floor loosely to the top. When that is done, it is suggested that you take the tent to a level spot in your yard, install it on a ridgeline of proper slope, and stake out the ground edges. When you are satisfied that your pins or basting stitches are properly located, take the tent back to the sewing machine and sew the floor securely to the top.

Next, sew the foot end to the tent; then the head end. If you want to be cautious, use the straight-pin or basting-stitch procedure with another trial setup in the yard.

The ridgeline. It is recommended that you use parachute cord or an avalanche cord for a ridgeline. Use a piece about 20 feet long and leave it permanently attached to the tent. It is secured by a knot to the cloth loops at the top of each end of the tent. Erect the tent in the yard and, by trial and error, secure the ridgeline so that when it is pulled taut the ridge of the tent material is smooth (free of wrinkles) but not stressed.

It is also recommended that you install about a 1-foot length of 1/8-inch-diameter shock cord in the ridgeline, adjacent to the front and foot ends of the tent (outside). Install the shock cord by first tying one end of it securely at the desired point in the ridgeline. Shock cord does not tie easily. Pull each part of the knot tight with pliers. Next, tie the other end of the shock cord into the ridgeline at such distance from the first point that when the shock cord is stretched to the desired degree, the ridgeline will have a definite sag in it between these two points. However, if the shock cord is stretched very much further, the ridgeline becomes parallel to it and the ridgeline takes the stress.

Use. The pitching of many tents requires two trees 10 to 15 feet apart, with a level area between, or poles (which must be carried). A level area is often difficult to find at the particular spot where you decide to camp. This tent only requires a tree or good-sized bush near the head end for fastening the ridgeline. A short stick near the foot end will keep that end at the proper height. It is best to erect the rain fly on a separate ridgeline about a foot higher than the tent ridgeline. If you feel you may lack a tree or bush for tying the head end of the tent, you can buy a single collapsible aluminum pole for this purpose. Both the ridgeline near the front end of the tent and that for the fly can be tied to this pole. Two additional lines tied at the top of the pole and angling to the ground will be required to hold the pole securely. The pole should be placed several feet out from the head end of the tent to allow room for entry.

Backpack tent with plastic fly for rain protection.

Backpack tent with coated-nylon cloth (waterproof) fly.

Correct method of using shock cord in ridgeline to provide give.

APPENDIX D

SOURCES FOR MAPS, TRAIL INFORMATION, AND BACKPACKING INFORMATION

Adirondack Mountain Club
Gabriels, New York 12939

Appalachian Mountain Club
5 Joy Street
Boston, Massachusetts 02108

The Appalachian Trail Conference
P.O. Box 236
Harpers Ferry, West Virginia 25425

Canadian Government Bureau of Tourism
Ottawa, Ontario K1A 0H6
Canada

Federations of Western Outdoor Clubs
201 South Ashdale Street
West Covina, California 94590

The Florida Trail Association
33 Southwest 18th Terrace
Miami, Florida 33129

Greb Hiking Bureau
1 Adam Street
Kitchener, Ontario N2H 5P6
Canada

Green Mountain Club
108 Merchants Row
Rutland, Vermont 05701

Mazamas
909 Northwest 19th Avenue
Portland, Oregon 97209

National Cartographic Information Center
U.S. Geological Survey
507 National Center
Reston, Virginia 22092

New York-New Jersey Trail Conference
G.P.O. Box 2250
New York, New York 10001

Potomac Appalachian Trail Club
1718 N Street N.W.
Washington, D.C. 20036

Parks Canada
(National Park Headquarters)
400 Laurier Avenue West
Ottawa, Ontario K1A 0H4
Canada

Secretaria de la Presidencia
Comisión de estudios
del territorio nacional
San Antonio Abad No. 24
Mexico 8, D.F.

The Sierra Club
1050 Mills Tower
San Francisco, California 94104

U.S. Forest Service
Washington, D.C. 20240
(and Regional Forest Service Offices)

U.S. Geological Survey
Federal Center
Denver, Colorado 80204

Wilderness Society
729 15th Street, N.W.
Washington, D.C. 20005

APPENDIX E

ORGANIZATIONS THAT PROMOTE CONSERVATION OF NATURAL RESOURCES

The following is a partial list of some well-known organizations that are fighting the uphill battle of conservation from one standpoint or another. You are urged to take an active interest in the programs of one or more of these organizations. If nothing more, you can become a dues-paying member. Don't delay! Write to them today!

American Forestry Association
919 17th Street, N.W.
Washington, D.C. 20006

American Planning and Civic Association
901 Union Trust Building
Washington, D.C. 20005

Appalachian Trail Conference
P.O. Box 236
Harpers Ferry, West Virginia 25425

The Conservation Foundation
1717 Massachusetts Avenue, N.W.
Washington, D.C. 20036

Defenders of Wildlife
1244 Nineteenth Street, N.W.
Washington, D.C. 20036

Environmental Policy Center
324 C Street, S.E.
Washington, D.C. 20003

Friends of the Earth
529 Commercial Street
San Francisco, California 94111

General Federation of Women's Clubs
1734 N Street, N.W.
Washington, D.C. 20036

The Izaak Walton League of America
1800 North Kent Street
Suite 806
Arlington, Virginia 22209

The Mountaineers
719 Pike Street
Seattle, Washington 98101

National Association of Soil and Water
  Conservation Districts
1424 K Street, N.W.
Washington, D.C. 20005

National Audubon Society
950 Third Avenue
New York, New York 10022

National Parks Association
1300 New Hampshire Avenue, N.W.
Washington, D.C. 20036

National Parks and Conservation Association
1701 18th Street, N.W.
Washington, D.C. 20009

National Resources Defense Council
15 West 44th Street
New York, New York 10036

National Wildlife Federation
1412 16th Street, N.W.
Washington, D.C. 20036

The Nature Conservancy
1522 K Street, N.W.
Washington, D.C. 20005

The Sierra Club
1050 Mills Tower
San Francisco, California 94104

The Wilderness Society
729 15th Street, N.W.
Washington, D.C. 20005

Wildlife Management Institute
709 Wire Building
Washington, D.C. 20005

APPENDIX F
SURVIVAL

The aspect of survival usually implies that you have had an emergency of some sort in the woods or other remote area. Yet, when one starts thinking and talking about survival, the discussion almost invariably centers on precautions to take so that actual survival circumstances are not encountered. When we get right down to fundamentals, your knowledge and experience in backwoods travel (under various conditions) are the most important tools at your disposal for either preventing circumstances from developing into a situation that calls for survival techniques or for successfully getting out of an emergency situation if one does occur. A situation that might cause one individual or a group to go into semi-panic might cause a more experienced individual or group only mild concern. Or the latter might simply look upon the situation as an interesting challenge. So if you want to avoid a serious emergency in the woods, take every opportunity to add to your knowledge and experience. This especially concerns travel and living in foul weather, staying oriented at all times, knowing where the next water supply is, first aid, and preparedness for emergencies.

As your knowledge and experience grow, you will become more sure of yourself. This in turn will lead to a frame of mind and an attitude toward the backwoods that can save your life in an emergency. Panic has caused more people to lose their lives under emergency situations than any other single factor. Many people who take to the woods are fine as long as the sun is shining and the birds are singing. But let a little foul weather move in or a slight emergency occur, and they start seeing hidden dangers behind every rock and tree. This is due to lack of knowledge and experience. There is nothing in the woods that can or will hurt you if you take reasonable precautions. You are in less danger there than in traveling around in a big city. That statement is made with full knowledge of a number of accidents that have involved campground bears, as well as other so-called hazards of the woods.

So take every opportunity to increase your knowledge and experience of the woods. If you are a beginner, when you go on a backpack trip, try to go with people who are knowledgeable. If this is not practical, go in an area that has well-marked and frequently used trails and don't get more than one or two days' travel away from the roadhead. Give some frequent thought to emergency situations that could occur, and mentally plan, step by step, what you would do about them. Do this often enough that if the emergency does occur, your reaction to the situation will be somewhat automatic, and it will not be such a shock.

Getting lost is probably the most frequent mishap that is likely to call for some survival techniques. When you enter a remote area, you should not only have a good map but also a good mental picture of the area. Is the overall area bounded on one side by a road? How many hours of travel is it from the vicinity that you will be in? Perhaps there are one or more streams in the area. Do they eventually lead to a small town or other habitation? In what general direction do they lie with respect to your planned route and, again, how many hours of travel would be required to reach them? What are the most prominent, unmistakable landmarks of the region? Are there occupied fire towers or survey stations in the area, and could you find your way to them if you had to?

Water is a most important factor. If you were lost, you might not be able to find your way to a spring or small lake, unless it was marked by very prominent landmarks. However, if you knew that a stream lay parallel to your general route of travel and about how many hours it would take to reach it, that could be extremely important information to your survival. You can live a long time without food, but your days are few if you don't have water. In some areas water supply may be no problem at any time. In other areas it may be at particular seasons. In still other regions water supply is something that must be continually considered in your planning.

Survival, under the conditions in which most backpackers would encounter the need for survival techniques, would probably be for a period of a few days or a week at the most.

Let's say that in a party of two or more backpackers, one member got sick or hurt. If the injured or sick person could not travel, you would ordinarily make him as comfortable as possible and go for help. You would leave him in the care of a third member of the party, if there is a third member. If there were only two persons in the party, the situation would take on somewhat different proportions. However, you would make certain that the injured person had ample water and food readily accessible and take off. There is nothing in the woods that will hurt him, and unless he is dying, he will be all right until you return with help.

You can backpack for years and never get lost. Most of our wilderness areas and national forests have well-marked main trails. If you stay on, or close to, those main trails, there is no reason to get lost. Backpackers being what they are, however, you will eventually want to push further into the backwoods, away from the main trails. (I admit to having been temporarily lost in the wilderness quite a few times.) When you leave the main, well-marked, frequently used trails, that is when you need to be alert to the possibility of getting lost and to be especially meticulous about keeping yourself oriented. Know where you are at all times with respect to major landmarks. As soon as you realize you are lost, try to backtrack if you can. That is, try to find your way back to a known trail, stream, or other landmark, rather than to keep pushing ahead. Frequently a party will be "lost" with respect to where they are going but not in regard to where they are. That is, they have an objective in mind that lies somewhere ahead, but the trail has "vanished," and they don't know where to find it. Yet, if they face the truth in time, they will be able to find their way back to where they came from. The answer is—backtrack! Forget the objective for this particular trip. Wait for a more favorable time or until assistance can be arranged with someone who is familiar with the area.

Let's assume, however, that not only are you lost with respect to the way ahead, but you aren't too sure of the way back. When you know you are really lost, make a firm and immediate resolution that you are going to pay particular attention to your frame of mind, or mental attitude, until the ordeal is over. Act slowly and very deliberately. Don't move hastily or do anything else hastily. Haste often leads to panic under such circumstances. Remember that the human body has far more mental strength, as well as physical endurance, than most people have ever put to the test. The "old woodsman" books say to sit down on a log and smoke your pipe. If that's what it takes, do it. (Check your match supply first!)

One of the first things to consider when you realize you are lost is water. How much water do you have with you? How far must you go in a certain direction before you are fairly certain of coming to a water supply? Do you recall passing a stream, spring, or other water supply during the past few hours? If possible, head back for it now. When you have found a water supply, stay with it until you have developed a positive plan for getting out of your predicament. Your water supply is always a foremost consideration when backpacking. When you are lost, it should be constantly considered.

Do you have any kind of container, aside from perhaps a one- or two-quart canteen? If not, unless you are in an area where water is abundant, you had better plan to camp awhile near the water supply you have found. Set up your "headquarters" there. From that headquarters you should carefully make short trips out in straight lines of travel in the most likely directions to pick up familiar landmarks. Mark your path out from your headquarters, or base camp, very carefully so that there will be no doubt about finding your way back again. Spend several days or more in making these reconnoitering trips if necessary. A little elevation can sometimes be a big help in orienting yourself. Try to find some higher ground from which you can scan the area you are in. If you find a tree that isn't too hard to climb, in a favorable location, give that a try. In the meantime try to make some additional water containers. A sheet of plastic, waterproof garment, or a ground cloth can be fashioned into a water pouch holding one to three gallons and carried on the end of a stick over your shoulder in hobo fashion.

Your knowledge and experience in backwoods travel are also very important, as stressed earlier. Hopefully you have substantial amounts of both; otherwise you should have stayed with the main, well-marked, frequently used trails. Other things to consider soon after you realize you are lost are protection from the elements and various ways of attracting attention, particularly from possible passing aircraft. There are very few areas in the United States these days that do not have an occasional passing aircraft. If you are in a national forest or wilderness area, it is quite likely that there will be aircraft within view almost daily, primarily Forest Service patrol planes.

Now, how do you attract their attention? Hopefully your normal backpack gear or your survival kit (which we will discuss later) contains a steel mirror. It is a very important item. A mirror is the most reliable means of attracting attention from passing aircraft. There are heavy glass mirrors, with sighting holes, made especially for signaling. However, with a little practice an ordinary steel mirror can be used and will be just as effective. (Do your practicing at home or on a routine hike, before the need for emergency use comes up.) The steel mirror will be lighter and will not be subject to breakage. The universal distress sign is three of a kind: a volley of three gunshots, three fires or three billows of smoke from one fire, three flashes of a mirror, and so on. Lacking a mirror, you can use a knife blade or the shiny surface of a cooking utensil or other metal container. These are not nearly as dependable, however.

Another good attention getter, especially in a forest, is smoke. Forest Service planes make regular patrols for the purpose of spotting forest fires. Fire towers are scattered throughout many of our forests for the prime purpose of locating forest fires and fixing their position. If you can build a fire and make enough smoke for it to be spotted (it doesn't take much), you can be reasonably sure that the fire will be investigated. One problem in the case of aircraft is having a fire going and enough greenery available to make the necessary smoke at the particular moment that a plane comes into view. A solution to this is a smoke-signal cartridge of the type shown in Chapter 11 of this book. With such a cartridge you have instantaneous smoke in good quantity when you need it. Such a smoke cartridge (or several) is recommended as an item for the survival kit of every party that ventures into the remote sections of the forests or wilderness areas.

By this time you are probably wondering When do we eat? For the most part, forget it. You can go a long time without eating. It is unlikely that any survival situation that the average backpacker would encounter would be of such duration that food would be a great problem. If you have some food with you, it should be rationed from the beginning of your emergency. Under such conditions one substantial portion of food per day is better than three smaller portions or frequent nibbling. Also, it is sometimes possible to eat off the land to some extent. Berries or nuts in season are obvious foods.

Hopefully your normal gear or survival kit included fishing line and hooks. Catch yourself a fish if you can. In shallow streams fish or minnows can sometimes be driven into very shallow pockets and clubbed or beached. A log or stick entranceway or "funnel" to the shallow area will help keep them there. Minnows are eaten whole.

Deadfalls and snares for the trapping of animals are usually associated with survival periods of weeks in extremely remote areas and would not normally be applicable. However, if you should come across a porcupine, take the time to "do it in" and take it along as a food supply. Also, snakes (including rattlesnakes) are a good source of food and can usually be easily killed if you see any. The best way to kill a rattlesnake is to use a stick four or five feet long to strike the snake sharply just back of the head. It is very difficult to kill a rattlesnake by throwing stones at it. Also,

don't follow a rattlesnake into dense cover. (You already have enough problems.) Frogs are a possibility, but don't eat toads. A rabbit will sometimes freeze in position hoping you don't see it, and you may be able to get one if you carry a stick or stone. Lastly, insects are an important source of food under such circumstances. Grubs (from rotted stumps or logs), grasshoppers, and so on, are good food. Practically all flying insects are satisfactory food, and a small light or fire at night, in season, will attract large numbers. They can be eaten as is or roasted on a flat stone after the stone has been heated in a fire.

Let's say that after three or four days of living in your headquarters camp, you have been unable to attract attention of aircraft, and you haven't been found by any surface-operating search parties. You have made regular reconnoitering trips out from your camp in straight line patterns like the spokes of a wheel. You have been unable to establish your position and pick up any firmly defined landmarks, although there are perhaps possibilities. You now have another decision to make. That is, whether to stay at your camp and make like Robinson Crusoe or to pack up food, water (depending upon the area), protective clothing, and other necessary gear, and strike out for civilization.

Hopefully, in your "mind pattern" of the general area you will remember that there is a road paralleling the north-south border that should lie perhaps twenty miles due east. Or it may be a railroad. Perhaps there is a logging area bordering the national forest you are in that is operating, and you are reasonably certain you can find it. Or your best way out may be a stream in some other direction that you know will lead to habita-

Cattail roots. These are good survival food. They are found over a large area of the country, and cattail is easily recognized. The roots can be eaten raw or boiled.

tion some thirty or forty miles distant. So you are ready to pack up and head out. Avoid the choice of a destination that, if you *miss* it, will simply take you *deeper* into the woods. A long stretch of road, a river, or a railroad are good places to head for because your chances of missing them are not nearly so great as a pinpoint objective, such as a logging camp or small town.

If the weather is hot, conserve your energy by traveling as soon as it is daylight and resting during the heat of the day. In hot weather it is just as important to keep your body cool as it is to ration your water. Avoid hurrying and any excessive exertion. Especially if your water is in short supply, take every precaution to avoid sweating (and loss of body water). Utilize shade when possible to save both a few degrees in temperature and water. Each time you come to a water supply, fill up your water containers. Have your signaling mirror and smoke cartridges handy. If you are following a river, you can of course dump most of your water supply while you are traveling with the stream.

Whether to follow mountain ridges or canyons in traveling is a question of terrain. Although there are exceptions, a lot of backpacking is done in fairly high country. To leave the country you will want to go down. If there is a canyon with a stream (or a trickle) of water at the bottom, it will be very wise to stay with it if it goes in the general direction you are heading. "Staying with it" does not necessarily mean walking in the bottom of the canyon. The canyon may be fairly wide at the bottom and provide relatively easy going, or it may be quite narrow, with possibly dangerous cliffs to be negotiated. In the latter case it will be better to stay on higher ground, probably the first ridge on one or the other side of the canyon. Canyon bottoms may also have almost impenetrable thickets and undergrowth because the bottom gets more rain runoff. So whether you travel the ridges or the canyon bottoms, or some of both, will depend upon the particular terrain. Again, if there is a trickle of water in that canyon bottom, keep it in sight as long as possible. You may also strike out through more open country. However, traveling through heavy timber without a trail to follow can be next to impossible. Downed timber and thickets will frequently be so dense as to simply rule this out. Also, attempting to travel in such a forest will probably get you "more lost" than you already are.

If you come to a trail and you are sure it is not a game trail, it will probably be best to follow it. That will depend on your knowledge of the area

Trail marker. Lightweight cloth strips, made up at home and numbered with a felt-tip pen, make excellent trail markers. They are tied to a tree limb or bush at conspicuous places along the trail, using a simple overhand knot. A note on the back trail is made on a 3-by-5-inch card, or in a small notebook. The note is numbered to correspond with the number on the cloth-strip marker.

and where the trail may lead. Certainly if it is a well-used trail, you would definitely follow it, rather than cross it and plunge into the woods again. The same applies to a road or a railroad or a power line. You would follow it with the probability that it would lead to habitation. Which way to follow it would, again, depend upon your knowledge of the area. Normally, however, you would follow in the direction that takes you to a generally lower elevation. When you come to such a trail or road, it would be a good idea to impale a 3-by-5-inch note card (another item for the survival kit) or tie it with a string on a branch in plain view of anyone who may travel the trail or road. The note card should give your name, address, phone number, and the fact that you are lost. Specify the date and the direction you are headed on the trail or road. Ask the person who sees the card to get in touch with authorities, and probably certain family members.

By following these procedures, you *may* arrive back at civilization. It cannot be stressed too strongly that before you go into a remote area, some responsible person or persons should be notified in advance that you are going, and of the general area you will be in and the date you will be back. They should also be told that if you are not back by that date, you have met with an emergency and they are to notify authorities to start a search for you. This immediately makes it apparent that the most favored choice for survival is to set up camp very near the place you became lost and make like Robinson Crusoe. Then the searchers will have perhaps a ten- or twenty-square-mile area to search for you instead of 100 or 200 square miles. You should only try to travel out if, for some reason, the odds are all against your being found where you are. If you are embarrassed by being lost and that is about to cause you to strike out into unfamiliar country, forget it. That too could cost you your life. Statistics have proven time and time again that if you are thoroughly lost, your best chance for survival is to "stay put." Find the best place for a "camp" in the area you are in, make yourself as comfortable as possible, and wait for rescue. Try to make camp in an area where there is open terrain nearby. In addition to a smoke-signaling fire, stamp out a pattern in the snow (if there is snow), use fire ashes to make a pattern, stake out a bright-colored tent or groundsheet, and use all other available means to aid aircraft in spotting your location.

And now some details about survival kits. Some of the items mentioned are simply those that you would normally carry as part of your routine backpacking gear, and they will be carried in a packsack pocket or wherever you normally carry them. However, a few items are "special," and it is recommended that you actually carry them in a small, separate kit, to be used only for survival purposes.

The following are items that are generally carried as a part of your normal backpacking gear. If not, they should be when you venture off the main trails of a wilderness or forest area.

1. Matches (several supplies stowed in different places in your pack and more than normally carried). Waterproof containers.

2. Long-burning candles. Two or more candles that will burn six hours or longer. Save your match supply by lighting a candle and using it for starting a fire each time you need fire.

3. First aid kit (the more remote the area, the more complete it should be).

4. Extra water containers. One or more collapsible plastic containers of one- or two-gallon capacity are good. During "normal" travel, they will probably be carried empty.

5. Heavy plastic or coated nylon (waterproof) tarp.

6. Cold-weather clothing if there is a possibility of low temperatures.

7. Map. Also a good homemade sketch of the area that has been drawn with the aid of a person who is thoroughly familiar with the area. It should show all important trails, sources of water, and recognizable landmarks that may not be included on a commercial map.

8. A good compass.

9. A canteen for each member of the party.

10. A good knife, and such items of cooking gear, equipment, and clothing as are normally carried by an experienced backpacker.

11. Good flashlight(s) and extra bulb. At least one flashlight in party should be a C or D size. Extra batteries.

12. A mirror.

13. Water purification tablets.

14. A whistle (shrill and loud, for signaling).

The following additional items should be carried, and many of these might be contained in a special, specific "survival" container.

1. Three or more smoke cartridges for signaling purposes.

2. Some survival foods. Meatbars, jerky, pemmican, and nuts are good (concentrated and rich in protein and fat). Carry extra salt.

3. Note cards, 3 by 5 inches (fifteen or twenty cards). A wood pencil. Enough transparent plastic map-covering material to cover ten or fifteen of the note cards and make them waterproof after the note is written. Some stout cord for hanging note cards (with a written message) in a prominent place along your trail or at "camps" to aid a search party in finding you.

4. Trail markers. Strips of very lightweight cloth, with a number added.

5. Some fishing line, a few hooks, and some split-shot sinkers.

6. Optional: some picture-frame wire for possible use as an animal snare.

7. Optional: about one square yard of nylon mosquito netting, preferably about 2 by 4 feet, to use for fashioning into a net to catch insects for food and for seining minnows or fish for food.

As a final item, it is important not to let your pack get lost. (It has happened to a few.) A hiker may throw off his pack and maybe walk to a certain vantage point perhaps only a short distance away, for a better view. He then returns for his pack and finds it isn't there. (It is still there, but he didn't return to the exact spot where he left his pack.) Obviously this is a serious situation. Your pack is your "house" when you are in the woods, and keeping it with you may very well decide the difference between surviving and not surviving.

APPENDIX G

CAMPING IN EXTREME COLD

James (Gil) Phillips of Albuquerque, New Mexico, a good friend of the author, is one of the foremost experts in the United States on camping in sub-zero weather. When temperatures plunge to 30° or 40° below zero, Gil heads for Wolf Creek Pass in southern Colorado. For a number of years, Gil has taken groups of interested persons into that area in January to instruct them on camping out in sub-zero weather and thoroughly enjoying it. He has developed a complete line of clothing and cold-weather gear for this type of camping, based on a unique approach to the problem of staying comfortable in cold weather. The purpose of the next few pages is not to make you an expert on cold-weather camping but rather to briefly describe Gil's techniques and equipment and perhaps spark your interest so that you will want to look into the subject further. Before describing the equipment in some detail, let's first briefly discuss some basic concepts that Gil has developed, largely through his own learning process of trial and error.

Basic concepts

FIRE. You do not need a fire or any source of artificial heat to keep warm at 40° below zero. As Gil says, suppose there was a blizzard or you could not find firewood. You would be in real trouble if you were depending on fire to keep you warm. The Eskimo never depends on fire for warmth. Under certain conditions you may want a fire, but look upon it as a luxury, never as a necessity.

FOOD. You do not need hot food for sub-zero camping. Your body derives no more energy from hot food than it does from cold food. That doesn't mean you can't have some hot meals but, again, look upon hot food as a luxury, not a necessity.

BODY MOVEMENTS. The concept that you must work fast and move fast at very low temperatures in order to keep warm is obsolete. In such temperatures you move very slowly and deliberately. It takes five to seven times as long to perform simple camp jobs in such weather as it does in normal temperatures.

SLEEP. Even many people well acquainted with the outdoors consider it a fact that if you go to sleep in sub-zero weather, you may never wake up. Gil Phillips claims this is essentially impossible to do. He says if you get cold enough, you will

wake up—shivering—just as you do in normally cold temperatures.

FEET AND HANDS. The extremities of the body, the feet and hands, are usually the first to get cold. The head usually gets cold last. To prevent heat loss from the body, you need to protect all areas from exposure. The saying "If your feet are cold, put your hat on" is not at all farfetched. Another point: If your hands, ears, or another part gets frostbitten, you do not rub it with snow; you rub the affected part with your hands to restore circulation. Or you place your feet (for example) against someone else's bare chest or stomach for warmth.

PLASTIC FOAM AND PLASTIC SHEETING. A basic part of Gil's approach to keeping warm in sub-zero temperatures involves the use of plastic (polyurethane) foam and plastic sheeting. The polyurethane foam is the basic thermal insulation and moisture remover. The plastic sheeting is the wind stop and vapor barrier at the bottom of the bed. Gil wraps a plastic sheet completely around his bed, as will be described later. He says if you should get low on air to breathe, you will wake up—fighting. He claims that only babies who lack the strength to work their way free from such an enclosed plastic sheet are in danger of suffocation.

Sleeping bag.

The sleeping bag that Gil uses for sub-zero camping is made of polyurethane foam. The right thickness for the sleeping bag is about 1 to 1½ inches. For some years, Gil took boy scout troops on winter camping trips into the Pecos Wilderness of northern New Mexico. He taught the scouts to make their own sleeping bags, as well as various articles of clothing, from polyurethane foam. Sleeping bags are always of mummy shape to conserve heat. The foam is glued together with automobile trim cement. A complete large-size sleeping bag weighs about 3½ pounds. In sub-zero temperatures you sleep with all clothes on, and at 40° below zero such a sleeping bag will be comfortable. The manner in which this sleeping bag is made into a "bed" is unique and will be described in some detail.

A 12-foot-square plastic sheet of about 4-mil thickness is a basic part of the bed. A polyurethane pad (without cover) 24 by 72 inches and 1 inch thick is also needed. Lastly, you need a piece of nylon cloth about the same size as the poly pad, or slightly larger. The polyurethane pad is not for the purpose of bone comfort but rather moisture comfort. It carries the ice-forming moisture away from the sleeping bag. The nylon cloth is placed beneath this pad and will be frozen stiff in the morning. It can be shaken out and hung in a breeze, and it will be dry — even in sub-zero temperatures.

The order of events in making up your bed for the night is as follows:

1. Lay the 12-by-12 foot plastic sheet down on the snow. The purpose of the plastic sheet is to form a waterproof barrier between your bed (sleeping bag) and the snow. It is also part of your wind barrier.

2. Lay the piece of nylon cloth on top of one side of the plastic sheet.

3. On top of the nylon cloth goes the 1-inch-thick polyurethane pad. On top of this you place your sleeping bag.

4. You now fold the free side of your plastic sheet over the top of the sleeping bag and tuck it under that part of the same plastic sheet that is already beneath the sleeping bag.

5. Next, that part of the plastic groundsheet extending out from the foot end of the sleeping bag is tucked underneath. The sleeping bag is now completely enclosed in the plastic sheet, with the plastic sheet tucked under one side and the foot end of the overall bed. There is still a slip-through "tunnel" formed by the plastic sheet extending beyond the head end of the bed. You maneuver through this end and slide into the sleeping bag when you are ready to go to bed, tucking the plastic sheet back under the bed at the sides, where it probably came untucked while you were getting into bed. Your supply of breathing air for the night comes through the tunnel of plastic extending out from the head end of the bed.

6. When you get into one of these beds for the night, you really get all the way in. Head, face, mouth, and nose go inside the hood of the sleeping bag, which is then drawn completely shut with the drawstring, which is held by a simple knot or drawstring clamp. Air can pass freely through the foam as you breathe, and there is no necessity of providing an opening at your face or nose.

Much of this procedure and technique seems contrary to the principles that many of us have long adhered to in using conventional sleeping bags of down, sleeping in small tents (if any shelter is used), fighting the problem of condensation, and so on. A good goose-down bag loses much of its insulating value when damp. The polyurethane bags apparently "eat up" the moisture.

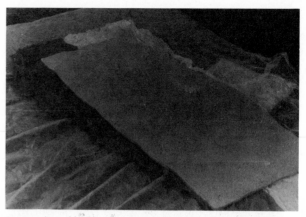

Preparation of bed. A 12-by-12-foot plastic sheet is first laid on the ground (snow). A sheet of nylon cloth slightly larger than the sleeping bag goes next. A 1-inch-thick polyurethane pad goes on top of the nylon cloth. The sleeping bag is placed on the foam pad. The free side of the plastic sheet is then folded over the top of the bed and tucked under at the side and at the foot end.

Gil Phillips explains the process like this: "Moisture given off by your body during the night will pass into and through the polyurethane sleeping bag. The moisture from the sleeping bag then passes into the poly pad beneath the sleeping bag. The nylon cloth beneath the poly pad will soak up this moisture and may be frozen stiff with frost in the morning. This is easily removed by 'beating' it out. It is dry 'water dust,' or sublimated evaporation. Also, the moisture that travels upward from your sleeping bag condenses on the inside surface of the cold plastic sheet. All of this moisture is 'dust' in the morning and is simply shaken from the plastic sheeting."

Clothes. At temperatures below zero, 1-inch-thick polyurethane foam is a basic part of the clothing. It is worn as underclothing next to the skin. You can use very large, loose-fitting mesh underwear to hold in place the panels of foam that are wrapped around the trunk of the body and around the thighs. The arms and legs are also wrapped in sheets of foam. Wool or synthetic (nylon) trousers and wool shirts are recommended, rather than cotton. Again, they should be very large and loose-fitting because of the bulkiness of the foam to be worn underneath. Now for a few remarks on outer clothing.

WATERPROOFING. For temperatures below freezing, clothing should not be waterproof. Our bodies require that moisture be emitted even at 50° below zero. If the clothing is waterproof, this moisture is forced to stay in the clothing insulation. The moisture then reduces the effectiveness of the clothing in retaining body heat. You should use clothing that permits the continuous passage of moisture to the outside air as it is being formed. Poly foam, if it is not enclosed in a waterproof cover, has this characteristic.

COAT. The coat should be large, loose-fitting, and preferably long enough to reach well below the hips. Gil Phillips favors a quilted Dacron-type coat with an outer shell of nylon. A most important part of the coat is an attached hood. The hoods that you will normally find attached to such coats, if you find them at all, will be too light in weight (one layer of cloth) and too small. They must be large enough to accommodate a foam hat and possibly a face tunnel, which will be discussed below. A suitable coat is so seldom found with a satisfactory hood that Gil finds it desirable to make his own hood and attach it to the coat after the coat is purchased. A quilted type of hood is best. A drawstring is very important to fit the hood around the face. The coat and the arms of the coat must be large enough that you can pull both arms out of the coat sleeves and cross them over your chest.

HAT. The hat is made of 1-inch-thick polyurethane foam. It is to come well down on the forehead in front and completely cover the back and sides of the neck.

FACE TUNNEL. The face tunnel might be considered part of the headgear. It is simply a piece of 1-inch-thick poly foam shaped into an essentially cylindrical form. Clothes-hanger wire is used to give shape to the tunnel.

MITTENS. Mittens are always used in sub-zero camping, never gloves. Your fingers need "companionship" to keep one another warm. The mittens are made of the 1-inch-thick poly foam, with generous gauntlet cuffs covering the cuffs of the coat. A very important part of the mittens is a substantial cord that goes around the neck and shoulders to connect with the mittens. Losing one or both mittens in sub-zero temperatures can be disastrous. You never lay your mittens in some "convenient spot" while you work. They stay with you constantly. In doing various camp chores, eating, and so on, you will slip your hands out of the mittens for a few minutes at a time. When your hands begin to get cold, you slip them back into the mittens — your portable pocket.

MUKLUKS. As in any other type of backpacking, your feet and the "shoes" that you put them in are of the utmost importance. In sub-zero hiking and camping (in contrast to normal backpack-

ing), a new dimension is added — the requirement to keep the feet warm. Thermal socks, leather boots, rubber boots, rubber boots with leather uppers, and so on, are all left at home when you go camping in sub-zero temperatures. Gil Phillips has found that the only satisfactory footwear is mukluks. He makes his own mukluks from a pair of over-sized galoshes with attached canvas uppers reaching almost to the knees. The galoshes are lined with 1-inch-thick polyurethane foam. He does not use socks. He takes a piece of 1-inch-thick polyurethane foam that is 29½ inches square and wraps each foot with this foam before inserting it in the mukluk. After a period of hiking, the foam wrapped about the foot will tend to compress and wear in the area beneath the foot. Therefore, each time the mukluks are put on, the foam is wrapped about the foot so that a different area falls beneath the sole of the foot.

BOOTIES. Your daytime footwear, the mukluks, are of course removed when you get into your sleeping bag. A foot "mitten" or "bootie" made of the polyurethane foam is worn at night to help keep the feet warm. Socks are not usually used, either for daytime or nighttime use.

Moisture control. Whether you are hiking, working in camp, or lying in your sleeping bag, you should take the necessary precautions to avoid perspiring. Whether you perspire will depend primarily on the temperature, amount of wind, and your level of exertion. If you find you are starting to perspire, slow down in your exertion, open up your clothing a bit, or remove some of your clothes (or do all of these). Remember to move very slowly and deliberately at sub-zero temperatures.

Shelter. Gil never uses tents in his sub-zero camping. He frequently makes his bed right out in the open on the snow, using the procedure described above. When he does build a shelter, it is most frequently a snow house. His course of instruction in sub-zero hiking and camping techniques always includes a considerable amount of time spent in building snow houses, which the students then live in. The snow houses are made with snow blocks, cut from the snow with an ordinary household saw. However, he does not consider a snow house or other such shelter to be really necessary, provided you are thoroughly trained and experienced in the other basic techniques. A snow cave can also be built and will provide adequate shelter. Gil sometimes builds igloos, but he says that, in general, these take too much time. Incidentally, Gil is an electrical engineer, and his work frequently takes him to the Aleutian Islands, off the coast of Alaska. A few years ago he took time off from his duties to instruct the Eskimos of the Barrow area on the building of igloos. (The use of igloos is primarily an art of the inhabitants of the far north of eastern Canada, not Alaska.) He and his son then lived in an igloo for two weeks. He has on many occasions, after building an igloo or snow house, slept outside on the windswept snow, just to prove the adequacy of his clothing, sleeping bag, and technique.

Travel.   A conventional backpack is carried for winter camping, and Gil states that it need not weigh more than 30 to 35 pounds. All traveling is done on snowshoes. He particularly warns against use of skis unless you are very expert

Mukluk. The mukluk is the only satisfactory footwear for sub-zero temperatures and deep snow, according to Gil Phillips. This is the chosen footwear of the Eskimos.

Polyurethane-foam hat and face tunnel. Gil Phillips is shown here with a poly-foam hat and face tunnel of the type he designed and has used for many years in his sub-zero backpacking and camping. Other articles of clothing, as well as the sleeping bag, are made of the same polyurethane foam.

Face tunnel. The face tunnel is used in this manner. The hood of the coat must be of generous size to accommodate the poly-foam hat and face tunnel. The snow goggles, being worn here, are very important as a preventive measure against snow blindness. Note the heavy cord connecting the mittens. Loss of one or both mittens could be a disaster.

with them. There is too much danger of a twisted ankle or knee—or worse. About five miles per day is all that should normally be counted on in winter camping. The question of using a sled or toboggan for hauling gear is frequently brought up by his students. Gil does not recommend these except where it is known that the terrain will be open and level. Snow goggles are an important item of gear and are worn almost constantly when you travel or work about camp. Snow blindness can be very serious.

Water supply. With snow covering the landscape one would think that water supply would be no problem. Yet there are difficulties in obtaining a water supply from snow, and Gil has a solution for this. In sub-zero temperatures all streams will probably be solidly frozen. Also, when the snow is several feet deep or more, the approach to a running stream, if it does exist, can be hazardous. You cannot eat enough snow to replace the water that your body uses every day. This amounts to a minimum of about 1½ quarts of water per day, and that is a lot of snow. To pass that much water through your mouth in the form of snow is essentially impossible. It will cause your lips to swell and crack, and you will have a terrible time. You could melt snow in a pan over a small stove used for backpacking, but Gil does not like to depend on fire or mechanical aids. His solution to the problem involves a large plastic bag with a wide-mouth opening. An ice bag with a large opening would also be satisfactory. He stuffs this full of snow and puts it next to his body. The body heat causes the snow to melt as you hike along or work about camp. He stresses that it is important to put more snow into the bag before you pour out the water that is already in the bag. Carrying a bag of snow inside your shirt or close to your skin may not sound very comfortable, but Gil says that you soon get used to this.

Food. The choice of food is more important in winter wilderness travel than in the summer. When you cannot depend upon fire for cooking, your choice is narrowed considerably. The food chosen should be high in protein and fat. Foods with sugar and starch bases are poor sources of lasting body heat and energy. Gil considers unprocessed foods to be best. The food should be cut in bite-sized chunks before you leave home. It is terrible to be hungry and to try to bite or cut a piece of cheese at 20° below zero. (It makes excellent structural material at this temperature.) Cheese and dried fat beef are good foods. (Most commercial jerky is too lean for this use.) Raisins, nuts, bacon, Tang, dried milk, and shredded coconut are good. Fresh-frozen fish and frozen beef can be eaten as is, with some practice. Soup and other common backpacking foods that require cooking should be considered luxury foods, rather than essential.

Where to go. A good place to go for your sub-zero backpacking and camping activity is to a ski area. In the dead of winter, in areas where sub-zero temperatures will be found, many roads will be hazardous or impassable. However, roads into ski areas will usually be kept open. After some persuasion Gil frequently convinces a ski-lift operator to haul him and his equipment to the top of a ski lift, and he takes off from there. For those just starting to learn the sub-zero hiking and camping techniques, it is a good idea to stay fairly close to civilization; for example, near an operating ski resort. As with other backpacking activity, you can increase the duration and distance of your trips as your knowledge and experience grow.

That, very briefly, is a description of the unusual techniques, clothing, and accessories that Gil Phillips uses in his hobby of backpacking and camping in sub-zero temperatures. In closing, Gil asked me to stress the fact that, for the most part, he has simply adapted the principles that the Eskimos have used for many years, and to be sure to give the Eskimos their due credit. He is a most unusual and interesting person, and you will be hearing more about him, I am sure. He is constantly experimenting, testing, and perfecting his gear and methods. If you would like to learn more about his techniques and equipment and have fun doing so, he will be glad to meet you at Wolf Creek Pass in southern Colorado—next January.

APPENDIX H

OTHER LITERATURE

Following is additional reading material dealing with some of the various aspects of backpacking with which you may want to become familiar.

1. *American Red Cross First Aid Textbook.* The American National Red Cross, 17th and D Streets, N.W., Washington, D.C. 20006

2. *Appalachian Trailway News.* A newsletter published three times yearly by the Appalachian Trail Conference, P.O. Box 236, Harpers Ferry, West Virginia 25425

3. *Backpacker.* A magazine published six times yearly. Subscription Department, Box 2946, Boulder, Colorado 80302.

4. *Backpacking Journal.* A magazine published four times yearly. Subscription Department, 229 Park Avenue South, New York, New York 10003

5. *Basic Mountaineering.* San Diego Chapter of the Sierra Club, San Diego, California 92112

6. *Carters' Map and Compass Manual.* Published by Carters Manual Company, P.O. Box 186, Estacada, Oregon 97023

7. *Composition of Foods.* Agriculture Handbook #8. Superintendent of Documents, U.S. Government Printing Office, Washington, D.C. 20402

8. Cunningham, Gerry, and Margaret Hansson, *Light Weight Camping Equipment and How to Make It.* (Published by Scribners; available from many suppliers listed in Appendix A.)

9. Danielson, John A., *Winter Hiking and Camping.* The Adirondack Mountain Club, Glen Falls, New York 12801

10. Darvill, Fred T., Jr., M.D., *Mountaineering Medicine.* The Skagit Mountain Rescue Unit, Inc., P.O. Box 2, Mount Vernon, Washington 98273

11. Fear, Eugene H., *Outdoor Living: Problems, Solutions, Guidelines.* Tacoma Unit, Mountain Rescue Council, P.O. Box 696, Tacoma, Washington 98401

12. *Fieldbook for Boys and Men.* Boy Scouts of America, New Brunswick, New Jersey 08901

13. Forgey, William W., M.D., *The Complete Guide to Trail Food Use.* Published by Indiana Camp Supply, P.O. Box 344, Pittsboro, Indiana 46167

14. Kjellstrom, Bjorn, *Be Expert with Map and Compass.* American Orienteering Service, La-Porte, Indiana 46350

15. LaChapelle, E. R., *The ABC of Avalanche Safety.* White Water Sports, 1203 N.E. 65th, Seattle, Washington 98115

16. Lathrop, Theodore G., M.D., *Hypothermia: Killer of the Unprepared.* Booklet published by Mazamas, 909 N.W. 19th Avenue, Portland, Oregon 97209

17. *Lightweight Equipment for Hiking, Camping, and Mountaineering.* Potomac Appalachian Trail Club, 1718 N Street, N.W., Washington, D.C. 20036

18. Manning, Harvey, *Backpacking: One Step at a Time.* A particularly comprehensive discussion of backpacking equipment. Recreational Equipment, Inc., 1525 11th Avenue, Seattle, Washington 98122

19. *Nutritive Value of Foods.* Home and Garden Bulletin #72, USDA. Superintendent of Documents, U.S. Government Printing Office, Washington, D.C. 20402

20. *1,000,000 Miles of Canoe and Hiking Routes.* Ohio Canoe Adventures, Inc., P.O. Box 2092, Sheffield Lake, Ohio 44054

21. *The Signpost.* A newsletter for backpackers and mountaineers in the northwestern U.S. Published at 16812 36th Avenue West, Lynwood, Washington 98036

22. *Trail Walker.* A newsletter published six times yearly by the New York-New Jersey Trail Conference, G.P.O. Box 2250, New York, New York 10001

23. *Wilderness Camping.* A magazine published six times yearly. Subscription address is P.O. Box 1186, Scotia, New York 12302

Index